Where to Stay in Southern California

WHERE TO STAY IN
SOUTHERN CALIFORNIA

Phil Philcox

SAN DIEGO PUBLIC LIBRARY
LA JOLLA BRANCH

HUNTER
PUBLISHING, INC
MPC

Hunter Publishing, Inc.
300 Raritan Center Parkway
Edison NJ 08818
(908) 225 1900
Fax (908) 417 0482

ISBN 1-55650-573-6

©1993 Hunter Publishing, Inc.

All rights reserved. No part of this publication may be reproduced, stored in a retrieval system, or transmitted in any form, or by any means, electronic, mechanical, photocopying, recording, or otherwise, without the written permission of the publisher.

Published in the UK by:
Moorland Publishing Co. Ltd.
Moor Farm Rd, Airfield Estate
Ashbourne, Derbyshire DE6 1HD
England

ISBN (UK) 0 86190 316 1

Cover photograph: *Pebble Beach* (James Hackett/Leo de Wys Inc.)

Contents

Introduction	13
Chain Hotels	15
Accommodations Directory	33
Adelanto	33
Agoura Hills	34
Alhambra	34
Anaheim and Anaheim Hills	35
Arcadia	48
Arroyo Grande	49
Artesia	49
Atascadero	50
Avalon	51
Avila Beach	53
Azusa	53
Baker	54
Bakersfield	54
Ballard	58
Baldwin Park	58
Banning	59
Barstow	60
Baywood Park	61
Beaumont	61
Bellflower	62
Beverly Hills	62
Big Bear and Big Bear Lake	65
Big Sur	67
Bishop	67
Borrego Springs	69
Brea	70
Buellton	70
Buena Park	71
Burbank	74
Camarillo	76
Calabasas	77
Calexico	78
Cambria	78
Canada Cove	80

Canoga Park	81
Capistrano Beach	81
Cardiff-By-The-Sea	82
Carlsbad	82
Carmel	85
Carpinteria	92
Carson	93
Castaic	94
Cayucos	94
Cerritos	95
Cathedral City	95
Chula Vista	96
Chatsworth	98
Chino	99
City of Commerce	99
City of Industry	100
Claremont	101
Coalinga	101
Coarsegold	102
Compton	102
Corcoran	103
Corona	103
Coronado	104
Costa Mesa	106
Covina	109
Culver City	110
Dana Point	111
Darwin	112
Death Valley	112
Delano	112
Del Mar	113
Desert Hot Springs	113
Diamond Bar	114
Downey	115
Duarte	116
Dublin	116
Dulzura	117
El Cajon	117
El Centro	118
El Granada	119
El Segundo	120
El Toro	121

Emeryville	121
Encinitas	122
Englewood	123
Escondido	123
Fallbrook	125
Fawnskin	126
Fillmore	127
Fish Camp	127
Fontana	128
Fresno	128
Fullerton	133
Gardena	134
Garden Grove	135
Glendale	136
Glendora	137
Goleta	137
Hanford	139
Hemet	139
Hermosa Beach	140
Hesperia	141
Hollister	142
Hollywood	142
Holtville	148
Huntington Beach	151
Huntington Park	152
Idyllwild	151
Indian Wells	152
Indio	153
Irvine	154
Jamestown	157
June Lake	157
Kernville	158
Klamath and Klamath River	159
La Canada	159
Laguna Beach	160
Laguna Hills	162
Laguna Niguel	163
La Habra	163
La Jolla	164
Lake Arrowhead	167
Lake Elsinore	168
Lakewood	168

La Mesa	169
La Mirada	169
Lancaster	170
La Puente	171
La Quinta	171
Lawndale	172
Lemon Cove	173
Lemon Grove	173
Lemoore	173
Lomita	174
Lompoc	174
Lone Pine	176
Long Beach	176
Los Alamos	182
Los Altos	182
Los Angeles	182
Airport Area	183
Downtown Area	186
Hollywood Area	195
Westside Area	196
Other Areas	202
Los Banos	205
Los Olivos	205
Los Osos	206
Lost Hills	206
Lynwood	206
Madera	207
Malibu	207
Manhattan Beach	208
Maricopa	209
Marina	209
Marina del Rey	210
Maywood	212
Merced	212
Mission Viejo	213
Mojave	213
Monrovia	214
Montecito	215
Monterey and Monterey Park	215
Moreno Valley	224
Morro Bay	225
Mountain View	229

National City	230
Newhall	231
Needles	231
New Cuyama	232
Newport Beach	232
Norco	234
North Fork	235
Norwalk	235
Oakhurst	236
Oceano	237
Oceanside	237
Ojai	239
Ontario	240
Orange	243
Oxnard	245
Pacific Beach	246
Pacific Grove	247
Palmdale	249
Palomar	250
Palm Desert	251
Palm Springs	253
Pasadena and South Pasadena	261
Paso Robles	264
Pismo Beach	265
Placentia	269
Pomona	269
Porterville	270
Port Hueneme	270
Poway	271
Ramona	271
Rancho Mirage	271
Rancho Santa Fe	272
Redlands	273
Redondo Beach	273
Reedley	275
Rialto	276
Ridgecrest	276
Riverside	277
Rosemead	279
Rowland Heights	280
Salinas	281
San Bernadino	282

San Clemente	284
San Diego	286
San Dimas	306
San Gabriel	306
Sanger	307
San Juan Capistrano	307
San Luis Obispo	308
San Marcos and Lake San Marcos	311
San Miguel	312
San Pedro	312
San Ramon	314
San Simeon	314
Santa Ana	316
Santa Barbara	319
Santa Clara	328
Santa Cruz	331
Santa Fe Springs	336
Santa Maria	337
Santa Monica	338
Santa Paula	342
Santee	343
Santa Maria	343
Santa Ynez	344
San Ysidro	345
Seal Beach	345
Seaside	346
Selma	346
Sepulveda	347
Sequoia National Park	347
Sherman Oaks	348
Shoshone	348
Simi Valley	348
Solano Beach	349
Soledad	349
Solvang	350
Spring Valley	352
Squaw Valley	352
Studio City	353
Summerland	353
Sun City	353
Tecopa	354
Tehachapi	354

Temecula	354
Templeton	356
Thousand Oaks	356
Three Rivers	357
Torrance	358
Tulare	359
Twentynine Palms	360
Universal City	361
Upland	362
Valencia	362
Van Nuys	363
Venice	364
Ventura	365
Victorville	367
Visalia	368
Vista	370
Warmer Springs	371
Wasco	371
West Covina	372
Westlake Village	373
Westminster	373
Westwood Village	374
Whittier	375
Woodland and Woodland Hills	376
Yorba Linda	378
Yucca Valley	379

Introduction

If you're California-bound for business or pleasure, this is the ultimate guide to finding a place to bed down for the night. Need a convenient downtown hotel with free airport transportation, exercise facilities, lighted tennis courts and meeting facilities? Prefer a waterfront apartment, a roadside motel or a high-rise condo with boat dock, completely equipped for move-in living? If elbow room is important, how about a rental home along the southern California coast or a two-bedroom duplex with swimming pool only a short drive from Disneyland? If you have special needs, this guide explains everything from where to find properties offering wheelchair access and rooms for the disabled to accommodations that provide free local telephone calls or that allow pets.

Included are the names and telephone numbers of regional rental sources that handle an assortment of accommodation options – from private homes to condos and apartments. These agencies are excellent sources of information on what's available in each area in different price ranges and most have toll-free numbers you can call for information.

You will also find, for the first time in any accommodations guide, toll-free and fax numbers you can call to request literature, rate cards and reservations. Many properties will fax their literature directly to your machine.

As of press time, the rates were current, based on interviews with the property owners. Rates are constantly changing and vary considerably with location and season, so use the rates listed to determine the price range of the property and always call prior to making your reservations. Use the toll-free number when available. Most toll-free numbers listed are valid from all states but some properties have outside-California or California-only numbers. If you reach an invalid number, check with the toll-free operator at 800-555-1212.

Properties in popular vacation areas often offer special discounts and programs for vacationers with children, seniors, frequent travelers and government employees. A list of chains with their California locations is included. Some resorts offer free shuttle transportation in and around areas with major attractions, discounts on admission tickets and other incentives. Call for further information. After the abbreviations section below, you'll find a list of chain hotels and motels, with special deals and offers available.

Abbreviations used in this guide

LS - low season – usually the lowest rates of the year.
MS - mid-season.
HS - high season – usually the highest rates of the year.
YRR - year-round rate.
SGL - single room – rate for one person.
DBL - double room – rate for two people sharing one room.
EFF - efficiency – usually one room with kitchen or kitchenette.
STS - suites.
1BR, 2BR, 3BR- 1-3-bedroom apartment condo, apartment, villa or townhouse with full kitchen facilities, washer/dryer, etc.
No-Smoking Rooms - rooms available for non-smokers.
No-Smoking - smoking not permitted on the property.
Child Care - babysitting services available.
Complimentary Breakfast - a free continental or full American breakfast is included in the room rate.
Airport Courtesy Car - free transportation to and from local airports.
Airport Transportation - transportation is available to and from local airports for a fee.
Meeting Facilities - the property can provide facilities for meetings and conferences.
$00-$000 - daily rate span.
$000W-$000W - weekly rate span.
$00/$000W - daily rate followed by weekly rate.

Chain Hotels:
Locations and Special Deals

BEST WESTERN Box 10203, Phoenix AZ 85064. 602-957-4200. Reservations 800-528-1234.

Most locations offer a 10% discount to senior travelers on a space-available basis with advanced reservations. The Government-Military Travel Program provides discounts to federal employees and military personnel. The Gold Crown Club provides points toward free stays and special amenities.

Locations: Alturas, Anaheim, Anderson, Antioch, Arcadia, Arroyo Grande, Atascadero, Auburn, Azusa, Bakersfield, Barstow, Beaumont, Benicia, Bishop, Blythen, Bodega Bay, Bridgeport, Buena Park, Camarillo, Cambria, Cameron Park, Canoga Park, Carlsbad, Carpinteria, Carmel, Chico, Chino, Clearlake, Concord, Corona, Coronado, Corte Madera, Costa Mesa, Crescent City, Davis, Dunnigan, El Cajon, Escondido, Eureka, Fairfield, Fallbrook, Fillmore, Fort Bragg, Fremont, Fresno, Fullerton, Garberville, Gilroy, Glendale, Gress Valley, Hanford, Hayward, Healdsburg, Hemet, Hollister, Hoopa, Huntington Beach, Jackson, Kettleman City, King City, La Hambra, Laguna Beach, Lake Tahoe, Lancaster, Lee Vining, Lemoore, Lodi, Lompac, Lone Pine, Long Beach, Los Angeles, Los Osos, Madera, Manteca, Maricopa, Merced, Modesto, Monterey, Morgan Hill, Morro Bay, Mount Shasta, Mountain View, Napa, Needles, Newport Beach, Oakland, Oceanside, Ojai, Ontario, Oroville, Pacific Grove, Palm Springs, Palo Alto, Pasadena, Paso Robles, Petaluma, Pismo Beach, Placerville, Rancho Cordova, Rancho Cucamonga, Redding, Redlands, Redondo Beach, Redwood City, Rialton, Riverside, Roseville, Rowland Heights, Sacramento, Salinas, San Bernadino, San Diego, San Francisco, San Jose, San Juan Capistrano, San Luis Obispo, San Mateo, San Pedro, Santa Barbara, Santa Clara, Santa Cruz, Santa Maria, Santa Monica, Santa Nella, Santa Rosa, Scotts Valley, Seaside, Selma, Smith River, Soledad, Solvang, Sonoma, Sonora, Stockton, Sunnyvale, Sunset Beach, Susanville, Tehachapi, Temecula, Thousand Oak, Three Rivers, Truckee, Tulare, Turlock, Twentynine Palms, Ukiah, Union City, Vacaville, Valencia, Ventura,

16 Chain Hotels:

Victorville, Visalia, Walnut Creek, Watsonville, Westminster, Whittier, Willows, Yountville.

BUDGET HOST INNS 2601 Jackboro Highway, Fort Worth TX 76114. 817-626-7064. Reservations 800-BUD-HOST.

Locations: *Banning, Beaumont, Blythe, Eureka, Inglewood, Los Angeles, Maywood, Midpines, Pico Rivera, South Gate.*

CLARION-CHOICE HOTELS 10750 Columbia Pike, Silver Spring MD 20901. 301-593-5600, Fax: 301-681-7478.

Reservation Numbers: Sleep Inn 800-62-SLEEP; Friendship Inn 800-453-4511, Econo Lodge 800-55-ECONO, Rodeway Inn 800-229-2000, Comfort Inn 800-228-5150, Quality Inn 800-228-5151, Clarion Hotels 800-CLARION.

Clarion and Choice Hotels consist of Sleep Inn, Comfort Inns, Friendship Inn, Econo Lodges, Rodeway Inns, Quality Inns and Clarion Hotels and Resorts. The Family Plan allows children to stay free when sharing a parent's room. Prime Time and Prime Time Senior Saver for people over age 60 offers a 10% discount at all hotels year-round and a 30% discount at limited locations when you call 800-221-2222 and ask for the Prime Time Senior Saver rate.

Special discounts of 10%-20% are available at participating locations for members of AAA and businesses with 100 employees or less enrolled in the Small Organizations Savings (SOS) Program. SOS-enrolled companies receive a 10% discount off the first 15 rooms used by company employees. The Weekender Rate Program offers special room rates of $20, $30 or $35 per night with an advanced reservation. All local, state and federal government employees and military personnel receive special per diem rates and upgrades when available at participating hotels.

Locations: *Anaheim, Arcata, Bakersfield, Barstow, Blythe, Calistoga, Camarillo, Canoga Park, Carson, Castaic, Costa Mesa, Downey, El Monte, El Toro, Fontana, Fremont, Glendora, Hay-*

ward, Hemet, Hollywood, Huntington Beach, Indio, Industry, La Mesa, Laguna Hill, Lancaster, Lawndale, Lompoc, Long Beach, Los Angeles, Mammoth Lakes, Manhattan Beach, Marina, Millbrae, Milpitas, Monterey, Moreno Valley, Mountain View, Napa, National City, Norwalk, Novato, Oakland, Oceanside, Ontario, Pacific Grove, Palm Springs, Pasadena, Petaluma, Pismo Beach, Placentia, Rancho Cordova, Redwood City, Sacramento, Salinas, San Bernardino, San Clemente, San Diego, San Dimas, San Francisco, San Gabriel, San Jose, San Luis Obispo, Santa Ana, Santa Barbara, Santa Clara, Santa Cruz, Santa Monica, Sepulveda, Simi Valley, Stanton, Sunnyvale, Temecula, Torrance, Upland, Vacaville, Vallejo, Ventura, West Covina, Williams, Wilmington, Woodland.

CO-Z 8 MOTELS
Reservations: 800-882-1985.

Locations: Mountain View, Palo Alto, Redwood City, Santa Clara, Sunnyvale.

DAYS INN
2751 Buford Highway, Atlanta GA 30324. 404-329-7466, Fax: 404-325-7731. Reservations 800-325-2525.

The September Days Club offers travelers over the age of 50 up to 40% discounts on rooms, 10% discounts on food and gifts, a quarterly club magazine, seasonal discounts and special tours and trips. The Inn Credible Card is designed for business travelers and provides up to 30% savings on room rates, free stays for spouses and other benefits. The Days Gem Club is a free travel club for military personnel and government employees that offers up to 30% savings on room rates. School Days Club for academic staff and eductors offers a minimum of 10% savings on room rates, special group rates and additional benefits. The Sport Plus Club is designed for coaches and team managers who organize team travel and offers 10% discounts on room rates, special team rates and late check-outs.

Locations: Adelanto, Anaheim, Bakersfield, Banning, Corning, Guerneville, Lompoc, Los Angeles, Monterey, Needles, Ontario,

18 Chain Hotels:

Palmdale, Palm Springs, Placerville, Redding, Riverside, Sacramento, San Diego, San Francisco, San Jose, Santa Clara, Santa Monica, Santa Rosa, Ventura, Victorville, Westley, Yosemite.

DOUBLETREE HOTELS 555 Madison Avenue, Suite 815, New York NY 10022. 212-754-7800, Fax: 212-754-7846. Reservations 800-528-0444.

Doubletree operates 38 hotels in the United States, including Doubletree Club Hotels that provide oversized rooms, complimentary, cooked-to-order breakfasts, club rooms and hosted evening receptions. Family Plans allow up to two children under the age of 18 to stay free when they share the rooms with their parents. For the business traveler, most hotels offer secretarial services, photocopying, fax machines and computer hook-up capabilities. A special discounted rate is available to seniors. A Corporate Plus Program is available at all business center locations.

Locations: *Burlingame, Los Angeles, Monterey, Ontario, Orange, Santa Ana, Palm Springs, Pleasanton, San Diego, Santa Clara, Santa Rosa, Temecula, Ventura, Walnut Creek.*

ECONOMY INNS OF AMERICA 755 Raintree Drive, Suite 200, Carlsbad CA 92009. 619-438-6661, Fax: 407-396-4979. Reservations 800-826-0778, 800-423-3018 in Florida.

Locations: *Bakersfield, Barstow, Carlsbad, Fairfield, Fresno, Lost Hills, Madera, Milpitas, San Diego, San Ysidro, Rancho Cordova, Tulare*

EMBASSY SUITES 222 Las Colinas Boulevard, Irving TX 75039. 214-556-1133, Fax: 214-556-8222. Reservations 800-528-1100.

Locations: *Anaheim, Arcadia, Brea, Buena Park, Burlingame, Covina, Downey, El Segundo, Irvine, Lompac, Los Angeles, Milpitas, Napa Valley, San Diego, San Francisco, San Rafael, Santa Ana, Santa Clara, Walnut Creek.*

Chain Hotels: 19

GUEST QUARTERS SUITE HOTELS 30 Rowes Wharf, Boston MA 02110. 617-330-1440, Fax: 716-737-8752, Reservations 800-424-2900.

Locations: *Santa Monica.*

HAMPTON INNS 6800 Poplar, Memphis TN 38138. 901-758-3100, Fax: 901-756-9479. Reservations 800-426-7866.

Locations: *Fairfield, Fresno, Los Angeles, Oakland, Palm Springs, Riverside, San Diego, Santa Barbara.*

HILTON HOTELS 9336 Civic Center Drive, Beverly Hills CA 90209. 213-278-4321, Fax: 213-205-4599, Reservations 800-HILTON.

Zip-Out/Quick Check-Out is available to travelers using major credit cards. An itemized statement of charges is provided the night before departure. Many Hilton locations have hotels-within-hotels, Tower and Executive accommodations offering room upgrades, use of a private lounge, access to business services, complimentary cocktails and continental breakfast and use of telex, fax machines and photocopying equipment.

The HHonors Guest Reward Program is a free program that earns points toward free or discounted stays at participating properties and members-only privileges that include rapid check-ins, free daily newspaper, free stay with spouse and free use of health club facilities when available.

The Corporate Rate Program offers business travelers guaranteed rates annually, speed reservations, Tower and Executive accommodations and Quick Check-Out facilities.

Hilton's Senior HHonors offers special amenities to travelers over the age of 60. Included are room discounts up to 50%, a 20% dinner discount and money-back guarantee, a private toll-free reservation number and automatic enrollment in Hilton's Guest Reward Programs. BounceBack Weekend offers a free, daily continental breakfast, children free in parents' rooms and special rates for Thursday to Sunday with a Saturday stay. During the summer these discounted rates apply Monday to Wednesday when a Saturday stay is included.

Hilton Leisure Breaks includes packages for honeymooners and special occasions with special rates. Hilton Meeting 2000 is a network of business meeting facilities available at some locations and includes special meeting room, audiovisual systems, refreshments and assistance in coordinating rooms and programs.

Locations: *Baldwin Park, Beverly Hills, Fremont, Los Angeles, Oakland, Oxnard, Pasadena, Pleasanton, San Bernardino, San Diego, San Francisco, Sunnyvale, Valencia.*

HOLIDAY INN 1100 Ashwood Parkway, Atlanta GA 30338. 404-551-3500,
Reservations 800-HOLIDAY.

When sharing a parent's rooms, children 12 and under stay free at all locations. Cribs are also free and in some participating hotels the age limit is extended to 18. The Forget Something Program offers complimentary shaving cream, razor, comb, toothbrush and toothpaste. Holiday Inn Preferred Senior Travelers Program and other Senior Savings Programs provide a 20% savings on rooms and a 10% discount at participating Holiday Inn restaurants. Great Rates provide up to 10% off the standard room rate with advance reservation.

Government-Military Rates are available to government employees, military personnel and contractors. Room upgrades, special room rates and a 10% dinner discount with free continental breakfast is available at participating locations. The Priority Club offers frequent travelers special rates, points toward free stays and additional benefits.

Locations: *Barstow, Belmont, Brentwood-Bel Air, Buena Park, Burbank, Chico, Costa Mesa, Fairfield, Foster City, Fresno, Fullerton, Glendale, Half Moon Bay, Hollywood, Huntington Beach, Irvine, Laguna Hills, Livermore, Long Beach, Los Ange-*

les, Marin, Milpitas, Modesto, Monrovia, Montebello, Monterey, Oakland, Ontario, Palm Desert, Palmdale, Palm Springs, Palo Alto, Pasadena, Pleasanton, Redondo, Redding, Riverside, Sacramento, San Clemente, San Diego, San Jose, San Francisco, San Simeon, Santa Barbara, Santa Cruz, Santa Monica, Santa Nelle, Solvang, Stockton, Sunnyvale, Thousand Oaks, Torrance, Union City, Vallejo, Van Nuys, Ventura, Victorville, Visalia, Walnut, Walnut Creek, West Covina, Woodland Hills

HOMEWOOD SUITES 3742 Lamar Avenue, Memphis TN 38195. 901-362-4663, Fax: 901-362-4663, Reservations 800-225-5466.

Locations: San Jose.

HOSPITALITY INTERNATIONAL INNS 1152 Spring Street, Suite A, Atlanta GA 30309. 404-873-5924, Reservations 800-251-1962.

Hospitality International consists of Red Carpet Inns, Scottish Inns, Passport Inns and Downtowner Motor Inns. The Identicard Program provides room discounts at participating inns and resorts.

Locations: Anaheim, Indio, Mohave, San Bernardino, Victorville.

HOWARD JOHNSON 3838 East Van Buren, Phoenix AZ 85038. 201-256-9030, Fax: 201-890-3051, Reservations 800-654-2000.

The Howard Johnson Road Rally Program offers discounts to senior travelers over the age of 60 and members of AARP and other national senior's organizations. With advanced reservations, a 30% discount is available at some location. The Family Plan lets children under the age of 12 stay free at all locations with some properties extending the age limit to 18.

Government Rate Programs offer special rates to federal employees, military personnel and government contractors. The

Chain Hotels:

Corporate Rate Program offers special rates to companies and business travelers. Howard Johnson Executive Section offers guests special rooms, complimentary wake-up coffee, newspapers and snacks. Kids Go Hojo provides children with free FunPacks filled with toys, puzzles, coloring books and games.

Locations: Anaheim, Baldwin Park, Barstow, Claremont, Colton, Corte Madera, Culver City, Dublin, Fresno, Hollywood, Huntington Beach, Long Beach, Los Angeles, Mill Valley, Monrovia, Norco, Ontario, Orange, Palm Desert, Pomona, Redwood City, Reseda, Riverside, Sacramento, San Bernardino, San Diego, San Francisco, San Jose, San Luis Obispo, Santa Ana, Santa Clara, Santa Maria, Sepulveda, Thousand Oaks, Torrance.

HYATT HOTELS INTERNATIONAL MADISON PLAZA, 200 West Madison, Chicago IL 60606. 312-720-1234, Fax: 312-750-8579, Reservations 800-228-9000.

Hyatt Gold Passport provides earned credits for free stays, a private toll-free reservation number, express check-in, special members-only rooms, free newspaper daily, complimentary morning coffee and use of fitness centers when available. Hyatt Reserved Upgrade coupon booklets are available for confirmed room upgrades. Hyatt Gold Passport At Leisure is available at over 155 locations worldwide and includes invitations to private receptions, room amenities, priority room and dining reservations and a quarterly newsletter with members-only offers.

The Regency Club is a hotel within a hotel offering VIP accommodations. Located on the topmost floors of participating hotels, the rooms are reached by special elevators requiring a passkey. Also include is a free morning paper, complimentary breakfast, afternoon hors d'ouevres, wine and cocktails.

Camp Hyatt is for children and their parents. Upon arrival at any Hyatt hotel or resort, children receive a free cap, frequent travel passport and a registration card. The program offers special childrens' menus in the dinning room, room discounts, kitchen tours and other pastimes.

Locations: Anaheim, Burlingame, Garden Grove, Hollywood, Indian Wells, Irvine, Long Beach, Los Angeles, Monterey, Newport Beach, Oakland, Palm Springs, Palo Alto, Sacramento, San Diego, San Francisco, San Jose, Westlake Village.

LAQUINTA INNS 10010 San Pedro, San Antonio TX 78279. 512-366-6000, Fax: 512-366-6100, Reservations 800-531-5900.

La Quinta has 200 inn locations around the United States. In addition to standard guest rooms, some properties offer King Plus and Executive King Rooms with king-size beds, two telephones, remote-control television and other amenities. Most properties offer free local telephone calls, complimentary morning coffee in the lobby, a complimentary issue of the current *Newsweek*, same-day laundry and dry cleaning service and free parking.

Rooms for the disabled are available at some locations and have lower dresser vanities, low-pile carpeting, portable shower heads, upper and lower closet racks, bath area railings and remote-control TV.

All active U.S. military and government employees receive special room rates at most locations. Children 18 and under stay free at all locations when sharing their parents' room. Cribs are available at no cost and roll-away beds are available at an extra charge.

Senior citizens age 55 and over receive a discount on room rates and many locations offer special rates on weekends. La Quinta Senior Class for travelers over the age of 60 provides a 20% discount at all Inns nationwide, no additional charge for a third or fourth person in a room, credits toward free night stays and guaranteed reservations. Upon applying for membership ($10), you receive a certificate good for $20 off the regular room rate.

La Quinta Per Diem Preferred offers credits and discounts to military personnel, U.S. government workers and cost reimbursable contractors. La Quinta Returns earns credits for free

24 Chain Hotels:

nights, special room rates, guaranteed reservations for late arrivals, account summaries and $50 check cashing privileges.

Locations: Bakersfield, Fresno, Chula Vista, Costa Mesa, Irvine, Rancho Penasquitos, Sacramento, San Bernardino, San Francisco, Stockton, Ventura, Vista.

MARRIOTT Marriott Drive, Washington DC 20053. 301-380-9000. Reservations 800-228-2800; 800-321-2211 (Courtyard); 800-331-3131 (Residence Inns); 800-228-9290 (Fairfield Inns).

Marriott consists of Marriott Hotels and Resorts, Marriott Suites, Courtyard by Marriott, Residence Inns and Fairfield Inns.

SuperSaver rates offer discounts on weekday and weekend stays at participating hotels. Discounts range from 10% and up. The TFB program (Two for Breakfast) offers discounts for weekend stays for two adults that includes complimentary breakfasts.

Advance Purchase Rates are discounts of up to 50% for advance, prepaid, non-refundable reservations 7, 14, 21 and 30 days in advance. Senior Citizen discounts for members of AARP and other senior groups are available at all participating hotels.

The Marriott Honored Guest Award offers special upgrades to members at participating hotels. After staying 15 nights during a 12-month period, members receive express checkout services, complimentary newspaper, check cashing privileges, free luggage tags and discounts.

Locations: Anaheim, Arcadia, Bakersfield, Campbell, Pleasant Hill, Costa Mesa, Fountain Valley, Fremont, Irvine, La Jolla, Livermore, Long Beach, Manhattan Beach, Mountain View, Ontario, Orange, Placentia, San Diego, Sacramento, San Mateo, San Ramon, Sunnyvale, Torrance.

MOTEL 6 14651 Dallas Parkway, Dallas TX 75240. 214-386-6161, Fax 214-991-2976, Reservations 800-437-7486

Locations: *Anaheim, Arcata, Atascadero, Bakersfield, Barstow, Bermuda Dunes, Big Bear, Blythe, Buellton, Buena Park, Buttonwillow, Camarillo, Carlsbad, Carpenteria, Chico, Chino, Coalinga, Corona, Davis, El Cajon, Escondido, Eureka, Fairfield, Fontana, Fremont, Fresno, Gilroy, Indio, King City, Lake Tahoe, Lompoc, Los Angeles, Lost Hills, Mammoth Lakes, Monterey, Merced, Modesto, Mojave, Morro Bay, Napa, Needles, Newark, Oakland, Oceanside, Ontario, Oroville, Palmdale, Palm Springs, Palo Alto, Petaluma, Pinole, Pismo Beach, Pittsburg, Porterville, Rancho California, Red Bluff, Redding, Redlands, Ridgecrest, Riverside, Rohnert Park, Sacramento, Salinas, San Bernardino, San Diego, San Jose, San Luis Obispo, Santa Ana, Santa Barbara, Santa Clara, Santa Maria, Santa Nella, Santa Rosa, San Ysidro.*

NATIONAL 9 INN 2285 South Main, Salt Lake City UT 84115. 801-466-9820, Fax 801-466-9856, Reservations 800-524-9999.

Locations: *Fresno, Lawndale, Livermore, Lone Pine, Redding.*

OMNI HOTELS 515 Madison Avenue, New York NY 10022. 212-308-4700, Fax 603-926-9122, Reservations 800-THE-OMNI.

The Omni Club Program is available at selected hotels and offers concierge service, private lounge facilities, complimentary breakfast, evening cocktails and hors d'oeuvres and specially-appointed rooms.

The Omni Hotel Select Guest Program provides special services, priority room availability, accommodations upgrade, complimentary coffee and morning newspaper and a newsletter announcing additional programs. The Omni Hotel Executive Service Plan is available to corporate members asnd includes a variety of special benefits. For planning and scheduling meetings, the Omni Hotels Gavel Service and Omni-Express Programs includes assistance by experienced meeting planners. City'scapes is a special weekend package that offers discounts and special amenities.

26 Chain Hotels:

Locations: San Diego.

PARK INN RESORTS 4425 West Airport Freeway, Irving TX 75062, Reservations 800-437-PARK.

The Silver Citizens Club offers a 20% room discount and 10% food discount at participating hotels, free morning paper and coffee, special directory, all-night emergency pharmacy telephone number and personal check cashing.

Locations: Palm Springs.

RADISSON HOTELS INTERNATIONAL Carlson Parkway, Minneapolis MN 55459. 612-540-5526, Fax 612-449-3400, Reservations 800-333-3333.

Radisson operates 270 hotels and affiliates worldwide. Plaza Hotels are usually in city centers or suburban locations. Suite Hotels offer oversized rooms with living room, mini-bar and kitchenette. Resort Hotels usually are near beaches, golf courses and recreational facilities.

Locations: City of Commerce, Fullerton, Irvine, Long Beach, Los Angeles, Oxnard, Rancho Bernardo, Sacramento, San Diego, San Francisco, San Jose, Santa Ana, Simi Valley, Sunnyvale, Visalia.

RAMADA INN Box 52106, Phoenix AZ 85072. Reservations 800-2-RAMADA.

Ramada Inn has 700 location world-wide consisting of Ramada Inns, Ramada Hotels and Ramada Renaissance Hotels. The Hotels are designed to five-star international standards and include convention and banquet facilities, restaurants, 24-hour room service, entertainment and lounges. Most Renaissance Hotels offer a club floor with concierge services, upgraded room amenities and lounge.

Membership in the Ramada Business Card Program earns points for trips and merchandise based on dollars spent at

Ramada properties. The card is available free. Membership includes favorable rates, automatic room upgrade when available, express check-in and check-out, free newspaper on business days, free same-room accommodations for your spouse when you travel together, extended check-out times, newsletter and points redeemable for hotel stays, air travel, car rentals and over 10,000 Service Merchandise catalog items.

Participating Ramada Inn properties offer SuperSaver Weekend discounts. These rates apply on Friday, Saturday and Sunday for one-, two- and three-night stays. Extra person rates may apply for a third or fourth person in the room. Because some hotels limit availability on some dates, reservations are recommended.

When traveling with family or friends, the Ramada 4-for-1 Program permits up to four people to share the same room and pay the single rate. At participating properties, the Best Years Seniors Program provides travelers over the age of 60 who are members of AARP, the Global Horizons Club, Catholic Golden Age, The Golden Buckeye Club, Humana Seniors Association, The Retired Enlisted Association, The Retired Officers Association and United Airlines Silver Wings Plus with a 25% discount off regular room rates.

The Ramada Per Diem Value Program is available at more than 350 locations. Properties honor the maximum lodging per diem rates set by the U.S. General Services Administration. Federal employees, military personnel and employees of Cost Reimbursable Contractors traveling on official government business are eligible. In addition to the per diem limits for lodging, the single person room rate at participating locations includes full American breakfast and all applicable taxes. All Ramada properties give corporate customers favorable rates. Companies need a minimum of ten travelers with a combined total of 100 room nights per year.

Locations: *Agoura Hills, Anaheim, Antioch, Artesia, Bakersfield, Buellton, Buena Park, Burbank, Burlingame, Carlsbad, Carson, Chatsworth, Chula Vista, Claremont, Commerce,*

28 Chain Hotels:

Compton, Culver City, Cypress, Davis, El Centro, El Montes, Fresno, Garden Grove, Hawthorne, Hemet, Hollywood, Long Beach, Los Angeles, Modesto, Monterey, Moreno Valley, Oakdale, Orange, Palmdale, Palm Springs, Salinas, San Bernardino, San Clemente, San Diego, San Francisco, Santa Ana, Santa Maria, Solano Beach, Sunset Beach, Temecula, Vallejo.

RITZ CARLTON HOTELS 3414 Peachtree Road NE, Atlanta GA 30326. 404-237-5500, Fax 404-261-0119, Reservations 800-241-3333.

Locations: *Laguna Beach, Rancho Mirage, Marina del Rey, San Francisco.*

SHERATON HOTELS, INNS AND RESORTS 60 State Street, Boston MA 02109. 617-367-3600, Fax 617-367-5676, Reservations 800-325-3535.

Sheraton Club International is a frequent guest program that offers free stays based on points earned. Membership includes upgraded accommodations, late check-outs and other benefits. The Sheraton Executive Traveler Plan provides guaranteed rooms rates year-round, earned credits, free newspaper daily, automatic upgrades, family plans, express check-outs and other benefits.

Locations: *Anaheim, Bakersfield, Burlingame, Cerritos, City of Industry, Concord, Fresno, La Jolla, Long Beach, Los Angeles, Milpitas, Monterey, Newport Beach, Norwalk, Pleasanton, Pomona, Rancho Cordova, Redondo Beach, Riverside, Rosemead, Sacramento, San Diego, San Francisco, San Jose, San Pedro, Sunnyvale, Santa Barbara, Santa Monica, Solvang, Universal City.*

SHILO INNS 11600 Southwest Barnes Road, Portland OR 97225. 503-641-6565, Reservations 800-222-2244.

Locations: *Corning, Delano, Mammoth Lakes, Oakhurst, Palm Springs, Pomona.*

SUNDOWNER MOTOR INNS Box 145, Goodlettesville TN 37072. 615-851-0942, Reservations 800-322-8029.

Sundowner International consists of Best Value Inns, Superior Motels, Sundowners Inns and Travel Host Motels.

Locations: *Los Angeles; Palm Springs; San Francisco; San Simeon.*

SUPER 8 MOTELS 1910 8th Avenue NE, Aberdeen SD 57402. 605-225-2272, Fax 605-225-1140, Reservations 800-800-8000, 800-848-8888.

Locations: *Alameda, Anaheim, Arcata, Arvin, Auburn, Bakersfield, Banning, Barstow, Blythe, Cameron Park, Costa Mesa, Fortuna, Gilroy, Hayward, Hemet, Hesperia, Indio, Inglewood, Martinez, Milpitas, Kettleman City, Modesto, Monterey, Ontario, Palm Springs, Palmdale, Pleasanton, Red Bluff, Redding, Riverside, Sacramento, San Bernardino, San Diego, San Francisco, San Luis Obispo, Santa Rosa, Selma, Truckee, Ukiah, Upper Lake, Vacaville, Willos, Yucca Valley.*

TRAVELODGE 1973 Friendship Drive, El Cajon CA 92020. 619-448-1884, Fax 619-562-0901, Reservations 800-255-3050.

The Business Break Club Program provides a 10% discount off the lowest published room rate, express check-in and check-out, free local telephone call and morning coffee and a special 800-number for fast reservations. The Corporate Business Break Club gives a 10% room discount and special amenities. Classic Travel Club is available to travelers over the age of 50. There are room discounts of 15%, a quarterly newsletter, check cashing privileges, free morning coffee, car rental discounts and express check-in, check-out services.

Under the Family Plan, there is no charge for children under the age of 17 when sharing a room with their parents. The Goverment Traveler-Value America Plan offers rates equal to or less than the prevailing per diem rates paid and is available to federal employees, military personnel and contractors on government business.

Locations: *Azusa, Bakersfield, Baldwin Park, Banning, Bellflower, Berkeley, Blythe, Buena Park, Burbank, Carlsbad, Castro Valley, Cerritos-Artesia, Chula Vista, Claremont, Compton, Corona, Costa Mesa-Newport Beach, Crescent City, Culver City, Duarte-Monrovia, Dunsmuir, El Cajon, El Toro, Encinitas, Escondido, Eureka, Fallbrook, Garden Grove, Harbor City, Hayward, Hemet, Hermosa Beach, Hollywood, Huntington Park, Imperial Beach, Indio, Inglewood, La Jolla, La Mesa, La Puente, Lake Elsinore, Lake Tahoe, Long Beach, Los Angeles, Lynwood, Mammoth Lakes, Merced, Millbrae, Mill Valley, Milpitas, Montebello, Monterey, Morena Valley, Morro Bay, Napa Valley, Novato, Oceanside, Ontario, Orange, Palms Springs, Palo Alto, Pasadena, Paso Robles, Pico Rivera, Poway, Rancho Bernardo, Redondo Beach, Rialto, Richmond, Riverside, Rosemead, Sacramento, San Bernardino, San Carlos, San Clemente, San Diego, San Francisco, San Jose, San Juan Capistrano, San Luis Obispo, San Marcos, San Ysidro, Santa Barbara, Santa Clara, Santa Clarita, Santa Cruz, Santa Monica, Santa Nella, Santa Paula, Santa Rosa, Simi Valley, Spring Valley, Tehachapi, Torrance, Ukiah, Vacaville, Vallejo, Van Nuys, Ventura, Victorville, Westminster, Whittier.*

VAGABOND INN Reservations 800-522-1555.

Vagabond Inns offer free continental breakfasts, free coffee, free weekday newspapers, free local telephone calls and a free toiletry pack with toothbrush, shampoo, etc. Children under 18 stay free in the same room with adult. Stay nine nights at any location and get the tenth night free.

Locations: *Bishop, Chula Vista, Costa Mesa, Fresno, Glendale, Hayward, Long Beach, Los Angeles, Modesto, Oxnard, Palm Springs, Palmdale, Pasadena, Redding, Redondo Beach, Rosemead, Sacramento, San Diego, Salinas, San Francisco, San Jose, San Luis Obispo, San Pedro, Santa Barbara, Santa Clara, Stockton, Sunnyvale, Ventura, Whittier, Woodland Hills.*

WESTIN HOTELS AND RESORTS The Westin Building, Seattle WA 98121. 206-443-5096, Fax 206-443-5096, Reservations 800-228-3000.

At Westin hotels or resorts there is no charge for children under the age of 18 when they share the same room with parents or guardians. If more than one room is required to accommodate a family, the single guest room rate will apply to each room, regardless of the number of people occupying the room.

Locations: Costa Mesa, Los Angeles, Rancho Mirage, San Francisco

WYNDHAM HOTELS AND RESORTS 2001 Bryan Street, Suite 2300, Dallas TX 75210. 214-978-4500, Reservations 800-822-4200.

Locations: Los Angeles, Commerce, Palm Springs, San Diego, Sunnyvale.

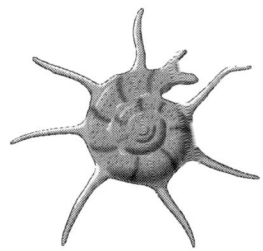

Accommodations Directory

Adelanto

Area Code 619
Adelanto Chamber of Commerce
Box 700
Adelanto CA 92301
246-5711

Best Western Inn (Highway 50, 95667; 622-9100, Fax 622-9376, 800-528-1234) 105 rooms, restaurant, lounge, swimming pool, fireplaces, fax service, meeting facilities, wheelchair-access rooms, no-smoking rooms, pets allowed. SGL/DBL$53-$130.

Cary House (300 Main Street, 95667; 622-4271) 24 rooms. SGL/DBL$40-$65.

Days Inn (11628 Bartlett Avenue, 92301; 246-8777, Fax 246-4350, 800-325-2525) 36 rooms and suites, swimming pool, pets allowed, wheelchair-access rooms, no-smoking rooms. SGL$35-$45, DBL$39-$49, STS$45-$65.

Days Inn (1332 Broadway, 95667; 622-3124, 800-325-2525) 45 rooms and suites, complimentary breakfast, swimming pool, free local telephone calls, children under 12 free, fax service, wheelchair-access rooms, no-smoking rooms, no pets. SGL/DBL$48-$61, STS$70-$80.

River Rock Inn (1756 Georgetown Drive, 95667; 622-7640) 4 rooms, bed and breakfast, complimentary breakfast. SGL$55, DBL$70.

Agoura Hills

Area Code 818
Agoura Hills Chamber of Commerce
29170 Agoura Road
Agoura Hills CA 91301
889-3150

Ramada Hotel Agoura Hills (30100 Agoura Road, 91301; 707-1220, Fax 707-6298) 282 rooms and suites, restaurant, wheelchair-access rooms, spa, valet laundry, fax service, room service, complimentary newspaper, gift shop, laundry room, children under 18 free, no-smoking rooms, exercise facilities, free parking. SGL/DBL$75-$95, STS$149-$195.

Alhambra

Area Code 818
Alhambra Chamber of Commerce
104 South First Street
Alhambra CA 91801
282-8481

Best Western Inn (2451 West Main Street, 91801; 284-5522, Fax 576-5937, 800-528-1234) 58 rooms, restaurant, complimentary breakfast, heated swimming pool, spa, laundry room, fax service, in-room refrigerators, children under 12 free, no-smoking rooms, no pets. SGL/DBL$80-$95.

Days Inn (15 North First Street, 91801; 308-0014, Fax 281-5996, 800-325-2525) 30 rooms, complimentary breakfast, swimming pool, in-room refrigerators and microwaves, children under 12 free, fax service, laundry room, jacuzzis, complimentary breakfast, no-smoking rooms. SGL$30-$40, DBL$35-$45.

Daystop (15 North First Street, 91801; 308-0014) 30 rooms. SGL/DBL$30-$45.

Quality Inn (2221 West Commonwealth Avenue, 91801; 816-300-0003, 800-221-2222) 72 rooms, restaurant, complimentary breakfast, swimming pool, wheelchair-access rooms, airport transportation, no-smoking rooms, no pets. SGL$60-$97, DBL$68-$109.

Anaheim and Anaheim Hills

Area Code 714
Anaheim Area Visitor and Convention Bureau
800 West Katella Avenue
Anaheim CA 92803
999-8999

Anaheim Chamber of Commerce
100 South Anaheim Boulevard #300
Anaheim CA 92805
758-0222

RENTAL SOURCES: Bed and Breakfast International (Box 282910, San Francisco 94128; 696-1690, Fax 696-1699, 800-872-4500) represents bed and breakfast and private home accommodations in the Anaheim area. All rates include complimentary breakfast. SGL/DBL$50-$125.

National Reservation Bureau, Inc. (19510 Ventura Boulevard, Tarzana CA 91357, 818-344-6776, 800-537-7666) represents hotels and inns in the Anaheim area. SGL/DBL$30-$200.

Anaheim Angel Inn (1800 East Katella Avenue, 92805; 634-9121, 800-435-4400, 800-358-440 in California) 61 rooms, restaurant, outdoor swimming pool, spa, in-room refrigerators, children under 13 stay free, in-room refrigerators, fax service, car rental, no-smoking rooms, microwaves and safes, child care, transportation to local attractions, complimentary coffee, wheelchair-access rooms, airport transportation, pets allowed, free parking. LS SGL$34-$45, DBL$39-$59; HS SGL$39-$59, DBL$45-$69.

Anaheim-Buena Park TraveLodge (735 South Beach Boulevard, 92804; 761-4255, Fax 821-0171, 800-869-8089, 800-255-3050) 40 rooms, restaurant, swimming pool, exercise facilities, wheelchair-access rooms, airport transportation, no pets. SGL$32-$35, DBL$35-$44.

Anaheim Cavalier Inn and Suites (11811 South Harbor Boulevard, 92802; 750-1000, Fax 971-3539, 800-821-2768, 800-621-5185 in California) 94 rooms and suites, complimentary breakfast, swimming pool, in-room refrigerators and microwaves, transportation to local attractions, free parking. LS SGL/DBL$32-$49, HS SGL/DBL$49-$65.

Anaheim Country Inn (856 South Walnut, 92802; 778-0150, 800-755-7801) 8 rooms, bed and breakfast, complimentary breakfast, hot tub, no smoking, no pets, free parking. DBL$55-$80.

Anaheim Harbor TraveLodge (2171 South Harbor Boulevard; 750-3100, Fax 748-9809, 800-255-3050) 128 rooms, restaurant, lounge, complimentary breakfast, swimming pool, spa, meeting facilities, laundry room, tours, car rental, transportation to local attractions. SGL/DBL$35-$59.

Anaheim Hilton and Towers (777 Convention Way, 92802; 750-4321, Fax 740-4252, 800-222-9923) 1,576 rooms and suites, four restaurants, lounges, outdoor and indoor swimming pools, spa, jacuzzi, tennis, concierge level, tours, exercise facilities, valet laundry, meeting facilities for 4,000, beauty and barber shop, wheelchair-access rooms, airport transportation, pets allowed. SGL/DBL$140-$200, STS$500-$1,100.

Anaheim International Inn and Suites (2060 South Harbor Boulevard, 92802; 972-9393, Fax 971-2706) 120 rooms, complimentary breakfast, heated swimming pool, jacuzzi, meeting facilities for 200, laundry room, transportation to local attractions, tours. SGL/DBL$49-$78.

Anaheim Maingate Inn (1211 South West Street, 92802; 533-2500, Fax 520-0578, 800-654-6175) 29 rooms and suites, outdoor spa, in-room refrigerators and microwaves, valet laundry, fax service, transportation to local attractions, laundry room, no-smoking rooms, tours, free parking. SGL/DBL$42-$68, STS$58-$98.

Anaheim Marriott Hotel (700 West Convention Way, 92802; 750-8000, Fax 750-9100, 800-228-9290) 1,043 rooms, three restaurants, lounges, two swimming pools, jacuzzis, concierge, exercise facilities, meeting facilities for 200, laundry room, transportation to local attractions, wheelchair-access rooms, airport transportation, pets allowed. SGL/DBL$89-$180.

Anaheim Park Vue Inn (1570 South Harbor Boulevard, 92802; 722-5721, 800-422-4470) 90 rooms and efficiencies, restaurant, complimentary breakfast, swimming pool. SGL$34-$53, DBL$38-$72, EFF$55-$120.

Anaheim Penny Sleeper Inn (1441 South Manchester Avenue, 92802; 991-8100, Fax 533-6430, 800-854-6118) 205 rooms, outdoor heated pool, laundry room, in-room refrigerators, valet laundry, fax service, transportation to local attractions, swimming pool, wheelchair-access rooms, no-smoking rooms, car rental, free parking. SGL/DBL$32-$55.

Best Western Abby's Anaheim Inn (1201 West Katella Avenue, 92802; 774-0211, 800-528-1234) restaurant, swimming pool, wheelchair-access rooms, no-smoking rooms, no pets. LS SGL$39-$42, DBL$42-$44; HS SGL$48-$58, DBL$58-$64.

Best Western Angels Inn (11851 South Harbor Boulevard, 92802; 971-0255, 800-528-1234) 55 rooms, restaurant, lounge, swimming pool, whirlpool, children under 12 free. SGL/DBL$36-$64.

Best Western Anaheim Inn (1630 South Harbor Boulevard, 92802; 774-1050, Fax 776-6305, 800-528-1234) 28 rooms, restaurant, heated swimming pool, whirlpool, sauna, valet laundry, wheelchair-access rooms, no-smoking rooms, no pets. SGL$55-$85, DBL$55-$85.

Best Western Anaheim Stardust (1057 West Ball Road, 92802; 774-7600, Fax 535-6953, 800-528-1234, 800-826-8932 in California) 103 rooms, restaurant, lounge, swimming pool, sauna, wheelchair-access rooms, no pets. SGL/DBL$42-$78.

Best Western Apollo Inn (1741 South West Street, 92802; 772-9759, Fax 772-5842, 800-854-8175, 800-528-1234) 136 rooms, swimming pool, sauna, whirlpool, children under 18 free, wheelchair-access rooms, no-smoking rooms. SGL/DBL$55-$90.

Best Western Courtesy Inn (1201 South West Street, 92804; 2470, Fax 774-3425, 800-233-8062, 800-528-1234) 35 rooms and suites, restaurant, lounge, complimentary breakfast, swimming pool, whirlpool, valet laundry, wheelchair-access rooms, free parking, no pets. SGL$36-$68, DBL$42-$70, STS$80-$125.

Best Western Park Place Inn (1544 Harbor Boulevard, 92802; 776-4800, Fax 758-1396, 800-854-8175, 800-528-1234) complimentary breakfast, swimming pool, wheelchair-access rooms, no pets. SGL/DBL$60-$95.

Best Western Station Inn (989 West Ball Road, 92802; 991-5500, 800-528-1234) 55 rooms, lounge, complimentary breakfast, swimming pool, no-smoking rooms, no pets. SGL$46-$78, DBL$56-$88.

Best Western Stovall's Inn (1110 West Katella Avenue, 92802; 778-1880, Fax 778-3805, 800-528-1234) 290 rooms, restaurant, lounge, two swimming pools, whirlpools, gift shop, tours, no-smoking rooms. SGL/DBL$50-$85.

Best Western Stovall's Pavilions (1176 West Katella Avenue, 92802; 776-0140, Fax 776-5801, 800-845-8157, 800-528-1234) 290 rooms, restaurant, lounge, swimming pool, whirlpool, children under 18 free, valet laundry, no-smoking rooms. SGL/DBL$50-$90.

Candy Cane Inn (1747 South Harbor Boulevard, 92802; 774-5284, Fax 772-5462, 800-321-3531) 272 rooms and suites, restaurant, complimentary breakfast, outdoor heated swimming pool, spa, exercise facilities, valet laundry, fax service, laundry room, wheelchair-access rooms, airport transportation, free parking. SGL/DBL$55-$79.

Carousel Inn and Suites (1530 South Harbor Boulevard, 92802; 758-0444, Fax 772-9965, 800-854-6767) 130 rooms and suites, complimentary breakfast, swimming pool, in-room refrigerators and microwaves, meeting facilities for 30, fax service, tours, wheelchair-access rooms, no-smoking rooms, no pets. SGL/DBL$51-$75.

Cavalier Inns and Suites (11811 South Harbor Boulevard, 92802; 750-1000, 800-821-2768) 94 rooms and suites, complimentary breakfast, outdoor swimming pool, jacuzzi, spa, children under 18 stay free, in-room refrigerators and microwaves, VCRs, fax service, meeting facilities for 15, tours, car rental, airport transportation, transportation to local attractions, no-smoking, no pets, wheelchair access. LS SGL$60, STS$70; HS SGL$75, STS$85.

Comfort Inn (2200 South Harbor Boulevard, 92802; 750-5211, 800-221-2222) 66 rooms, restaurant, complimentary breakfast, heated swimming pool, spa, whirlpool, children under 18 free, valet laundry, tours, wheelchair-access rooms, no pets. SGL$39-$69, DBL$44-$79.

Comfort Inn North (1251 North Harbor Boulevard, 92801; 635-6461, 800-221-2222) 119 rooms, restaurant, swimming pool, whirlpool, tours, laundry room, wheelchair-access rooms, no pets. SGL/DBL$34-$65.

Comfort Suites (201 North Via Cortez Street, 92806; 921-1100, 800-221-2222, 800-228-5150) 163 rooms, restaurant, complimentary breakfast, outdoor heated swimming pool, sauna, whirlpool, spa, exercise facilities, in-room refrigerators, valet laundry, fax service, laundry room, no pets. SGL$64-$74, DBL$74-$94.

Conestoga Hotel (1240 Walnut Street, 92802; 535-0300, Fax 491-8953, 800-321-3531, 800-321-3530 in California) 252 rooms, restaurant, swimming pool, meeting facilities for 200, no-smoking rooms, exercise facilities, airport transportation. SGL/DBL$89-$109.

Country Inn Bed and Breakfast (856 Walnut Street, 92802; 778-0150) 8 rooms, bed and breakfast, complimentary breakfast. SGL/DBL$37-$80.

Crown Sterling Suites (3100 East Frontera, 92806; 632-1221, Fax 632-9963, 800-433-4600) 224 suites, swimming pool, sauna, fireplaces, meeting facilities for 200, children under 12 free, laundry room, child care, wheelchair-access rooms, no-smoking rooms. SGL/DBL$110-$150.

Days Inn (1500 South Raymond Avenue, 92631; 635-9000, Fax 520-5831) 250 rooms, two restaurants, swimming pool, whirlpool, laundry room, gift shop, children under 12 free, fax service, wheelchair-access rooms, no-smoking rooms. SGL$69-$85, DBL$79-$95.

Days Inn Disneyland (1030 West Ball Road, 92802; 520-0101, Fax 758-9406, 800-325-2525) 45 rooms and suites, complimentary breakfast, outdoor heated swimming pool, tours, fax service, children under 12 free, in-room refrigerators and microwaves, laundry room, wheelchair-access rooms, no-smoking rooms, car rental, free parking. SGL/DBL$39-$69, STS$59-$99.

Disneyland Hotel (1150 West Cerritos Avenue, 92802; 778-6600, Fax 956-6597) 1,174 rooms, 11 restaurants, lounges, three swimming pools, marina, wheelchair-access rooms, airport transportation, meeting facilities for 200, child care, room service, tennis, transportation to local attractions, no-smoking rooms. SGL$99-$195, DBL$99-$215, STS$400-$1,750.

Econo Lodge (837 South Beach Boulevard, 92804; 952-0898, 800-424-4777) 60 rooms, restaurant, swimming pool, wheelchair access, no pets, children under 18 free. SGL/DBL$30-$35.

Econo Lodge East (871 South Harbor Boulevard, 92805; 535-7878, Fax 567-5870, 800-424-4777) 34 rooms, restaurant, swimming pool, kitchenettes, whirlpools, wheelchair-access rooms, children under 18 free. SGL/DBL$35-$70.

Econo Lodge Stadium (1914 South Anaheim Boulevard, 92805; 533-2666, 800-424-4777) 64 rooms, restaurant, complimentary breakfast, swimming pool, whirlpool, children under 18 free, transportation to local attractions, airport transportation, spas, kitchenettes, VCRs, no pets. SGL/DBL$35-$60.

Eden Rock Motel (1830 South West Street, 92802; 971-5511) 48 rooms and suites, restaurant, kitchenettes, swimming pool, free parking. SGL/DBL$32-$45, STS$40-$85.

Friendship Inn Sunrise (705 South Beach Boulevard, 92804; 761-4200, 800-424-4777) 65 rooms, restaurant, indoor swimming pool, whirlpools, tennis, no-smoking rooms, children under 18 free. SGL/DBL$33-$41.

Granada Inn (2375 West Lincoln Avenue, 92801; 774-7370, 800-648-8685, 800-648-8686 in California) 80 suites, restaurant, outdoor swimming pool, complimentary breakfast, children under 16 stay free, fax service, free parking. SGL$59-$69, DBL$65-$75, STS$72-$82.

Grand Hotel (One Hotel Way, 92802; 772-7777, Fax 774-7281, 800-421-6662, 800-352-6688 in California) 242 rooms and suites, swimming pool, exercise facilities, wheelchair-access rooms, no-smoking rooms. SGL/DBL$85-$120, STS$125-$235.

Hampton Inn (300 East Katella Way, 92802; 772-8713, Fax 778-1235, 800-HAMPTON) 136 rooms, complimentary breakfast, swimming pool, meeting facilities, pets allowed, wheelchair-access rooms. SGL/DBL$61-$80.

Hilton Hotel and Towers (777 Convention Way, 92802; 750-4321, Fax 750-4943, 800-HILTONS) 1,600 rooms and suites, restaurant, swimming pool, meeting facilities for 200, exercise facilities, wheelchair-access rooms, no-smoking rooms. SGL/DBL$140-$200.

Holiday Inn (1850 South Harbor Road, 92802; 750-2801, Fax 971-4754, 800-624-6855, 800-HOLIDAY) 312 rooms, restaurant, transportation to local attractions, meeting facilities for 500, laundry room, gift shop, tours, no pets. SGL/DBL$85-$95.

Holiday Inn (1221 South Harbor Road, 92802; 213-435-8511, 800-HOLIDAY) 224 rooms, restaurant, swimming pool, jacuzzi, wheelchair-access rooms, child care, room service, gift shop, valet laundry, meeting facilities for 200, transportation to local attractions, free parking, exercise facilities, no pets. SGL/DBL$69-$79.

Holiday Inn (1850 South Harbor Road, 92802; 750-2801, Fax 971-4754, 800-624-6855, 800-HOLIDAY) 314 rooms, restaurant, swimming pool, wheelchair-access rooms, no-smoking rooms, gift shop, meeting facilities, room service, concierge, transportation to local attractions, free parking. airport transportation. SGL/DBL$85-$95.

Holiday Inn Express (435 West Katella Avenue, 92802; 772-7755, Fax 772-2727, 800-833-7888) 105 rooms and suites, outdoor heated swimming pool, sauna, exercise facilities, in-room refrigerators, valet laundry, fax service, laundry room, wheelchair-access rooms, free parking. SGL$36-$56, DBL$46-$62.

Holiday Inn Fullerton (222 West Houston Avenue, 92632; 992-1700, 800-465-4329) 289 rooms, restaurant, swimming pool, meeting facilities for 350. SGL/DBL$50-$85+.

Howard Johnson Hotel-Disneyland (1380 South Harbor Road; 776-6120, Fax 533-3578, 800-854-0303, 800-422-4228 in California) 318 rooms and suites, restaurant, two outdoor swimming pools, transportation to local attractions, valet laundry, concierge, children under 18 free, room service, child care, fax service, gift shop, laundry rooms, no-smoking rooms, free parking, airport courtesy car. SGL$59-$78, STS$145+.

Anaheim and Anaheim Hills 43

Hyatt Regency Alicante (Box 4669, 92803; 971-3000, Fax 740-0465, 800-972-2929) 398 rooms and suites, two restaurants, lounges, outdoor swimming pool, jacuzzi, transportation to local attractions, tennis, meeting facilities for 200, child care, pets allowed, exercise facilities, wheelchair-access rooms, airport transportation. SGL$79-$129, DBL$79-$149.

Inn At The Park Hotel (1855 South Harbor Boulevard, 92802; 750-1811, Fax 971-3626, 800-352-6686) 500 rooms and one-bedroom suites, restaurant, swimming pool, room service, meeting facilities for 200, children under 12 free, wheelchair-access rooms, airport transportation. SGL$79-$109, DBL$89-$119, 1BR$180-$380+.

Jolly Roger Inn (640 West Katella Avenue, 92802; 772-7621, Fax 772-2308, 800-854-3184) 237 rooms, restaurant, lounge, swimming pool, wheelchair-access rooms, meeting facilities for 250, room service, airport transportation, no-smoking rooms. SGL/DBL$65-$95.

Marco Polo Hotel (1604 South Harbor Boulevard, 92802; 635-3630, 800-854-8005, 800-624-3940 in California) 58 rooms, restaurant, swimming pool. SGL$38-$70, DBL$75-$120.

Marriott Residence Inn (1700 South Clementine Street, 92802; 533-3555, Fax 535-7626, 800-331-3131) 200 suites, swimming pool, meeting facilities for 50, in-room microwaves, room service, transportation to local attractions, free parking, pets allowed. SGL$38-$46, DBL$42-$50.

Motel 6 (1440 North State College, 92806; 956-9690, 505-891-6161) 127 rooms. SGL/DBL$29-$35.

Motel 6 (921 South Beach Boulevard, 92804; 220-2866, 505-891-6161) 54 rooms. SGL/DBL$27-$33.

Motel 6 (100 West Freedman Way, 92802; 520-9696, 505-891-6161) 222 rooms. SGL/DBL$36-$42.

Pan Pacific Hotel (1717 South West Street, 92802; 999-0999, Fax 999-0745) 508 rooms, restaurant, swimming pool, wheelchair-access rooms, meeting facilities for 200, child care, children under 17 free, room service, airport transportation, no-smoking rooms. SGL/DBL$99-$165.

Parcher Bed and Breakfast (Bed and Breakfast International) 3 rooms, complimentary breakfast, no smoking. SGL/DBL$45-$55.

Plaza Resort Hotel (1700 South Harbor Boulevard, 92802; 772-5900, Fax 772-8386, 800-228-1357) 308 rooms and suites, restaurant, outdoor swimming pool, valet laundry, child care, meeting facilities for 200, fax service, gift shop, laundry room, wheelchair-access rooms, no-smoking rooms airport transportation. SGL/DBL$69-$79, STS$175-$600.

Quality Hotel and Conference Center (616 Convention Way, 92802; 750-3131, Fax 750-9027, 800-777-1455, 800-221-2222, 800-852-5215) 284 rooms, restaurant, lounge, swimming pool, whirlpool, tours, transportation to local attractions, exercise facilities, pets allowed, wheelchair-access rooms, meeting facilities for 200, laundry room, no-smoking rooms, airport transportation, SGL$62-$85, DBL$67-$90.

Quality Inn (711 Brookhurst Street, 92804; 999-1220, 800-221-2222) 91 rooms, restaurant, lounge, heated swimming pool, sauna, whirlpool, transportation to local attractions, meeting facilities, wheelchair-access rooms, no pets. SGL$42-$68, DBL$52-$78.

Quality Inn West (727 South Beach Boulevard, 92804; 220-0100, 800-221-2222) 100 rooms, restaurant, heated swimming pool, whirlpool, sauna, transportation to local attractions, room service, tours, wheelchair-access rooms, no pets. SGL/DBL$36-$72.

Raffles Inn and Suites (2040 South Harbor Boulevard, 92802; 750-6100, Fax 740-0639, 800-233-6593) 122 rooms and suites, complimentary breakfast, outdoor heated swimming pool, children under 12 free, kitchenettes, gift shop, no-smoking rooms, pets allowed, wheelchair-access rooms, airport transportation. SGL/DBL$55-$69, STS$69-$129.

Ramada Hotel (5865 Katella Avenue, 90630; 827-1010, Fax 220-0543, 800-228-2828) 180 rooms, restaurant, lounge, swimming pool, exercise facilities, children under 18 free, wheelchair-access rooms, airport transportation, no-smoking rooms, transportation to local attractions, SGL/DBL$86-$116.

Ramada Maingate Hotel Anaheim (1460 South Harbor Boulevard, 92804; 800-447-4048) 465 rooms, restaurant, heated swimming pool, children under 18 free, spa, gift shop, laundry room, in-room refrigerators and safes, transportation to local attractions. SGL/DBL$79-$99.

Rodeway Inn (800 South Beach Boulevard, 92804; 955-5700, 800-628-3400) 74 rooms and efficiencies, restaurant, complimentary breakfast, heated swimming pool, spa, wheelchair-access rooms, children under 18 free, meeting facilities, VCRs, laundry room. SGL/DBL$44-$58.

Rodeway Inn Harbor Park (1104 North Harbor Boulevard, 92703; 554-1177, Fax 554-7538, 800-445-0226) 90 rooms, complimentary breakfast, swimming pool, wheelchair-access rooms, exercise facilities, no-smoking rooms. SGL$44-$45, DBL$80-$120.

Scottish Inn (2225 West Lincoln Avenue, 92801; 774-7774, 800-251-1962) 41 rooms, heated swimming pool, laundry room, whirlpool, wheelchair-access rooms. SGL$29-$31, DBL$31-$40.

Sheraton Anaheim Hotel (1015 West Ball Road, 92802; 778-1700, Fax 535-3889, 800-325-3535) 500 rooms and suites, indoor and outdoor restaurants, lounge, complimentary breakfast, outdoor heated swimming pool, 24-hour room service, wheelchair-access rooms, transportation to local attractions, laundry room, meeting facilities for 1,000, room service, airport transportation, no-smoking rooms. SGL$70-$105, DBL$80-$120.

Sterling Suites (3100 South Frontera Street, 92806; 632-1221, Fax 632-9963) 224 suites, restaurant, complimentary breakfast, swimming pool, wheelchair-access rooms, airport transportation, no-smoking rooms. SGL$109-$129, DBL$119-$139.

Stovall's Inn (1110 West Katella Avenue, 92802; 778-1880, Fax 778-3805, 800-854-8175) 292 rooms and suites, restaurant, lounge, two outdoor heated swimming pools, spa, valet laundry, gift shop, laundry room, no-smoking rooms, free parking. SGL/DBL$55-$75, STS$110-$150.

Super 8 Motel (915 South West Street, 92802; 778-0350, Fax 778-3878, 800-800-8000) 113 rooms, restaurant, outdoor heated swimming pool, spa, complimentary breakfast, transportation to local attractions, wheelchair-access rooms, laundry room, fax service, no-smoking rooms, no pets. LS SGL/DBL$39; HS SGL/DBL$42-$54.

TraveLodge (328 North Stanton Avenue, 92801; 229-0101, 800-255-3050) 60 rooms and suites, restaurant, lounge, swimming pool, spa, sauna, valet laundry, meeting facilities, tennis, no pets. SGL$32-$42, DBL$42-$52.

TraveLodge (505 West Katella Avenue, 92802; 774-8710, 800-255-3050) 50 rooms, restaurant, lounge, complimentary breakfast, swimming pool, car rental, laundry room, free local telephone calls, pets allowed. LS SGL/DBL$35-$49; HS SGL/DBL$49-$52.

TraveLodge (1765 South West Street, 92802; 774-6427, Fax 635-1502, 800-255-3050) 39 rooms, restaurant, lounge, swimming pool, spa, car rental, tours, valet laundry, fax service, no pets. SGL/DBL$40-$65.

TraveLodge (1700 East Katella, 92805; 634-1920, Fax 634-0366, 800-255-3050) 72 rooms and efficiencies, restaurant, lounge, swimming pool, spa, in-room refrigerators, kitchenettes, tours, car rental, meeting facilities for 50, transportation to local attractions, tennis, no pets. SGL$45-$55, DBL$50-$60.

Anaheim and Anaheim Hills 47

TraveLodge At The Park (1717 South Harbor Boulevard, 92802; 635-6550, Fax 635-1502, 800-545-1275) 254 rooms and suites, restaurant, complimentary breakfast, outdoor heated swimming pool, spa, in-room refrigerators and microwaves, valet laundry, concierge, fax service, child care, transportation to local attractions, laundry room, no pets, wheelchair-access rooms, airport transportation, car rental, free parking, no-smoking rooms. SGL$69-$79, DBL$79-$89.

TraveLodge Convention Side (735 West Katella Avenue, 92802; 774-8065, Fax 635-1502, 800-255-3050) 36 rooms, restaurant, lounge, swimming pool, spa, tennis, car rental, tours, meeting facilities, no pets. LS SGL$45-$60, DBL$50-$60; HS SGL/DBL$60-$75.

TraveLodge Suites (2141 South Harbor Boulevard, 92802; 971-3553, Fax 971-4609, 800-255-3050, 800-526-9444) 95 suites, restaurant, lounge, complimentary breakfast, swimming pool, spa, in-room refrigerators and microwaves, transportation to local attractions, tours, wheelchair-access rooms, no-smoking rooms, airport transportation, no pets, free parking. SGL/DBL$58-$118.

TraveLodge Westgate (1759 South West Street, 92802; 774-2136, Fax 635-1502, 800-255-3050) 56 rooms, restaurant, lounge, swimming pool, tours, car rental, laundry room, no pets. LS SGL$45-$65, DBL$55-$65; HS SGL$60-$70, DBL$65-$75.

Westwood Ho Seven Seas (415 Katella Avenue, 92802; 778-6900, 800-777-7123) 176 rooms and suites, heated outdoor swimming pool, jacuzzi, no-smoking rooms, tours, airport transportation, free parking. SGL$39-$46, DBL$44-$54, STS$60-$75.

Woodfine Suite Hotel (720 The City Drive, 92668; 740-2700, Fax 971-1692, 800-237-8811) 124 suites, restaurant, complimentary breakfast, swimming pool, wheelchair-access rooms. SGL$121-$160, DBL$136-$175.

Arcadia

Area Code 818
Arcadia Chamber of Commerce
388 West Huntington Drive
Arcadia CA 91006
447-2159

Best Western Westerner Inn (161 Colorado Place, 91006; 447-3501, Fax 447-4739, 800-528-1234) 70 rooms, restaurant, complimentary breakfast, outdoor heated swimming pool, spa, meeting facilities for 75, fax service, exercise facilities, no pets. SGL/DBL$47-$93.

Embassy Suites Hotel Arcadia (211 East Huntington Drive; 445-8525, Fax 445-8548, 800-EMBASSY) 194 suites, restaurant, complimentary breakfast, outdoor swimming pool, spa, in-room refrigerators, kitchenettes, vale laundry, fax service, child care, complimentary newspaper, laundry room, wheelchair-access rooms, no-smoking rooms, pets allowed, car rental, free parking. SGL/DBL$104-$145.

Hampton Inn (311 East Huntington Drive, 91006; 574-5600, Fax 446-2748, 800-426-7866) 131 rooms, complimentary breakfast, heated swimming pool, pets allowed, meeting facilities, wheelchair-access rooms, no-smoking rooms. SGL$50-$57, DBL$55-$66.

Marriott Residence Inn (321 East Huntington Drive, 91006; 446-6500, Fax 446-5824, 800-331-3131) one- and two-bedroom suites, complimentary breakfast, airport transportation, heated swimming pool, whirlpool, room service, exercise facilities, meeting facilities for 30, laundry room, in-room microwaves, wheelchair-access rooms, no-smoking rooms, pets allowed, free parking. SGL/DBL$110-$140.

Motel 6 (225 Colorado Place, 91006; 446-2660, 505-891-6161) 87 rooms. SGL/DBL$35-$40.

Arroyo Grande

Area Code 805
Arroyo Grande Chamber of Commerce
200 East Branch Street
Arroyo Grande 93420
489-1488

Arroyo K Lodge (611 El Camino Real, 93420; 489-9300, 800-366-3391) 42 rooms, outdoor heated swimming pool, children under 12 free, wheelchair access, pets allowed, no-smoking rooms. SGL$59-$69, DBL$69-$79.

Arroyo Village Inn (407 El Camino Real, 93420; 489-5926) 7 rooms, bed and breakfast, complimentary breakfast. SGL/DBL$50-$200+.

Best Western Casa Grande Inn (850 Oak Park Road, 93420; 805-481-7398, Fax 805-481-4895, 800-528-1234) 113 rooms, restaurant, complimentary breakfast, heated swimming pool, spa, kitchenettes, fax service, meeting and conference facilities, wheelchair-access rooms, no-smoking rooms, no pets. SGL$58-$71, DBL$63-$115.

E-Z 8 Motel (555 Camino Mercado, 93420; 481-4774) 100 rooms. SGL/DBL$25-$35.

Village Inn Bed and Breakfast (407 El Camino Real, 93420; 489-5926) 7 rooms. SGL/DBL$88-$165.

Artesia

Area Code 310
Artesia Chamber of Commerce
18634 Pioneer Boulevard
Artesia CA 90701
924-6397

50 Atascadero

Best Western Pioneer Motor Inn (16905 South Pioneer Boulevard, 90701; 402-2202, Fax 924-3623, 800-826-7479, 800-528-1234) 163 rooms and suites, swimming pool, jacuzzi, whirlpools, complimentary breakfast, children under 18 free, fax services, in-room refrigerators, no-smoking rooms. SGL/DBL$44-$95.

Ramada Inn (17510 South Pioneer Boulevard, 90701; 924-6700, Fax 924-7756, 800-2-RAMADA) 66 rooms and suites, restaurant, swimming pool, jacuzzis, valet laundry, gift shop, free parking, airport transportation, exercise facilities, meeting facilities, child care, wheelchair-access rooms, no-smoking rooms. SGL$65, DBL$75, STS$125.

TraveLodge (1185 Artesia Boulevard, 90701; 213-402-0070, Fax 213-402-0070, 800-255-3050) 49 rooms, restaurant, lounge, tours, car rental, swimming pool, airport transportation. SGL/DBL$42-$44.

Atascadero

Area Code 805
Atascadero Chamber of Commerce
6550 El Camino Real
Atascadero CA 93422

Atascadero Inn (6505 Morro Road, 93442; 466-6853) 30 rooms, restaurant, whirlpool, wheelchair access, no-smoking rooms. SG$50, DBL$55.

Best Western Colony Inn (3600 El Camino Real, 93422; 466-4449, 800-528-1234) 75 rooms, restaurant, swimming pool, exercise facilities, pets allowed, wheelchair-access rooms, no-smoking rooms. SGL/DBL$52-$80.

Avalon

Area Code 213
Avalon-Catalina Island Chamber of Commerce
Box 217
Avalon CA 90704
510-1520

Atwater Hotel (125 Sumner, 90704; 510-1788, 800-428-2566 in California) 100 rooms, LS SGL/DBL$34-$68; HS SGL/DBL$52-$100.

Banning House Lodge (Box 5044, 90704; 510-0303, Fax 510-0303) 11 rooms, restaurant, lounge, bed and breakfast, complimentary breakfast, no-smoking rooms, transportation to local attractions, meeting facilities, SGL/DBL$100-$175.

Catalina Canyon Hotel and Conference Center (888 Country Club Drive, 90704; 510-0325, Fax 510-0900, 800-253-9391 in California) 81 rooms and suites, restaurant, jacuzzi, sauna, swimming pool, meeting facilities, balconies, airport transportation, exercise facilities, free parking. SGL/DBL$135-$155, STS$350-$500.

Catalina Hotel (129 Whittley Avenue, 90704; 510-0027) 34 rooms. SGL/DBL$85-$110.

Catalina Island Inn (125 Metropole Avenue, 90704; 510-1623) 36 rooms, complimentary breakfast, ocean view, balconies, beach. SGL$45-$75, DBL$85-$160.

El Terado Terrace (230 Marilla Avenue, 90704; 510-0831) 20 rooms and suites. SGL/DBL$100-$120, STS$150-$170.

Glenmore Plaza Hotel (120 Sumner Avenue, 90704; 510-0017, 800-422-8254 in California) 50 rooms and suites, complimentary breakfast, boat dock. SGL/DBL$85-$200, STS$200-$400.

Avalon

The Gull House (Box 1381, 90704; 510-2547, Fax 624-9746) 4 rooms and suites, bed and breakfast, complimentary breakfast, swimming pool, no-smoking rooms. SGL/DBL$100-$110, STS$135-$145.

Inn On Mt. Ada (Box 2560, 90704; 510-2030) 6 rooms, bed and breakfast, complimentary breakfast. SGL/DBL$190-$580.

Hotel Metropole (205 Crescent Avenue, 90704; 510-1884, Fax 510-2543, 800-541-8528 in California) 47 rooms and suites, complimentary breakfast, airport transportation, swimming pool, ocean view, balconies, meeting facilities, wheelchair-access rooms, no-smoking rooms. SGL$85-$225, DBL$100-$225, STS$225-$350.

Pavilion Lodge (513 Crescent Avenue, 90704; 510-1788, 800-428-2566 in California) 6 rooms, bed and breakfast, restaurant, complimentary breakfast, no-smoking rooms, beach. LS SGL/DBL$59; HS SGL/DBL$99.

Hotel St. Lauren (Box 497, 90704; 510-2299, Fax 510-2762) 42 rooms, restaurant, complimentary breakfast, spa, meeting facilities, exercise facilities, wheelchair-access rooms, tennis, golf. SGL/DBL$85-$200.

Seaport Village (119 Maiden Lane, 90704; 510-0344, 800-222-8254 in California, 800-CATALINA) 29 rooms and efficiencies, wheelchair-access rooms, airport transportation. SGL/DBL$49-$139.

Hotel Villa Portofino (111 Crescent Avenue, 90704; 510-0555) 34 rooms, restaurant, complimentary breakfast, beach. SGL/DBL$80-$200.

Hotel Vista Del Mar (417 Crescent Avenue, 90704; 510-0416, Fax 510-2917) 15 rooms and suites, restaurant, spas, complimentary breakfast, ocean view, balconies, in-room refrigerators and mini-bars, hot tubs, fireplaces, rooms service, fax service, complimentary newspaper, no-smoking rooms, beach, free parking. SGL/DBL$65-$155, STS$195-$275.

Avila Beach

Area Code 805

San Luis Bay Inn (Avila Beach Road and Hartford Drive, 93424; 595-2333, 800-592-5928 in California) 77 rooms and suites, restaurant, swimming pool, airport courtesy car, tennis, golf, free parking. SGL$104-$124, DBL$114-$134, STS$180-$280.

Surfside Motel (256 Front Street, 93424; 592-2300) 32 rooms and efficiencies. SGL/DBL$50-$150.

Sycamore Mineral Springs (1215 Avila Beach Road, 92324; 595-7302, Fax 595-2956, 800-234-5831) 28 rooms and cottage suite, restaurant, outdoor heated swimming pool, spa, children under 12 free, in-room refrigerators, fax service, gift shop, free parking, wheelchair-access rooms, no pets. SGL$99-$140, STS$140-$160.

Azusa

Area Code 818
Azusa Chamber of Commerce
213 East Foothill Boulevard
Azusa CA 91702
334-1507

Best Western (433 South Azusa Avenue, 91702; 818-969-4221, Fax 818-334-6661, 800-528-1234) 60 rooms, restaurant, swimming pool, spa, whirlpools, fax service, kitchenettes, no-smoking rooms, no pets. SGL/DBL$36-$52.

TraveLodge (469 East Arrow Highway, 91702; 818-966-7777, 800-255-3050) 60 rooms, restaurant, no pets. SGL$30-$33, DBL$35-$40.

Baker

Area Code 619

Arne's Royal Hawaiian Hotel (200 West Baker Boulevard, 92309; 733-4326, Fax 733-4615) 43 rooms, swimming pool, pets allowed. SGL/DBL$22-$43.

Bakersfield

Area Code 805
Bakersfield Convention Bureau
1333 Truxton Avenue
Bakersfield CA 93301
325-5051

Best Western Hill House (700 Truxton Avenue, 93301; 327-4064, Fax 327-1247, 800-528-1234) 99 rooms, restaurant, complimentary breakfast, swimming pool, fax service, children under 12 free, wheelchair-access rooms, no-smoking rooms, pets allowed. SGL/DBL$55-$65.

Best Western Inn (2620 Pierce Road, 93308; 327-9651, Fax 334-1820, 800-528-1234) 196 rooms, restaurant, swimming pool, whirlpool, fax service, laundry room, meeting facilities for 300, no-smoking rooms, airport transportation, pets allowed. SGL/DBL$52-$70.

Best Western Oak Inn (889 Oak Street, 93304; 324-9686, Fax 334-1820, 800-528-1234) 42 rooms, restaurant, lounge, complimentary breakfast, swimming pool, fax service, no-smoking rooms, pets allowed. SGL/DBL$44-$58.

California Inn (3400 Chester Lane, 93309; 328-1100, Fax 378-0433) 74 rooms, complimentary breakfast, swimming pool, wheelchair-access rooms, no-smoking rooms. SGL$41-$43, DBL$45+.

Comfort Inn (2514 White Lane, 93304; 833-8000, 800-221-2222) 64 rooms, restaurant, complimentary breakfast, swimming pool, whirlpool, laundry room, in-room refrigerators and microwaves, wheelchair-access rooms, no pets. SGL/DBL$34-$$65.

Comfort Inn (830 Wible Road, 93304; 831-1922, 800-221-2222) 53 rooms and efficiencies, restaurant, complimentary breakfast, exercise facilities, swimming pool, whirlpool, in-room refrigerators and microwaves, wheelchair-access rooms, no pets. SGL/DBL$35-$65.

Courtyard by Marriott (3601 Marriott Drive, 93308; 324-6660, 800-321-2211) 146 rooms, restaurant, swimming pool, exercise facilities, wheelchair-access rooms, no-smoking rooms. SGL/DBL$69-$79.

Days Inn (3540 Rosedale Highway, 93308; 326-1111, Fax 326-1513, 800-325-2525) 122 rooms, restaurant, lounge, swimming pool, spa, meeting facilities, gift shop, valet laundry, fax service, children under 12 free, exercise facilities, wheelchair-access rooms, no-smoking rooms. SGL$55-$80, DBL$60-$85+.

Econo Lodge (200 Trask Street, 93312; 764-5221, 800-424-4777) 53 rooms, restaurant, swimming pool, wheelchair-access rooms. SGL$33-$37, DBL$37-$44.

Econo Lodge (1230 East Main Street, 92311; 619-256-2133, 800-424-4777) 50 rooms, free parking, children under 18 stay free. SGL/DBL$32-$39.

Economy Inns of America (6501 Colony Street, 93307; 831-9200, 800-826-0778) 139 rooms, restaurant, complimentary breakfast, swimming pool, wheelchair-access rooms, pets allowed, no-smoking rooms. SGL/DBL$25-$35.

Bakersfield

Economy Inns of America (6100 Knudsen Drive, 93308; 392-1800, 800-826-0778, 800-423-3018) 156 rooms, swimming pool. SGL$24, DBL$30.

E-Z 8 Motel (2604 Pierce Road, 93308; 322-1901, 800-326-6835) 100 rooms, outdoor swimming pool, children under 10 free, free local telephone calls, wheelchair-access rooms, pets allowed. SGL/DBL$24-$31.

E-Z 8 Motel (5200 Olive Tree court, 93308; 392-1511, 800-326-6835) 101 rooms, outdoor swimming pool, children under 12 free, free local telephone calls, in-room refrigerators, airport transportation, wheelchair access, pets allowed. SGL/DBL$23-$33.

La Quinta Motor Inn (3232 Riverside Drive, 93308; 325-7400, Fax 324-6032, 800-531-5900) 130 rooms, restaurant, meeting facilities, swimming pool, wheelchair-access rooms, free local telephone calls, pets allowed, airport courtesy car, no-smoking rooms. SGL/DBL$45-$75.

Marriott Residence Inn (4241 Chester Lane, 93309; 321-9800, 800-331-3131) restaurant, complimentary breakfast, meeting facilities for 30, in-room microwaves, wheelchair-access rooms, exercise facilities, no-smoking rooms, pets allowed. SGL/DBL$89+.

Motel 6 (8223 East Brundage Lane, 93307; 366-7231, 505-891-6161) 112 rooms. SGL/DBL$26-$32.

Motel 6 (350 Oak Street, 93304; 326-1222, 505-891-6161) 71 rooms. SGL/DBL$24-$30.

Motel 6 (5241 Olive Tree Court, 93308; 392-9700, 505-891-6161) 149 rooms. SGL/DBL$22-$28.

Motel 6 (2727 White Lane, 93304; 834-2828, 505-891-6161) 102 rooms. SGL/DBL$14-$30.

Quality Inn (1011 Oak Street, 93304; 325-0772, Fax 325-4646, 800-221-2222) 89 rooms, restaurant, complimentary breakfast, swimming pool, whirlpool, sauna, exercise facilities, balconies, laundry room, wheelchair-access rooms, no-smoking rooms. SGL$38-$51, DBL$42-$56.

Quarter Circle U Rankin Ranch (23500 Walker Basin Road, 93304; 867-2511) 18 rooms and cabins, restaurant, swimming pool, airport courtesy car, exercise facilities, lighted tennis courts, wheelchair-access rooms, no-smoking rooms. SGL/DBL$68-$78.

Ramada Inn (3535 Rosedale Highway, 93308; 327-0681, Fax 327-0681, 800-2-RAMADA) 197 rooms, restaurant, lounge, swimming pool, spa, free parking, meeting facilities for 400, wheelchair-access rooms, pets allowed, meeting facilities, airport courtesy car. SGL$49-$63, DBL$55-$69.

Red Lion Inn (3100 Camino Del Rio Court, 93308; 327-0681, Fax 323-0331) 262 rooms and suites, restaurant, lounge, swimming pool, wheelchair-access rooms, meeting facilities for 200, exercise facilities, no-smoking rooms, airport transportation. pets allowed. SGL/DBL$75-$105, STS$125+.

Rio Bravo Resort (11200 Lake Ming Road, 93306; 872-5000, Fax 872-6546, 800-282-5000 in California) 112 rooms, restaurant, lounge, complimentary breakfast, swimming pool, sauna, meeting facilities for 200, airport courtesy car, in-room refrigerators, fireplaces, no-smoking rooms, exercise facilities, tennis, golf. SGL$66, DBL$76.

Rio Mirada Motor Inn (4500 North Pierce Road, 93308; 324-5555, Fax 324-5555, 800-822-3050) 208 rooms, complimentary breakfast, swimming pool, sauna, laundry room, fireplaces, wheelchair-access rooms, exercise facilities, pet allowed, airport courtesy car, no-smoking rooms. SGL/DBL$39-$60.

Sheraton Inn (5101 California Avenue, 93309; 325-9700, Fax 323-3508, 800-325-3535) 198 rooms, two restaurants, lounge, complimentary breakfast, outdoor swimming pool, jacuzzi, meeting facilities for 1,200, business center, gift shop, child care, exercise facilities, wheelchair-access rooms, airport transportation, no-smoking rooms. SGL$70-$95, DBL$80-$105.

Super 8 Motel (901 Real Road, 93309; 322-1012, Fax 322-7636, 800-800-8000) 89 rooms, outdoor swimming pool, spa, free local telephone calls, complimentary newspaper, fax service, meeting facilities, wheelchair-access rooms, no pets. SGL/DBL$47-$51.

TraveLodge Bakersfield Plaza Inn (1030 Wible Road, 93304; 834-3377, Fax 834-4439, 800-255-3050) 61 rooms, restaurant, lounge, complimentary breakfast, swimming pool, spa, sauna, laundry room, meeting facilities for 40, tennis, no pets. SGL$39-$49, DBL$43-$53.

TraveLodge (3620 Wible Road, 93309; 833-1000, 800-255-3050) 60 rooms and efficiencies, restaurant, lounge, complimentary breakfast, swimming pool, spa, laundry room, wheelchair-access rooms, no-smoking rooms. SGL/DBL$40-$60.

Ballard

Area Code 805

Ballard Inn (2436 Baseline Avenue, 93463; 688-7770) 15 rooms, restaurant, complimentary breakfast, wheelchair-access rooms, no-smoking rooms. SGL/DBL$125+.

Baldwin Park

Area Code 818
Baldwin Park Chamber of Commerce
4141 North Maine Avenue
Baldwin Park CA 91706
960-4848

Hilton San Gabriel (14635 Baldwin Park Centre, 91706; 962-6000) 215 rooms, restaurant, swimming pool, meeting facilities for 430, business services. SGL/DBL$90-$130.

Howard Johnson (14624 East Dalewood, 91706; 962-8761, Fax 338-7989, 800-654-2000) 69 rooms, restaurant, complimentary breakfast, swimming pool, laundry room, meeting facilities, wheelchair-access rooms, no pets. SGL$40-$65, DBL$50-$75.

Motel 6 (14510 Garvey Avenue, 91706; 960-5011, 505-891-6161) 75 rooms. SGL/DBL$30-$35.

TraveLodge (13921 Francisquito Avenue, 91706; 814-0808, Fax 337-1190, 800-255-3050) 107 rooms, restaurant, lounge, complimentary breakfast, swimming pool, spa, laundry room, meeting facilities for 50, free local telephone calls, no pets. SGL/DBL$38-$60.

Banning

Area Code 619
Banning-San Gorgonio Pass Chamber of Commerce
123 East Ramsey
Banning CA 92220
849-4695

Days Inn (2320 West Ramsey Street, 92220; 849-0092, Fax 849-0509, 800-325-2525) 43 rooms, restaurant, heated swimming pool, jacuzzis, fax service, children under 12 free, wheelchair-access rooms, no-smoking rooms. SGL$44, DBL$46.

Super 8 Motel (1690 West Ramsey Street, 92220; 849-6887, 800-800-8000) 51 rooms, restaurant, complimentary breakfast, outdoor swimming pool, free local telephone calls, wheelchair-access rooms, no-smoking rooms, pets allowed. SGL/DBL$32-$40.

TraveLodge (1700 West Ramsey Street, 92220; 849-1000, Fax 849-4071, 800-255-3050) 41 rooms, restaurant, lounge, complimentary breakfast, swimming pool, spa, sauna, free local telephone calls, meeting facilities, no pets. SGL$36-$46, DBL$40-$50.

Barstow

Area Code 619
Barstow Area Chamber of Commerce
270 East Virginia Way
Barstow CA 92311
256-8617

Best Western Desert Villa Motor Inn (1984 East Main Street, 92311; 256-1781, Fax 256-9265) 79 rooms and efficiencies, restaurant, lounge, complimentary breakfast, swimming pool, room service, children under 12 free, laundry room, fireplaces, whirlpool, valet laundry, wheelchair-access rooms, no pets, SGL/DBL$48-$60.

Econo Lodge (1230 East Main Street, 92311; 256-2133, 800-424-4777) 50 rooms, children under 18 stay free, pets allowed. SGL$24-$35, DBL$29-$49.

Economy Motels of America (1590 Coolwater Lane, 92311; 256-1737, 800-826-0778) 113 rooms, swimming pool, pets allowed. SGL$23, DBL$30.

El Rancho Motel (112 East Main Street, 92311; 256-2401) 91 rooms and efficiencies, swimming pool. SGL/DBL$45-$55.

Economy Inns of America (1590 Coolwater Lane, 92311; 256-1737, 800-826-0778) 113 rooms, swimming pool, wheelchair-access rooms, pets allowed. SGL/DBL$22-$35.

Holiday Inn Barstow (1511 East Main Street, 92311; 256-5673, Fax 256-5917, 800-HOLIDAY) 148 rooms, restaurant, lounge, swimming pool, room service, complimentary newspaper, meeting facilities for 250, wheelchair-access rooms, children under 19 free, no-smoking rooms, no pets. SGL$65-$68, DBL$70-$73.

Howard Johnson (1431 East Main Street, 92311; 256-0661, Fax 256-8392, 800-146-4056) 64 rooms, restaurant, complimentary breakfast, swimming pool, no-smoking rooms, children under 18 free, laundry room, meeting facilities, valet laundry, pets allowed. SGL$40-$30, DBL$45-$90.

Quality Inn (1520 East Main Street, 92311; 256-6891, Fax 256-8392, 800-221-2222) 100 rooms, restaurant, swimming pool, meeting facilities, wheelchair-access rooms, no-smoking rooms, pets allowed. SGL/DBL$46-$64.

Sleep Inn (1861 West Main Street, 92311; 256-1300, 800-221-2222) 65 rooms, restaurant, complimentary breakfast, swimming pool, wheelchair-access rooms, no pets. SGL/DBL$31-$39.

Vagabond Inn (1243 East Main Street, 92311; 256-5601, Fax 256-1451, 800-522-1555) 67 rooms, complimentary breakfast, in-room refrigerators, heated swimming pool, pets allowed, wheelchair-access rooms, airport transportation, free local telephone calls, no-smoking rooms, children under 18 free, fax service, complimentary newspaper. SGL$41-$47, DBL$46-$57.

Baywood Park

Area Code 805

Baywood Bed and Breakfast Inn (1370 Second Street, 93402; 528-8888) 15 rooms, bed and breakfast, complimentary breakfast, wheelchair-access rooms. SGL$60, DBL$70.

Beaumont

Area Code 714
Beaumont Chamber of Commerce

450 East Fourth Street
Beaumont CA 92223
845-9541

Best Western El Rancho Motor Inn (550 Beaumont Avenue, 92223; 845-2176, 800-528-1234) 52 rooms, restaurant, lounge, no-smoking rooms, no pets. SGL/DBL$40-$72.

Highland Springs Hotel Resort (10600 Highland Springs Avenue, 92233; 845-1151, Fax 845-8090, 800-735-2948) 94 rooms and cottages, restaurant, lounge, complimentary breakfast, heated swimming pool, whirlpool, in-room refrigerators, meeting facilities, child care, sauna, tours, exercise facilities, tennis, golf. SGL$120-$230, DBL$140-$255.

Bellflower

Area Code 213
Bellflower Chamber of Commerce
Box 1236
Bellflower CA 90706
867-1744

Comfort Inn (1711 Clark Avenue, 90706; 920-8853, 800-228-5150) 70 rooms, outdoor heated swimming pool. SGL/DBL$45-$60.

Motel 6 (17220 Downey Avenue, 90706; 531-3933, 505-891-6161) 36 rooms. SGL/DBL$50-$60.

TraveLodge (8730 Artesia Boulevard, 90706; 213-633-7689, 800-255-3050) 61 rooms, restaurant, lounge, swimming pool, airport transportation, tennis, no pets. SGL/DBL$38-$48.

Beverly Hills

Area Code 213
Beverly Hills Visitors Bureau

239 South Beverly Drive
Beverly Hills CA 90212
271-8174

Beverly Crest Hotel (125 South Spalding Drive, 90212; 274-6801, Fax 273-6614, 800-247-6432) 54 rooms, restaurant, lounge, outdoor swimming pool, children under 16 free, fax service, meeting facilities for 10, airport transportation, wheelchair-access rooms, no pets. no-smoking rooms. SGL$95-$105, DBL$110-$120+.

Beverly Hills Hotel and Bungalows (9641 Sunset Boulevard, 90210; 276-2251, Fax 271-0319, 800-283-8885, 800-792-7637 in California) 269 rooms and bungalows, two restaurants, lounge, outdoor swimming pool, spa, meeting facilities, child care, valet laundry, 24-hour room service, fax service, complimentary newspaper, exercise facilities, wheelchair-access rooms, lighted tennis courts, car rental. SGL/DBL$205-$320+.

Beverly Hills St. Moritz (120 South Reeves, 90212; 276-1031) 50 suites, airport transportation, exercise facilities. SGL$35-$50, DBL$45-$55.

Beverly Hilton Hotel (9876 Wilshire Boulevard, 90210; 247-7777, Fax 285-1313, 800-445-8667) 589 rooms and suites, three restaurants, lounges, two outdoor swimming pools, exercise facilities, airport transportation, meeting facilities for 4,000, valet laundry, fax and business services, transportation to local attractions, pets allowed, wheelchair-access rooms, beauty and barber shop, gift shop, travel agency, no-smoking rooms, car rental. SGL$175-$215, DBL$195-$235, STS$450-$1,000.

Beverly House Hotel (140 South Lasky Drive, 90210; 271-2145, Fax 276-8431, 800-432-5444) 50 rooms, continental breakfast, no pets, children under 12 free, fax service, free parking. SGL$78-$98, DBL$88-$98.

Beverly Pavilion (9360 Wilshire Boulevard, 90212; 273-1400, Fax 859-8551, 800-421-0545, 800-441-505 in California) 110 rooms, restaurant, lounge, outdoor swimming pool, saunas, in-room refrigerators, valet laundry, fax service, transportation to local attractions, meeting facilities, room service, gift shop, wheelchair-access rooms, airport transportation, no-smoking rooms, free parking. SGL$130-$160, DBL$150-$180, STS$250-$390.

Beverly Plaza Hotel (8384 West Third Street, Los Angeles, 90048; 658-6600, 800-624-6835, 800-62-HOTEL, 800-33-HOTEL in California) 97 rooms, restaurant, outdoor swimming pool, saunas, spa, valet laundry, 24-hour room service, fax service, child care, complimentary newspaper, transportation to local attractions, beauty and barber shop, wheelchair-access rooms, no-smoking rooms, exercise facilities. SGL/DBL$98-$168+.

Beverly Rodeo Hotel (360 North Rodeo Drive, 90210; 263-0300, Fax 859-8730, 800-356-7575, 800-441-5050) 88 rooms and suites, restaurant, lounge, no-smoking rooms, laundry room, valet laundry, room service, fax service, complimentary newspaper. SGL/DBL$125-$180, STS$250-$350+.

J.W. Marriott Hotel At Century City (2151 Avenue of the Stars, 90067; 277-2777, Fax 785-9240, 800-228-9290) 375 rooms, restaurant, swimming pool, wheelchair-access rooms, airport transportation, exercise facilities, no-smoking rooms. SGL$249-$269, DBL$275-$2,500.

L'Ermitage Hotel (9291 Burton Way, 90210; 278-3344, Fax 278-8247, 800-424-4443) 112 rooms and suites, restaurant, swimming pool, spa, meeting facilities, child care, wheelchair-access rooms, airport transportation, tennis, no-smoking rooms. SGL$275-$335, DBL$375-$545.

The Peninsula Beverly Hills (9882 Santa Monica Boulevard, 90212; 273-4888, Fax 858-6663, 800-462-7899) 184 rooms and suites, restaurant, swimming pool, sauna, spa, wheelchair-access rooms, laundry room, pets allowed, valet laundry, 24-hour room service, fax service, transportation to local attractions, free parking, airport transportation, exercise facilities, no-smoking rooms. SGL/DBL$285-$340, STS$400-$2500.

Regent Beverly Wilshire Hotel (9500 Wilshire Boulevard, 90212; 275-5200, Fax 274-2851, 800-545-4000, 800-421-4354) 363 rooms and suites, restaurant, lounge, swimming pool, sauna, child care, meeting facilities, exercise facilities, wheelchair-access rooms, no-smoking rooms. SGL/DBL$255-$395, STS$425-$4000.

St. Moritz Hotel (120 South Reeves Drive, 90212; 275-2108, Fax 347-4326) 100 rooms. SGL/DBL$50-$100.

Big Bear and Big Bear Lake

Area Code 714
Big Bear Chamber of Commerce
Box 2860
Big Bear CA 92315
866-5652

RENTAL SOURCES: All of the following rent condos and homes in the Big Bear Lake area: **All Seasons Resort Rental** (41320 Big Bear Boulevard, 92315; 866-5851); **Big Bear Real Estate** (40703 Lakeview Drive, 92315; 866-3744); **Big Bear Information and Reservation Service** (40588 Big Bear Boulevard, 92315; 866-4601); **First Cabin Resort Reservations** (Box 1872, 92315; 866-9689, Fax 866-6265); **Front Desk Holiday Rentals** (1288 Clubview, 92315; 866-5753); **Mountain Shore Vacation Rentals** (40090 Lakeview Drive, 92315; 866-9404); **Sleepy Forest Rentals** (426 Eureka Drive, 92315; 866-7567).

Big Bear Inn (42200 Moonridge Road, 92315; 866-3471, 800-232-7466 in California) 80 rooms, restaurant, lounge, swimming pool, meeting facilities, wheelchair-access rooms, fireplaces, no-smoking rooms. SGL/DBL$85-$200.

Big Bear Lake Inn (39471 Big Bear Lake Boulevard, 92315; 866-3471, 800-843-0103) 52 rooms, complimentary breakfast, outdoor swimming pool, jacuzzi, children under 14 free, free local telephone calls, in-room refrigerators, kitchenettes, meeting facilities for 40, wheelchair-access rooms, no-smoking, no pets. SGL$50, DBL$61-$76.

Eagle's Nest (41675 Big Bear Boulevard, 92315; 866-6465) 5 rooms, complimentary breakfast, transportation to local attractions, fireplaces. SGL/DBL$70-$140.

Escape For All Seasons (Box 1909, 92315; 714-866-7504, Fax 714-866-7504, 800-722-4366) 70 rooms and efficiencies, restaurant, heated swimming pool, wheelchair-access rooms, fireplaces, airport transportation, no-smoking rooms, tennis. SGL/DBL$95-$140.

Gold Mountain Manor (1117 Anita Avenue, 92314; 585-6997) 7 rooms, bed and breakfast, complimentary breakfast, no pets, no children. SGL/DBL$75-$180.

Knickerbocker Mansion (Box 3661, 92315; 866-8221) 10 rooms, bed and breakfast, complimentary breakfast, whirlpool, balconies, fireplaces. SGL/DBL$85-$165.

Marina Riviera Resort (40770 Lakeview Drive, 92315; 866-4643) 22 rooms, complimentary breakfast, swimming pool, whirlpool, in-room refrigerators, beach, no-smoking rooms, SGL/DBL$70-$120.

Robinhood Inn (40797 Lakeview Drive; 866-4643) 22 rooms, complimentary breakfast, whirlpool, fireplaces. SGL/DBL$59-$89.

Shore Acres Lodge (40090 Lakeview Drive, 92315; 866-8200, Fax 866-3248, 800-524-6600 in California) 11 rooms, swimming pool, fireplaces, spa, pets allowed. SGL$60-$85, DBL$85-$120.

Smoketree Lodge (40210 Big Bear Boulevard, 92315; 866-2415) 18 rooms, heated outdoor swimming pool, spa, airport transportation, pets allowed. LS SGL/DBL$65-$75, 1BR $70-$98, 2BR$100-$145; HS SGL/DBL$80-$86, 1BR$90-$105, 2BR$115-$167.

Big Sur

Area Code 408
Big Sur Chamber of Commerce
Box 87
Big Sur CA 93920
667-2100

Big Sur Lodge (Box 190, Pfeiffer State Park, 93920; 667-2171) 61 rooms, restaurant, swimming pool, free parking. SGL$60-$100, DBL$100-$120, STS$70-$120.

Ventana Inn (Highway One, 93920; 667-2171, 800-628-6500 in California) 62 rooms, restaurant, complimentary breakfast, swimming pool, wheelchair-access rooms, exercise facilities. SGL/DBL$155-$275.

Bishop

Area Code 619
Bishop Chamber of Commerce
690 North Main Street
Bishop CA 93514
873-8405

Mono County Chamber of Commerce
Box 315
Bishop CA 93514
387-2723

Best Western Holiday Spa Lodge (1025 North Main Street, 93514; 873-3543, Fax 872-4777, 800-528-1234) 89 rooms, restaurant, heated swimming pool, in-room refrigerators, whirlpool, fax service, wheelchair-access rooms, laundry room, pets allowed, no-smoking rooms. SGL$50-$67, DBL$57-$100.

Best Western Bishop Westerner Motel (150 East Elm Street, 93514; 873-3564, Fax 873-6939, 800-356-3221, 800-528-

1234) 55 rooms, restaurant, swimming pool, fax service, airport courtesy car, no-smoking rooms, pets allowed. SGL/DBL$45-$59.

Bishop Inn (805 North Main Street, 93514; 873-4284) 30 rooms, restaurant, heated swimming pool, whirlpool, wheelchair-access rooms, in-room refrigerators, pets allowed. SGL/DBL$43-$58.

Chalfant House (213 Academy Street, 93514; 872-1790) 6 rooms, bed and breakfast, complimentary breakfast, no-smoking. SGL/DBL$50-$60.

Matlick House (1313 Rowan Lane, 93514; 873-3133) 4 rooms, bed and breakfast, complimentary breakfast, airport courtesy car, no-smoking. SGL/DBL$65-$75.

National 9 Sierra Lodge (1005 North Main Street, 93514; 873-8426) 52 rooms, restaurant, heated swimming pool, whirlpool, in-room refrigerators, airport courtesy car, wheelchair-access rooms, no-smoking rooms. SGL$40-$45, DBL$50-$55.

Sierra Gateway Motel (606 North Main Street, 93514; 873-3548) 51 rooms and suites, wheelchair-access rooms, pets allowed, tennis, golf. SGL$33-$37, DBL$37-$41+.

Thunderbird Motel (190 West Pine Street, 873-4215) 23 rooms, airport transportation, no-smoking rooms, pets allowed. SGL/DBL$30-$45.

Vagabond Inn (1030 North Main Street, 93514; 873-6351, Fax 873-3067, 800-522-1555) 80 rooms, complimentary breakfast, heated swimming pool, in-room refrigerators, airport transportation, free local telephone calls, no-smoking rooms, children under 18 free, fax service, complimentary newspaper. SGL$46-$51, DBL$51-$61.

Borrego Springs

Area Code 619
Borrego Springs Chamber of Commerce
622 Palm Canyon Drive
Borrego Springs CA 92004
767-5555

La Casa Del Zorro Resort Hotel (3845 Yaqui Pass Road, 92004; 767-5323, Fax 767-5923, 800-824-1884) 79 rooms and suites, restaurant, lounge, swimming pool, lighted tennis courts, fireplaces, concierge, golf, airport courtesy car, wheelchair-access rooms, beauty shop, no-smoking rooms. SGL/DBL$98+, STS$145-$450.

Overland Junction Resort (221 Palm Canyon Drive, 92004; 767-5341, Fax 767-4073, 800-242-0044 in California) 44 rooms, restaurant, swimming pool, pets allowed, wheelchair-access rooms. SGL/DBL$65-$85.

Palm Canyon Resort (221 Palm Canyon Drive, 92004; 767-5341, Fax 767-4074, 800-242-0044 in California) 44 rooms, restaurant, swimming pool, spa, sauna, gift shop, children under 12 free, laundry room, child care, meeting facilities, wheelchair-access rooms, pets allowed, airport courtesy car. SGL/DBL$85, STS$129+.

Stanlund's Resort Motel (2771 Borrego Springs Road, 92004; 767-5501, 800-647-5812) 21 rooms and suites, outdoor heated swimming pool, kitchenettes, wheelchair access, laundry room. SGL/DBL$48-$125, STS$75-$150.

Villas Borrego (Box 185, 92004; 767-5371) one- and two-bedroom condos, swimming pool. 1BR$100/$600W, 2BR$130/$780W.

Whispering Sands Motel (1234 Borrego Springs Road, 92004; 767-3322) 36 rooms. SGL/DBL$45+.

Brea

Area Code 714
Brea Chamber of Commerce
Civic Center Circle
Brea CA 92621
529-4938

Embassy Suites Hotel (900 East Birch Street, 92621; 990-6000, Fax 990-1653, 800-EMBASSY) 229 suites, restaurant, complimentary breakfast, swimming pool, meeting facilities for 575, gift shop, room service, meeting facilities, child care, valet laundry, exercise facilities, wheelchair-access rooms, free parking, no-smoking rooms. SGL/DBL$129-$149.

Woodfin Suites (3100 East Imperial Highway, 92621; 579-3200, Fax 996-5984, 800-237-8811) 88 suites, complimentary breakfast, children under 16 free, meeting facilities for 30, laundry room, fax service, business services, free parking, wheelchair access, no-smoking rooms, pets. SGL$89-$109, DBL$99-$119, STS$99-$120.

Buellton

Area Code 805
Buellton Chamber of Commerce
140 West Highway 246
Buellton CA 93427
688-7829

Best Western Pea Soup Andersen's Inn (51 East Highway 246, 93427; 688-3216, Fax 688-9767, 800-PEA-SOUP, 800-528-1234) 97 rooms, restaurant, lounge, complimentary breakfast, swimming pool, children under 12 free, whirlpool, in-room refrigerators and microwaves, fax service, putting green, wheelchair-access rooms, no-smoking rooms, no pets. SGL/DBL$53-$69.

Country Lane Motel (412 Avenue of Flags, 93427; 688-4181) 14 rooms. SGL/DBL$35-$45.

Econo Lodge (630 Avenue of Flags, 93427; 688-0022, 800-424-4777) 60 rooms, restaurant, wheelchair-access rooms, no-smoking rooms, no pets. SGL$33-$50, DBL$50-$80.

Farm House Motel (590 Avenue of Flags, 93427; 688-5145) 21 rooms and efficiencies, pets allowed. SGL/DBL$25-$35.

Frederick's Holiday Inn (555 McMurray Road, 93427; 688-1000, 800-638-8882, 800-HOLIDAY) 149 rooms and suites, restaurant, lounge, swimming pool, meeting facilities for 750, wheelchair-access rooms, children under 18 free, exercise facilities. SGL/DBL$68-$127.

Motel 6 (333 McMurray Road, 93427; 688-7797, 505-891-6161) 59 rooms, swimming pool, no-smoking rooms, pets allowed. SGL/DBL$29-$45.

Ramada Inn At The Windmill (114 East Highway, 93427; 688-8448, Fax 686-1338, 800-228-2828) 110 rooms, restaurant, lounge, complimentary breakfast, swimming pool, meeting facilities for 250, wheelchair access, no-smoking rooms. SGL/DBL$45+.

Red Rose Court (435 Avenue of Flags, 93427; 688-5611) 22 rooms and efficiencies. SGL/DBL$25-$45.

San Marcos Motel (536 Avenue of Flags, 93427; 688-5511) 19 rooms, swimming pool, no-smoking rooms. SGL/DBL$35-$55.

Sleepy Hollow Motel (550 Avenue of Flags, 93427; 688-6638) 20 rooms, no-smoking rooms, pets allowed. SGL/DBL$45-$65.

Buena Park

Area Code 714
Buena Park Visitor and Convention Bureau

Buena Park

7711 Beach Boulevard
Buena Park CA 90620
994-1511

Chamber of Commerce
6280 Manchester Boulevard
Buena Park CA 90621
521-0261

Best Inn Capri Motel (7860 Beach Boulevard, 90620; 522-7221, Fax 522-3310, 800-237-8466) 67 rooms and efficiencies, complimentary breakfast, swimming pool. SGL$35, DBL$45.

Best Western Aztec Motel (7620 Beach Boulevard, 90620; 522-8433, 800-528-1234) 50 rooms, restaurant, swimming pool, laundry rooms, tours, no-smoking rooms, no pets. SGL/DBL$32-$80.

Best Western Buena Park Inn (8580 Stanton Avenue, 90620; 828-5211, Fax 826-3716, 800-654-2889, 800-528-1234) 63 rooms, restaurant, lounge, swimming pool, room service, children under 12 free, wheelchair-access rooms, no-smoking rooms. SGL$32-$36, DBL$39-$82.

Buena Park Hotel and Convention Center (7675 Crescent Avenue, 90620; 995-1111, Fax 828-8590, 800-854-8792) 350 rooms and suites, restaurant, heated swimming pool, children under 12 free, in-room refrigerators, free parking, airport transportation, SGL$75-$95, DBL$85-$105, STS$150-$500.

Buena Park Inn (8580 Stanton, 90620; 828-5211, 800-654-2889 in California) 63 rooms, complimentary breakfast, swimming pool, wheelchair-access rooms, no-smoking rooms. SGL$36-$45, DBL$40-$55.

Buena Park Motor Inn (7921 Beach Boulevard, 90621; 739-5885) 53 rooms and suites, swimming pool, wheelchair-access rooms. SGL/DBL$75-$95.

Courtyard by Marriott (7621 Beach Boulevard, 90620; 670-6600, Fax 670-0360, 800-321-2211) 145 rooms and suites, restaurant, heated swimming pool, exercise facilities, wheelchair access/room, in-room refrigerators, laundry room, meeting facilities, no-smoking rooms. SGL$80-$90, DBL$90-$100, STS$95-$110.

Embassy Suite Hotels (7762 Beach Boulevard, 90620; 739-5600, Fax 521-9650, 800-EMBASSY) 203 suites, restaurant, complimentary breakfast, heated outdoor swimming pool, spa, meeting facilities for 125, gift shop, room service, business services, valet laundry, transportation to local attractions, airport transportation, fireplaces, pets allowed, exercise facilities, wheelchair-access rooms, no-smoking rooms. SGL$109-$175, DBL$119-$185.

Fairfield Inn (7032 Orangethorpe Avenue, 90621; 523-1488) 135 rooms, restaurant, heated swimming pool, children under 18 free, meeting facilities, wheelchair-access rooms, no-smoking rooms. SGL$42-$56, DBL$45-$60.

Friendship Inn Farm De Ville (7800 Crescent Avenue, 90620; 527-2201, 800-424-4777) 35 rooms, restaurant, whirlpool, saunas, children under 18 free. SGL/DBL$35-$44.

Hampton Inn Buena Park (7828 Orangethorpe Avenue, 90620; 670-7200, Fax 522-3319, 800-HAMPTON) 184 rooms, restaurant, complimentary breakfast, heated swimming pool, spa, meeting facilities, laundry room, wheelchair-access rooms, no-smoking rooms. SGL/DBL$57-$62.

Holiday Inn Plaza Hotel (7000 Beach Boulevard, 90620; 522-7000, 800-HOLIDAY) 246 rooms, restaurant, lounge, complimentary breakfast, swimming pool, sauna, spa, meeting facilities for 200, laundry room, child care, exercise center, airport transportation, wheelchair-access rooms, no-smoking rooms.

Motel 6 (7051 Valley View, 90622; 522-1200, 505-891-6161) 188 rooms. SGL/DBL$28-$34.

Burbank

Plaza Inn (7039 Orangethorpe Avenue, 90621; 521-9220, 800-854-8299, 800-854-8299, 800-854-7725 in California) 83 rooms, restaurant, complimentary breakfast, swimming pool, wheelchair-access rooms, no-smoking rooms, free parking. SGL$38-$46, DBL$42-$50.

Quality Inn (7555 Beach Boulevard, 90620; 522-7360, 800-228-5151) 65 rooms, swimming pool, exercise facilities. SGL/DBL$45-$65.

Ramada Inn (7555 Beach Boulevard, 90620; 522-7360, Fax 523-2883, 800-522-7360) 190 rooms, complimentary breakfast, swimming pool, jacuzzi, sauna, transportation to local attractions, free parking, no-smoking rooms, exercise facilities. SGL/DBL$55-$85.

Siesta Inn (7930 Beach Boulevard, 90620; 994-6480, 800-854-6031) 79 rooms and suites, restaurant, complimentary breakfast, swimming pool, free parking. SGL$39-$55, DBL$65-$85.

Traveler's Inn (7121 Beach Boulevard, 90620; 670-9000, Fax 522-7280, 800-633-8300) 132 rooms and suites, complimentary breakfast, swimming pool, wheelchair-access rooms, no-smoking rooms. SGL/DBL$49.

TraveLodge (7640 Beach Boulevard, 90620; 522-8461, 800-255-3050) 68 rooms, restaurant, lounge, swimming pool, spa, tours, car rental, laundry room, airport transportation, no-smoking rooms. SGL/DBL$32-$45.

Burbank

Area Code 818
Burbank Chamber of Commerce
200 West Magnolia Boulevard
Burbank CA 91502 846-3111

Greater Burbank Visitor and Convention Center
425A South Victory Boulevard

Burbank CA 91502
845-4266

RENTAL SOURCES: Apartments For Travelers (952-1336) rental source for one- and two-bedroom apartments in the Burbank area. SGL/DBL$65-$100.

Bed and Breakfast International (Box 282910, 94128; 696-1690, Fax 696-1699, 800-872-4500) represents bed and breakfast accommodations throughout California. Accommodations available in private home, houseboats on the Bay and inns. All rates include complimentary breakfast. SGL/DBL$50-$125.

Belair Bed and Breakfast (941 North Frederic Avenue, 91505; 848-9227) 12 rooms and suites, bed and breakfast, complimentary breakfast, free parking. SGL$30, DBL$40, STS$40-$50.

Burbank Hilton Hotel and Convention Center (2500 Hollywood Way, 91505; 843-6000, Fax 842-8126, 800-HOTEL-RM, 800-HILTONS, 800-643-7400 in California) 500 rooms and suites, restaurant, outdoor swimming pool, spa, sauna, in-room refrigerators and mini-bars, child care, meeting facilities for 2,000, fax service, airport courtesy car, gift shop, laundry room, exercise facilities, pets allowed, free parking. SGL/DBL$65-$119, STS$85-$275.

Holiday Inn (150 East Angeleno, 91502; 818-841-4770, 800-HOLIDAY) 370 rooms, restaurant, lounge, swimming pool, car rental, meeting facilities for 300. SGL$81, DBL$91.

Holiday Lodge (3901 Riverside Drive, Toluca Lake, 91505; 818-843-1121, Fax 559-6424) 28 rooms, outdoor swimming pool, spa, no-smoking rooms. SGL/DBL$49-$85.

Ramada Inn (2900 North San Fernando Boulevard, 91504; 843-5955, Fax 845-9030, 800-2-RAMADA) 144 rooms, restaurant, lounge, swimming pool, free parking, airport courtesy car, wheelchair-access rooms, no-smoking rooms. SGL$82-$92, DBL$92-$102.

The Royal Equestrian (1200 Riverside Drive, 91506; 843-2441, Fax 843-0948) 50 suites, swimming pool, exercise facilities, pets allowed, free parking. STS$50-$75.

Safari Inn (1911 West Olive Avenue, 91506; 845-8586, Fax 845-0054, 800-782-4373, 800-845-5544 in California) 130 rooms and suites, restaurant, lounge, heated swimming pool, jacuzzi, in-room refrigerators, fax service, meeting facilities for 100, free parking, airport courtesy car, no pets, SGL$55-$80, DBL$58-$80, STS$63/$434W-$504W.

TraveLodge (1112 North Hollywood Way, 91505; 818-845-2408, 800-255-3050) 28 rooms, restaurant, lounge, swimming pool, airport transportation, tennis. SGL$47-$57, DBL$50-$60.

Camarillo

Area Code 805
Camarillo Chamber of Commerce
1000 Paseo Camarillo
Camarillo, CA 93010
484-4383

Best Western Inn (295 Daily Drive, 93010; 987-4991, Fax 338-3679, 800-528-1234) 58 rooms, restaurant, swimming pool, whirlpool, fax service, no pets. SGL/DBL$50-$70.

Candlelight Motel (2050 East Ventura Boulevard, 93010; 482-0777) 26 rooms and efficiencies, swimming pool, no pets. SGL/DBL$55-$65.

Comfort Inn (984 West Ventura Boulevard, 93010; 987-4188, 800-221-2222) 70 rooms and suites, complimentary breakfast, swimming pool, whirlpools, spa, meeting facilities, valet laundry, wheelchair-access rooms, no pets. SGL/DBL$45-$65.

Country Inn At Camarillo (1405 Del Norte Road, 93010; 983-7171, Fax 983-1838, 800-44-RELAX) 100 rooms, restaurant, complimentary breakfast, swimming pool, in-room refrigerators and microwaves, fireplaces, wheelchair-access rooms, no-smoking rooms, no pets. SGL/DBL$75-$135.

Courtyard by Marriott (4994 Verdugo Way, 93010; 388-1020, Fax 987-6274, 800-321-2211) 65 rooms, restaurant, lounge, meeting and banquet facilities. SGL$64, DBL$74.

Days Inn Camarillo (165 Daily Drive, 93010; 482-0761, Fax 987-7985, 800-325-2525) 82 rooms, complimentary breakfast, swimming pool, children under 12 free, fax service, valet laundry, banquet facilities, wheelchair-access rooms, no-smoking rooms, no pets. SGL$45-$59, DBL$60-$69.

Del Norte Inn at Camarillo (4444 Central Avenue, 93010; 485-3999, 800-44-RELAX) 110 rooms and suites, complimentary breakfast, heated swimming pool, spa, kitchenettes, in-room refrigerators, wheelchair-access rooms, no-smoking rooms. SGL/DBL$50-$90.

Motel 6 (1641 East Daily Drive, 93010; 388-3467) 505-891-6161) 84 rooms, swimming pool, pets allowed. SGL/DBL$30-$45.

Calabasas

Area Code 818
Calabasas Chamber of Commerce
23632 Calabasas Road
Calabasas CA 91302
992-7600

The Country Inn At Calabasas (23627 Calabasas Road, 91302; 887-2900, Fax 347-4326, 800-44-RELAX) 120 rooms, restaurant, lounge, complimentary breakfast, heated swimming pool, spa, meeting facilities, laundry room, fireplaces, wheelchair-access rooms, no-smoking rooms. SGL$85-$91, DBL$93-$99+.

Calexico

Area Code 619
Calexico Chamber of Commerce
1100 West Imperial Avenue
Calexico CA 92231
357-1365

De Anza Motel (233 East Fourth Street, 92231; 357-1112) 82 rooms, restaurant, lounge, swimming pool, laundry room. SGL/DBL$45-$50.

Cambria

Area Code 805
Cambria Chamber of Commerce
767 Main Street
Cambria CA 93428
927-3624

The Beach House (6360 Moonstone Beach Drive, 93428; 927-3136) 7 rooms, bed and breakfast, complimentary breakfast, no-smoking rooms. SGL/DBL$100-$135.

Best Western Fireside Inn By The Sea (6700 Moonstone Beach Drive, 93428; 927-8661, Fax 926-8584, 800-528-1234) 46 rooms, restaurant, complimentary breakfast, heated swimming pool, whirlpool, spa, no-smoking rooms, no pets. SGL/DBL$90-$110.

Best Western Mariner's Inn (6180 Moonstone Beach Drive, 93428; 927-4624, 800-528-1234) 26 rooms, restaurant, complimentary breakfast, spa, whirlpool, in-room refrigerators, ocean view, no-smoking rooms, pets allowed. SGL/DBL$40-$70.

Blue Dolphin Motel (6470 Moonstone Beach Drive, 93428; 927-3300) 18 rooms, complimentary breakfast, beach, wheelchair-access rooms, no-smoking rooms. SGL/DBL$75-$150+.

Bluebird Motel (1880 Main Street, 93428; 927-4643) 33 rooms. SGL/DBL$35-$80.

Cambria Landing Inn (6530 Moonstone Beach Drive, 93428; 927-1619) 20 rooms, bed and breakfast, complimentary breakfast, wheelchair-access rooms, in-room refrigerators, fireplaces, no-smoking rooms. SGL/DBL$65-$170.

Cambria Palms Motel (2662 Main Street, 93428; 927-4485) 18 rooms. SGL$34-$54, DBL$36-$58.

Cambria Pines Lodge (2905 Burton Drive, 93428; 927-4200, 800-445-6868) 120 rooms and suites, restaurant, lounge, indoor swimming pool, jacuzzi, exercise facilities, in-room refrigerators and microwaves, fax service, meeting facilities for 200, gift shop, free parking, wheelchair-access rooms, no-smoking, no pets. SGL/DBL$60-$100.

Cambria Shores Motel (6276 Moonstone Beach Drive, 93428; 927-8644, 800-433-9179 in California) 24 rooms, restaurant, complimentary breakfast, ocean view, in-room refrigerators. SGL/DBL$65-$95.

The Castle Inn (6620 Moonstone Beach Drive, 93428; 927-8605, 800-525-7227 in California) 31 rooms, complimentary breakfast, swimming pool, in-room refrigerator, ocean view. SGL/DBL$55-$100.

Creekside Inn (2618 Main Street, 93428; 927-4021) 21 rooms, wheelchair-access rooms. SGL/DBL$45-$75.

Moonstone Inn (5860 Moonstone Beach Drive, 93428; 927-4815) 7 rooms, complimentary breakfast. SGL/DBL$90-$130.

Olallieberry Inn (2476 Main Street, 93428; 927-3222) 18 rooms, bed and breakfast, complimentary breakfast. SGL/DBL$60+.

The J. Patrick House (2990 Burton Drive, 93428; 927-3812) 8 rooms, complimentary breakfast, no-smoking. SGL/DBL$90-$120.

Pickford House (2555 MacLeod Way, 93428; 927-8619) 8 rooms, bed and breakfast, complimentary breakfast. SGL/DBL$65-$75.

Canada Cove

Area Code 415

Cypress Inn (407 Mirada Road, 94019; 726-6002, 800-83-BEACH) 8 rooms, restaurant, complimentary breakfast, beach, wheelchair-access rooms, no-smoking. SGL/DBL$130-$250.

Half Moon Bay Lodge (2400 South Carbrillo Highway, 94019; 726-9000, 800-368-2468) 82 rooms, two restaurants, fireplaces, swimming pool, spa, no-smoking rooms, meeting facilities for 100, wheelchair access. SGL$74-$104, DBL$84-$114.

Holiday Inn (300 South Cabrillo Highway, 94019; 726-3400, Fax 726-3616, 800-HOLIDAY) 52 rooms, complimentary breakfast, wheelchair-access rooms, meeting facilities for 12. SGL$65-$72, DBL$70-$90.

Mill Rose Inn (615 Mill Street, 94019; 726-9794, 800-829-1794) 5 rooms, bed and breakfast, complimentary breakfast, private baths, meeting facilities for 30, no-smoking rooms. SGL$145, DBL$225.

Old Thyme Inn (779 Main Street, 94019; 726-1616) 7 rooms, complimentary breakfast, no-smoking, whirlpools, meeting facilities for 20, fireplaces. SGL$45-$155, DBL$60-$150.

San Benito Inn (356 Main Street, 94019; 726-3425) 12 rooms, restaurant, swimming pool, no-smoking rooms, meeting facilities for 72. SGL/DBL$55-$112.

Zaballa House (324 Main Street, 94019; 726-9123, 800-77-BNB4U) 9 rooms, bed and breakfast, complimentary breakfast.

Canoga Park

Area Code 818
Canoga Park Chamber of Commerce
7248 Owensmouth Avenue
Canoga Park CA 91303
884-4222

Best Western Inn (20122 Vanowen Street, 91306; 883-1200, Fax 883-1202, 800-479-4484, 800-528-1234) 46 rooms, restaurant, lounge, complimentary breakfast, swimming pool, spa, whirlpool, sauna, jacuzzi, meeting facilities, fax service, SGL$49-$64, DBL$49-$119.

Clarion Suites Warner Palms Hotel (20200 Sherman Way, 91306; 883-8250, Fax 883-8268, 800-221-2222) 100 suites, swimming pool, free parking, wheelchair-access rooms. STS$80-$115.

Days Inn (20128 Roscoe Boulevard, 91306; 341-7200, Fax 341-5741) 57 rooms and suites, indoor swimming pool, jacuzzis, sauna, in-room refrigerators and microwaves, children under 12 free, fax service, wheelchair-access rooms, no-smoking rooms, pets allowed. SGL$50-$65, DBL$55-$80, STS$70-$80.

Capistrano Beach

Area Code 714
Capistrano Beach Chamber of Commerce
Box 2335
Capistrano Beach CA 92624, 496-1017

Edgewater Inn (34744 Pacific Coast Highway, 92624; 240-0150, Fax 493-3692) 42 rooms. SGL/DBL$70+.

Surfside Inn Capistrano (34680 Pacific Coast Highway, 92624; 240-7681) 74 rooms. SGL/DBL$100-$145.

Cardiff-By-The-Sea

Area Code 619
Cardiff-By-The-Sea Chamber of Commerce
119 Aberdeen Avenue
Cardiff-By-The-Sea CA 92007
753-0431

Cardiff-By-The-Sea Lodge (142 Chesterfield, 92007; 944-6474) 17 rooms, wheelchair access, no-smoking rooms. SGL$65, DBL$75-$85.

Country Side Inn (1661 Villa Cardiff Drive, 92007; 944-0427, Fax 944-7708, 800-322-9993) 104 rooms and suites, complimentary breakfast, heated swimming pool, jacuzzi, children under 12 free, kitchenettes, in-room refrigerators, fax service, meeting facilities for 25, car rental, airport transportation, wheelchair-access rooms, no-smoking rooms, no pets. SGL$59-$65, DBL$66-$74.

Carlsbad

Area Code 619
Carlsbad Convention and Visitors Bureau
Elm and RR Tracks
Carlsbad CA 92008
438-5540

Carlsbad Chamber of Commerce
5411 Avenida Encinas
Carlsbad CA 92008
729-5924

Carlsbad 83

Beach Terrace Inn (2775 Ocean Street, 92008; 729-5951, Fax 729-1078, 800-433-5415, 800-662-3224 in California) 79 rooms and suites, complimentary breakfast, swimming pool, beach. LS SGL/DBL$105-$185, STS$130-$190; HS SGL/DBL$125-$220, STS$125-$200.

Beach View Lodge (3180 Carlsbad Boulevard, 92008; 729-1151, Fax 729-1078, 800-535-5588, 800-BEACH-VU in California) 47 rooms and efficiencies, swimming pool, beach, no pets. LS SGL/DBL$66-$92, STS$100-$140; HS SGL/DBL$80-$104, STS$90-$160.

Best Western Andersen Inn (850 Palomar Airport Road, 92008; 438-7880, Fax 931-0499, 800-528-1234) 148 rooms and suites, restaurant, lounge, swimming pool, spa, jacuzzi, whirlpool, kitchenettes, children under 12 free, fax service, wheelchair access, no-smoking rooms. SGL$50-$90, DBL$58-$98.

Best Western Beach Terrace Inn (2775 Ocean Street, 92008; 729-5951, Fax 729-1078, 800-433-5415, 800-ON-BEACH in California) 49 rooms, swimming pool, whirlpool, fireplaces, meeting facilities, balconies, no pets, laundry room, fax service. SGL$104-$115, DBL$115-$125.

Best Western Beach View Lodge (3180 Carlsbad Road, 92008; 729-1151, Fax 729-1078, 800-232-2488, 800-528-1234) 41 rooms and suites, complimentary breakfast, outdoor heated swimming pool, spa, kitchenettes, in-room refrigerators and safes, valet laundry, meeting facilities, fireplaces, fax service, laundry room, wheelchair access, no-smoking rooms, no pets, free parking. SGL/DBL$66-$120, STS$115-$140.

Carlsbad Inn Beach Resort (3075 Carlsbad Boulevard, 92008; 434-7020, Fax 431-4594, 800-235-3939) 198 rooms, suites and condos, restaurant, lounge, swimming pool, airport transportation, meeting facilities, child care, laundry room, fireplaces, exercise facilities, tennis, wheelchair-access rooms. SGL$100-$125, DBL$115-$130.

Carlsbad

Economy Inns of America (751 Raintree Drive, 92009; 931-1185, 800-826-0778) 122 rooms, complimentary breakfast, heated swimming pool, wheelchair-access rooms, no-smoking rooms, pets allowed. SGL$40, DBL$50-$55.

La Costa Hotel and Spa (Costa Del Mar Road, 92009; 438-9111, Fax 438-3758, 800-854-5000) 500 rooms and suites, restaurant, swimming pool, sauna, spa, airport transportation, meeting facilities for 200, child care, lighted tennis courts, golf, exercise facilities, wheelchair-access rooms, no-smoking rooms. SGL/DBL$215-$400, STS$375-$1,500.

Motel 6 (1006 Carlsbad Village Drive, 92008; 434-7135, 505-891-6161) 109 rooms. SGL/DBL$26-$32.

Motel 6 (750 Raintree Drive, 92009; 431-0745, 505-891-6161) 160 rooms, swimming pool. SGL/DBL$25-$32.

Ocean Manor Motel (2950 Ocean Street, 92008; 729-2493, 800-341-8000) 47 rooms and suites, swimming pool. LS SGL/DBL$47-$64/$235W-$315W, STS$60-$81/$300W-$405W; HS SGL/DBL$67-$95/$390W-$570W, STS$93-$126/$690W-$750W.

Pelican Cove Inn (320 Walnut Avenue, 92008; 434-5995) 8 rooms and suites, bed and breakfast, complimentary breakfast, wheelchair access, pets allowed, free parking. SGL/DBL$85-$150, STS$190-$275.

Ramada Inn Suites (751 Macadamia, 92008; 438-2285, Fax 438-4547, 800-2-RAMADA) 120 suites and one- and two-bedroom apartments, complimentary breakfast, swimming pool, children under 16 free, wheelchair-access rooms, no-smoking rooms, free parking, pets allowed. SGL/DBL$55+.

Sun Coast Inn (3700 Pio Pico Drive, 92008; 720-0808) 47 rooms, swimming pool. SGL/DBL$35-$45.

Surf Motel (3136 Carlsbad Boulevard, 92008; 729-7961) 38 rooms and efficiencies, restaurant, swimming pool, ocean view. SGL#35-$6, DBL$40-$75, EFF$55-$110.

Tamarack Beach Resort (3200 Carlsbad Boulevard, 92008; 729-3500, Fax 434-5942, 800-334-2199) 77 rooms and one- and two-bedroom condos, restaurant, outdoor heated swimming pool, spa, jacuzzi, exercise facilities, free local telephone calls, children under 12 free, in-room refrigerators, VCRs, wheelchair access, no pets. LS SGL/DBL$95-$125, 1BR$120/$780W, 2BR$150/$975W; HS SGL/DBL$95-$125, 1BR$150/$1,105W, 2BR$200/$1,300W.

Travel Inn Motel (3666 Pio Pico Drive, 92008; 729-4941) 40 rooms, swimming pool. SGL/DBL$50+.

TraveLodge (760 Macadamia Drive, 92009; 438-2828, Fax 438-8181, 800-255-3050) 128 rooms and suites, restaurant, lounge, complimentary breakfast, swimming pool, meeting facilities for 40, laundry room, children under 15 free, in-room refrigerators and microwaves, no pets. SGL/DBL$44-$63.

Carmel

Area Code 408
Carmel Business Association
Vandervort Court
Carmel CA 93921
624-2522

Carmel-By-The-Sea Chamber of Commerce
Box 3333
Carmel-By-The-Sea CA 93921
624-2522

Carmel Valley Chamber of Commerce
Box 288
Carmel Valley CA 93924
659-4000

RENTAL SOURCES: Garden Court Realty (Box 171, 93921; 625-1400); **Pine Cone Property Management** (22613 Carmel Center Place, 93922; 626-8163); **San Carlos Agency** (Box 22123, 93922; 624-3846; Fax 624-4465) represents over 100 rental homes, cottages and estates on the Monterey peninsula; **Tourist Information and Finder's Service** (Box 7430, 93921; 624-1711).

Acacia Lodge (Box 87, 93924; 659-2297) 18 rooms and efficiencies, complimentary breakfast, swimming pool, no children, no pets. SGL/DBL$58-$90.

Adobe Inn (Box 4115, 93921; 624-3933, 800-624-8636 in California) 20 rooms, restaurant, complimentary breakfast, heated swimming pool, sauna, wheelchair-access rooms, free parking, no-smoking rooms. SGL/DBL$135-$180+.

Best Western Bay View Inn (Box 3719, 93921; 624-1831, 800-528-1234) 56 rooms, restaurant, lounge, complimentary breakfast, heated swimming pool, free parking, fireplaces, no pets, children under 12 free. SGL/DBL$79-$130.

Best Western Carmel Mission Inn (3665 Rio Road, 93923; 624-1841, Fax 624-8684, 800-528-1234) 165 rooms, restaurant, lounge, swimming pool, room service, fax service, children under 12 free, no-smoking rooms, free parking. SGL$69-$139, DBL$69-$149.

Best Western Carmel's Town House Lodge (Box 3547, 93921; 624-1261, 800-528-1234) 28 rooms, restaurant, swimming pool, free parking, no pets. SGL$64-$96, DBL$64-$125+.

Blue Sky Lodge (Box 233, 93924; 659-2256) 30 rooms and efficiencies, rooms, swimming pool, pets allowed. SGL/DBL$49-$84.

Candle Light Inn (Box 101, 93921; 624-6451, 800-422-4732) 20 rooms and efficiencies, complimentary breakfast, heated swimming pool, in-room refrigerators, children under 12 free,

free local telephone calls, wheelchair access, no pets, no-smoking rooms. SGL/DBL$89-$139.

Carmel's Hidden Valley Inn (102 West Carmel Valley Road, 93924; 659-5361, 800-367-3336) 25 rooms and suites, complimentary breakfast, outdoor heated swimming pool, in-room refrigerators, kitchenettes, fax service, no pets, no-smoking rooms, free parking. SGL$79-$109, DBL$99-$129, STS$129-$169.

Carmel River Inn (26600 Oliver Road, 93923; 624-1575) 43 rooms, heated swimming pool, wheelchair-access rooms, fireplaces. SGL/DBL$60-$85.

Carmel Sands Lodge (Box 1616, 93921; 624-1255) 40 rooms, restaurant, complimentary breakfast, swimming pool, wheelchair-access rooms, no-smoking rooms. SGL/DBL$70-$115+.

Carmel Studio Lodge (Box 2388, 93921; 624-8515) 19 rooms, complimentary breakfast, swimming pool, no-smoking rooms. SGL$45-$90, DBL$60-$90+.

Carmel's Tally Ho Inn (Monte Verde Avenue, 93921; 624-2232, Fax 624-2661) 14 rooms, bed and breakfast, complimentary breakfast, free parking. SGL$95-$200, DBL$105-$250.

Carmel Valley Inn (Box 115, 93924; 659-3131, Fax 373-4258) 46 rooms, restaurant, swimming pool, tennis, pets allowed. SGL/DBL$54-$119.

Carmel Valley Ranch Resort (One Old Ranch Road, 93923; 625-9500, Fax 624-2858, 800-4-CARMEL) 100 rooms, restaurant, lounge, swimming pool, meeting facilities, room service, airport courtesy car, tennis, golf, wheelchair-access rooms, free parking. SGL/DBL$235-$700.

Carriage House Inn (Box 101, 93921; 625-2585, Fax 624-2967, 800-422-4732) 13 rooms and suites, complimentary breakfast, jacuzzi, free local telephone calls, no children, no-smoking rooms, no pets, wheelchair access. SGL/DBL$135-$225+.

Coachman's Inn (Box C-1, 93921; 624-6421, 800-336-6421) 30 rooms, complimentary breakfast, pets allowed, free parking. SGL/DBL$90-$145.

The Cobblestone Inn (Box 3185, 93921; 625-5222) 22 rooms and suites, bed and breakfast, complimentary breakfast. SGL/DBL$95-$175.

Comfort Inn (Carpenter Street, 93921; 624-3113, 800-221-2222) 28 rooms, restaurant, complimentary breakfast, swimming pool, whirlpool, sauna, no pets. SGL$69-$89, DBL$69-$105.

Cypress Inn (Box Y, 93921; 624-3871, 800-443-7443) 30 rooms, complimentary breakfast, pets allowed, no-smoking rooms, meeting facilities. SGL/DBL$78-$190.

The Dolphin Inn (4th and San Carlos, 93921; 624-5356, Fax 624-2967, 800-422-4632) 27 rooms, restaurant, complimentary breakfast, heated swimming pool, in-room refrigerators, children under 12 free, fireplaces, no-smoking rooms. SGL/DBL$69-$175.

Green Lantern Inn (Seventh and Casanova, 93921; 624-4392) 19 rooms. SGL/DBL$65-$125.

Happy Landing Inn (Fifth Avenue and Monte Verde Street, 93921; 624-7917) 9 rooms, complimentary breakfast, swimming pool, free parking. SGL/DBL$90-$145.

Hidden Valley Inn (102 West Carmel Valley Road; 624-3801, 800-445-9516, 800-367-3336 in California) 27 rooms and suites, complimentary breakfast, outdoor heated swimming pool, meeting facilities for 20, wheelchair access, no-smoking rooms, no pets. SGL/DBL$79-$109, STS$129-$189.

Highlands Inn (Highway 1, 93921; 624-3801, Fax 626-1574, 800-682-4811) 142 rooms, restaurant, lounge, swimming pool, sauna, spa, kitchenettes, airport transportation, pets allowed, balconies, fireplaces, child care, ocean view, wheelchair-access rooms, exercise facilities, free parking. SGL/DBL$225-$550.

The Hofsas House (Box 1195, 93921; 624-2745, 800-221-2548) 624-2745, 800-221-2548) 38 rooms and suites, complimentary breakfast, outdoor heated swimming pool, free parking, no-smoking rooms, no pets. SGL/DBL$75-$140.

Horizon Inn (Junipero Street and Third Avenue, 93921; 624-5327) 20 rooms, complimentary breakfast, swimming pool, fireplaces, in-room refrigerators, ocean view. SGL/DBL$79-$155.

La Playa Hotel (Camino and 8th Avenue, 93921; 624-6476, Fax 624-7966, 800-582-8900) 80 rooms and cottage suites, restaurant, lounge, outdoor heated swimming pool, children under 12 free, in-room refrigerators, meeting facilities for 100, laundry room, free parking, child care, no pets. wheelchair-access rooms. SGL/DBL$110-$200, STS$200-$475.

Lamplighter Inn (Ocean Avenue and Camino Real, 93921; 624-7372) 9 rooms and efficiencies. SGL/DBL$70-$130.

Lobos Lodge (Ocean Avenue, 93921; 624-3874; 624-3874) 30 rooms, complimentary breakfast, fireplaces, in-room refrigerators. SGL/DBL$84-$160.

Los Laureles Lodge (Carmel Valley Road, 93925; 659-2233, Fax 659-0481) 30 rooms, bed and breakfast, complimentary breakfast, restaurant, swimming pool, no pets. SGL/DBL$95-$125, STS$150-$350.

Mission Ranch Resort (26270 Delores, 93923; 624-6436) 26 rooms, restaurant, complimentary breakfast, child care, pets allowed, tennis, wheelchair-access rooms. SGL/DBL$55-$130.

Monte Verde Inn (Box 394, 93921; 624-6046, 800-328-7707 in California) 10 rooms, bed and breakfast, complimentary breakfast. SGL$65, DBL$75.

Normandy Inn (Ocean and Monte Verde Avenues, 93921; 624-3825, 800-343-3825 in California) 45 rooms and suites, complimentary breakfast. SGL/DBL$89-$390.

Pine Inn (Ocean Avenue, 93921; 624-3851, Fax 624-3030, 800-228-3851) 49 rooms and suites, restaurant, room service, wheelchair-access rooms, transportation to local attractions, meeting facilities, SGL/DBL$85-$185+.

Quail Lodge Resort and Golf Course (8205 Valley Greens Drive, 93923; 624-1581, Fax 624-3626, 800-682-9303, 800-538-9516 in California) 100 rooms and cottages, restaurant, lounge, swimming pool, airport transportation, hot tubs, pets allowed, wheelchair-access rooms, no-smoking rooms, meeting facilities, fireplaces, child care, exercise facilities, tennis, golf, free parking, no pets allowed. LS SGL/DBL$195-$235; HS SGL/DBL $275-$515.

River Inn (Highway One, 93922; 624-1575) 43 rooms. SGL/DBL$55-$110.

Robles Del Rio Lodge (100 Punta Del Monte, 93924; 659-3705, Fax 659-5157, 800-833-0843) 33 rooms, restaurant, lounge, swimming pool, spa, sauna, child care, kitchenettes, fireplaces, meeting facilities, airport courtesy car, wheelchair access, tennis, no pets. SGL/DBL$80-$125.

Sandpiper Inn At The Beach (2408 Bay View, 93923; 624-6433) 16 rooms, bed and breakfast, complimentary breakfast, airport transportation, no-smoking rooms, free parking. SGL/DBL$69-$195.

Sea View Inn (Box 4138, 93921; 624-8778) 8 rooms, bed and breakfast, complimentary breakfast. SGL/DBL$80-$110.

Stonehouse Inn (Box 2517, 93921; 624-4569) 6 rooms, bed and breakfast, complimentary breakfast, no-smoking rooms. SGL/DBL$95-$125.

Carmel 91

Stonepine Estate Resort (150 East Carmel Valley Road, 93924; 659-2245, Fax 659-5160) 12 rooms, restaurant, complimentary breakfast, airport transportation, swimming pool, tennis, no-smoking rooms. SGL/DBL$75-$550.

Studio Lodge (Box 2388, 939212; 624-8518) 19 rooms. SGL/DBL$40-$150.

Sundial Lodge (Monte Verde and 7th Avenue, 93921; 624-8578) 20 rooms, restaurant, complimentary breakfast. SGL/DBL$99-$165.

Svendsgaards Inn (Box 101, 93921; 624-1511, Fax 624-2967, 800-422-4732) 34 rooms, complimentary breakfast, heated swimming pool, in-room refrigerators, fireplaces, no-smoking rooms. SGL/DBL$69-$185.

Tally Ho Inn (Box 3726, 93921; 624-2232) 14 rooms, bed and breakfast, restaurant, complimentary breakfast. SGL/DBL$95-$200+.

Tickle Pink Motor Inn (155 Highland Drive, 93923; 624-1244, Fax 626-9516, 800-635-4774) 35 rooms and suites, complimentary breakfast, wheelchair access, no pets. SGL/DBL$109-$159, STS$199-$259.

Torres Inn (Ocean Avenue and Torres Street, 93921; 624-3387) 17 rooms, complimentary breakfast. SGL/DBL$100+.

Tradewinds Inn (Box 3403, 93921; 624-2776) 27 rooms and suites, complimentary breakfast, heated swimming pool, fireplaces. SGL/DBL$95-$175.

Vagabond's House Inn (Box 2747, 93921; 624-7738, Fax 626-1243, 800-262-1262) 11 rooms and suites, bed and breakfast, complimentary breakfast, kitchenettes, pets allowed, SGL/DBL$79-$135.

Valley Lodge (Carmel Valley Road, 93924; 659-2261, Fax 659-4558, 800-641-4646) 49 rooms and cottages, complimentary breakfast, swimming pool, sauna, spa, meeting facilities, fireplaces, exercise facilities, wheelchair-access rooms, pets allowed. SGL/DBL$85-$215.

The Wayfarer Inn (Box 1896, 93921; 624-2711, 800-533-2711 in California) 17 rooms and suites, bed and breakfast, complimentary breakfast, children under 18 free, no smoking, no pets. SGL$63-$83, DBL$73-$93.

Carpinteria

Area Code 805
Carpinteria Valley Chamber of Commerce
5036 Carpinteria Avenue
Carpinteria CA 93013
684-5479

All Star Inn (5550 Carpinteria Avenue, 93013; 684-8602) 138 rooms, indoor, swimming pool, wheelchair-access rooms, no-smoking rooms, pets allowed. SGL/DBL$30-$35.

Best Western Inn (4558 Carpinteria Avenue, 93013; 805-684-0473, Fax 805-684-4015, 800-528-1234) 143 rooms, restaurant, lounge, heated swimming pool, spa, meeting facilities, fax service, LS SGL/DBL$89-$99; HS SGL/DBL$105-$115.

Casa Del Sol Motel (5585 Carpinteria Avenue, 93013; 684-4307) 21 rooms, swimming pool. SGL/DBL$35-$65.

Coast Village Inn (1188 Coast Village Road, 93108; 969-3266) 25 rooms, restaurant, complimentary breakfast, swimming pool. SGL/DBL$50-$110.

Eugenia Motel (5277 Carpinteria Avenue, 93108; 684-4416) 10 rooms and efficiencies. SGL/DBL$35-$55.

Friendship Inn (4160 Via Real Road, 93013; 684-4176, 800-453-4511) 45 rooms, indoor swimming pool. SGL/DBL$36-$44.

Motel 6 (4200 Via Real Road, 93013; 684-6921, 505-891-6161) 124 rooms, swimming pool, wheelchair-access rooms, no-smoking rooms, pets allowed. SGL/DBL$30-$36.

Reef Motel (4160 Via Real, 93013; 684-4176) 51 rooms and efficiencies, swimming pool, wheelchair-access rooms. SGL/DBL$35-$55.

Carson

Area Code 213
Carson Chamber of Commerce
9426 West Carson Street
Carson CA 90749
320-0551

Clarion Hotel Conference Center (Two Civic Plaza Drive, 90745; 830-9200, Fax 518-2969, 800-221-2222) 224 rooms and suites, restaurant, lounge, swimming pool, jacuzzi, whirlpools, meeting facilities, exercise center, airport courtesy car, no pets. SGL/DBL$70-$90.

Comfort Inn (1325 East Carson Street, 90745; 830-8044, 800-221-2222) 31 rooms, restaurant, swimming pool, whirlpools, wheelchair-access rooms, no pets. SGL/DBL$43-$62.

Days Inn (415 West Carson Street, 90745; 328-2622, Fax 328-4815, 800-325-2525) 35 rooms and suites, complimentary breakfast, swimming pool, sauna, no pets, fax service, children under 12 free, wheelchair-access rooms, no-smoking rooms. SGL/DBL$50-$60, STS$75-$85.

Hampton Inn (767 Albertoni Street, 90746; 768-8833, Fax 768-2022, 800-HAMPTON, 800-465-4329) 137 rooms, complimentary breakfast, swimming pool, jacuzzi, exercise center, free parking, meeting facilities. SGL/DBL$48-$55, STS$56-$60.

Ramada Inn South (850 East Dominguez Street, 90746; 538-5500, Fax 715-2957, 800-228-2828) 167 rooms and suites, restaurant, lounge, swimming pool, meeting facilities for 250, wheelchair-access rooms, no-smoking rooms, free parking, airport transportation. SGL$54-$75, DBL$56-$85.

Castaic

Area Code 805

Comfort Inn Magic Mountain (31558 Castaic Road, 91384; 295-1100, 800-221-2222) 120 rooms, restaurant, complimentary breakfast, swimming pool, wheelchair-access rooms. LS SGL/DBL$43-$50; HS SGL/DBL$49-$60.

Econo Lodge of Castaic (31410 Castaic Road, 91348; 295-1070, Fax 295-9775, 800-348-4219) 54 rooms and suites, complimentary breakfast, outdoor swimming pool, spa, in-room refrigerators, fax service, wheelchair-access rooms, no-smoking rooms. SGL/DBL$35-$80, STS$120+.

South Lake Inn (31410 Castaic Road, 91384; 295-1070, Fax 295-9775, 800-5ECONO1) 54 rooms, complimentary breakfast, free local telephone calls, heated swimming pool, jacuzzi, fax service, wheelchair-access rooms, no-smoking rooms. SGL/DBL$49-$64.

Cayucos

Area Code 805
Cayucos Chamber of Commerce
151 Cayucos Drive
Cayucos CA 93430
995-1200

Cayucos Motel (20 South Ocean Avenue, 93430; 995-3670) 6 rooms and efficiencies. SGL/DBL$35-$45.

Estero Bay Motel (25 South Ocean Avenue, 93430; 995-3614, Fax 995-2813, 800-736-1292) 12 rooms and efficiencies, restaurant, wheelchair-access rooms, pets allowed, free local telephone calls, airport transportation, free parking. SGL$30-$$72, DBL$45-$85.

Shoreline Inn (34 North Ocean Avenue, 93430; 995-3681) 28 rooms, wheelchair-access rooms. SGL/DBL$50-$150.

Cerritos

Area Code 213
Cerritos Chamber of Commerce
19141 Bloomfield Avenue
Cerritos CA 90701
809-2262

Sheraton Cerritos Hotel At Towne Center (12725 Center Court Drive, 90701; 809-1500, Fax 403-2081, 800-325-3535) 203 rooms and suites, restaurant, lounge, outdoor heated swimming pool, spa, child care, gift shop, car rental, meeting facilities for 200, exercise center, airport transportation, wheelchair-access rooms, no-smoking rooms. SGL$95-$115, DBL$110-$130.

Cathedral City

Area Code 619
Cathedral City Chamber of Commerce
68-703 Perez Road #5
Cathedral City 92234
328-1213

Days Inn (69-151 East Palm Canyon Drive, 92234; 324-5939, Fax 324-3034, 800-325-2525) 97 rooms and efficiencies, heated swimming pool, whirlpool, valet laundry, laundry room, meeting facilities, children under 16 free, no pets, fax service. SGL$59-$93, DBL$69-$113.

Desert Princess (Visto Chino at Landau, 92263; 322-7000, 800-637-0577, 800-528-0444) 300 rooms and suites, restaurant, swimming pool, golf, tennis, airport courtesy car, exercise facilities. SGL/DBL$49, STS$135.

Lawrence Welk's Desert Oasis Resort (34567 Cathedral Canyon Drive, 92234; 321-9000, Fax 749-5263, 800-932-9355, 800-824-8224 in California) 132 rooms and suites, restaurant, lounge, two outdoor heated swimming pools, spa, jacuzzi, fax service, golf, lighted tennis courts, meeting facilities for 300, gift shop, valet laundry, free parking, wheelchair-access rooms, no-smoking rooms, pets allowed. LS SGL/DBL$90-$110, STS$150-$220.

Royce Resort Hotel (34567 Cathedral Canyon Drive, 92264; 321-9000, 800-327-0475 in California) 162 rooms, restaurant, swimming pool, golf, tennis. SGL/DBL$85-$135.

Chula Vista

Area Code 619
Chamber of Commerce
233 Fourth Street
Chula Vista CA 92010
420-6602

All Seasons Inn (699 E Street, 92010; 585-1999, Fax 427-3748, 800-537-8483) 108 rooms, complimentary breakfast, swimming pool, sauna, fireplaces, laundry room, airport transportation, wheelchair access, no-smoking rooms. SGL$44-$57, DBL$49-$62.

Best Western Cavalier Motor Hotel (710 E Street, 92010; 420-5198, 800-528-1234) 76 rooms, restaurant, lounge, swimming pool, in-room refrigerators, children under 12 free, no-smoking rooms, no pets. SGL$39-$49, DBL$48-$58.

Days Inn (225 Bay Boulevard, 92010; 425-8200, Fax 426-7411, 800-325-2525) 118 rooms, restaurant, swimming pool, children under 12 free, fax service, wheelchair-access rooms, no-smoking rooms, pets allowed. SGL$36-$49, DBL$44-$45.

Chula Vista

Grosvenor Inn (4450 Otay Valley Road, 91910; 422-2600, Fax 425-4605) 120 rooms, restaurant, complimentary breakfast, swimming pool, airport courtesy car, wheelchair-access rooms, no-smoking rooms. SGL/DBL$50-$75.

La Quinta Motor Inn (150 Bonita Road, 92010; 691-1121, Fax 427-0135, 800-531-5900) 142 rooms, restaurant, lounge, heated swimming pool, meeting facilities, wheelchair access, no-smoking rooms, pets allowed. SGL/DBL$46-$56.

Motel 6 (745 E Street, 91010; 422-4200, 505-891-6161) 176 rooms. SGL/DBL$28-$34.

Otay Valley Inn (4450 Otay Valley Road, 91911; 422-2600, Fax 425-2605) 131 rooms. SGL/DBL$48-$68.

Ramada Inn (91 Bonita Road, 91910; 425-9999, Fax 425-8934, 800-228-2828) 97 rooms and suites, restaurant, lounge, swimming pool, children under 18 free, meeting facilities for 60, wheelchair-access rooms, no-smoking rooms, beauty and barber shops. SGL/DBL$55-$72.

Rodeway Inn (778 Broadway, 91910; 476-9555) 49 rooms, swimming pool, ocean view, in-room refrigerators and microwaves, children under 18 free, no-smoking rooms, wheelchair-access rooms, no-smoking rooms. SGL$40-$50, DBL$45-$55.

Royal Vista Inn (632 E Street, 91910; 426-2500, Fax 476-8635) 80 rooms, restaurant, swimming pool. SGL$35-$50, DBL$40-$55.

Traveler Motel Kitchen Suites (235 Woodlawn Avenue, 92010; 427-9170, Fax 427-5247) 85 suites, swimming pool, no-smoking rooms, child care, laundry room, pets allowed. STS$39-$72.

TraveLodge (394 Broadway, 91910; 420-6600, Fax 420-5556, 800-255-3050) 63 rooms, restaurant, lounge, swimming pool, whirlpool, VCRs, laundry room, meeting facilities, tennis, no pets. SGL/DBL$41-$64.

Vagabond Inn (230 Broadway, 91910; 422-8305, Fax 425-3645, 800-522-1555) 91 rooms, restaurant, lounge, complimentary breakfast, heated swimming pool, pets allowed, airport transportation, free local telephone calls, no-smoking rooms, children under 18 free, fax service, complimentary newspaper.

Chatsworth

Area Code 818
Chatsworth Chamber of Commerce
10305 Vassar Avenue
Chatsworth CA 91311
341-2428

The Chatsworth Hotel (9777 Topanga Canyon Boulevard, 91311; 709-7054, Fax 998-3573, 800-676-9641) 148 rooms and suites, restaurant, exercise center, meeting facilities, wheelchair-access rooms, no-smoking rooms, free parking. SGL/DBL$87-$97, STS$130-$165.

Ramada Inn (21340 Devonshire Street, 91311; 998-5289, Fax 990-0257, 800-2-RAMADA) 74 rooms and suites, restaurant, lounge, swimming pool, in-room refrigerators, free parking, airport transportation, wheelchair-access rooms, no-smoking rooms. SGL/DBL$80-$110.

7 Star Suites Hotel (21603 Devonshire Street, 91311; 998-8888, Fax 718-6666, 800-782-7872) 75 rooms and suites, outdoor heated swimming pool, jacuzzi, children under 18 free, in-room refrigerators, fax service, meeting facilities for 20, free parking, wheelchair-access rooms, no-smoking, no pets. SGL/DBL$59-$79, STS69-$150. STS$150+.

Summerfield Suites (21902 Lassen Chat, 91311; 773-0707) 114 suites and condos, swimming pool, exercise facilities. SGL/DBL$120-$150.

Topanga Inn (9817 Topanga Canyon Road, 91311; 709-7054; Fax 998-3574) 49 rooms, complimentary breakfast, swimming pool, airport transportation, wheelchair access, no-smoking rooms. SGL/DBL$100-$125.

Chino

Area Code 714
Chino Valley Chamber of Commerce
12134 Central Avenue
Chino CA 91710
591-6336

Best Western Pine Tree Motel (12018 Central Avenue, 91710; 628-6021, 800-528-1234) 44 rooms, restaurant, swimming pool, balconies, wheelchair access, no-smoking rooms, no pets. SGL$39-$56, DBL$45-$63.

Motel 6 (12266 Central Avenue, 91710; 591-3877, 505-891-6161) 95 rooms. SGL/DBL$27-$33.

City of Commerce

Area Code 213

Best Western (7810 East Telegraph Road, 90040; 806-3791. Fax 806-4741) 120 rooms, complimentary breakfast, free parking, children under 12 free, no pets, no-smoking rooms, wheelchair-access rooms, airport courtesy car. SGL/DBL$50-$64.

Radisson Hotel (6300 East Telegraph Road, 90040; 722-7000, Fax 888-9629, 800-333-3333) 283 rooms and suites, restaurant, swimming pool, exercise facilities, airport transportation, pets allowed, free parking. SGL$79-$99, DBL$94-$114, STS$175-$250.

Ramada Inn (7272 Gage Avenue, 90040; 806-4777, Fax 806-4777, 800-547-4777) 159 rooms and suites, restaurant, heated swimming pool, meeting facilities, free parking, airport transportation, exercise facilities, wheelchair access, no-smoking rooms, pets allowed. SGL$61-$75, STS$75-$125.

TraveLodge Suites Hotel (7701 East Slauson Avenue, 90040; 728-5165, Fax 721-1039, 800-426-0580) 70 suites, restaurant, lounge, complimentary breakfast, in-room refrigerators and microwaves, tours, car rental, meeting facilities for 62, business services, laundry room, wheelchair-access rooms, no-smoking rooms, free parking. SGL/DBL$39-$65.

Wyndham Garden Hotel (575 Telegraph Road, 90040; 887-8100, Fax 887-4343) 201 rooms, restaurant, lounge, swimming pool, whirlpool, saunas, meeting facilities for 600, wheelchair-access rooms, no-smoking rooms, exercise center, SGL/DBL$100-$120.

City of Industry

Area Code 818

Best Western Executive Inn (18880 East Gale Avenue, 91748; 810-1818, Fax 810-3222, 800-874-2858) 135 rooms and suites, outdoor heated swimming pool, in-room refrigerators, fax services, transportation to local attractions, wheelchair-access rooms, no-smoking rooms, free parking. SGL/DBL$60-$72, STS$78-$86.

Industry Hills and Sheraton Resort (One Industry Hills Parkway, 91744; 965-0861, Fax 964-9535, 800-325-3535) 296 rooms and suites, three restaurants, lounge, two swimming pools, spa, meeting facilities for 1,600, car rental, lighted tennis courts, golf, exercise facilities, airport transportation, wheelchair-access rooms, no-smoking rooms, free parking. SGL$85-$120, DBL$95-$135, STS$150-$450.

Claremont

Area Code 714
Claremont Convention and Visitors Bureau
205 North Yale Avenue
Claremont CA 91711
621-9644

Griswold's Claremont Center (555 West Foothill Boulevard, 626-2411, Fax 624-056, 800-854-5722, 800-821-0341 in California) 273 rooms and suites, restaurant, lounge, swimming pool, sauna, transportation to local attractions, meeting facilities, exercise facilities, airport courtesy car, wheelchair-access rooms, no-smoking rooms. SGL$75, DBL$125-$195.

Howard Johnson Lodge (721 South Indian Hills Boulevard, 91711; 626-2431, Fax 624-7051, 800-654-2000) 62 rooms, restaurant, complimentary breakfast, swimming pool, meeting facilities, airport courtesy car, wheelchair-access rooms, free parking. SGL$49, DBL$49.

Ramada Inn (840 South Indian Hill Boulevard, 621-4831, Fax 626-8452) 126 rooms, restaurant, lounge, swimming pool, lighted tennis courts, meeting facilities, jacuzzis, airport courtesy car, wheelchair access/room, no-smoking rooms. SGL$55, DBL$60.

TraveLodge (736 South Indian Hill Boulevard, 91711; 626-5654, 800-255-3050) 52 rooms, restaurant, swimming pool, no pets. SGL/DBL$39-$55.

Coalinga

Area Code 209
Coalinga Chamber of Commerce
193 East Elm Street

Coalinga CA 93210
935-2948

The Inn At Harris Ranch (24485 West Dorris, 93210; 935-0717, Fax 935-5061, 800-942-2333) 123 rooms and suites, restaurant, lounge, complimentary breakfast, outdoor heated swimming pool, children under 12 free, fax service, meeting facilities for 50, gift shop, airport transportation, wheelchair access, pets allowed, no-smoking rooms. SGL$77-$215, DBL$83-$215.

Coarsegold

Area Code 209

Black Hawk Lodge (28543 Highway 41, 93614; 868-3596) 11 rooms, no-smoking rooms, pets allowed. LS SGL/DBL$49; HS SGL/DBL$65.

Lakeshore Resort (61953 Huntington Lane, 93614; 893-3193) 65 rooms. SGL/DBL$65-$115.

Southern Manor Inn (Box 262, 93614; 682-4303, 800-735-4525) 6 rooms and efficiencies, no-smoking rooms, pets allowed, wheelchair access. LS SGL/DBL$30-$35; HS SGL/DBL$45-$70.

Compton

Area Code 213
Compton Chamber of Commerce
499 East Compton Boulevard
Compton CA 90224
631-8611

Best Western (1919 West Artesia Boulevard, 90220; 537-6300, Fax 661-2142) 96 rooms. SGL/DBL$60-$90.

Budget Host Inn (1408 Longbeach Boulevard, 90221; 635-2900) 27 rooms. SGL/DBL$35-$45.

Ramada Hotel and Convention Center (111 East Artesia Boulevard, 90221; 632-1234, Fax 632-3307, 800-2-RAMADA) 292 rooms, restaurant, lounge, swimming pool, spa, exercise facilities, meeting facilities, wheelchair-access rooms, no-smoking rooms. SGL/DBL$35-$100.

TraveLodge (1116 Long Beach Boulevard, 90221; 213-763-9700, 800-255-3050) 40 rooms, restaurant, whirlpools, no pets. SGL/DBL$40-$55.

Corcoran

Area Code 209
Corcoran Chamber of Commerce
Box 771
Corcoran CA 93212
992-4514

Shilo Inn (1224 Whitley Avenue, 93212; 992-3171) 45 rooms, complimentary breakfast, complimentary newspaper, laundry room. SGL/DBL$47-$55.

Corona

Area Code 714
Corona Chamber of Commerce
904 East Sixth Street
Corona CA 91719
737-3352

Best Western Kings Inn (1084 Pomona Road, 91720; 734-4241, Fax 279-5371, 800-892-5464, 800-528-1234) 87 rooms, restaurant, complimentary breakfast, swimming pool, in-room refrigerators and microwaves, whirlpools, wheelchair-access rooms, no-smoking rooms, no pets. SGL/DBL$49-$64.

Days Inn-Kings Inn (1084 Pomona Road, 91720; 734-4241, 800-528-1234) 88 rooms, restaurant, swimming pool. SGL/DBL$46-$66.

Executive Inn and Suites (1805 West Sixth Street, 91720; 3781-7185, 800-523-9321) 56 rooms and suites, restaurant, outdoor swimming pool, spa, children under 12 free, free parking, wheelchair-access rooms, no-smoking rooms, no pets. SGL/DBL$42, STS$55-$60.

Motel 6 (200 North Lincoln Avenue, 91719; 735-6408, 505-891-6161) 126 rooms. SGL/DBL$22-$28.

TraveLodge (210 South Lincoln Avenue, 91720; 272-4800, Fax 913-8859, 800-255-3050) 67 rooms and suites, restaurant, lounge, swimming pool, whirlpool, kitchenettes, no pets. SGL/DBL$38-$55.

TraveLodge (1701 West Sixth Street, 91720; 735-5500, 800-255-3050) 45 rooms, restaurant, lounge, swimming pool, spa, kitchenettes, airport transportation, SGL/DBL$33-$47.

Coronado

Area Code 619
Coronado Chamber of Commerce
720 Orange Street
Coronado CA 92118
435-9260

Coronado Visitor Information Center
111 Orange Avenue
Coronado CA 92118
436-8788

Best Western Suites Hotel (275 Orange Avenue, 92118; 437-1666, Fax 437-0188, 800-528-1234) 63 rooms, restaurant, complimentary breakfast, swimming pool, jacuzzi, laundry room, free parking, in-room refrigerators and microwaves, fax service, no-smoking rooms, wheelchair-access rooms, no pets. SGL$74-$129, DBL$82-$129, STS$114-$130.

Coronado Inn (266 Orange Avenue, 92118; 435-4121) 24 rooms and apartments, swimming pool, kitchenettes, laundry room. SGL/DBL$58-$68, EFF$68/$350W.

Coronado Victorian House (1000 8th Street, 92118; 435-2200) 6 rooms, bed and breakfast, complimentary breakfast, wheelchair-access rooms, no-smoking rooms. SGL/DBL$150-$450.

Coronado Village Inn (1017 Park Place, 92118; 435-9318) 20 rooms, jacuzzis. SGL/DBL$45-$60.

Crown City Inn (520 Orange Avenue, 92118; 435-3116, Fax 435-6750, 800-422-1173) 33 rooms and suites, restaurant, heated outdoor swimming pool, in-room refrigerators, children under 16 free, fax service, free parking, wheelchair access, no-smoking, no pets. SGL/DBL$69-$109, STS$85-$125.

Hotel Del Coronado (1500 Orange Avenue, 92118; 522-8000, Fax 522-8262, 800-HOTEL-DEL) 690 rooms and suites, restaurant, lounge, swimming pool, spa, wheelchair access/room, in-room mini-bars, exercise facilities, tennis, boat rentals. SGL/DBL$149-$995.

Del Island Motel (308 Orange Avenue, 92118; 435-9722) 30 rooms and one- and two-bedroom apartments, laundry room, in-room refrigerators. SGL/DBL$55, 1BR$75+, 2BR$85+.

El Cordova Hotel (1351 Orange Avenue, 92118; 435-4231, 800-367-6467) 39 rooms and suites, restaurant, swimming pool, pets allowed. SGL/DBL$60-$75, STS$94-$145.

El Rancho Motel (370 Orange Avenue, 92118; 435-2251) 6 rooms, in-room refrigerators and microwaves, free parking. SGL/DBL$45-$85.

Glorietta Bay Inn (1630 Glorietta Boulevard, 92118; 435-3101, Fax 435-6182, 800-283-9383) 98 rooms and suites, restaurant, swimming pool, meeting facilities, free parking, kitchenettes, SGL$79-$105, DBL$89-$115, STS$165-$265.

Holiday Motel (301 Orange Avenue, 92118; 435-0935) 12 rooms and efficiencies, in-room refrigerators, airport transportation. SGL$40-$45, DBL$40-$50, EFF$60-$75.

La Avenida Motel (1315 Orange Avenue, 92118; 435-3191) 28, one- and two-bedroom suites, restaurant, heated swimming pool, kitchenettes, LS SGL/DBL$46-$54, STS$125; HS SGL/DBL$66-$74, STS$180.

Le Meridien San Diego at Coronado (2000 Second Street, 92118; 435-3000, Fax 435-3032, 800-543-4300) 300 rooms, suites and villas, restaurant, lounge, swimming pool, sauna, spa, meeting facilities, business services, child care, wheelchair-access rooms, no-smoking rooms, exercise facilities, lighted tennis courts. SGL/DBL$155-$215, STS$350-$650.

Loews Coronado Bay Resort (4000 Coronado Bay Road, 92118; 424-4000, Fax 424-4400, 800-23-LOEWS) 440 rooms and suites, three restaurants, lounge, three swimming pools, sauna, child care, fireplaces, business services, meeting facilities for 200, marina, lighted tennis courts, wheelchair-access rooms, airport transportation. SGL$180-$375, DBL$200-$395, STS$275-$1,200.

Villa Capri (1417 Orange Avenue, 92118; 435-4137, 800-231-3954, 800-325-2756 in California) 14 suites and apartments, swimming pool, kitchenettes, free local telephone calls, airport transportation. SGL$68-$90, DBL$78-$88, STS$98-$615.

Costa Mesa

Area Code 714
Costa Mesa Chamber of Commerce
1901 Newport Boulevard #135

Costa Mesa

Costa Mesa CA 92629
650-1490

All Star Inn (1441 Gisler Avenue, 92626; 957-3063) 66 rooms. SGL/DBL$31-$37.

Ana Mesa Suites (3597 Harbor Boulevard, 92626; 662-3500, Fax 549-7126) 51 suites. SGL/DBL$59+.

Best Western Newport Mesa Inn (2642 Newport Boulevard, 92627; 650-2030, Fax 642-1220, 800-528-1234, 800-554-2378 in California) 97 rooms, restaurant, swimming pool, spa, meeting facilities, children under 12 free, exercise facilities, wheelchair-access rooms, no-smoking rooms, airport courtesy car. SGL/DBL$45-$99.

The Beverly Heritage Hotel (3350 Avenue of the Arts, 92626; 751-5100, Fax 751-0129, 800-443-4455) 238 rooms and suites, restaurant, lounge, complimentary breakfast, swimming pool, meeting facilities, airport courtesy car, exercise center, wheelchair-access rooms, no-smoking rooms. SGL/DBL$95-$180+.

Comfort Inn (2430 Newport Boulevard, 92626; 631-7840, 800-221-2222) 58 rooms, complimentary breakfast, swimming pool, whirlpool, wheelchair-access rooms, no pets. SGL$43-$51, DBL$48-$58.

Countryside Inn and Suites (325 Bristol Street, 92626; 549-0300, Fax 662-0828, 800-322-9992) 285 rooms and suites, restaurant, complimentary breakfast, swimming pool, airport courtesy car, exercise facilities, wheelchair-access rooms, no-smoking rooms. SGL$85, DBL$95, STS$95-$120.

The Cozy Inn (325 West Bay, 92627; 650-2055) 29 rooms and efficiencies, swimming pool, wheelchair-access rooms. SGL$40-$45, DBL$45-$50.

Harbor Mesa Inn (3151 Harbor Boulevard, 92626; 540-8571, Fax 979-9647) 50 rooms, complimentary breakfast, swimming pool, pets allowed. SGL/DBL$42-$60.

Costa Mesa

Holiday Inn Airport (3131 Bristol Street, 92676; 557-3000, Fax 957-8185, 800-221-7220, 800-HOLIDAY) 230 rooms and suites, restaurant, lounge, swimming pool, sauna, spa, laundry room, meeting facilities for 600, exercise center, airport transportation, wheelchair-access rooms, no-smoking rooms, no pets. SGL$75-$85, DBL$85-$95.

La Quinta Inn (1515 South Coast Drive, 92626; 975-5841, Fax 432-7159, 800-531-5900) 162 rooms, restaurant, lounge, swimming pool, wheelchair-access rooms, meeting facilities, airport courtesy car, no-smoking rooms. SGL$51-$56, DBL$56-$61+.

Marriott Residence Inn (881 Baker Street, 92626; 241-8800, Fax 546-4308, 800-331-3131) in-room microwaves, airport transportation, exercise facilities, wheelchair-access rooms, no-smoking rooms, pets allowed. SGL/DBL$99-$139.

Marriott Suites (500 Anton Boulevard, 92626; 957-1100, Fax 966-8495, 800-228-9290) 254 suites, restaurant, lounge, complimentary breakfast, swimming pool, sauna, exercise facilities, airport courtesy car, VCRs, wheelchair-access rooms, no-smoking rooms, pets allowed. SGL/DBL$120-$160, STS$300+.

Newport Bay Inn (2070 Newport Boulevard, 92627; 631-6000, Fax 631-4952, 800-284-3229) 60 rooms, complimentary breakfast, wheelchair access, no-smoking rooms. SGL$50-$60, DBL$55-$65.

Red Lion Hotel At The Airport (3050 Bristol Street, 92626; 540-7000, Fax 540-9176, 800-547-8010) 484 rooms and one-bedroom suites, restaurant, lounge, swimming pool, sauna, meeting facilities, child care, exercise facilities, airport courtesy car, wheelchair-access rooms, no-smoking rooms, pets allowed. SGL$120-$170, DBL$130-$175, STS$450+.

Super 8 Motel (2645 Harbor Boulevard, 92626; 545-9471, 432-8129, 800-800-8000) 49 rooms, complimentary breakfast, outdoor heated swimming pool, sauna, spa, free local telephone calls, fax service, kitchenettes, complimentary newspaper, no-smoking rooms, no pets. SGL/DBL$42-$45.

TraveLodge (2450 Newport Boulevard, 92627; 642-8226, Fax 650-6961) 93 rooms, restaurant, lounge, complimentary breakfast, swimming pool, whirlpool, in-room refrigerators and microwaves, tours, car rental, laundry room, no pets, airport transportation, meeting facilities for 15. SGL/DBL$39-$49.

TraveLodge (1951 Newport Boulevard, 92627; 650-2999, Fax 650-7579, 800-255-3050) 57 rooms, restaurant, lounge, complimentary breakfast, swimming pool, sauna, in-room refrigerators and microwaves, tours, car rental, meeting facilities for 20, airport transportation, no pets. SGL$35-$39, DBL$39-$45.

Vagabond Inn (3205 Harbor Boulevard, 92626; 557-8360) 130 rooms and suites, restaurant, lounge, swimming pool, sauna, meeting facilities, exercise center, pets allowed, airport transportation, free local telephone calls, no-smoking rooms, children under 18 free, fax service, complimentary newspaper. SGL$38-$43, DBL$43-$53.

Westin South Coast Plaza (666 Anton Boulevard, 92626; 540-2500, Fax 754-7996, 800-228-3000) 400 rooms and one-bedroom suites, 4 restaurants, lounge, outdoor swimming pool, spa, meeting facilities, wheelchair-access rooms, no-smoking rooms, exercise center, airport courtesy car, lighted tennis courts. SGL$134-$174, DBL$154-$194, STS$215-$945.

Covina

Area Code 818
Covina Chamber of Commerce
128 East College Street
Covina CA 91723
967-4191

Embassy Suites Hotel (1211 East Garvey Street, 91724; 915-3441, Fax 331-0773, 800-EMBASSY) 264 suites, restaurant, lounge, complimentary breakfast, swimming pool, sauna, meeting facilities for 350, gift shop, car rental, room service, airport transportation, wheelchair access, no-smoking rooms, pets allowed. SGL/DBL$99-$129, STS$99+.

Culver City

Area Code 213
Culver City Convention and Visitors Bureau
1000 Washington Boulevard
Culver City CA 90232
204-6422

Culver City Chamber of Commerce
4491 Sepulveda Boulevard
Culver City CA 90203
397-2626

Howard Johnson Plaza Hotel (5990 Green Valley Circle, 90230; 641-7740, Fax 645-7045, 800-654-2000) 200 rooms, restaurant, lounge, swimming pool, gift shop, meeting facilities, valet laundry, free parking, fax service, wheelchair-access rooms, no-smoking rooms. airport courtesy car. SGL/DBL$59-$98.

Pacifica Hotel and Conference Center (6161 Centinela Avenue, 90230; 649-1776, Fax 649-4411, 800-854-2608, 800-542-6082 in California) 368 rooms and suites, restaurant, swimming pool, meeting facilities, airport courtesy car, wheelchair-access rooms, no-smoking rooms, exercise facilities. free parking. SGL/DBL$85-$95, STS$190-$515.

Ramada Hotel Airport (6333 Bristol Parkway, 90230; 670-3200, Fax 641-8925) 260 rooms and suites, restaurant, lounge, swimming pool, exercise center, airport courtesy car, children under 18 free, car rental, pets allowed, meeting facilities for 300, no-smoking room. SGL/DBL$62-$105, STS$175-$250.

TraveLodge (11180 Washington Place, 90232; 839-1111, Fax 839-4628, 800-255-3050) 35 rooms and suites, restaurant, wheelchair access, no-smoking rooms, no pets, free parking. SGL/DBL$55-$66, STS$115-$131.

Vista Motel (4900 Sepulveda Boulevard, 90230; 390-2014) 22 rooms and suites, free parking. SGL/DBL$35-$40, STS$40-$60.

Dana Point

Area Code 714
Dana Point Chamber of Commerce
34221 Golden Lantern
Dana Point CA 92629
496-1555

Blue Lantern Inn (34343 Street of the Blue Lantern, 92629; 661-1304) 29 rooms, bed and breakfast, complimentary breakfast, exercise facilities, free parking. SGL/DBL$125-$275.

Best Western Marina Inn (24800 Dana Point Harbor Drive, 92629; 496-1203, Fax 248-0360, 800-528-1234) 136 rooms, restaurant, lounge, swimming pool, beach, marina, meeting facilities, fax service, in-room refrigerators and safes, balconies, no pets. LS SGL$56-$75, DBL$76-$86; HS SGL/DBL$125-$150.

Dana Point Resort (25135 Park Lantern, 92629; 661-5000, Fax 661-3688, 800-533-9748) 340 rooms and suites, restaurant, lighted tennis courts, golf, exercise facilities, beach, airport transportation, wheelchair-access rooms, no-smoking rooms, pets allowed. SGL$170-$280, DBL$190-$300, STS$300+.

Hilton All Suites Resort (34402 Pacific Coast Highway, 92629; 661-1100, Fax 489-0628, 800-63-HILTON) 200 suites, restaurant, lounge, swimming pool, sauna, jacuzzi, meeting facilities for 150, beach, wheelchair-access rooms, kitchenettes, no-smoking rooms. SGL/DBL$99-$165.

Darwin

Area Code 619

Panamint Springs Resort (Box 45, 93522; no phone) 26 rooms. SGL/DBL$36.

Death Valley

Area Code 619

Furnace Creek Ranch (Box 192328, 92328; 786-2345, 800-528-6367) 70 rooms and cabins, restaurant, swimming pool, tennis, pets allowed. SGL/DBL$60-$94.

Stovepipe Wells Village (State Highway 190, 92328; 786-2387) 74 rooms, restaurant, swimming pool, pets allowed. SGL/DBL$65-$85.

Delano

Area Code 805
Delano Chamber of Commerce
931 High Street
Delano CA 93215
725-2518

Shilo Inn (2231 Girard Street, 93215; 725-7551, 800-222-2233) 48 rooms, complimentary breakfast, outdoor swimming pool, spa, meeting facilities for 20, complimentary newspaper, airport courtesy car, wheelchair-access rooms, no-smoking rooms. SGL/DBL$49-$55, STS$60+.

Del Mar

Greater Del Mar Chamber of Commerce
1401 Carmino Del Mar #101
Del Mar CA 92014
755-4844

Del Mar Hilton (15575 Jimmy Durante Boulevard, 92014; 792-5200, 800-HILTONS) 260 rooms and suites, restaurant, outdoor swimming pool, meeting facilities for 850, business services, wheelchair access, no-smoking rooms. SGL$75-$150, DBL$90-$165, STS$225+.

Del Mar Inn (720 Camino Del Mar, 92014; 755-9765, 800-451-4515) 80 rooms, complimentary breakfast, swimming pool, no-smoking rooms. SGL/DBL$80-$100+.

The Inn L'Auberge Del Mar (1540 Camino Del Mar, 92014; 259-1515, Fax 755-4940, 800-553-1336) 123 rooms and suites, restaurant, swimming pool, airport transportation, lighted tennis courts, exercise facilities, wheelchair-access rooms, no-smoking rooms. SGL/DBL$156-$225, STS$325-$1,000.

Stratford Inn of Del Mar (710 Camino Del Mar, 92014; 619-755-1501, Fax 755-4704, 800-367-6567) 111 rooms and suites, complimentary breakfast, swimming pool, wheelchair-access rooms, no-smoking rooms. SGL/DBL$70-$100, STS$90-$185.

Desert Hot Springs

Area Code 619.
Desert Hot Springs Chamber of Commerce
Box 848
Desert Hot Springs CA 92240
329-6403

Best Western Ponce De Leon (11000 Palm Drive, 92240; 329-6484, 800-528-1234, 800-922-6484) 105 rooms, restaurant, swimming pool, airport transportation, pets allowed. SGL/DBL$64-$89.

Cactus Springs Lodge (68075 Club Circle Drive, 92240; 329-5776) 11 rooms, swimming pool, no-smoking rooms. SGL/DBL$50-$75.

Desert Hot Springs Hotel and Spa (10805 Palm Drive, 92240; 329-6495, Fax 329-6915, 800-843-6053 in California) 50 rooms and suites, restaurant, swimming pool, tennis. LS SGL/DBL$49-$109; HS SGL/DBL$79-$119.

Stardust (66-634 Fifth Street, 92240; 329-5443) 17 rooms, swimming pool, airport transportation, pets allowed. SGL/DBL$85-$95.

Two Bunch Palms Resort and Spa (67-425 Two Bunch Palms Trail, 92240; 329-8791, Fax 329-1317, 800-472-4334) 45 rooms and suites, restaurant, complimentary breakfast, outdoor heated swimming, spas, no children under 18, in-room refrigerators and microwaves, fax service, meeting facilities for 15, lighted tennis courts, wheelchair-access rooms, no pets allowed. SGL/DBL$105-$220, STS$220-$396.

Travellers Repose (66920 First Street, 92240; 329-9584) 3 rooms, bed and breakfast, complimentary breakfast, swimming pool, airport courtesy car, no-smoking rooms. SGL$45-$68, DBL$50-$75.

Diamond Bar

Area Code 714
Diamond Bar Chamber of Commerce
1081 Grand Avenue
Diamond Bar CA 91765
861-2121

Best Western (21725 East Gateway Drive, 91765; 860-5440, Fax 860-8224, 800-325-2525) 184 rooms, restaurant, swimming pool, wheelchair-access rooms, no-smoking rooms. SGL$49-$85, DBL$59-$95.

Best Western Hotel (259 Gentle Springs Lane, 91765; 860-3700, Fax 860-2100, 800-528-1234) 94 rooms, complimentary breakfast, swimming pool, airport transportation, no-smoking rooms, wheelchair-access rooms, no pets. SGL$55-$75, DBL$60-$130.

Days Inn Hotel (21725 East Gateway Drive, 91765; 396-0363, Fax 860-8224, 800-325-2525) 184 rooms, restaurant, lounge, swimming pool, valet laundry, airport transportation, gift shop, meeting facilities, children under 12 free, fax service, exercise facilities. SGL/DBL$75-$85.

Ramada Suites (259 Gentle Springs Lane, 91765; 860-3700, Fax 860-2705, 800-2-RAMADA) 100 suites, restaurant, complimentary breakfast, swimming pool, airport transportation, wheelchair access, no-smoking rooms. SGL/DBL$65-$125.

Downey

Area Code 213
Downey Chamber of Commerce
11131 Brookshire Avenue
Downey CA 90241
923-2191

Comfort Inn (9438 East Firestone Boulevard, 90241; 803-3555, 800-221-2222) 33 rooms, restaurant, complimentary breakfast, whirlpool, meeting facilities, in-room refrigerators, no-smoking rooms, wheelchair-access rooms, no pets. SGL/DBL$39-$72, DBL$39-$82.

Embassy Suites Hotel (8425 Firestone Boulevard, 90241; 861-1900, Fax 923-5847, 800-EMBASSY) 220 suites, restaurant, lounge, complimentary breakfast, swimming pool, spa, sauna, child care, meeting facilities, gift shop, car rental, room service, transportation to local attractions, valet laundry, airport transportation, wheelchair access, pets allowed. SGL$104-$134, DBL$114-$145.

Duarte

Area Code 818
Duarte Chamber of Commerce
2229 East Huntington Drive
Duarte CA 91010
358-6102

Rodeway Inn (1533 East Huntington Drive, 91010; 303-4544, 800-424-4777) 50 rooms, swimming pool, whirlpools, children under 18 free, wheelchair-access rooms, no pets. SGL/DBL$40-$100.

TraveLodge (1200 East Huntington Drive, 91010; 818-357-0907, Fax 912-7243, 800-255-3050) 59 rooms and suites, complimentary breakfast, swimming pool, spa, in-room refrigerators, fax service, 24-hour room service, complimentary newspaper, wheelchair-access rooms, no-smoking rooms, meeting facilities for 30, no pets, free parking. SGL/DBL$30-$47, STS$55+.

Dublin

Area Code 415
Dublin Chamber of Commerce
7986 Amador Valley Boulevard
Dublin CA 94568
828-6200

Howard Johnson Hotel (6680 Regional Street, 94568; 828-7750, Fax 828-3650, 800-223-4656, 800-654-2000, 800-422-4656 in California) 224 rooms and suites, restaurant, lounge, swimming pool, whirlpool, spa, valet laundry, meeting facilities for

300, fireplaces, exercise facilities, wheelchair-access rooms, airport transportation. SGL$69-$79, DBL$79-$89.

Dulzura

Area Code 619

Brookside Farm (1373 Marron Valley Road, 91917; 468-3043) 10 rooms, bed and breakfast, complimentary breakfast, wheelchair-access rooms. SGL/DBL$66-$76.

El Cajon

Area Code 619
El Cajon Chamber of Commerce
109 Rea Avenue
El Cajon CA 92120
440-6161

Best Western Continental Inn (650 North Mollison Avenue, 92021; 442-0601, Fax 442-0152, 800-528-1234) 97 rooms and efficiencies, restaurant, complimentary breakfast, swimming pool, wheelchair access/room, spas, jacuzzi, meeting facilities, in-room refrigerators, kitchenettes, no pets. LS SGL$44-$54, DBL$53-$63; HS SGL/DBL$80-$90.

Best Western Courtesy Inn (1355 East Main Street, 92021; 440-7378, 800-528-1234) 47 rooms, restaurant, complimentary breakfast, swimming pool, in-room refrigerators, jacuzzis, laundry room, wheelchair-access rooms, children under 12 free, no-smoking rooms. SGL$38-$48, DBL$44-$90.

Budget House Hacienda (588 North Mollison Avenue, 92021; 579-1444) 77 rooms. SGL/DBL$32-$35.

Days Inn (1250 El Cajon Boulevard, 92020; 588-8808, 800-325-2525) 110 rooms, swimming pool, jacuzzi, meeting facilities, children under 12 free, fax service, wheelchair-access rooms, no-smoking rooms, no pets. SGL$29-$39, DBL$35-$45.

Motel 6 (550 Montrose Court, 92020; 588-6100, 505-891-6161) 183 rooms. SGL/DBL$27-$33.

Penny Lodge Bed and Breakfast (1556 East Main Street, 92021; 442-9617) 84 rooms. SGL/DBL$39-$52.

Plaza International Inn (683 North Mollison Avenue, 92021; 442-0973, 800-652-3030 in California) 60 rooms, restaurant, swimming pool, golf, wheelchair-access rooms, no-smoking rooms. SGL$30-$35, DBL$35-$40.

Singing Hills Lodge (3007 Dehesa Road, 92019; 442-3425, Fax 442-9574) 102 rooms and suites, restaurant, swimming pool, lighted tennis courts, golf, wheelchair-access rooms. SGL/DBL$75-$135, STS$95-$210.

TraveLodge (471 North Magnolia Avenue, 92020; 447-3999, Fax 447-8403, 800-255-3050) 47 rooms and suites, restaurant, car rental, laundry room, swimming pool. SGL/DBL$32-$45.

TraveLodge (1220 West Main Street, 92020; 442-2576; 442-2576, Fax 579-7562, 800-255-3050) 37 rooms and suites, restaurant, swimming pool, in-room refrigerators, business services, wheelchair-access rooms, no-smoking rooms, pets allowed. SGL$45-$55, DBL$45-$60, STS$80-$160.

El Centro

Area Code 619
El Centro Chamber of Commerce
Box 3006
El Centro CA 92244 352-3681

Best Western El Dorado Motel (1464 Adams Avenue, 92234; 352-7333, 800-874-5532) 72 rooms and suites, swimming pool, no-smoking rooms, airport transportation, pets allowed. SGL$38-$43, DBL$43-$54.

Brunners Motel (215 North Imperial Avenue, 92243; 352-6431, Fax 352-6431, 800-435-8581 in California) 88 rooms, restaurant, swimming pool, airport courtesy car, no-smoking rooms, pets allowed. SGL/DBL$50-$75.

Executive Inn (725 State Street, 92243; 352-8500) 43 rooms and suites, swimming pool, free parking. SGL/DBL$27-$32, STS$45-$55.

E-Z 8 Motel (455 Wake Avenue, 92234; 352-6620, 800-326-6835) 49 rooms. SGL/DBL$24-$34.

Motel 6 (395 Smoketree Drive, 92243; 353-6766, 505-891-6161) 65 rooms. SGL/DBL$24-$35.

Ramada Inn (1455 Ocotillo Drive, 92243; 352-5152, Fax 337-1567, 800-238-8000) 150 rooms, restaurant, lounge, swimming pool, meeting facilities for 150, wheelchair-access rooms, no-smoking rooms, free parking, airport courtesy car, no-smoking rooms, pets allowed. SGL$45-$55, DBL$52-$65.

Vacation Inn TraveLodge (2000 Cottonwood Circle, 92243; 352-9523, Fax; 352-9523, 800-255-2050, 800-268-3330 in California) 193 rooms, restaurant, swimming pool, wheelchair-access rooms, no-smoking rooms. SGL/DBL$50-$60.

El Granada

Area Code 415

Harbor View Inn (11 Avenue Alhambra, 94018; 726-2329) 17 rooms. SGL$62, DBL$72.

El Segundo

Area Code 213
El Segundo Chamber of Commerce
427 Main Street
El Segundo CA 90245
322-1220

Compi Hotel Airport (1985 East Grand Avenue, 90245; 322-0999, Fax 322-4758, 800-426-6774) 215 rooms and suites, swimming pool, exercise facilities, free parking. SGL$88, DBL$98, STS$125.

Crown Sterling Suites (1440 East Imperial Avenue, 90245; 640-3600, Fax 322-0954, 800-433-4600) 350 suites, restaurant, swimming pool, wheelchair access, airport transportation, no-smoking rooms, free parking. SGL/DBL$124-$164.

Doubletree Club Hotel Airport (1985 East Grand Street, 90245; 213-322-0999, Fax 213-322-4758, 800-528-0444) 209 rooms and suites, restaurant, lounge, outdoor heated swimming pool, spa, exercise facilities, airport courtesy car, free parking. SGL/DBL$100-$130.

Embassy Suites Hotel LAX Imperial (1440 East Imperial Avenue, 90245; 640-3600, Fax 322-0954, 800-362-2779) 351 suites, restaurant, swimming pool, pets allowed, airport courtesy car, free parking, wheelchair access, no-smoking rooms. SGL$124-$154, DBL$139-$169.

Hacienda Hotel LAX (525 El Sepulveda Boulevard, 90245; 615-0015, Fax 615-0217) 645 rooms, restaurant, lounge, swimming pool, sauna, spa, laundry room, child care, meeting facilities, airport transportation, wheelchair-access rooms, no-smoking rooms. SGL/DBL$55-$75.

LAX Hotel (1804 East Sycamore, 90245; 615-0133, Fax 322-4475, 800-421-5781, 800-854-1349 in California) 94 rooms and suites, outdoor heated swimming pool, children under 12 free, in-room refrigerators, airport courtesy car, wheelchair access, pets allowed, free parking, no-smoking rooms. SGL$58-$62, DBL/STS$64-$70.

El Toro

Area Code 714

Best Western Laguna Inn (23702 Rockfield Boulevard, 92630; 458-1900, Fax 830-3325, 800-528-1234) 100 rooms, restaurant, lounge, swimming pool, spa, sauna, children under 12 free, laundry room, fax service, wheelchair-access rooms, no-smoking rooms, no pets. LS SGL$55-$65, DBL$61-$71; HS SGL/DBL$115-$140.

Quality Suites (23192 Lake Center Drive, 92630; 380-9888, 800-221-2222) 90 rooms, restaurant, lounge, complimentary breakfast, swimming pool, whirlpools, in-room microwaves, meeting facilities, VCRs, exercise facilities, wheelchair-access rooms, no pets. SGL$69-$99, DBL$79-$109.

TraveLodge (23150 Lake Center Drive, 92630; 855-1000, Fax 830-4447) 127 rooms, restaurant, lounge, complimentary breakfast, heated swimming pool, whirlpool, in-room refrigerators and microwaves, laundry room, exercise center, meeting facilities for 30, wheelchair access, no-smoking rooms. SGL$48-$50, DBL$58-$60.

Emeryville

Area Code 510
Emeryville Chamber of Commerce
2000 Powell Street
Emeryville CA 94608
654-7820

Days Inn Bay Bridge (1603 Powell Street, 94608; 547-7888, Fax 652-4426, 800-325-2525) 154 rooms and suites, restaurant, swimming pool, wheelchair-access rooms, no-smoking rooms, no pets, free parking. SGL$70-$85, DBL$80-$95, STS$98-$115.

Holiday Inn (1800 Powell Street, 94608; 658-9300, Fax 547-8166, 800-HOLIDAY) 280 rooms and suites, restaurant, outdoor swimming pool, airport transportation, wheelchair-access rooms, pets allowed, free parking. SGL$85-$125, DBL$95-$125.

Encinitas

Area Code 619
Encinitas-Leucadia Chamber of Commerce
930 First Street
Encinitas CA 92024
753-6041

Budget Motels of America (133 Encinitas Boulevard, 92024; 944-0260, 800-624-1257) 124 rooms, restaurant, wheelchair-access rooms, room service, no-smoking rooms. SGL/DBL$35-$50.

Friendship Inn (410 North Highway 101, 92024; 436-4999, 800-453-4511, 800-424-4777) 30 rooms, in-room microwaves, VCRs, wheelchair-access rooms, no-smoking rooms. LS SGL/DBL$34-$40, HS SGL/DBL$45-$55.

Moonlight Beach Motel (233 Second Street, 92024; 753-0623, 800-323-1259) 24 rooms and efficiencies, complimentary breakfast, children under 16 free, free parking, wheelchair access, no pets. SGL$$62-$70, DBL$72-$86.

Radisson Inn Encinitas (85 Encinitas Boulevard, 92024; 942-7455, 800-333-3333) 96 rooms and suites, restaurant, swimming pool, exercise facilities, wheelchair access, no-smoking rooms. SGL/DBL$75.

TraveLodge (186 North Highway 101; 619-944-0301, Fax 619-944-0642, 800-255-3050) 39 rooms and suites, restaurant, lounge, whirlpool, in-room refrigerators and microwaves, laundry room, meeting facilities, no pets. LS SGL$39-$45, DBL$45-$51; HS SGL$43-$48, DBL$48-$53.

Englewood

Area Code 310

Days Inn Airport (901 West Manchester Boulevard, 90301; 649-0800, Fax 674-1137, 800-231-2508) 47 rooms and suites, restaurant, swimming pool, no-smoking rooms, free parking. SGL/DBL$47-$59, STS$60-$72.

Escondido

Area Code 619
Escondido Convention and Visitors Bureau
720 North Broadway
Escondido CA 92025
745-4741 or 800-848-3336

Best Western Escondido Hotel (1700 Nutmeg Street, 92026; 740-1700, Fax 740-9832, Fax 740-9832, 800-528-1234, 800-752-1719 in California) 100 rooms, complimentary breakfast, swimming pool, meeting facilities for 100, in-room refrigerators and microwaves, wheelchair-access rooms, no-smoking rooms, no pets. SGL/DBL$45-$97.

Castle Creek Inn Resort and Spa (29850 Circle R Way, 92026; 751-8800, 800-253-5341) 30 rooms, restaurant, complimentary breakfast, lounge, outdoor swimming pool, sauna, children under 12 free, golf, tennis, exercise facilities, wheelchair-access rooms, meeting facilities for 75, no-smoking rooms, no pets. SGL/DBL$140.

Civic Center Inn (435 West Washington Avenue, 92025; 745-2800) 56 rooms, restaurant, swimming pool, wheelchair-access rooms, meeting facilities, no-smoking rooms.

Econo Lodge (1250 West Valley Parkway, 92029; 741-7117, 800-446-6900, 800-424-4777) 100 rooms, restaurant, heated swimming pool, spa, children free, room service, meeting facilities, whirlpools, wheelchair-access rooms, children under 18 free. SGL/DBL$44-$54.

Escondido Daystop (2650 South Escondido Boulevard, 92025; 743-9733) 44 rooms, restaurant, meeting facilities, wheelchair-access rooms. SGL/DBL$29-$45.

Lake Wohlford Resort (Route 1, 92027; 749-2755) 10 rooms, restaurant, swimming pool, pets allowed. SGL/DBL$110-$145.

Lawrence Welk Resort and Greens Executive Conference Center (8860 Lawrence Welk Drive, 92026; 800-932-WELK) 134 rooms and suites, lounge, restaurant, swimming pool, meeting facilities, room service, no-smoking rooms, lighted tennis courts, wheelchair-access rooms, pets allowed. SGL/DBL$85-$225, STS$200-$250.

Motel 6 (900 North Quince Street, 92025; 745-6669, 505-891-6161) 131 rooms. SGL/DBL$27-$33.

Motel Mediteran (2336 South Escondido Boulevard, 92025; 743-1061, 800-441-3118) 35 rooms and suites, complimentary breakfast, outdoor swimming pool, children under 16 free, fax service, wheelchair-access rooms, no-smoking rooms, free parking, pets allowed. SGL$34, DBL$38.

Mt. Vernon Inn (501 West Mission, 92025; 745-6100, 800-824-2244, 800-782-8822 in California) 79 rooms and efficiencies, outdoor swimming pool, children under 10 free, in-room refrigerators, meeting facilities for 35, tennis, wheelchair access, pets allowed, no-smoking rooms. SGL$48, DBL$56, EFF$55-$65.

Nendels Inn (528 West Washington Avenue, 92025; 747-3711, 800-426-6071) 75 rooms, complimentary breakfast, heated swimming pool, spa, no-smoking rooms, laundry room, kitchenettes, free parking, meeting facilities, wheelchair-access rooms, no-smoking rooms. SGL/DBL$65-$85.

Palms Inn (2650 Escondido Boulevard, 92025; 743-9733, 800-727-8932) 44 rooms and suites, restaurant, outdoor swimming pool, sauna, spa, meeting facilities for 20, free parking, laundry room, no-smoking rooms, pets allowed. SGL$50-$60, DBL$65-$75.

Pine Tree Lodge (425 West Mission Avenue, 92025; 745-7613) 38 rooms, restaurant, swimming pool. SGL/DBL$50-$60.

Sheridan Inn (1341 North Escondido Boulevard, 92026; 743-8338, Fax 743-0840, 800-258-8527) 59 rooms and suites, restaurant, complimentary breakfast, heated swimming pool, spa, meeting facilities, wheelchair-access rooms, no-smoking rooms, pets allowed. SGL$51-$58.

Super 7 Motel (515 West Washington Avenue, 92925; 743-7979, 800-777-9479) 74 rooms and suites, restaurant, swimming pool, wheelchair access, no-smoking rooms, pets allowed. SGL$35-$45, DBL$48-$68.

TraveLodge West (1290 West Valley Parkway, 92029; 489-1010, Fax 489-7847, 800-255-3050, 800-541-6012 in California) 96 rooms and suites, restaurant, complimentary breakfast, swimming pool, whirlpool, meeting facilities for 45, room service, wheelchair-access rooms, no-smoking rooms, no pets. SGL$48-$53, DBL$$51-$56.

Fallbrook

Area Code 619
Fallbrook Chamber of Commerce
300 North Main Street #10
Fallbrook CA 92028
728-5848

Best Western Franciscan Inn (1635 South Mission Road, 92028; 728-6184, Fax 731-6040, 800-528-1234) 52 rooms, complimentary breakfast, swimming pool, whirlpool, fax service, wheelchair-access rooms. SGL$45-$70, DBL$50-$80.

La Estancia Inn (3135 Highway 395, 92028; 723-2888, 800-852-3660) 40 rooms and suites, outdoor heated swimming pool, jacuzzi, children under 11 free, meeting facilities for 100, in-room refrigerators, airport transportation, free parking, wheelchair-access rooms, pets allowed. SGL/DBL$68-$78, STS$199.

Pala Mesa Resort (2001 Old Highway 395, 92028; 728-5881, 800-822-4600, 800-722-4700 in California; 133 rooms, restaurant, lounge, meeting facilities for 300, swimming pool, golf, lighted tennis courts, airport transportation, no-smoking rooms. SGL$110-$140, DBL$140-$190+.

TraveLodge (1608 South Mission Road, 92028; 723-1127, 800-255-3050) 36 rooms. SGL$50-$60, DBL$55-$60.

Village Inn Motel (1433 Mission Road, 92020; 728-8355) 29 rooms, restaurant, swimming pool, wheelchair access. SGL/DBL$46-$59.

Fawnskin

Area Code 714

French's Cottages (39544 Barbara Lee Lane, 92333; 866-4573) 12 cottages, no pets. SGL/DBL$60-$70.

The Inn At Fawnskin (Box 378, 92333; 866-3200) 4 rooms, bed and breakfast, complimentary breakfast. SGL$45, DBL$55+.

Windy Point Inn (Box 357, 92333; 866-2746) 4 rooms, bed and breakfast, complimentary breakfast, wheelchair-access rooms. SGL/DBL$50-$60.

Fillmore

Area Code 805
Fillmore Chamber of Commerce
344 Central Avenue
Fillmore CA 93015
524-0351

Best Western La Posada Motel (827 Ventura Street, 93015; 524-0440, Fax 524-1463, 800-528-1234) 49 rooms, restaurant, swimming pool, no-smoking rooms, no pets. SGL/DBL$37-$55.

Fish Camp

Area Code 209

Apple Tree Inn (Box 41, 93623; 683-5111) 6 rooms, bed and breakfast, complimentary breakfast. SGL/DBL$75-$90.

Karen's Bed and Breakfast Yosemite Inn (Box 8, 93623; 683-4550, 800-346-1443) 3 rooms, bed and breakfast, complimentary breakfast, free parking, no smoking, no pets. SGL$80, DBL$85.

Marriott's Tenya Lodge at Yosemite (1122 Highway 41, 93623; 683-6555, Fax 683-8624, 800-635-5807) 242 rooms, restaurant, swimming pool, exercise facilities, wheelchair-access rooms, no-smoking rooms, free parking. SGL$138-$175, DBL$153-$190, STS$250-$350.

The Narrow Gauge Inn (48571 Highway 41, 93623; 683-7720) 28 rooms, restaurant, swimming pool. SGL/DBL$70-$105.

The Owl's Nest (Box 33, 93623; 683-3484) 2 rooms, bed and breakfast, complimentary breakfast. SGL/DBL$55-$80.

Scotty's Bed and Breakfast (1223 Highway 41, 93623; 683-6936) 1 rooms, bed and breakfast, complimentary breakfast, no-smoking rooms. SGL$65, DBL$75.

White Chief Mountain Lodge (Box 79, 93623; 683-5444) 26 rooms, wheelchair access. SGL/DBL$55-$100.

Yosemite Fish Camp Inn (Box 25, 93623; 683-7426) 3 rooms. SGL/DBL$55-$65.

Fontana

Area Code 714
Fontana Area Chamber of Commerce
8575 Sierra Avenue
Fontana CA 92335 822-4433

Comfort Inn (16780 Valley Boulevard, 92335; 822-3350, 800-221-2222) 50 rooms, restaurant, swimming pool, wheelchair-access rooms, no pets. SGL/DBL$43-$53.

Fresno

Area Code 209
Fresno City and County Visitors Bureau
317 North Van Ness Avenue
Fresno CA 93717
486-4636

Fresno Chamber of Commerce
2331 Fresno Street
Fresno CA 93716
233-4651

RENTAL SOURCES: Yosemite Four Seasons Vacation Rentals (454-2080) reservation service for rental homes; **Yosemite Reservation** (5410 East Home Avenue, 93727; 252-4848) SGL/DBL$27-$91.

All Star Inn (1240 North Crystal Avenue, 93728; 237-0855) 64 rooms. SGL/DBL$20-$25.

All Star Inn (4080 Blackstone Avenue, 93726; 222-2431) 54 rooms. SGL/DBL$20-$30.

Best Western Parkside Inn (1415 West Olive Avenue, 93728; 237-2086, Fax 264-9304, 800-528-1234, 800-442-2284 in California) 46 rooms, restaurant, lounge, swimming pool, spa, children under 12 free, fax service, laundry room, no-smoking rooms, no pets. SGL/DBL$48-$68.

Best Western Tradewinds Motor Inn (2141 North Parkway Drive, 93705; 237-1881, Fax 237-9719, 800-528-1234) 110 rooms, restaurant, lounge, swimming pool, spa, children under 12 free, whirlpool, fax service, no-smoking rooms. SGL/DBL$44-$59.

Best Western Village Inn (3110 North Blackstone, 93704; 226-2110, Fax 226-0539, 800-528-1234) 153 rooms, restaurant, swimming pool, spa, children under 12 free, fax service, airport courtesy car, complimentary breakfast, no-smoking rooms. SGL/DBL$47-$60.

Best Western Water Tree Inn (4141 North Blackstone, 93726; 222-4445, Fax 226-4589, 800-762-9071, 800-528-1234) 136 rooms, restaurant, swimming pool, in-room refrigerators, children under 12 free, fax service, computer hookups, no-smoking rooms, no pets. SGL/DBL$50-$66.

Chateau By Piccadilly Inn (5113 East McKinley Avenue, 93727; 456-1418) 78 rooms, airport courtesy car, wheelchair-access rooms, no-smoking rooms. SGL/DBL$50-$65.

Country Victorian Bed and Breakfast (1003 South Orange Avenue, 93702; 233-1988) 3 rooms, bed and breakfast, complimentary breakfast. SGL$50, DBL$60.

Courtyard by Marriott (140 East Shaw Avenue, 93710; 221-6000, Fax 221-0368) 146 rooms, restaurant, swimming pool, exercise facilities, wheelchair-access rooms, no-smoking rooms. SGL$75, DBL$85.

Econo Lodge (1804 West Olive Avenue, 93728; 442-1082, 800-424-4777) 49 rooms, swimming pool, wheelchair-access rooms, children under 18 free, no pets. SGL/DBL$40-$50.

Economy Inns of America (2570 South East Street, 93760; 486-1188, 800-826-0778) 121 rooms, swimming pool, wheelchair-access rooms, no-smoking rooms, pets allowed. SGL/DBL$30-$45.

Economy Inns of America (5021 North Barcus Avenue, 93722; 276-1910, 800-826-0778) 86 rooms, swimming pool. SGL$26, DBL$33.

Executive Suites of Fresno (109 North Glenn Street, 93707; 237-7444) 65 suites, swimming pool, spa, sauna, laundry room, exercise facilities, fireplaces, tennis, airport transportation, no-smoking rooms. SGL/DBL$160W-$300W.

Hampton Inn (1551 North Peach Avenue, 93727; 251-5200, Fax 454-0552, 800-HAMPTON) 118 rooms, swimming pool, exercise facilities, airport transportation, meeting facilities. SGL/DBL$61-$77.

Hilton Hotel (1055 Van Ness Avenue, 93721; 485-9000, Fax 485-7666) 194 rooms and suites, restaurant, outdoor swimming pool, jacuzzi, meeting facilities for 900, exercise facilities free parking, airport courtesy car, wheelchair-access rooms, no-smoking rooms, pets allowed. SGL/DBL$80-$110.

Holiday Inn Airport (5090 East Clinton, 93727; 252-3611, 800-HOLIDAY) 210 rooms and suites, restaurant, lounge, swimming pool, spa, laundry room, putting green, meeting facilities for 300, teens free with parents, wheelchair-access rooms, airport transportation, pets allowed, no-smoking rooms. SGL$75-$110, DBL$80-$120.

Fresno   131

Holiday Inn Downtown (2233 Ventura Street, 93721; 268-1000, Fax 486-6625, 800-HOLIDAY) 320 rooms and suites, restaurant, lounge, swimming pool, spa, sauna, gift shop, beauty and barber shop, meeting facilities for 1,500, exercise facilities, wheelchair-access rooms, pets allowed, airport transportation. SGL/DBL$65-$114.

Howard Johnson Hotel (4061 North Blackstone Avenue, 93726; 222-5641, 800-692-7070 in California, 800-654-2000) 115 rooms, restaurant, lounge, swimming pool, room service, meeting facilities for 300, free local telephone calls, pets allowed, wheelchair-access rooms, airport courtesy car. SGL$36-$46, DBL$42-$52.

La Quinta Inn (2926 Tulare Avenue, 93721; 442-1110, Fax 237-0415, 800-531-5900) 130 rooms, restaurant, lounge, swimming pool, meeting facilities, airport courtesy car, pets allowed. SGL$48-$65, DBL$56-$64.

Motel 6 (933 North Parkway Drive, 93728; 233-3913, 505-891-6161) 155 rooms. SGL/DBL$20-$25.

Motel 6 (4245 North Blackstone Avenue, 93726; 221-0800, 505-891-6161) 84 rooms. SGL/DBL$25-$30.

Motel 6 (445 North Parkway Drive, 93726; 485-5011, 505-891-6161) 60 rooms. SGL/DBL$25-$30.

Piccadilly Inn Airport (5115 East McKinley, 93727; 251-6000, Fax 251-6956, 800-468-3587) 185 rooms, restaurant, swimming pool, airport courtesy car, exercise facilities, wheelchair-access rooms, no-smoking rooms. SGL/DBL$85-$95, STS$175+.

Piccadilly Inn Shaw (2305 West Shaw, 93711; 226-3850, Fax 226-2448, 800-468-3587) 197 rooms and suites, restaurant, swimming pool, exercise facilities, airport transportation, wheelchair-access rooms, no-smoking rooms. SGL/DBL$78-$90, STS$150-$220.

Fresno

Piccadilly Inn University (4961 North Cedar, 93726; 224-4200, Fax 227-2382, 800-468-3587) 191 rooms and suites, swimming pool, exercise facilities, airport courtesy car, wheelchair-access rooms, no-smoking rooms. SGL$80, DBL$88, STS$175+.

Ramada Inn (324 East Shaw Avenue, 93710; 224-4040, Fax 222-4017, 800-228-2828) 170 rooms, restaurant, lounge, swimming pool, sauna, free parking, meeting facilities, room service, airport courtesy car, no-smoking rooms. SGL/DBL$60-$70.

San Joaquin Hotel (1309 West Shaw, 93711; 225-1309, Fax 225-6021) 68 suites and efficiencies, restaurant, complimentary breakfast, swimming pool, spa, meeting facilities, kitchenettes, airport courtesy car, wheelchair-access rooms, no-smoking rooms. SGL/DBL$75.

Sheraton Smuggler's Inn (3737 North Blackstone, 93726; 226-2200, Fax 222-7147, 800-325-3535) 205 rooms and suites, restaurant, lounge, outdoor swimming pool, spa, meeting facilities for 350, in-room refrigerators, exercise facilities, airport courtesy car, no-smoking rooms. SGL/DBL$70-$85.

Travelers Inn (2655 East Shaw Avenue, 93710; 294-0224, Fax 292-0851) 113 rooms. SGL/DBL$30-$45.

Travelers Inn (6730 North Blackstone Avenue, 93710; 431-3557, Fax 439-7824) 153 rooms, swimming pool, wheelchair access, no-smoking rooms. SGL/DBL$30-$45.

Travelers Inn (2640 South Second Street, 93706; 237-6644, Fax 237-0705) 153 rooms, swimming pool, no-smoking rooms. SGL/DBL$24-$40.

Vagabond Hill House (1101 North Parkway Drive, 93728; 268-6211, Fax 268-6211, 800-522-1555) 100 rooms, restaurant, swimming pool, wheelchair-access rooms, pets allowed, in-room refrigerators, airport transportation, free local telephone calls, no-smoking rooms, children under 18 free, fax service, complimentary newspaper. SGL$33-$38, DBL$38-$48.

Hotel Virginia (2125 Kern Street, 93721; 268-8926) 34 rooms, restaurant, airport transportation, pets allowed. SGL$17, DBL$22+.

Fullerton

Area Code 714
Fullerton Chamber of Commerce
Box 529
Fullerton CA 92632
871-3100

All Star Inn (1415 South Euclid Avenue, 92632; 992-0660) 67 rooms. SGL/DBL$30-$36.

Best Western Heritage Inn (333 East Imperial Highway, 92635; 447-9200, Fax 773-0685, 800-528-1234) 124 rooms, restaurant, lounge, complimentary breakfast, heated swimming pool, spa, laundry room, meeting facilities, in-room refrigerator, fax service, no-smoking rooms, no pets. SGL$48-$68, DBL$53-$73.

Days Inn (1500 South Raymond Avenue, 92631; 635-9000, Fax 520-5831, 800-325-2525) 250 rooms and suites, two restaurants, lounge, swimming pool, room service, meeting facilities for over 200, whirlpool, laundry room, gift shop, children under 12 free, fax service, tours, exercise facilities, wheelchair-access rooms, no-smoking rooms. SGL/DBL$70-$110, STS$130-$250+.

Fullerton Hacienda Hostel (1700 North Harbor Boulevard, 92635; 738-3721) 15 beds, kitchen, no-smoking rooms, free parking. SGL$12-$15.

Griswold Hotel (1500 South Raymond Avenue, 92631; 635-9000, Fax 520-5831) 260 rooms, restaurant, swimming pool, exercise facilities, no-smoking rooms, pets allowed. SGL$56-$70, DBL$66-$80.

Holiday Inn (222 West Houston, 92632; 992-1700, Fax 992-4843, 800-HOLIDAY) 289 rooms and suites, restaurant, lounge, swimming pool, laundry room, tours, gift shop, meeting facilities for 500, wheelchair-access rooms, no pets. SGL/DBL$80-$100.

Marriott University Hotel (2701 East Nutwood Avenue, 92631; 738-7800, Fax 738-0288, 800-228-9290) 225 rooms and suites, restaurant, lounge, swimming pool, airport courtesy car, room service, meeting facilities, exercise facilities, wheelchair-access rooms, no-smoking rooms, pets allowed. SGL$129, DBL$140, STS$250+.

Radisson Suites (2932 East Nutwood Avenue, 92631; 579-7400, Fax 528-7945, 800-333-3333) 96 suites, restaurant, complimentary breakfast, swimming pool, exercise facilities, wheelchair-access rooms, no-smoking rooms. STS$100+.

Sunset Inn (1000 South Euclid, 92632; 871-7200, Fax 870-5058, 800-225-7343, 800-445-4044 in California) 60 rooms and suites, complimentary breakfast, lounge, outdoor heated swimming pool, fax service, wheelchair access, no-smoking rooms, free parking. SGL$30-$35, DBL$35-$45, STS$40-$50.

Gardena

Area Code 310
Gardena Chamber of Commerce
1204 West Gardena Boulevard
Gardena CA 90247
532-9905

Best Western Palace Hotel (1641 West Redondo Beach Boulevard West, 90247; 327-5757, Fax 327-5370, 800-528-1234) 101 rooms, restaurant, lounge, swimming pool, whirlpool, in-room refrigerators and microwaves, laundry room, wheelchair-access rooms, no-smoking rooms, no pets. SGL/DBL$62-$175.

Days Inn (16427 South Western Avenue, 90247; 213-329-1188, Fax 213-532-3285, 800-325-2525) 40 rooms, swimming pool, jacuzzis, fax service, children under 12 free, wheelchair-access rooms, no-smoking rooms, no pets. SGL$45, DBL$50+.

Pacific Square Inn (1624 West Redondo Beach Boulevard, 90247; 532-5200) 47 rooms. SGL/DBL$48-$55.

Garden Grove

Area Code 714
Garden Grove Chamber of Commerce
11400 Stanford Avenue
Garden Grove CA 92640
638-7950

The Best Inn (8062 Garden Grove Boulevard, 92664; 898-3500) 131 rooms. SGL/DBL$20-$39.

Best Western Plaza International (7912 Garden Grove Boulevard, 92641; 894-7568, 800-528-1234) 123 rooms, restaurant, heated swimming pool, meeting facilities for 40, free parking. SGL/DBL$46-$50.

Ramada Inn (10022 Garden Grove Boulevard, 92644; 534-1818, Fax 539-9930, 800-228-2828) 126 rooms and suites, restaurant, lounge, heated swimming pool, spa, children under 18 free, meeting facilities, transportation to local attractions, wheelchair-access rooms, no-smoking rooms, airport transportation, free parking. SGL$55-$65, DBL$65-$75, STS$85-$95.

Rodeway Inn Disneyland South (12052 Garden Grove Boulevard, 92643; 636-1555, 800-424-4777) 77 rooms, complimentary breakfast, swimming pool, transportation to local attractions, meeting facilities, children under 18 free, wheelchair-access rooms, tours. SGL/DBL$39-$62.

Royal Plaza International Inn (7912 Garden Grove Boulevard, 92641; 894-7568, Fax 894-6308) 101 rooms, restaurant, swimming pool, wheelchair-access rooms, no-smoking rooms. SGL$40-$50, DBL$45-$55.

Tahiti Motel (12625 Harbor Boulevard, 92640; 893-7521) 60 rooms, swimming pool. SGL$35, DBL$38.

TraveLodge (14052 Brookhurst Street, 92643; 714-636-4890, Fax 714-530-8712, 800-255-3050) 55 rooms, restaurant, lounge, swimming pool, whirlpool, tours, car rental, no pets. SGL$35-$45, DBL$44-$54.

Glendale

Area Code 818
Glendale Chamber of Commerce
200 South Louise Street
Glendale CA 91209
240-7870

RENTAL SOURCES: Apartments For Travelers (The Valley; 952-1336) rental source for one- and two-bedroom apartments in the Burbank area. SGL/DBL$65-$100.

Best Western Golden Key Motor Hotel (123 West Colorado Street, 91204; 247-0111, Fax 545-9393, 800-528-1234) 55 rooms, restaurant, lounge, complimentary breakfast, swimming pool, whirlpool, meeting facilities, in-room refrigerators and microwaves, no-smoking rooms. SGL/DBL$72-$118.

Econo Lodge (1437 East Colorado Street, 91205; 246-8367, 800-424-4777) 30 rooms, complimentary breakfast, swimming pool, whirlpool, children under 18 free, no pets. SGL/DBL$50-$90.

Friendship Inn (200 West Colorado Street, 91204; 246-7331, 800-453-4511)

25 rooms, restaurant, swimming pool, airport transportation, meeting facilities, children under 18 free, laundry room, free parking, no-smoking rooms. SGL$38-$42, DBL$42-$46.

Holiday Inn (600 North Pacific, 91203; 956-0202, 800-HOLIDAY) 600 rooms and efficiencies, restaurant, lounge, car rental, kitchenettes, wheelchair-access rooms. SGL/DBL$75-$105.

Red Lion Hotel Glendale (100 West Glenoaks Boulevard, 91203; 956-5466, Fax 956-5490, 800-547-8010) 350 rooms and suites, restaurant, swimming pool, exercise facilities, airport transportation, no-smoking rooms, free parking. SGL/DBL$65-$100.

Vagabond Inn Glendale (120 West Colorado Street, 91204; 240-1700, Fax 548-8428, 800-468-2251, 800-522-1555 in California) 52 rooms, complimentary breakfast, outdoor swimming pool, valet laundry, pets allowed, airport transportation, free local telephone calls, no-smoking rooms, children under 18 free, fax service, complimentary newspaper. SGL$68, DBL$73-$78.

Glendora

Area Code 818
Glendora Chamber of Commerce
200 South Louise Street
Glendora CA 91209
963-4128

Comfort Inn (606 West Alosta Avenue, 91740; 963-9361, 800-221-2222) 38 rooms, restaurant, complimentary breakfast, wheelchair-access rooms, no pets. SGL$44-$69, DBL$54-$79.

20th Century Motor Lodge (1345 East Alosta Avenue, 91740; 335-3348) 22 rooms, swimming pool, wheelchair access, no-smoking rooms, pets allowed. SGL/DBL$30-$50.

Goleta

Area Code 805
Goleta Valley Chamber of Commerce
300 North Los Carneros Road
Goleta CA 93116
967-4618

Circle Bar B Guest Ranch (6021 Hollister Avenue, 93117; 967-5591) 13 rooms, complimentary breakfast, swimming pool, no-smoking rooms. SGL/DBL$45-$65.

Hampton Inn (5620 Calle Real, 93117; 967-3200, 800-426-7866) 121 rooms, swimming pool. SGL/DBL$82-$103.

Holiday Inn (5650 Calle Real, 93117; 805-964-6241, 800-HOLIDAY) 156 rooms, restaurant, lounge, meeting facilities for 300, airport transportation, children under 18 free, tennis, airport transportation. SGL/DBL$85-$135.

Motel 6 (5897 Calle Real, 93117; 964-3596, 505-891-6161) 88 rooms, swimming pool, no-smoking rooms, pets allowed. SGL/DBL$35-$40.

Pilot House Motel (Santa Barbara Airport, 93117; 967-2336) 24 rooms, swimming pool, airport courtesy car. SGL/DBL$40-$60.

South Coast Inn (5620 Calle Real, 93117; 967-3200, Fax 683-4466, 800-350-3614) 121 rooms, complimentary breakfast, swimming pool, exercise facilities, wheelchair access, no-smoking rooms. SGL/DBL$80-$105.

Hanford

Area Code 209
Hanford Chamber of Commerce
213 West Seventh Street
Hanford CA 93230
582-0483

Best Western Inn (755 Cadillac Lane, 93230; 583-7300, 800-528-1234) 40 rooms, restaurant, lounge, swimming pool, laundry room, wheelchair-access rooms, no-smoking rooms, no pets. SGL/DBL$42-$55.

Downtown Motel (101 North Redington Street, 93239; 582-9036) 29 rooms. SGL$30-$35, DBL$35-$40.

Irwin Street Inn (522 North Irwin Street, 93230; 583-8791) 30 rooms and suites, bed and breakfast, complimentary breakfast, swimming pool, wheelchair-access rooms, pets allowed. SGL$65-$75, DBL$75-$85, STS$85-$95.

Hemet

Area Code 714
Hemet Chamber of Commerce
2627 West Florida #200
Hemet CA 92343
658-3211

Best Western Motor Inn (2625 West Florida Avenue, 92434; 925-6605, Fax 925-7095, 800-528-1234) 72 rooms, restaurant, lounge, complimentary breakfast, swimming pool, kitchenettes, fax service, computer hookups, no-smoking rooms. no pets. SGL$44-$58, DBL$54-$99.

Hemet East Motel (2688 East Florida Avenue, 92343; 658-9811) 28 rooms. SGL$35, DBL$45.

Quality Inn (800 West Florida Avenue, 92343; 929-6366, 800-221-2222) 65 rooms, restaurant, complimentary breakfast, swimming pool, whirlpools, meeting facilities, exercise center, wheelchair-access rooms, pets allowed. SGL/DBL$45-$70.

Ramada Inn (3885 West Florida Avenue, 92343; 929-8900, Fax 925-3716) 100 rooms and suites, restaurant, lounge, complimentary breakfast, swimming pool, children under 18 free, room service, airport transportation, free parking, car rental, meeting facilities for 125, wheelchair-access rooms, no-smoking rooms. SGL/DBL$45-$70, STS$65-$75.

Super 8 Motel (3510 West Florida, 92343; 658-2281, 800-800-8000) 69 rooms, restaurant, complimentary breakfast, outdoor heated swimming pool, spa, meeting facilities, kitchenettes, in-room refrigerators, wheelchair-access rooms, no-smoking rooms, pets allowed. SGL/DBL$38-$43.

TraveLodge (1201 West Florida Avenue, 92343;; 766-1902, Fax 766-7739, 800-255-3050) 46 rooms and suites, restaurant, lounge, swimming pool, spa, in-room refrigerators and microwaves, meeting facilities for 60, laundry room, kitchenettes, no pets. SGL/DBL$35-$58.

Hermosa Beach

Area Code 213
Hermosa Beach Chamber of Commerce
323 Pier Avenue
Hermosa Beach CA 90254
376-0951

RENTAL SOURCES: ABC Travel Agency (18039 Crenshaw Boulevard, Torrance 90504; 376-3704, Fax 379-6615) rents ocean-front homes and apartments in the Hermosa Beach area.

The Grand View Hotel (55 14th Street, 90254; 374-8981) 18 rooms. SGL/DBL$60-$100.

Hotel Hermosa (2515 Pacific Coast Highway, 90254; 318-6000, Fax 318-6936, 800-331-9979) 81 rooms and suites, complimentary breakfast, outdoor swimming pool, spa, exercise facilities, ocean view, kitchenettes, valet laundry, fax service, complimentary newspaper, laundry room, wheelchair-access rooms, no-smoking rooms, free parking. SGL/DBL$60-$125, STS$115-$125.

TraveLodge Hermosa Beach (901 Aviation Boulevard, 90254; 213-374-2666, Fax 213-379-3979, 800-255-3050, 800-553-1145) 68 rooms and suites, restaurant, complimentary breakfast, ocean view, in-room refrigerators, kitchenettes, valet laundry, fax service, complimentary newspaper, laundry room, airport transportation, tennis, wheelchair access, no-smoking rooms, no pets, free parking. SGL/DBL$59-$69, STS$75-$145.

Hesperia

Area Code 619
Hesperia Chamber of Commerce
Box 782
Hesperia CA 92345
244-0265

Days Inn (14865 Bear Valley, 92345; 948-0600, 800-325-2525) 29 rooms and suites, complimentary breakfast, swimming pool, in-room refrigerators, free local calls, children under 12 free, fax service, wheelchair-access rooms, no-smoking rooms, pets allowed. SGL$39-$49, DBL$45-$55.

Super 8 Motel (12033 Oakwood Avenue, 92345; 949-3231, Fax 949-2045, 800-800-8000) 45 rooms, restaurant, indoor swimming pool, spa, laundry room, kitchenettes, fax service, wheelchair-access rooms, no-smoking rooms, no pets. SGL/DBL$33-$36.

Hollister

Area Code 408
San Benito County Chamber of Commerce
649 San Benito Street
Hollister CA 95023
637-5315

Best Western San Benito Inn (660 San Felipe Road, 95023; 637-9248, Fax 637-4584, 800-528-1234) 42 rooms, complimentary breakfast, swimming pool, wheelchair-access rooms, fax service, no-smoking rooms, no pets. SGL/DBL$44-$70.

Cinderella Motel (110 San Felipe Road, 95023; 637-5761, Fax 636-9212) 20 rooms, complimentary breakfast, airport transportation, no-smoking rooms, pets allowed. SGL/DBL$35-$85.

Ridemark Golf and Country Club (3800 Airline Highway, 95023; 637-8151, Fax 636-3168, 800-924-1033 in California) 32 rooms, restaurant, tennis, wheelchair access. SGL$70-$80, DBL$80-$90, STS$90-$105+.

San Juan Inn (Highway One, 95023; 623-4380) 36 rooms. SGL/DBL$45-$60.

Hollywood

Area Code 213
Hollywood Chamber of Commerce
6290 Sunset Boulevard #525
Hollywood CA 90028
469-8311

City of West Hollywood
8611 Santa Monica Boulevard West
Hollywood CA 90069
854-7475

RENTAL SOURCES: Bed and Breakfast International (Box 282910, 94128; 696-1690, Fax 696-1699, 800-872-4500) represents bed and breakfast accommodations throughout California. Accommodations available in private home, houseboats on the Bay and inns. All rates include complimentary breakfast. SGL/DBL$50-$125

Banana Bungalow Hollywood Hotel (2775 Cahuenga Boulevard West, 90068; 851-1129, Fax 851-2022, 800-446-7835, 800-4-HOSTEL) 45 rooms and suites/bungalows, kitchenettes, restaurant, lounge, transportation to local attractions, outdoor heated swimming pool, laundry room, no-smoking rooms, free parking. SGL/DBL$39+, STS$49-$59.

Bel Age Hotel (1020 North San Vincente Boulevard, 90069; 854-1111, 800-424-4443) 198 suites, restaurant, lounge, swimming pool, jacuzzi, kitchenettes, child care, free parking. STS$225-$350.

Best Western Hollywood (6141 Franklin Avenue, 90028; 464-5181, 800-528-1234) 85 rooms and efficiencies, restaurant, swimming pool, airport transportation, pets allowed, free parking. SGL$54-$64, DBL$59-$69, STS$105-$130.

Best Western Hollywood Plaza Inn (2100 North Highland Avenue, 90068; 851-1800, Fax 851-1836, 800-528-1234) 81 rooms and suites, restaurant, outdoor swimming pool, in-room refrigerators, fax service, transportation to area attractions, complimentary newspapers, meeting facilities, laundry room, free parking, wheelchair-access rooms, no-smoking rooms, car rental. SGL/DBL$63-$85, STS$100-$125.

Best Western Mikado Hotel (12600 Riverside Drive, 91607; 818-763-9141, Fax 818-752-1045, 800-528-1234) 58 rooms, restaurant, lounge, complimentary breakfast, swimming pool, kitchenettes, whirlpool, children under 12 free, no pets. SGL/DBL$80-$90.

Best Western Sunset Plaza Hotel (8499 Sunset Boulevard, 90069; 654-0750, Fax 650-6146, 800-421-3652, 800-252-0645 in

California) 87 rooms and suites, located in the Sunset Strip area, restaurant, complimentary breakfast, outdoor heated swimming pool, in-room refrigerators, kitchenettes, fax service, complimentary afternoon tea and newspaper, laundry room, free parking. SGL/DBL$69-$92, STS$139-$155.

Beverly Garland Hotel (4222 Vineland Avenue, 91602; 800-BEVERLY, 800-238-3759 in California) 258 rooms and suites, restaurant, lounge, outdoor swimming pool, sauna, in-room refrigerators, fax service, airport courtesy car, tennis, free parking, located within walking distance of Universal Studios, putting green, child's playground, car rental, wheelchair-access rooms, no-smoking rooms. SGL/DBL$69-$99, STS$175-$300.

Campbell Ranch Inn (1475 Canyon Road, 95441; 707-857-3476) 5 rooms, complimentary breakfast, swimming pool, tennis. SGL$50, DBL$60.

Chateau Marmont Hotel (8221 Sunset Boulevard, 90046; 656-1010, Fax 655-5311, 800-CHATEAU) 63 rooms and suites, restaurant, swimming pool, in-room refrigerators, kitchenettes, wheelchair-access rooms, pets allowed, free parking. SGL/DBL$150, STS$170-$500.

Consort Renaissance Hotel (1160 North Vermont Avenue, 90029; 660-1788) 130 rooms and suites, restaurant, swimming pool, exercise facilities, airport transportation. SGL/DBL$85-$90, 1BR$80-$175.

Econo Lodge (777 North Vine Street, 90038; 466-1691, 800-446-6900) 43 rooms, outdoor swimming pool, free parking, no pets, wheelchair-access rooms. SGL/DBL$35-$40.

French Cottage (6757 Sunset Boulevard, 90028; 464-9144) 40 rooms, restaurant, kitchenettes, complimentary breakfast and newspaper, outdoor swimming pool. SGL/DBL$30-$55.

Friendship Inn (5333 Hollywood Boulevard, 90027; 466-1691, 800-424-4777) 39 rooms, swimming pool, kitchenettes, children under 18 free. SGL/DBL$32-$42.

Gilboa Bed and Breakfast (Bed and Breakfast International) 1 room, complimentary breakfast, no smoking. SGL/DBL$50.

Hallmark Hotel (7023 West Sunset Boulevard, 90028; 464-8344, 800-255-7249, 800-346-7723 in California) 74 rooms and suites, swimming pool, jacuzzi, kitchenettes, airport transportation, free parking. SGL$54-$65, DBL$58-$75, STS$100+.

Hastings Hotel (6162 Hollywood Boulevard, 90028; 464-4136) 85 rooms. SGL$20-$25, DBL$25-$35.

Hilton and Towers (555 Universal Terrace Parkway, 91608; 506-2500, Fax 509-2058) 485 rooms, restaurant, no-smoking rooms. SGL/DBL$150-$180.

Holiday Inn Hollywood (1755 North Highland, 90028; 462-7181, Fax 466-9072, 800-HOLIDAY) 492 rooms and suites, restaurant, lounge, outdoor swimming pool, wheelchair-access rooms, exercise facilities, in-room refrigerators and safes, valet laundry, child care, transportation to area attractions, gift shop, car rental, pets allowed, free parking. SGL/DBL$85-$114, STS$130-$195.

Hollywood Celebrity Hotel (1775 Orchid Avenue, 90028; 850-6464, 800-222-7090 in California) 38 rooms and suites, complimentary breakfast, child care, free parking, pets allowed. SGL$65, DBL$75-$90, STS$90-$120.

Hollywood Downtowner Hotel (5601 Hollywood Boulevard, 90028; 464-7191) 38 rooms and suites, swimming pool, airport transportation, kitchenettes, free parking. SGL/DBL$38-$48, STS$80-$90.

Hollywood 8 Motel (1822 North Cahuenga Boulevard, 90028; 467-2252) 24 rooms, near Universal Studios, refrigerators in rooms, free parking. SGL/DBL$30-$45.

Hollywood International Hostel (6561 Franklin Street, 90028; 850-6287) 5 rooms, kitchen, no-smoking rooms. SGL$10.

Hollywood Legacy Hotel (1160 North Vermont Avenue, 90028; 660-1789, Fax 660-8069, 800-445-6120) 130 rooms, restaurant, outdoor swimming pool, valet laundry, child care, fax service, transportation to area attractions, laundry room, sauna, car rental, no-smoking rooms, free parking, travel agency. SGL/DBL$56-$80.

Hollywood Metropolitan Hotel (5825 Sunset Boulevard, 90028; 962-5800, Fax 465-1380, 800-962-5800) 90 rooms and suites, restaurant, lounge, complimentary breakfast, in-room refrigerators, fax service, child care, complimentary newspaper, wheelchair-access rooms, no-smoking rooms, gift shop, travel agency, car rental. SGL/DBL$85-$95, STS$105-$115.

Hollywood Palm Hotel (2005 North Highland Avenue, 90068; 850-5811, Fax 876-3272, 800-338-7256) 153 rooms and suites, restaurant, lounge, swimming pool, spa, meeting facilities, child care, wheelchair-access rooms, free parking. SGL/DBL$85-$95, STS$120-$140.

Hollywood Roosevelt Hotel (7000 Hollywood Boulevard, 90028; 466-7000, Fax 462-8056, 800-950-7667) 330 rooms and suites, two restaurants, swimming pool, spa, sauna, in-room refrigerators and mini-bars, kitchenettes, child care, exercise facilities, airport transportation, meeting rooms, wheelchair-access rooms, no-smoking rooms. SGL/DBL$110-$145, STS$160-$1500.

Hollywood Vine Motel (1133 Vine Street, 90038; 466-7501) 58 rooms and suites, swimming pool, kitchenettes, free parking. SGL$40-$5, DBL$40-$50, STS$50-$60.

Howard Johnson (4222 Vineland Avenue, 91602; 818-980-8000, 800-238-3579, 800-654-2000) 258 rooms, restaurant, lounge, swimming pool, valet laundry, putting green, gift shop, car rental, fax service, meeting facilities, tours, wheelchair-access rooms, airport courtesy car. SGL/DBL$80-$350.

Hyatt On Sunset (8401 Sunset Boulevard, 90069; 656-1234, Fax 650-7024, 800-233-1234) 262 rooms and suites, restaurant, lounge, swimming pool, wheelchair-access rooms, meeting facilities, room service, no-smoking rooms, airport transportation. SGL/DBL$140-$160, STS$350-$550.

Le Dufy Hotel (1000 Westmount Drive, 90069; 657-7400) 121 suites, swimming pool, jacuzzi, laundry room, kitchenettes, free parking. STS$135-$215.

Le Parc Hotel (733 North West Knoll Drive, 90069; 855-8888, Fax 659-7812) 154 rooms and suites, restaurant, swimming pool, exercise facilities, tennis, no-smoking rooms, pets allowed. SGL$165+, DBL$185+, STS$200-$250.

Le Reve Hotel (8822 Cynthia Street, 90069; 854-1114, 800-424-5554 in California) 80 suites, swimming pool, free parking. STS$95-$155.

Magic Hotel (7025 Franklin Avenue, 90068; 851-0800, Fax 851-4926) 40 rooms and suites, swimming pool, airport transportation, laundry room, kitchenettes, pets allowed, free parking. SGL$52-$62, DBL$67-$78, STS$81-$129.

Mondrian Hotel De Grand Luxe (8440 Sunset Boulevard, 90069; 650-8999, Fax 650-5215, 800-424-4443) 138 suites, restaurant, swimming pool, exercise facilities, child care, wheelchair access/room, no-smoking rooms, free parking. SGL/DBL$145-$275.

Park Sunset Hotel (8462 Sunset Boulevard, 90069; 654-6470, 800-821-3660) 74 rooms and suites, restaurant, swimming pool, laundry room, child care, kitchenettes, tours, no-smoking rooms. SGL$75, DBL$80, STS$140+.

Quality Inn (5410 Hollywood Boulevard, 90027; 463-7171, 800-221-2222) 60 rooms, restaurant, complimentary breakfast, swimming pool, valet laundry, no pets. SGL/DBL$46-$110.

Ramada Inn (8585 Santa Monica Boulevard, 90069; 652-6400, Fax 652-2135) 177 rooms and suites, restaurant, lounge, complimentary breakfast, swimming pool, beauty shop, airport transportation, exercise facilities, wheelchair-access rooms, no-smoking rooms. SGL/DBL$100-$110, STS$140-$270.

Saharan Motor Lodge (7212 Sunset Boulevard, 90046; 874-6700, Fax 876-2625) 63 rooms and suites, kitchenettes, fax service, outdoor swimming pool, kitchenettes, laundry room, beauty shop, free parking. SGL/DBL$38-$55, STS$50-$75.

Sportsmen's Lodge Hotel (12825 Ventura Boulevard, 91604; 769-4700, Fax 877-3898, 800-821-8511, 800-821-1625 in California) 196 rooms and suites, restaurant, swimming pool, exercise facilities, free parking. SGL$88-$98, DBL$98-$108, STS$145-$150.

Sunset Marquis Hotel and Villas (1200 North Alta Loma Road, 90069; 657-1333, 800-858-9758) 120 suites, restaurant, lounge, jacuzzi, room service, laundry room, kitchenettes, child care, exercise facilities, free parking. STS$165-$255.

TraveLodge (7051 Sunset Boulevard, 90028; 462-0905, Fax 465-6088, 800-255-3050) 43 rooms, restaurant, swimming pool, no pets. SGL/DBL$52-$67.

TraveLodge Hollywood/LA (1401 North Vermont Avenue, 90027; 665-5735, Fax 665-0879, 800-255-3050) 70 rooms, restaurant, lounge, located in downtown area, fax service, tours, outdoor swimming pool, no-smoking rooms, free parking, no pets, car rental. SGL/DBL$39-$60.

Valadon Hotel (900 Hammons Street, 90069; 855-1115, Fax 657-9192, 800-424-4443) 136 suites, restaurant, swimming pool, child care, room service, lighted tennis courts, wheelchair-access rooms, no-smoking rooms. STS$135-$215.

Holtville

Area Code 619
Holtville Chamber of Commerce
Box 185

Holtville CA 92250
356-2923

Barbara Worth Country Club and Inn (2050 Country Club Drive, 92250; 356-2806, Fax: 356-GOLF, 800-356-3806) 103 rooms and suites, restaurant, swimming pool, golf. SGL$50-$60, DBL$55-$65, STS$160+.

Huntington Beach

Area Code 714
Huntington Beach Chamber of Commerce
2213 Main Street #32
Huntington Beach CA 92648
536-8888

RENTAL SOURCES: Bed and Breakfast International (Box 282910, 94128; 696-1690, Fax 696-1699, 800-872-4500) represents bed and breakfast accommodations throughout California. Accommodations available in private homes, houseboats on the Bay and inns. All rates include complimentary breakfast. SGL/DBL$50-$125; **House Guests USA** (Box 1185; 891-3736, 800-333-4678, Fax 964-4250, 800-333-HOST) reservation service for condo and home rentals in Huntington Beach and surrounding areas.

Best Western Inn (21112 Pacific Coast Highway, 92648; 536-1421, Fax 969-1644, 800-528-1234) 92 rooms. SGL/DBL$65-$95.

Best Western Regency Inn (19360 Beach Boulevard, 92648; 962-4244, Fax 963-4724, 800-528-1234) 65 rooms and efficiencies, outdoor swimming pool, spa, kitchenettes, fax service, wheelchair-access rooms, no-smoking rooms, no pets. SGL$63-$85, DBL$63-$120.

Colonial Inn Youth Hostel (421 Eighth Street; 536-3315, Fax 536-9485) 50 beds, kitchen, free parking. SGL$10-$12.

Huntington Beach

Comfort Suites (16301 Beach Boulevard, 92647; 841-1812, 800-221-2222) 103 rooms, restaurant, complimentary breakfast, outdoor heated swimming pool, valet laundry, fax service, meeting facilities, laundry room, wheelchair-access rooms, exercise facilities, no-smoking rooms, no pets. LS SGL$39-$89, DBL$49-$89; HS SGL$39-$99, DBL$49-$99.

Enochs Bed and Breakfast (Bed and Breakfast International) 2 rooms, complimentary breakfast, no smoking. SGL/DBL$55.

Friendship Beach Inn (18112 Beach Boulevard; 841-6606) 38 rooms and efficiencies, outdoor swimming pool, hot tub, in-room refrigerators, whirlpools, wheelchair-access rooms, no pets, children under 18 free. SGL/DBL$45-$63.

Hilton Waterfront Beach Resort (21100 Pacific Coast Highway, 92648; 960-7873, Fax 960-3791., 800-822-7873) 292 rooms and suites, restaurant, lounge, complimentary breakfast, swimming pool, in-room refrigerators, child care, valet laundry, concierge, room service, fax service, gift shop, meeting facilities for 650, free parking, lighted tennis courts, exercise center, wheelchair-access rooms, no-smoking rooms, free parking. SGL/DBL$99-$195, STS$195-$1,200.

Holiday Inn (7667 Center Avenue, 92647; 891-0123, Fax 895-4591, 800-HOLIDAY) 224 rooms and suites, restaurant, swimming pool, airport transportation, exercise facilities, wheelchair-access rooms, no-smoking rooms, no pets. SGL$75-$100, DBL$85-$115, STS$160.

Howard Johnson Hotel (75 West Thousand Oaks Boulevard, 91360; 805-497-3701, Fax 805-497-1875, 800-654-2000) 107 rooms, restaurant, swimming pool, spa, fax service, laundry room, meeting facilities, wheelchair-access rooms, airport transportation, no-smoking rooms. SGL$47-$77, DBL$55-$85.

Howard Johnson (17251 South Beach Boulevard, 92647; 375-0250, 800-464-7064) 65 rooms and suites, wheelchair-access rooms, laundry room, no-smoking rooms. SGL/DBL$48-$68.

Huntington Shores Motel (21002 Pacific Coast Highway; 536-8861, 800-554-6799) 50 rooms and efficiencies, restaurant, complimentary breakfast, outdoor heated swimming pool, airport transportation, wheelchair-access rooms, no-smoking rooms, no pets. SGL/DBL$55-$88.

Quality Inn (800 Pacific Coast Highway, 92648; 536-7500, 800-221-2222) 50 rooms, restaurant, complimentary breakfast, whirlpools, spa, fireplaces, in-room refrigerators, ocean view, wheelchair-access rooms, no pets. SGL$65-$99, DBL$69-$110.

The Waterfront Hilton (21100 Pacific Coast Highway; 960-7873, 800-822-SURF) 324 rooms and suites, two restaurants, lounge, outdoor heated swimming pool, jacuzzi, children under 12 free, child care, lighted tennis court, free parking, gift shop, airport transportation, exercise facilities, wheelchair-access rooms, no-smoking rooms, pets allowed. SGL/DBL$125-$195, STS$225-$250.

Huntington Park

Area Code 213
Huntington Park Chamber of Commerce
2650 Zoe Avenue
Huntington Park CA 90255
585-1155

TraveLodge (2786 Florence Avenue, 90255; 588-8889, Fax 588-0733, 800-255-3050) 52 rooms and suites, restaurant, lounge, whirlpool, no pets. SGL/DBL $39-$51.

Idyllwild

Area Code 714
Idyllwild Chamber of Commerce

54274 North Circle Drive
Idyllwild CA 92349
659-3259

Strawberry Creek Inn (26-370 Highway 243, 92349; 659-3202, 800-262-8969) 15 rooms, restaurant, complimentary breakfast. SGL/DBL$85-$125.

Indian Wells

Area Code 619

Erawan Garden Hotel (76-477 Highway 111, 92210; 346-8021, 800-237-2926) 225 rooms and suites, restaurant, swimming pool, exercise facilities. LS SGL/DBL$55-$85; HS SGL/DBL$90-$140, STS$220-$350.

Hyatt Grand Champions Resort (44-600 Indian Wells Lane, 92210; 341-1000, Fax 568-2236, 800-233-1234, 800-826-1112 in California) 336 rooms and suites, three restaurants, lounge, swimming pool, spa, sauna, free parking, meeting facilities for over 1,000, room service, lighted tennis courts, exercise facilities, golf, beauty shop, wheelchair-access rooms, no-smoking rooms. LS SGL/DBL$89-$180; HS SGL/DBL$199-$280, STS$180-$925.

Indian Wells Hotel (76-661 Highway 111, 92210; 345-6466, 800-248-3220) 151 rooms and suites, restaurant, lounge, swimming pool, spa, transportation to local attractions, meeting facilities, no-smoking rooms, wheelchair-access rooms. LS SGL/DBL$95-$125; HS SGL/DBL$165-$185, STS$245-$440.

Indian Wells Racquet Club Resort (46-765 Bay Club Drive, 92210; 345-2811) 56 rooms and suites, restaurant, swimming pool, golf. SGL/DBL$90+, STS$235+.

Ramada Inn (76-661 Highway 111, 92210; 345-6466, 800-2-RAMADA) 190 rooms, restaurant, swimming pool, tennis, golf, exercise facilities, wheelchair-access rooms, no-smoking rooms. LS SGL/DBL$39-$48; HS SGL/DBL$89-$130.

Stouffer Esmeralda (44-400 Indian Wells Lane, 92210; 773-4444, Fax 773-9250) 560 rooms and suites, restaurant, swimming pool, lighted tennis courts, golf, airport transportation, wheelchair-access rooms, no-smoking rooms. LS SGL/DBL$145-$205; HS SGL/DBL$260-$340.

Indio

Area Code 619
Indio Chamber of Commerce
82-503 Highway 111
Indio CA 92202
347-0676

Best Western Date Tree Motor Hotel (81-909 Indio Boulevard, 92201; 347-3421, Fax 347-3421, 800-528-1234, 800-292-5599) 120 rooms, restaurant, complimentary breakfast, swimming pool, spa, kitchenettes, laundry room, children under 18 free, airport courtesy car, no-smoking rooms, no pets. SGL/$48-$76, DBL$58-$105.

Comfort Inn (43505 Monroe Street, 92201; 347-4044, 800-221-2222) 63 rooms, restaurant, swimming pool, meeting facilities, no-smoking rooms, no pets. LS SGL/DBL$39-$59; HS SGL/DBL$44-$60.

Date Tree Motor Hotel (81-909 Indio Boulevard, 92201; 347-3421) 120 rooms and suites. LS SGL/DBL$42-$64; HS SGL/DBL$46-$76, STS$82-$125.

Friendship Inn (84115 Indio, 92201; 342-4747, 800-453-4511, 800-424-4777) 35 rooms, two restaurants, 2 outdoor swimming pools, whirlpool, children under 18 free, pets allowed. SGL/DBL$45+.

154 Irvine

Indian Palms Resort and Country Club (48-630 Monroe Street, 92201; 347-0688) 59 rooms, restaurant, swimming pool, golf, tennis. SGL$65, DBL$85+.

Rodeway Inn (84096 Indio Springs Drive, 92201; 342-6344, 800-424-4777) 125 rooms, restaurant, swimming pool, whirlpools, gift shop, meeting facilities, children under 18 free, wheelchair-access rooms. SGL$42, DBL$49.

Royal Plaza Inn (82-347 Highway 111, 92201; 347-0911, 800-228-9559) 99 rooms, restaurant, swimming pool, pets allowed, wheelchair access. SGL$30-$45, DBL$44-$55.

Super 8 Motel (81753 Highway 111, 92201; 342-0264, 800-800-8000) 70 rooms and suites, restaurant, complimentary breakfast, outdoor heated swimming pool, free local telephone calls, wheelchair-access rooms, no-smoking rooms, pets allowed. SGL/DBL$40-$44.

TraveLodge (80-651 Highway 111, 92201; 342-0882, 800-255-3050) 50 rooms and suites, restaurant, lounge, whirlpool, laundry room, no pets. LS SGL/DBL$40-$58; HS SGL/DBL$62-$82.

Irvine

Area Code 714
Irvine Chamber of Commerce
2815 McGraw
Irvine CA 92174
360-9112

Airporter Inn Hotel (18700 MacArthur Boulevard, 92715; 833-2770, Fax 757-1228, 800-854-3012, 800-432-7018 in California) 211 rooms and suites, restaurant, complimentary breakfast, swimming pool, airport courtesy car, exercise facilities, wheelchair-access rooms, no-smoking rooms. SGL/DBL$75-$85, STS$85-$190.

Irvine   155

Best Western Motel (1717 East Dyer Road, 92705; 261-1515, Fax 261-1265) 150 rooms and suites, restaurant, swimming pool, airport courtesy car, exercise facilities, no-smoking rooms. SGL$60-$75, DBL$65-$85, STS$170-$225.

Embassy Suites (2120 Main Street, 92714; 553-8332, Fax 261-5301, 800-828-1832) 293 suites, restaurant, lounge, complimentary breakfast, indoor swimming pool, sauna, whirlpool, gift shop, meeting and conference facilities, airline ticket office, room service, valet laundry, airport courtesy car, wheelchair-access rooms, free parking, no-smoking rooms. SGL$125-$140, DBL$135-$150.

Holiday Inn of Irvine (17941 Von Karman, 92714; 714-863-1999, Fax 714-474-7236, 800-HOLIDAY) 340 rooms and suites, restaurant, indoor swimming pool, meeting facilities for 500, car rental, exercise facilities, wheelchair-access rooms, no-smoking rooms, airport transportation, pets allowed. SGL$81, DBL$94.

Hyatt Regency Irvine (17900 Jamboree Boulevard, 92714; 714-975-1234, Fax 714-363-0532, 800-233-1234) 536 rooms and suites, restaurant, outdoor heated swimming pool, whirlpool, spa, airport courtesy car, lighted tennis courts, exercise facilities, wheelchair-access rooms, no-smoking rooms, pets allowed. SGL$120-$140, DBL$140-$160, STS$250+.

Irvine Hilton and Towers (17900 Jamboree Road, 92714; 714-863-3111) 550 rooms, restaurant, swimming pool, exercise facilities, lighted tennis courts. SGL$98-$138, DBL$113-$153, 1BR$250-$1,200.

La Quinta Inn (14972 Sand Canyon Avenue, 92718; 714-551-0909, Fax 714-551-2945, 800-531-5900) 150 rooms, restaurant, swimming pool, jacuzzi, airport courtesy car, meeting facilities, pets allowed. SGL$58-$63, DBL$63-$68.

Marriott Hotel (18000 Von Karman Avenue, 92175; 553-0100, Fax 261-7059) 490 rooms and suites, restaurant, airport courtesy car, lighted tennis courts, exercise facilities, wheelchair-access rooms, meeting facilities for 25, in-room microwaves and

156 Irvine

Best Western Motel (1717 East Dyer Road, 92705; 261-1515, Fax 261-1265) 150 rooms and suites, restaurant, swimming pool, airport courtesy car, exercise facilities, no-smoking rooms. SGL$60-$75, DBL$65-$85, STS$170-$225.

Embassy Suites (2120 Main Street, 92714; 553-8332, Fax 261-5301, 800-828-1882) 293 suites, restaurant, lounge, complimentary breakfast, indoor swimming pool, sauna, whirlpool, gift shop, meeting and conference facilities, airline ticket office, room service, valet laundry, airport courtesy car, wheelchair-access rooms, free parking, no-smoking rooms. SGL$125-$140, DBL$135-$150.

Holiday Inn of Irvine (17941 Von Karman, 92714; 714-863-1999, Fax 714-474-7236, 800-HOLIDAY) 340 rooms and suites, restaurant, indoor swimming pool, meeting facilities for 500, car rental, exercise facilities, wheelchair-access rooms, no-smoking rooms, airport transportation, pets allowed. SGL$81, DBL$94.

Hyatt Regency Irvine (17900 Jamboree Boulevard, 92714; 714-975-1234, Fax 714-863-0532, 800-233-1234) 536 rooms and suites, restaurant, outdoor heated swimming pool, whirlpool, spa, airport courtesy car, lighted tennis courts, exercise facilities, wheelchair-access rooms, no-smoking rooms, pets allowed. SGL$120-$140, DBL$140-$160, STS$250+.

Irvine Hilton and Towers (17900 Jamboree Road, 92714; 714-863-3111) 550 rooms, restaurant, swimming pool, exercise facilities, lighted tennis courts. SGL$98-$138, DBL$113-$153, 1BR$250-$1,200.

La Quinta Inn (14972 Sand Canyon Avenue, 92718; 714-551-0909, Fax 714-551-2945, 800-531-5900) 150 rooms, restaurant, swimming pool, jacuzzi, airport courtesy car, meeting facilities, pets allowed. SGL$58-$63, DBL$63-$68.

Marriott Hotel (18000 Von Karman Avenue, 92175; 553-0100, Fax 261-7059) 490 rooms and suites, restaurant, airport courtesy car, lighted tennis courts, exercise center, wheelchair-access rooms, meeting facilities for 25, in-room microwaves and

VCRs, no-smoking rooms, pets allowed. SGL/DBL$80-$160, STS$250+.

Marriott Residence Inn (10 Morgan Street, 92718; 714-380-3000, Fax 714-588-7743, 800-331-3131) 112 rooms, airport transportation, wheelchair-access rooms, no-smoking rooms, pets allowed. SGL/DBL$110.

Radisson Plaza Hotel (18800 MacArthur Boulevard, 92715; 833-9999, 800-333-3333) 285 rooms, restaurant, lounge, outdoor heated swimming pool, free parking, airport courtesy car, exercise facilities, lighted tennis courts, computer hookups, transportation to local facilities. SGL/DBL$105+.

Jamestown

Area Code 209

Jamestown Hotel (Box 539, 95327; 984-3902) 8 rooms, restaurant, complimentary breakfast. SGL/DBL$55-$85.

National Hotel (Box 502, 95327; 984-3446) 11 rooms, restaurant, complimentary breakfast, airport courtesy car, pets allowed. SGL/DBL$65-$75.

Royal Hotel (Box 219, 95327; 984-5271) 19 rooms, bed and breakfast, complimentary breakfast. SGL/DBL$45+.

Sheets n' Eggs (Box 657, 95327; 984-0915) 3 rooms, bed and breakfast, complimentary breakfast. SGL$65, DBL$75.

June Lake

Area Code 619
June Lake-Loop Chamber of Commerce

Box 2
June Lake CA 93529
648-7584

Boulder Lodge (Box 68, 93529; 648-7533, Fax 648-7330) 32 rooms, suites and cottages, swimming pool, tennis, no-smoking rooms. SGL/DBL$50-$70, STS$80-$220.

Gull Lake Lodge (Box 25, 93529; 648-7516, 800-631-9081 in California) 14 rooms and efficiencies, pets allowed. SGL/DBL$53-$100.

June Lake Lodge (Box 98, 93529; 648-7547, 800-648-6835 in California) 20 rooms and cabins, restaurant, pets allowed. SGL/DBL$55.

Kernville

Area Code 619
Kernville Chamber of Commerce
11447 Kernville Road
Kernville CA 93238
376-2629

Hi-Ho Resort Lodge (11901 Sierra Way, 93238; 376-2671) 8 cottages, swimming pool, pets allowed. SGL/DBL$50+.

Kern River Inn (Box 1725, 93238; 376-6750) 6 rooms, bed and breakfast, complimentary breakfast. SGL$50, DBL$60.

Maple's McCambridge Lodge Motel (13525 Sierra Way, 93238; 376-2299) 10 rooms, swimming pool, transportation to local attractions, no-smoking rooms. SGL/DBL$40-$46.

Whispering Pines Lodge (13745 Sierra Way, 93238; 376-2334, Fax 376-3735) 12 rooms, bed and breakfast, complimentary breakfast, meeting facilities, swimming pool, spa, no-smoking. SGL/DBL$80-$130.

Klamath and Klamath River

Area Code 707
Klamath River Chamber of Commerce
Box 750
Klamath River CA 96050
465-2224

Camp Marigold Motel (16101 Highway 101, 95548; 482-3585) 16 rooms and cottages. SGL/DBL$32-$55.

Motel Trees (15495 Highway 101, 95548; 848-2982) 23 rooms, restaurant. SGL/DBL$36+.

Requa Inn (451 Requa Road, 95548; 482-8205) 10 rooms, bed and breakfast, complimentary breakfast, no-smoking. SGL/DBL$50-$75.

Trees Motel (Box 309, 95548; 482-3152, Fax 482-2005) 25 rooms, restaurant, tennis. SGL/DBL$34-$50.

La Canada

Area Code 818
La Canada Chamber of Commerce
4529 Angeles Crest Highway
La Canada CA 91011
790-4289

RENTAL SOURCES: Apartments for Travelers (1611 Verdugo Boulevard, 91011; 952-1336) rents apartments and condos, swimming pools, exercise facilities, pets allowed, free parking. $65-$100.

Laguna Beach

Area Code 714
Laguna Beach Chamber of Commerce
357 Flenneyre Avenue
Laguna Beach CA 92652
494-1018

RENTAL SOURCES: Laguna Beach Hospitality Association (Box 395, 92652; 497-9229, 800-734-3714) reservation and referral service for accommodations in Laguna Beach. Accommodations range from bed and breakfast inns to full-service hotels; **Bed and Breakfast International** (1181B Solana Avenue, Albany, 94706; 415-525-4569, 800-872-4500) represents local bed and breakfasts.

Aliso Creek Resort (31106 South Coast Highway, 92677; 499-2271) 62 suites, restaurant, swimming pool, golf, wheelchair-access rooms, no-smoking rooms. SGL/DBL$110-$180.

Best Western Laguna Reef Inn (30806 Coast Highway, 92651; 714-499-2227, Fax 714-499-5575, 800-528-1234) 43 rooms, restaurant, complimentary breakfast, heated swimming pool, sauna, whirlpool, meeting facilities, beach, no-smoking rooms. LS SGL$67-$77, DBL$82-$92; HS SGL/DBL$110-$120.

Capri Laguna Hotel (1441 South Coast Highway, 92651; 494-6533) 46 rooms, complimentary breakfast, swimming pool. SGL/DBL$50-$210.

The Carriage House (1322 Catalina Street, 92651; 494-8945) 6 suites, bed and breakfast, complimentary breakfast, restaurant, free parking. SGL/DBL$95+.

Casa Laguna Inn (2510 South Coast Highway, 92651; 494-2996) 25 rooms and suites, restaurant, complimentary breakfast, fireplaces, swimming pool. SGL/DBL$100-$120, STS$150-$225.

Eilers Inn (741 South Coast Highway, 92651; 494-3004) 11 rooms, complimentary breakfast, restaurant. SGL$100-$170, DBL$100-$175.

Hotel Firenze (1289 South Coast Highway, 92651; 497-2446, Fax 497-3770) 20 rooms, restaurant, complimentary breakfast, airport transportation, no-smoking rooms, pets allowed. SGL$80-$100, DBL$80-$120.

Holiday Inn (25205 La Paz Road, 92653; 586-5000, Fax 581-7410, 800-HOLIDAY) 148 rooms, restaurant, swimming pool, airport courtesy car, wheelchair-access rooms, no-smoking rooms. SGL$70-$100, DBL$80-$110.

Hotel Laguna (425 South Coast Highway, 92651; 714-494-1151, Fax 497-2163, 800-524-2927) 68 rooms and one- and two-bedroom suites, restaurant, lounge, complimentary breakfast, meeting facilities, room service, free parking, beach. LS SGL/DBL$65-$105; HS SGL/DBL$80-$130.

The Inn At Laguna Beach (211 North Pacific Coast Highway, 92651; 497-9722, Fax 497-9972, 800-544-4479) 70 rooms, restaurant, swimming pool, child care, sauna, wheelchair-access rooms, beach. SGL/DBL$140-$300.

Laguna Riviera Beach Resort (825 South Coast Highway, 92651; 494-1196) 41 rooms and suites, complimentary breakfast, swimming pool. SGL/DBL$95-$185, STS$120-$185.

Hotel St. Maarten (696 South Coast Highway, 92651; 714-494-9436, Fax 497-7101, 800-772-2539, 800-228-5691 in California) 54 rooms and one-bedroom suites, restaurant, complimentary breakfast, swimming pool, beach. LS SGL$69-$89, DBL$79-$99+, 1BR$109-$139+; HS SGL$80-$100, DBL$90-$110, 1BR$135-$155+.

162 Laguna Hills

Surf and Sand (1555 South Coast Highway, 92651; 497-4477, Fax 494-7653, 800-524-8621) 157 rooms and suites, two restaurants, outdoor heated swimming pool, children under 12 free, no pets, wheelchair-access rooms, no-smoking rooms. SGL/DBL$160-$275, STS$375-$575.

Tides of Laguna Motel (460 North Pacific Coast Highway, 92651; 494-2494, Fax 497-5209) 23 rooms. SGL/DBL$45+.

Vacation Village Motel (647 South Coast Highway, 92651; 494-8566) 33 rooms. SGL/DBL$65+.

Laguna Hills

Area Code 714
Saddleback Regional Chamber of Commerce
25301 Cabor Road #201
Laguna Hills CA 92653
837-3000

Comfort Inn (23061 Avenue De La Carlota, 92653; 859-0166, 800-221-2222) 76 rooms, restaurant, complimentary breakfast, swimming pool, whirlpool, sauna, wheelchair-access rooms, no pets. SGL/DBL$52-$68.

Holiday Inn (25205 La Paz Road, 92653; 586-5000, 800-HOLIDAY) 147 rooms, restaurant, swimming pool, wheelchair-access rooms, meeting facilities for 400, exercise center, airport transportation, no pets. SGL/DBL$69-$109.

Hyatt Lodge (23932 Paseo De Valencia, 923653; 830-2550, Fax 581-0819) 132 rooms. SGL/DBL$195-$450.

The Ritz-Carlton (33533 Ritz-Carlton Drive, 92677; 240-2000, 800-241-3333) 390 rooms and suites, restaurant, swimming pool, exercise facilities, free parking. SGL/DBL$175-$310, STS$550-$1,500.

Laguna Niguel

Area Code 714
Laguna Niguel Chamber of Commerce
3 Monarch Bay Plaza
Laguna Niguel CA 92677
240-2112

Ritz-Carlton (33533 Ritz-Carlton Drive, 92677; 240-2000, Fax 240-0829, 800-241-3333) 393 rooms and suites, restaurant, lounge, complimentary breakfast, swimming pool, sauna, spa, airport transportation, beach, tennis, golf, wheelchair-access rooms, no-smoking rooms. SGL/DBL$195-$380.

La Habra

Area Code 310
La Habra Chamber of Commerce
321 East La Habra Boulevard
La Habra CA 90631
697-1704

All Star Inn (870 North Beach Boulevard, 90631; 694-2158) 44 rooms. SGL/DBL$31-$37.

Best Western Inn (700 North Beach Boulevard, 90631; 694-1991, Fax 690-2867, 800-528-1234) 82 rooms, restaurant, lounge, complimentary breakfast, swimming pool, fax service, meeting facilities, no-smoking rooms. SGL/DBL$45-$65.

Sunset Inn (1001 South Beach Boulevard, 90631; 694-1515) 61 rooms, free parking. SGL$28-$35, DBL$35-$45.

La Jolla

Area Code 619
La Jolla Town Council
1055 Wall Street
La Jolla CA 92038
454-1444

RENTAL SOURCES: Bed and Breakfast International (Box 282910, 94128; 696-1690, Fax 696-1699, 800-872-4500) represents bed and breakfast accommodations throughout California. Accommodations available in private homes, houseboats on the Bay and inns. All rates include complimentary breakfast. SGL/DBL$50-$125.

Andrea Villa Inn (2402 Torrey Pines Road, 92037; 459-3311, 800-367-6467) 49 rooms and efficiencies, restaurant, complimentary breakfast, swimming pool. SGL/DBL$75-$85.

Bed and Breakfast Inn At La Jolla (7753 Draper Avenue, 92037; 456-2066) 16 rooms, complimentary breakfast, wheelchair-access rooms, no-smoking rooms. SGL/DBL$85-$200+.

Best Western Inn By The Sea (7830 Fay Avenue, 92037; 459-4461, Fax 456-2578, 800-528-1234) 132 rooms, restaurant, complimentary breakfast, swimming pool, spa, airport transportation, meeting facilities, car rental, fax service, children under 12 free, no-smoking rooms, wheelchair-access rooms, exercise facilities. LS SGL$84-$95, DBL$890$99; HS SGL$91-$102, DBL$120-$130.

Colonial Inn (910 Prospect, 92037; 454-2181, Fax 454-5679, 800-826-1278) 75 rooms, restaurant, lounge, complimentary breakfast, swimming pool, airport transportation, no-smoking rooms, transportation to local attractions. SGL/DBL$150-$200, STS$200+.

Costello Bed and Breakfast (Bed and Breakfast International) 1 room, complimentary breakfast, no smoking. SGL/DBL$70.

Embassy Suites (4550 La Jolla Village Drive, 92037; 453-0400, Fax 453-4226) 335 suites, restaurant, complimentary breakfast, swimming pool, exercise facilities, wheelchair-access rooms, no-smoking rooms. STS$110-$160.

Empress Hotel of La Jolla (7766 Fay Avenue, 92037; 454-3001, 800-525-6552, 800-468-3555 in California) 75 rooms, restaurant, complimentary breakfast, swimming pool, exercise facilities, airport transportation, wheelchair-access rooms. SGL/DBL$95-$125.

Hyatt Regency La Jolla (3777 La Jolla Village Drive, 92037; 552-1234, Fax 552-6066, 800-233-1234) 400 rooms and suites, restaurant, swimming pool, exercise facilities, airport transportation, tennis, golf, wheelchair-access rooms, no-smoking rooms. SGL/DBL$135-$185, STS$200-$400.

The Inn At La Jolla (5440 La Jolla Boulevard, 92037; 454-6121, Fax 544-1257, 800-367-6467) 45 rooms, swimming pool, spa, free parking, no pets. SGL/DBL$57-$84.

Inn By The Sea Hotel (7830 Fay Avenue, 92037; 459-4461, 800-462-9732, 800-526-4545 in California) 134 rooms and suites, restaurant, heated swimming pool, spa, meeting facilities for 50, airport transportation, ocean view. SGL/DBL$85-$250.

La Jolla Beach and Tennis Club (2000 Spindrift Drive, 92037; 454-7126, Fax 456-3805) 90 rooms. SGL/DBL$60-$245.

La Jolla Cove Motel (1155 Coast Boulevard, 92037; 459-2621, Fax 454-3522, 800-248-2683) 120 rooms, swimming pool, sauna, spa, exercise facilities, child care, laundry room, meeting facilities, airport transportation. SGL/DBL$55-$120.

La Jolla

La Jolla Village Inn (3299 Holiday Court, 92037; 453-5500, Fax 453-5550, 800-345-9995) 196 rooms, restaurant, swimming pool, tennis, exercise facilities, airport courtesy car, wheelchair-access rooms, no-smoking rooms. SGL$65-$119, DBL$75-$129.

La Jolla Palms Inn (6705 La Jolla Boulevard, 92037; 454-7101, Fax 454-6957, 800-451-0358) 59 rooms and suites, restaurant, complimentary breakfast, swimming pool, pets allowed. SGL/DBL$60-$100, STS$80-$150.

La Jolla Shores Inn (5390 La Jolla Boulevard, 92037; 454-0175, 800-367-6467) 39 rooms and suites, swimming pool. SGL/DBL$55-$85, STS$130+.

La Valencia Hotel (1132 Prospect Street, 92037; 454-0771, 800-451-0772, 454-0771, 800-451-0772) 100 rooms and suites, three restaurant, outdoor heated swimming pool, fax service, airport courtesy car, meeting facilities for 100, no pets, exercise facilities. SGL/DBL/STS$135-$285, STS$300-$600.

Marriott Residence Inn (8901 Gilman Drive, 92037; 587-1770, Fax 552-0387, 800-332-3131) 288 suites, restaurant, complimentary breakfast, swimming pool, lighted airport courtesy car, meeting facilities for 65, in-room microwaves, wheelchair-access rooms, no-smoking rooms, pets allowed. STS$85-$139.

Palms Inn (6705 La Jolla Boulevard, 92037; 454-7101, Fax 454-6957) 65 rooms. SGL/DBL$59-$99.

Sands of La Jolla (5417 La Jolla Boulevard, 92037; 459-3336, Fax 231-8026) 39 rooms. SGL/DBL$64-$94.

Sands Motel (5417 La Jolla Boulevard, 92037; 459-3336, 800-367-6467) 38 rooms and suites, complimentary breakfast, swimming pool. SGL/DBL$65-$95, STS$90-$120.

Sea Lodge Hotel (8110 Camino Del Oro, 92037; 459-8271, Fax 456-9346, 800-237-5211) 128 rooms, restaurant, lounge, swimming pool, sauna, spa, room service, laundry room, airport transportation, wheelchair access, no-smoking rooms. SGL$100-$260, DBL$115-$275+.

Sheraton Grande Torrey Pines (10950 North Torrey Pines Road, 92037; 558-1500, Fax 558-1131, 800-325-3535) 417 rooms and suites, restaurant, lounge, outdoor heated swimming pool, whirlpool, spa, sauna, exercise center, meeting facilities for 1,000, business services, lighted tennis courts, golf, airport transportation, wheelchair-access rooms, no-smoking rooms. SGL/DBL$145,STS$155+.

Summer House Inn (7995 La Jolla Shores Drive, 92037; 459-0261, Fax 459-7649, 800-666-0261) 80 rooms and suites, restaurant, lounge, swimming pool, laundry room, meeting facilities, room service, airport courtesy car, tennis. SGL/DBL$100-$130, STS$145-$300+.

Torrey Pines Inn (11480 North Torrey Pines, Road, 92037; 453-4420, Fax 453-0691, 800-448-8355) 71 rooms, restaurant, lounge, swimming pool, child care, balconies, ocean view, meeting facilities for 350, airport courtesy car, exercise facilities, golf. no-smoking rooms. SGL$79-$89, DBL$85-$95.

TraveLodge (6750 La Jolla Boulevard, 92037; 454-0716, Fax 454-1075, 800-255-3050) 44 rooms and suites, restaurant, swimming pool, laundry room, airport transportation, no pets. SGL/DBL$53-$73.

TraveLodge (1141 Silverado Street, 92037; 454-0791, Fax 459-8543, 800-255-3050) 30 rooms, restaurant, no pets. SGL/DBL$39-$59.

Village Inn (3299 Holiday Court, 92037; 453-5500, Fax 453-5550) 204 rooms. SGL/DBL$69-$149.

Lake Arrowhead

Area Code 714
Lake Arrowhead Chamber of Commerce

Box 155
Lake Arrowhead CA 92352
337-3715

Bluebelle House (Box 2177, 92352; 336-3292, 800-429-BLUE in California) 5 rooms, bed and breakfast, complimentary breakfast. SGL$55, DBL$65.

Hilton Arrowhead Lodge (Box 1699, 92352; 336-1511, Fax 336-1378, 800-HILTONS) 261 rooms and suites, restaurant, swimming pool, spa, kitchenettes, valet laundry, child care, fax service, transportation to local attractions, beauty salon, meeting facilities for 800, lighted tennis courts, airport transportation, exercise facilities, wheelchair-access rooms, no-smoking rooms, free parking. SGL/DBL$89-$219, STS$275-$450.

Saddleback Inn (300 Highway 173, 92357; 336-3571) 34 cottages, restaurant, complimentary breakfast. SGL/DBL$200-$380.

Tree Top Lodge (27992 Rainbow Drive, 92353; 337-2311) 20 rooms, swimming pool, no-smoking rooms. SGL/DBL$65-$105, STS$75-$100+.

Lake Elsinore

Area Code 714
Lake Elsinore Valley Chamber of Commerce
132 West Graham Avenue
Lake Elsinore CA 92330, 674-2577

TraveLodge (31620 Casino Drive, 92230; 245-8998, Fax 674-9749, 800-255-3050) 60 rooms, restaurant, swimming pool, whirlpool, meeting facilities for 50, no pets. SGL/DBL$35-$42.

Lakewood

Area Code 310

Lakewood Chamber of Commerce
Box 160
Lakewood CA 90714, 920-7737

Best Western Inn (11727 East Carson Street, 90715; 402-4200, Fax 402-8761, 800-528-1234) 48 rooms, swimming pool, fax service, wheelchair-access rooms, no pets. SGL/DBL$46-$59.

La Mesa

Area Code 619

Allstar Inn (7621 Alvarado Road, 92041; 464-7151) 12 rooms. SGL/DBL$28-$34.

Comfort Inn (8000 Parkway Drive, 92041; 698-7747, 800-228-5150) 127 rooms. SGL/DBL$45-$82.

Econo Lodge (4210 Spring Street, 92041; 589-7288, 800-446-6900) 54 rooms. SGL/DBL$38-$45.

E-Z 8 Motel (7851 Fletcher Parkway, 92042; 698-9444, 800-326-6835) 105 rooms. SGL/DBL$27-$30.

TraveLodge Grossmont (9550 Murray Drive, 92041; 466-0200, 800-255-3050) 78 rooms and suites, restaurant, lounge, swimming pool, meeting facilities for 50, no pets. SGL/DBL$35-$50.

La Mirada

Area Code 714
La Mirada Chamber of Commerce
15052 Rosecrans Avenue
La Mirada CA 90638
521-1702

170 Lancaster

Gateway Holiday Inn (14299 Firestone Boulevard, 90638; 739-8500, 800-356-6873) 300 rooms, restaurant, lounge, swimming pool, car rental, gift shop, meeting facilities for 1,200, no pets. exercise facilities. SGL/DBL$88-$100.

Lancaster

Area Code 805
Lancaster Chamber of Commerce
44943 North Tenth Street
Lancaster CA 93534
948-4518

All-Star Inn (43540 17th Street, 93534; 948-0435) 36 rooms. SGL/DBL$26-$30.

Bermuda Resort (43019 Sierra Highway, 93534; 942-1493; 342-SLIM) 35 rooms, restaurant, complimentary breakfast, exercise facilities, wheelchair access. SGL$60-$65, DBL$65-$70.

Best Western Antelope Valley Inn (44055 North Sierra Highway, 93534; 948-4651, Fax 948-4651, 800-528-1234) 148 rooms, restaurant, lounge, complimentary breakfast, swimming pool, wheelchair-access rooms, computer hookups, in-room refrigerators, children under 18 free, meeting facilities, no-smoking rooms, pets allowed. LS SGL/DBL$49-$65; HS SGL/DBL$55-$71.

Bon Reussite (43019 North Sierra Highway, 93534; 942-1493, Fax 942-7115) 32 rooms. SGL/DBL$100+.

Desert Inn Motor Hotel (44219 North Sierra Highway, 93534; 942-8401, Fax 942-8950, 800-942-8401) 147 rooms, restaurant, complimentary breakfast, swimming pool, sauna, spa, transportation to local attractions, exercise facilities, wheelchair-access rooms. SGL/DBL$60-$80.

Essex House Hotel and Racquet Club (44916 North Tenth Street, 93534; 948-0961) 234 rooms, restaurant, lounge, swimming pool, sauna, spa, meeting facilities, laundry room, complimentary breakfast, swimming pool, exercise facilities, no-smoking rooms. SGL$55-$80, DBL$65-$90.

E-Z 8 Motel (43530 17th Street West, 93534; 945-9477, 800-326-6835) 102 rooms. SGL/DBL$25-$40.

Quality Inn (43321 North Sierra Highway, 93534; 948-2691, Fax 945-2363, 800-221-2222) 87 rooms, restaurant, lounge, swimming pool, whirlpool, meeting facilities, no pets. SGL/DBL$39-$75.

Rio Mirada Motor Inn (1651 West Avenue K, 93534; 949-3423, Fax 949-0896, 800-522-3050) 178 rooms and suites, restaurant, lounge, complimentary breakfast, swimming pool, meeting facilities, airport courtesy car, wheelchair-access rooms, no-smoking rooms. SGL/DBL$50-$125.

La Puente

Area Code 818
La Puente Chamber of Commerce
15917 Main Street
La Puente CA 91747
330-3216

TraveLodge (15412 Francisquito Avenue, 91744; 918-2315, Fax 917-5608, 800-255-3050) 46 rooms, fax service, wheelchair-access rooms. SGL/DBL$35-$45.

La Quinta

Area Code 619
La Quinta Chamber of Commerce
Box 255
La Quinta CA 92253
564-3199

La Quinta Hotel Golf and Tennis Resort (49-499 Eisenhower Drive, 92253; 564-4111, 800-472-4316) 640 rooms and suites, restaurant, swimming pool, tennis, golf. LS SGL/DBL$65-$110; HS SGL/DBL$255-$295.

Lawndale

Area Code 310
Lawndale Chamber of Commerce
14704 Hawthorne Boulevard
Lawndale CA 90260
679-3306

Best Western South Bay Hotel (15000 Hawthorne Boulevard, 90260; 973-0998, Fax 978-0022, 800-528-1234) 101 rooms, restaurant, lounge, complimentary breakfast, heated swimming pool, spa, in-room refrigerators, fax service, airport transportation, no-smoking rooms, no pets. SGL/DBL$48-$80.

Comfort Inn (14814 Hawthorne Boulevard, 90260; 676-1111, 800-221-2222) 103 rooms, restaurant, complimentary breakfast, swimming pool, sauna, meeting facilities, wheelchair-access rooms, no pets. SGL/DBL$49-$62.

Days Inn Los Angeles Airport South (15636 Hawthorne Boulevard, 90260; 213-676-7378, Fax 213-676-3138, 800-325-2525) 43 rooms and suites, complimentary breakfast, swimming pool, spa, children under 12 free, fax service, wheelchair-access rooms, no-smoking rooms, free parking. SGL/DBL$52-$64, STS$85-$100.

Friendship Inn (14808 Hawthorne Boulevard, 90260; 675-5228, Fax 676-3226, 800-424-4777) 40 rooms, whirlpools, wheelchair-access rooms, exercise facilities, laundry room, in-room refrigerators, fax service, children under 18 free, no pets. SGL/DBL$45-$55.

TraveLodge Southbay (15636 Hawthorne Boulevard, 90260; 676-7378, Fax 674-1137, 800-233-8058) 45 rooms and suites, free parking. SGL$45-$54, DBL$49-$59, STS$70-90.

Lemon Cove

Area Code 209

Lemon Cove Bed and Breakfast (33038 Sierra Drive, 93244; 597-2555) 7 rooms, bed and breakfast, complimentary breakfast. SGL$55, DBL$75.

Lemon Grove

Area Code 619
Lemon Grove Chamber of Commerce
3443 Main Street
Lemon Grove CA 92045
469-9621

E-Z 8 Motel (7458 Broadway, 91945; 462-7022) 39 rooms. SGL/DBL$23-$39.

National 9 Inn (8429 Broadway, 91945; 463-9353, Fax 461-0971) 62 rooms. SGL/DBL$30-$60.

Lemoore

Area Code 209
Lemoore Chamber of Commerce
218 West D Street
Lemoore CA 93245
924-6401

Best Western Vineyard Inn (877 East D Street, 93245; 924-1261, Fax 924-4270, 800-528-1234) 67 rooms, restaurant, lounge, swimming pool, tennis, laundry room, meeting facilities, free local telephone calls, fax service, wheelchair-access rooms, pets allowed. SGL$40-$50, DBL$42-$53.

Lomita

Area Code 310
Lomita Chamber of Commerce
24300 Narbonne Avenue
Lomita CA 90717
326-6378

Best Western Eldorado Inn (2037 Pacific Coast Highway, 90717; 534-0700, Fax 539-5223, 800-528-1234) 60 rooms, restaurant, complimentary breakfast, swimming pool, jacuzzi, in-room refrigerators, fax service, whirlpool, no-smoking rooms, pets allowed. SGL$46-$50, DBL$53-$57.

Lompoc

Area Code 805
Lompoc Valley Chamber of Commerce
119 East Cypress Avenue
Lompac CA 93436
736-4567

All-Star Inn (1425 North H Street, 93436; 735-7631) 36 rooms. SGL/DBL$20-$30.

Best Western Flagwaver Inn (937 H Street, 93436; 736-5605, Fax 736-6423, 800-528-1234) 56 rooms, restaurant, lounge, complimentary breakfast, heated swimming pool, spa, children under 12 free, fax service, no pets. SGL$35-$55, DBL$40-$80.

Days Inn (1122 North H Street, 93436; 735-7744, Fax 736-0421, 800-325-2525) 90 rooms, restaurant, complimentary breakfast, indoor heated swimming pool, spa, in-room refrigerators and microwaves, VCRs, laundry room, meeting facilities, fax service, children under 12 free, exercise center, wheelchair-access rooms, no-smoking rooms. SGL$46-$51, DBL$50-$57.

Embassy Suites (1117 North H Street, 93436; 735-8311, Fax 735-8459, 800-433-0680, 800-433-3182) 156 suites, restaurant, complimentary breakfast, heated swimming pool, spa, exercise center, meeting facilities for 125, valet laundry, wheelchair access, free parking, no-smoking rooms, no pets. SGL$69, DBL$79, STS$89-$99.

The Inn of Lompac (1122 North H Street, 93436; 735-7744, 800-548-8231) 90 rooms, complimentary breakfast, indoor heated swimming pool, spa, meeting facilities, in-room refrigerators, exercise facilities, no-smoking rooms. SGL/DBL$51-$57.

Motel 6 (1415 East Ocean Avenue, 93436; 736-6514, 505-891-6161) 48 rooms. SGL/DBL$20-$30.

Porto Finale Inn (940 East Ocean Avenue, 93436; 735-7731, 800-776-7375) 85 rooms, restaurant, lounge, complimentary breakfast, swimming pool, sauna, airport transportation, wheelchair-access rooms, no-smoking rooms. SGL$28-$45, DBL$33-$55.

Quality Inn and Executive Suites (1621 North H Street, 93436; 735-8555, 800-221-2222) 225 rooms and suites, restaurant, complimentary breakfast, heated swimming pool, spa, whirlpool, laundry room, wheelchair access, no-smoking rooms, pets allowed. SGL$48-$60, DBL$58-$70.

Tally Ho Motor Inn (1020 East Ocean Avenue, 93436; 735-6444) 57 rooms, complimentary breakfast, sauna, spa, wheelchair-access rooms, laundry room, pets allowed, no-smoking rooms. SGL/DBL$30-$60.

Valley Oaks Inn (3955 Highway One, 93436; 733-4502) 63 rooms, restaurant, swimming pool, exercise facilities, no-smoking rooms, pets allowed. SGL/DBL$55-$75.

Lone Pine

Area Code 619
Lone Pine Chamber of Commerce
126 South Main Street
Lone Pine CA 93545
876-4702

Best Western Frontier Motel (10008 South Main Street, 93545; 876-5571, Fax 876-5357, 800-528-1234) 73 rooms, complimentary breakfast, swimming pool, jacuzzis, meeting facilities, fax service, laundry room, wheelchair-access rooms, pets allowed. SGL/DBL$40-$75.

Dow Villa (310 South Main Street, 876-5521, Fax 876-5643, 800-824-9317) 96 rooms and suites, restaurant, outdoor swimming pool, spa, free local telephone calls, in-room refrigerators, free parking, airport courtesy car, wheelchair-access rooms, no-smoking rooms, pets allowed. SGL/DBL$23-$58.

Long Beach

Area Code 213
Long Beach Area Convention and Visitors Bureau
180 East Ocean Boulevard
Long Beach CA 90802
436-3645)

Long Beach Chamber of Commerce
One World Trade Center #350
Long Beach CA 90831
436-1251

RENTAL SOURCES: Bed and Breakfast International (Box 282910, 94128; 696-1690, Fax 696-1699, 800-872-4500) represents bed and breakfast accommodations throughout California. Accommodations available in private homes, houseboats on the Bay and inns. All rates include complimentary breakfast.

SGL/DBL$50-$125; **House Guests USA** (Box 1185, Huntington Beach, 92647; 891-3736, Fax 964-4250, 800-333-HOST) represents more than 1,000 host properties in southern California with 200 properties in the Long Beach area.

All-Star Inn (5665 East Seventh Street, 90804; 597-1311) 21 rooms. SGL/DBL$35-$40.

Appleton Place Bed and Breakfast Inn (935 Cedar Avenue, 90813; 432-2312) 5 rooms, bed and breakfast, complimentary breakfast, no-smoking.

At Ocean Motel (50 Atlantic Avenue, 435-8369) 38 rooms and suites, pets allowed, free parking. SGL$38-42, DBL$42-$45, STS$60+.

Best Western Inn (1725 Long Beach Boulevard, 90813; 310-599-5555, Fax 310-599-1212, 800-528-1234) 102 rooms, complimentary breakfast, swimming pool, wheelchair-access rooms, complimentary newspaper, laundry room, fax service, meeting facilities, no pets. SGL$48-$78, DBL$54-$88.

Best Western Golden Sails Hotel (6285 East Pacific Coast Highway, 90803; 310-596-1631, Fax 310-596-1631, 800-528-1234) 175 rooms and suites, restaurant, lounge, swimming pool, whirlpool, complimentary newspaper, meeting facilities for 1,000, balconies, in-room refrigerators, transportation to local attractions, fax service, wheelchair-access rooms, airport courtesy car, no-smoking rooms, no pets. SGL/DBL$90-$130.

Best Western Queen City Motel (3555 East Pacific Coast Highway 90804; 310-597-4455, Fax 310-494-3186, 800-528-1234) 44 rooms, complimentary breakfast, swimming pool, children under 12 free, laundry room, balconies, fax service, no-smoking rooms, no pets. SGL$50-$60, DBL$52-$62.

Brittany Inn (1500 East Pacific Coast Highway, 90806; 591-0088, Fax 591-6390) 47 rooms, restaurant, complimentary breakfast, swimming pool, laundry room, wheelchair access, no-smoking rooms. SGL/DBL$50-$75.

Brooks College (4825 East Pacific Coast Highway, 90804; 597-6611) 300 rooms available between during the summer months, dining room, swimming pool, laundry room. SGL$15+.

Clarion Edgewater Hotel (6400 East Pacific Coast Highway, 90803; 434-8451, Fax 598-6028, 800-221-2222) 249 rooms and suites, two restaurants, lounge, swimming pool, whirlpools, jacuzzi, wheelchair-access rooms, no-smoking rooms, free parking. SGL/DBL$79-$124.

Colonial Motel (802 East Pacific Coast Highway, 90806; 591-8327) 60 rooms, kitchenettes. SGL/DBL$35-$45.

Comfort Inn (3201 East Pacific Coast Highway, 90804; 597-3374, 800-221-2222, 800-228-5150) 65 rooms and suites, restaurant, complimentary breakfast, swimming pool, jacuzzi, whirlpools, laundry room, wheelchair-access rooms, no pets. SGL/DBL$60-$95.

Days Inn (5950 Long Beach Boulevard, 90805; 423-9898, 800-325-2525) 76 rooms, complimentary breakfast, swimming pool, jacuzzi, spa, fax service, wheelchair-access rooms, no-smoking rooms. SGL/DBL$48-$51.

Econo Lodge (150 Alamitos Avenue, 90802; 435-7621, Fax 436-4011, 800-446-6900) 60 rooms, swimming pool, complimentary newspaper. SGL/DBL$35-$75.

Friendship Inn (50 Atlantic Avenue, 90802; 435-8369, Fax 432-3799, 800-453-4511) 40 rooms and suites, in-room refrigerators. SGL$50, DBL$55.

Long Beach Hilton (Two World Trade Center, 90831; 983-3400, Fax 983-1200, 800-HILTONS) 397 rooms, restaurant, swimming pool, meeting facilities, exercise facilities, airport transportation. SGL/DBL$75+.

Holiday Inn Airport (2640 Lakewood Boulevard, 90815; 597-4401, Fax 597-0601, 800-235-9556, 800-HOLIDAY) 231 rooms and suites, restaurant, outdoor heated swimming pool, meeting facilities for 250, wheelchair-access rooms, airport courtesy car, exercise facilities, pets allowed. SGL/DBL$80-$110.

Holiday Inn Downtown (500 East First Street, 90802; 435-8511, Fax 435-1370, 800-HOLIDAY) 224 rooms, restaurant, swimming pool, airport transportation, exercise facilities, wheelchair-access rooms, no-smoking rooms, no pets. SGL/DBL$70+.

Howard Johnson Plaza Hotel (1133 Atlantic Avenue, 90813; 590-8858, Fax 983-1607, 800-654-2000) 135 rooms, restaurant, lounge, swimming pool, jacuzzi, meeting facilities, fax service, VCRs, wheelchair-access rooms, free parking, airport transportation, no-smoking rooms. SGL$71-$95, DBL$79-$103.

Hyatt Edgewater (6400 East Pacific Coast Highway, 90803; 434-8451, 800-228-9000) 249 rooms, restaurant, marina, airport courtesy car. SGL$86-$99, DBL$95-$114.

Hyatt Regency (200 South Pine Avenue, 90802; 491-1234, Fax 432-1972, 800-233-1234) 521 rooms and suites, restaurant, lounge, swimming pool, spa, exercise facilities, wheelchair-access rooms, no-smoking rooms. SGL/DBL$80-$150.

International Inn (200 East Willow Street, 90806; 426-7611) 74 rooms, swimming pool. SGL/DBL$35-$50.

Lord Mayor's Inn (435 Cedar Avenue, 90802; 436-0324) 5 rooms, bed and breakfast, complimentary breakfast, free parking. SGL$65, DBL$75.

Mageean Bed and Breakfast (Bed and Breakfast International) one-room apartment, complimentary breakfast, no smoking. SGL/DBL$72.

Marriott Airport (4700 Airport Plaza Drive, 90815; 425-5210, Fax 425-2744, 800-333-3333, 800-228-9290) 311 rooms and suites, restaurants, indoor and outdoor swimming pool, whirlpool, children under 18 stay free, exercise facilities, airport transportation, wheelchair-access rooms, no-smoking rooms. SGL$50+.

Marriott Residence Inn (4111 East Willow Street, 90815; 595-0909, Fax 988-0587, 800-331-3131) one- and two-bedroom suites, airport transportation, in-room microwaves, meeting facilities for 65, no-smoking rooms, pets allowed. SGL/DBL$125-$145.

Nashin Bed and Breakfast (Bed and Breakfast International) one room, complimentary breakfast, no smoking. SGL/DBL$55.

Oak Creek Inn (4201 East Pacific Coast Highway, 90804; 597-7701, 800-228-9669) 49 rooms, complimentary breakfast, swimming pool, exercise facilities. SGL$50-$60, DBL$60-$70.

Ramada Inn (5325 East Pacific Coast Highway, 90804; 597-1341, Fax 597-1664, 800-228-2828) 143 rooms and suites, restaurant, lounge, heated swimming pool, meeting facilities, exercise center, children under 18 stay free, airport courtesy car, wheelchair-access rooms, no-smoking rooms, pets allowed. SGL/DBL$65-$95.

Ramada Renaissance Hotel (111 East Ocean Boulevard, 90802; 437-5900, Fax 437-3813, 800-228-9898) 380 rooms and suites, three restaurants, lounge, swimming pool, spa, meeting facilities, airport transportation, children under 18 stay free, exercise center, wheelchair-access rooms, no-smoking rooms. SGL/DBL$120-$155, STS$175+.

Residence Inn by Marriott (4111 East Willow Street, 90815; 595-0909, 800-331-3131) one- and two-bedroom suites, complimentary breakfast, swimming pool, whirlpool, fireplaces, meeting facilities. SGL/DBL$65-$135.

Sandpiper Inn (3624 East Pacific Coast Highway, 90804; 498-7544) 24 rooms and efficiencies, no-smoking rooms, pets allowed. SGL/DBL$35-$55.

Sheraton Long Beach at Shoreline Square (333 East Ocean Boulevard, 90802; 436-3000, Fax 436-9176, 800-325-3535) 426 rooms and suites, restaurant, lounge, outdoor heated swimming pool, saunas, meeting facilities for 2,200, business services, exercise center, airport courtesy car, wheelchair-access rooms, no-smoking rooms. SGL/DBL$100-$145.

Super 8 Motel (4201 East Pacific Coast Highway, 90804; 597-7701, 800-800-8000) 49 rooms, complimentary breakfast, swimming pool, sauna, jacuzzi, in-room refrigerators, complimentary newspaper, free local telephone calls, exercise facilities. SGL/DBL$50-$56.

Travel Inn (2900 East Pacific Coast Highway, 90804; 494-4394) 29 rooms. SGL/DBL$40-$50.

TraveLodge (80 Atlantic Avenue, 90802; 310-435-2471;, Fax 310-437-1995, 800-255-3050) 63 rooms, restaurant, lounge, swimming pool, in-room refrigerators, tours, car rental, airport transportation, pets allowed. SGL/DBL$50-$65.

TraveLodge (700 Queensway Drive, 90802; 310-437-0866, Fax 437-0866, 800-255-3050) 194 rooms and suites, restaurant, lounge, swimming pool, exercise facilities, room service, tours, car rental, ocean view, meeting facilities, lighted tennis courts, airport transportation, no-smoking rooms, no pets. SGL/DBL$79-$99.

The Vagabond Inn Long Beach (185 Atlantic Avenue, 90802; 435-3791, Fax 436-7510, 800-522-1555) 74 rooms, restaurant, complimentary breakfast, outdoor heated swimming pool, spa, pets allowed, airport transportation, free local telephone calls, in-room refrigerators, no-smoking rooms, children under 18 free, fax service, complimentary newspaper. SGL$48-$55, DBL$53-$65.

Viscount Hotel Resort and Marina (700 Queensway Drive, 90801; 435-7676, Fax 437-0866, 800-255-3050) 200 rooms, restaurant, swimming pool, tennis, airport transportation, wheelchair access, no-smoking rooms. SGL$90-$100, DBL$100-$110+.

Los Alamos

Area Code 805

Skyview Motel (9150 Highway 101, 93440; 344-3770) 32 rooms and efficiencies, swimming pool, airport transportation, wheelchair-access rooms, no-smoking rooms. SGL/DBL#35-$58.

Union Hotel and Annex (362 Bell Street, 93440; 344-2744) 20 rooms, restaurant, swimming pool, no-smoking rooms. SGL/DBL$75-$125.

Los Altos

Area Code 415
Los Altos Chamber of Commerce
321 University Avenue
Los Altos CA 94002
948-1455

Best Western Sea Pines Golf Resort (1945 Solano Avenue, 93402; 528-5252, Fax 528-8231) 20 rooms, restaurant, lounge, children under 18 free, meeting facilities, no-smoking rooms, no pets. SGL/DBL$79-$99.

Los Angeles

Area Code 213
Los Angeles Visitors and Convention Bureau
515 South Figueroa Street
Los Angeles CA 90071, 624-7300

RENTAL SOURCES: Bed and Breakfast Exchange (1458 Lincoln Avenue, Calistoga, 94515; 707-942-5900) reservation service for local bed and breakfasts. **Bed and Breakfast International** (Box 282910, 94128; 696-1690, Fax 696-1699, 800-872-4500) represents bed and breakfast accommodations throughout California. Accommodations available in private homes, houseboats on the Bay and inns. All rates include complimentary breakfast. SGL/DBL$50-$125. **Southern California Hotel Reservation Center** (800-537-7666, 800-527-9997 in California) represents hotels in the Los Angeles area. **Hotel Reservation Network** (8140 Walnut Hill Lane, Dallas TX 75231; 214-361-7351, Fax 361-7299, 800-92-HOTEL) hotel reservation service in Los Angeles and other California cities. **Southern California Hotel Reservation Center** (800-537-7666, 800-527-9997 in California) represents hotels in the Los Angeles area.

Airport Area

Airport Marina Hotel (8601 Lincoln Boulevard, 90045; 670-8111, Fax 337-1883, 800-225-8126) 761 rooms and suites, restaurant, outdoor swimming pool, valet laundry, fax service, transportation to local attractions, gift shop, travel agency, no-smoking rooms, free parking. SGL/DBL$89-$110, STS$195-$265.

Best Western Airpark Hotel (640 West Manchester Boulevard, 90301; 677-7378, Fax 674-1137, 800-528-1234) 72 rooms and suites, complimentary breakfast, outdoor swimming pool, spa, in-room refrigerators, complimentary newspaper, fax service, airport courtesy car, wheelchair access, no-smoking rooms, car rental, free parking. SGL/DBL$56-$82, STS$95-$120.

Best Western Airport Plaza Inn (1730 Centinela Avenue, 90301; 568-0071, Fax 337-1919, 800-528-1234, 800-233-8061 in California) 54 rooms, complimentary breakfast, in-room refrigerators, wheelchair access, tour service, laundry room, no-smoking rooms, exercise facilities, free parking, car rental. SGL/DBL$52-$82.

Best Western Inn and Suites (5005 West Century Boulevard, 90304; 310-677-7733, Fax 310-674-1137, 800-528-1234) 82 rooms, complimentary breakfast, outdoor swimming pool, spa, airport courtesy car, tours, in-room refrigerators, wheelchair access, laundry room, no-smoking rooms, no pets, free parking. SGL/DBL$69-$89, STS$69-$105.

Embassy Suites LAX-Century (9801 Airport Boulevard, 90045; 215-1000, Fax 215-1952, 800-362-2779) 215 suites, restaurant, lounge, indoor swimming pool, spa, exercise facilities, in-room refrigerators and mini-bars, valet laundry, fax service, computer hookups, meeting facilities for 300, laundry room, wheelchair access, no-smoking rooms, pets allowed, airport courtesy car, gift shop, car rental. SGL/DBL$154-$174.

Holiday Inn Los Angeles International Airport (9901 La Cienega Boulevard, 90045; 649-5151, Fax 670-3619, 800-HOLIDAY) 402 rooms and suites, restaurant, outdoor swimming pool, spa, free parking, fax and business services, babysitting services, valet laundry, complementary newspaper, gift shop, laundry room, exercise center, wheelchair access, airport transportation, meeting facilities for 300, no-smoking rooms, car rental, free parking. SGL/DBL$49-$102, STS$250-$500+.

Holiday Inn Crowne Plaza (5985 West Century Boulevard, 90045; 642-7500, Fax 417-3608, 800-HOLIDAY) 615 rooms and suites, restaurant, swimming pool, exercise center, meeting facilities for 750, concierge, wheelchair access, free parking, airport transportation, no pets. SGL$112-$131, DBL$127-$146, STS$200-$400.

Howard Johnson LAX Hotel (8620 Airport Boulevard, 90045; 645-7700, Fax 645-2958, 800-654-2000) 160 rooms and suites, restaurant, complimentary breakfast, outdoor swimming pool, spa, valet laundry, fax service, transportation to local attractions, in-room refrigerators, complimentary newspaper, tour service, airport courtesy car, wheelchair access, gift shop, car rental, free parking. SGL/DBL$71-$100.

Hyatt Regency Airport (6225 West Century Boulevard, 90045; 310-672-1234, Fax 310-641-6924, 800-233-1234) 594 rooms and suites, two restaurants, lounges, outdoor swimming pool, spa, meeting facilities, in-room refrigerators, mini-bars and safes, valet laundry, babysitting services, fax service, wheelchair access, no-smoking rooms, exercise facilities, airport courtesy car, pets allowed, gift shop, beauty and barber shop, car rental. SGL/DBL$115-$155, STS$300-$425.

Los Angeles Airport Hilton and Towers (5711 West Century Boulevard, 90045; 410-4000, Fax 410-6177, 800-445-8667) 1,279 rooms and suites, two restaurants, lounge, outdoor swimming pool, spa, in-room refrigerators and mini-bars, valet laundry, child care, fax and business services, transportation to local attractions, exercise facilities, wheelchair access, meeting facilities for 1,600, airport transportation, gift shop, car rental, pets allowed. SGL$130-$175, STS$295-$500.

Los Angeles Marriott Hotel Airport (5855 West Century Boulevard, 90045; 641-5700, 800-228-9290) 1,012 rooms and suites, restaurant, swimming pool, airport courtesy car, pets allowed, free parking. SGL$105-$140, DBL$105-$160, STS$275-$1,200

Quality Hotel Airport (5249 West Century Boulevard, 90045; 645-2200, 800-221-2222) 274 rooms and suites, restaurant, swimming pool, exercise facilities, wheelchair access, no-smoking rooms, no pets. SGL$56, DBL$64, STS$75.

Ramada LAX Airport South (5250 West El Segundo Boulevard, 90250; 536-9800, Fax 536-9535) 169 rooms and suites, restaurant, swimming pool, airport courtesy car, children under 18 free, free parking. SGL$85-$95, DBL$95-$105, STS$110-$130.

Ramada Renaissance LAX (9620 Airport Boulevard, 90045; 337-2800, Fax 216-6681) 505 rooms and suites, hospitality suites, restaurant, lounge, outdoor swimming pool, spa, in-room refrigerators, mini-bars and safes, valet laundry, babysitting services, children under 18 free, 24-hour room service, fax and business services, wheelchair access, no-smoking rooms, exercise facilities, gift shop, car rental. SGL/DBL$95-$175, STS$175-$800.

Roadway Inn LAX (4922 West Century Boulevard, 90304; 671-7213, Fax 671-1804, 800-999-1277) 136 rooms and suites, swimming pool, airport courtesy car, free parking. SGL$49-$55, DBL$54-$60, STS$59-$64.

Sheraton Plaza La Reina (6101 Century Boulevard, 90045; 642-1111, Fax 410-1267, 800-325-3535) 807 rooms and suites, two restaurants, lounge, outdoor heated swimming pool, spa, in-room mini-bars, valet laundry, 24-hour room service, meeting facilities for 1,000, complimentary newspaper, fax service, exercise center, airport courtesy car, laundry room, wheelchair access, no-smoking rooms, pets allowed, beauty and barber shop, gift shop, travel agency. SGL/DBL$115-$155, STS$195-$500.

Stouffer Concourse Hotel (5400 West Century Boulevard, 90045; 216-5858, Fax 670-1948, 800-468-3571) 750 rooms and suites, restaurant, lounge, complimentary breakfast, outdoor swimming pool, spa, saunas, in-room refrigerators and mini-bars, valet laundry, child care, 24-hour room service, fax and business services, complimentary newspaper, exercise facilities, no-smoking rooms, airport courtesy car, gift shop, car rental. SGL/DBL$105-$155, STS$450-$800.

TraveLodge (9750 Airport Boulevard, 90045; 310-338-9618, Fax 310-338-9618, 800-255-3050) 552 rooms and suites, restaurant, lounge, heated swimming pool, in-room refrigerators, tours, car rental, laundry room, wheelchair access, no-smoking rooms, meeting facilities for 1,100, exercise facilities, airport courtesy car. SGL/DBL$69-$79.

Downtown Area

Best Western Inn Towne Hotel (925 South Figueroa Street, 90015; 628-2222, Fax 687-0566, 800-528-1234) 168 rooms and suites, restaurant, lounge, outdoor swimming pool, free parking, no pets, valet laundry, meeting facilities, fax service, tours, car rental. SGL/DBL$60-$86, STS$120-$140.

Best Western Dragon Gate Inn (818 North Hill Street, 90012; 617-3077, Fax 680-3653, 800-528-1234) 50 rooms, restaurant, wheelchair access, no-smoking rooms, in-room safes, valet laundry, children under 12 free, no pets, transportation to local attractions, fax service, barber and beauty shop, gift shop. SGL/DBL$49-$63.

Best Western The Mayfair (1256 West 7th Street, 90017; 484-9789, Fax 484-2769, 800-528-1234) 295 rooms, restaurant, outdoor swimming pool, spa, private sauna, free parking, in-room refrigerators and microwaves, transportation to local attractions, meeting and conference facilities for 200, room service, no-smoking rooms, gift shop, valet laundry, wheelchair access, exercise facilities, pets allowed. SGL$75-$115, DBL$85-$130, STS$130-$250.

Best Western Executive Motor Inn Mid-Wilshire (603 South New Hampshire Avenue, 900005; 385-4444, Fax 380-5413, 800-528-1234, 800-325-2525) 90 rooms, restaurant, complimentary breakfast, swimming pool, laundry room, fax service, exercise facilities, free parking, no-smoking rooms. SGL/DBL$52-$62.

The Biltmore Hotel (506 South Grand Avenue, 90071; 624-1011, Fax 612-1545, 800-421-8000, 800-252-0175 in California) 700 rooms and suites, two restaurants, 24-hour room service, indoor swimming pool, spa, exercise facilities, airport courtesy car, downtown shuttle, babysitting services, tours, wheelchair access, no-smoking rooms, valet laundry. SGL/DBL$175-$275, STS$400-$1,800.

Budget Inn (1710 West Seventh Street, 90016; 483-3470, Fax 484-2142) 50 rooms, swimming pool, free parking. SGL/DBL$35-$65.

Century City Inn (10330 West Olympic Boulevard, 90064; 553-1000, Fax 277-1633, 800-553-1005) 40 rooms and suites, airport transportation, lighted tennis courts, exercise facilities, wheelchair access, no-smoking rooms, pets allowed. SGL$99-$119, DBL$109-$129, STS$129-$159.

Chancellor Hotel and Residence (535 South Grand Avenue, 90071; 624-0000, Fax 626-9906, 800-628-4900) 114 rooms and suites, restaurant, lounge, outdoor swimming pool, spa, exercise facilities, valet laundry, computer and fax outlets, limousine service. SGL/DBL$175-$225, STS$350-$1,000.

The Checkers Hotel (535 South Grand Avenue, 90071; 624-0000, Fax 626-9906, 800-628-4900) 188 rooms and suites, restaurant, lounge, swimming pool, jacuzzi, airport transportation, room service, exercise facilities, pets allowed, tours, wheelchair access, no-smoking rooms. SGL/DBL$175-$225, STS$350-$1,000.

City Center Motel (1135 West Seventh Street, 90017; 628-7141) 42 rooms and suits, swimming pool, airport transportation, room service, laundry room, free parking. SGL/DBL$35-$49.

Comfort Inn Eagle Rock (2300 Colorado Boulevard, 90041; 256-1199, Fax 255-7768, 800-221-2222) 58 rooms, restaurant, complimentary breakfast, outdoor swimming pool, whirlpool, spa, room service, laundry room, fax service, wheelchair access, free parking, no pets, located near Rose Bowl. SGL/DBL$48-$100.

Comfort Inn Towne (4122 South Western Avenue, 90062; 294-5200, 800-221-2222) 41 rooms, restaurant, whirlpools, meeting facilities, wheelchair access, no pets. SGL$52-$70, DBL$57-$62.

Comfort Inn Wilshire (3400 West 3rd Street, 90020; 385-0061, 800-221-2222) 130 rooms, restaurant, swimming pool, meeting facilities, no pets, free parking. SGL/DBL$49-$54, DBL$53-$59.

Figueroa Hotel (939 South Figueroa Street, 90015; 627-8971, Fax 689-0305, 800-421-9092, 800-331-5151 in California) 285 rooms and suites, restaurant, outdoor swimming pool, spa, airport transportation, transportation to local attractions, laundry room, tours, free parking, valet laundry, fax service, SGL/DBL$64-$98, STS$120+.

Halekulani Los Angeles (Eighth and Figueroa Street, 90071; 278-9699, Fax 278-5436) 390 rooms and suites, restaurant, indoor and outdoor swimming pools, spa, exercise facilities, in-room refrigerators, mini-bars and safes, fax service, car rental, beauty and barber shop, no-smoking rooms, wheelchair access. SGL/DBL$115-$135.

Hilton Midtown (400 North Vermont Avenue, 90004; 662-4883, Fax 662-2974, 800-950-4458 in California) 205 rooms and suites, in-room mini-bars, restaurant, lounge, complimentary newspaper, outdoor swimming pool, spa, sauna, wheelchair access, no-smoking rooms, fax service, business center, meeting facilities for 600, airport transportation, exercise facilities, car rental, travel agency, SGL/DBL$89-$154+, STS$225-$575+.

Hilton and Towers (930 Wilshire Boulevard, 90017; 629-4321, Fax 488-9869) 900 rooms and suites, four restaurants, lounge, outdoor swimming pool, spa, exercise facilities, wheelchair access, valet laundry, babysitting services, no-smoking rooms, beauty and barber shops, car rental, travel agency, SGL$155-$205, DBL$175-$225, STS$370+.

Hilton University (3540 South Figueroa Street, 90007; 748-4141, Fax 748-0043) 241 rooms and suites, restaurant, outdoor swimming pool, spa, fax service, wheelchair access, free parking, no-smoking rooms, car rental, gift shop, SGL/DBL$89-$129.

Holiday Inn (750 South Garland Avenue, 90017; 628-5242, Fax 628-1201, 800-HOLIDAY) 205 rooms and suites, restaurant, lounge, outdoor swimming pool, car rental, meeting facilities for 150, valet laundry, fax services, laundry room, free parking, wheelchair access, no-smoking rooms. SGL/DBL$70-$120, STS$135-$149.

Holiday Inn Convention Center (1020 South Figueroa, 90015; 748-1291, Fax 748-6028, 800-HOLIDAY) 195 rooms, restaurant, outdoor swimming pool, spa, exercise facilities, wheelchair access, airport transportation, valet laundry, meeting facilities for 300, fax services, transportation to area attractions, gift shop, wheelchair access, no-smoking rooms. free parking, pets allowed. SGL$80-$120, DBL$95-$135, STS$160-$250.

Hotel Intercontinental at California Plaza (251 South Olive Street, 90012; 670-7284; Fax 216-9521) 469 rooms and suites, restaurant, lounge, in-room refrigerators and mini-bars, valet laundry, fax services, restaurant, outdoor swimming pool, exercise facilities, wheelchair access, gift shop. SGL$95+, DBL$105+.

Howard Johnson Downtown (1640 Marengo Street, 90033; 223-3841, Fax 222-4039, 800-654-2000) 122 rooms, restaurant, lounge, outdoor swimming pool, wheelchair access, valet laundry, meeting facilities, tours, fax service, airport transportation, transportation to local attractions, room service, pets allowed, free parking, car rental, no-smoking rooms. SGL/DBL$64-$74+.

Hyatt Regency Los Angeles (711 South Hope Street, 90017; 683-1235, Fax 612-3179, 800-233-1234) 487 rooms and suites, outdoor spa, mini-bars, two restaurants, transportation to local attractions, computer hookups, meeting facilities, lounge, exercise center, pets allowed, airport courtesy car, wheelchair access, no-smoking rooms. SGL$79-$175, DBL$89-$100, STS$250-$650.

Hyatt Wilshire (3513 Wilshire Boulevard, 90010; 381-7411) 396 rooms, restaurant, swimming pool, exercise facilities, airport transportation. SGL$110-$130, DBL$130-$150, STS$450-$650.

The Inn at 657 (657 West 23rd Street, 90007; 741-2200, 800-347-7512) 7 rooms and suites, bed and breakfast, complimentary breakfast, some suites with full kitchen, fax service, no-smoking rooms, free parking. SGL/DBL$65+, STS$95+.

Kawada Hotel (200 South Hill Street, 90012; 621-4455, Fax 687-4455, 800-752-9232) 116 rooms and suites, restaurant, lounge, in-room refrigerators, kitchenettes, valet laundry, restaurant, babysitting services, wheelchair access. SGL/DBL$55-$75+, STS$125+.

Kent Inn Motel (920 South Figueroa Street, 90015; 626-8701) 91 rooms, restaurant, lounge, swimming pool, laundry room, babysitting services, tours, room service, free parking. SGL$40-$45, DBL$50-$55.

Los Angeles Athletic Club (431 West Seventh Street, 90014; 625-2211, Fax 689-1194) 72 rooms and suites, restaurant, lounge, complimentary breakfast, indoor swimming pool, spa, exercise facilities, fax service, no-smoking rooms, beauty and barber shops, gift shop. SGL/DBL$110-$135, STS$185+.

Los Angeles Hamilton Tourist Inn (3160 West Eighth Street, 90005; 384-7768, 800-443-5300) 40 rooms, restaurant, lounge, spa, in-suite saunas, complimentary breakfast, in-room refrigerators, valet laundry, 24-hour room service, fax service, transportation to Universal Studios, gift shop, travel agency, free parking. SGL/DBL$59-$99+.

Los Angeles Hilton and Towers (930 Wilshire Boulevard, 90017; 629-4321) 900 rooms and suites, restaurant, swimming pool, airport transportation, wheelchair access, no-smoking rooms, exercise facilities. SGL/DBL$160-$201+, STS$375-$525+.

Los Angeles Inn (1240 West Seventh Street, 90017; 626-3590) 26 rooms, tours, complimentary newspaper. SGL$49-$69, DBL$59-$89.

Mayfair Hotel (1256 West Seventh Street, 90017; 484-9789, Fax 484-2769, 800-821-8682) 296 rooms and suites, restaurant, lounge, room service, babysitting services, airport courtesy car, exercise facilities, free parking. SGL$95-$110, DBL$110-$125, STS$150-$350.

Metro Plaza Hotel (701 North Main Street, 90012; 680-0200, Fax 620-0200, 800-223-2223) 81 rooms and suites, in-room microwaves and refrigerators, jacuzzis, restaurant, airport transportation, valet laundry, beauty and barber shop, car rental, babysitting services, wheelchair access, no-smoking rooms, free parking. SGL/DBL$59-$79, STS$99-$150+.

Milner Hotel (813 South Flower Street, 90017; 627-6981, 800-521-0592) 175 rooms, restaurant, lounge, laundry room, kitchenettes, airport transportation. SGL$35-$40, DBL$40-$60, STS$60-$65.

Miyako Hotel (328 East First Street, 90012; 617-2000, Fax 617-2700, 800-228-6596) 174 rooms and suites, restaurant, spa, exercise facilities, in-room refrigerators and safes, valet laundry, wheelchair access, no-smoking rooms, fax, business services, travel agency, car rental. SGL/DBL$85-$107, STS$194-$204.

Morrison Hotel (1246 South Hope Street, 90015; 748-6442) 111 rooms, restaurant, complimentary breakfast, valet laundry, laundry room, no-smoking rooms. SGL/DBL$45-$65.

Motel De Ville (1123 West Seventh Street, 90017; 624-8474, Fax 624-7652) 60 rooms, restaurant, outdoor swimming pool, spa, airport courtesy car, car rental, fax service, free parking. SGL/DBL$35-$45.

New Olympian Hotel (1903 West Olympic Boulevard, 90006; 385-7141, 800-421-9620, 800-252-0489 in California) 126 rooms and suites, two restaurants, lounge, outdoor swimming pool, spa, shopping center, in-room refrigerators, mini-bars and safes, airport transportation, transportation to the downtown area, 24-hour room service, babysitting services, beauty and barber shop, travel agency, fax service, no-smoking rooms, free parking. SGL/DBL$48-$72, STS$65-$92.

The New Otani Hotel and Garden (120 South Los Angeles Street, 90012; 629-1200, Fax 622-0980, 800-421-8795, 800-252-0197 in California) 440 rooms and suites, restaurant, lounge, airport transportation, babysitting services, tours, wheelchair access, no-smoking rooms. pets allowed. SGL/DBL$135-$195, STS$385-$750.

Oasis Motel (2200 West Olympic Boulevard, 90006; 385-4191, Fax 480-1682) 70 rooms, swimming pool, kitchenettes, tours, free parking, in-room refrigerators. SGL$36-$40, DBL$39-$48.

The Orchid Hotel (819 South Flower Street, 90017; 624-5855, Fax 624-8740) 65 rooms and suites, restaurant, transportation to local attractions, fax service, laundry room, tours, laundry room, travel agency. SGL/DBL$30-$42, STS$50+.

Rotex Plaza Hotel (3411 West Olympic Boulevard, 90019; 734-7373) 66 rooms and suites, restaurant, lounge, airport courtesy car, laundry room, babysitting services, pets allowed, tours, free parking. SGL$79-$84, DBL$89, STS$150.

Royal Host Olympic Motel (901 West Olympic Boulevard, 90015; 626-6255) 54 rooms, restaurant, outdoor swimming pool, in-room refrigerators, tours, kitchenettes, free parking. SGL/DBL$36-$50.

Sheraton Grande Hotel (333 South Figueroa Street, 90071; 617-1133, Fax 613-0291, 800-325-3535) 469 rooms and suites, three restaurants, lounge, outdoor heated swimming pool, exercise center, in-room refrigerators, mini-bars and safes, fax service, meeting facilities for 1,500, gift shop, complimentary newspaper, transportation to area attractions, wheelchair access, airport transportation, no-smoking rooms, car rental. SGL$175-$200, DBL$200-$225, STS$250-$900.

Sheraton Town House (2961 Wilshire Boulevard, 90010; 382-7171, Fax 487-7148, 800-325-3535) 272 rooms and suites, two restaurants, outdoor heated swimming pool, sauna, lighted tennis courts, meeting facilities for 1,000, gift shop, airport transportation, wheelchair access, no-smoking rooms. SGL$88-$123, DBL$100-$138, STS$175-$250.

Stillwell Hotel (838 Grand Avenue, 90017; 627-1151, Fax 622-8940, 800-553-4774) 250 rooms and suites, restaurant, no-smoking rooms, valet laundry, fax service, beauty and barber shop, laundry room, travel agency. SGL/DBL$39-$69.

University Hilton Hotel (3540 South Figueroa, 90007; 748-4141, Fax 748-0043, 800-445-8667, 800-872-1104) 250 rooms and suites, restaurant, swimming pool, jacuzzi, meeting facilities for 850, airport transportation, wheelchair access. SGL/DBL$90-$145, STS$400-$600.

Vagabond Inn USC (3101 South Figueroa Street, 90007; 746-1530, 800-522-1555) 72 rooms and suites, restaurant, complimentary breakfast, heated swimming pool, pets allowed, laundry room, kitchenettes, tours, airport transportation, free local telephone calls, no-smoking rooms, children under 18 free, fax service, complimentary newspaper. SGL$59-$64, DBL$64-$74.

Vagabond Inn Downtown (1904 West Olympic Boulevard, 90006; 380-9393, Fax 487-2662, 800-522-1555) 54 rooms, restaurant, complimentary breakfast, swimming pool, pets allowed, free parking, airport transportation, free local telephone calls, no-smoking rooms, children under 18 free, fax service, complimentary newspaper. SGL$50-$54, DBL$55-$64.

Vermont Motel (1717 South Vermont Avenue, 90006; 730-1578) 38 rooms, jacuzzi, free parking. SGL$30-$40, DBL$40-$50, STS$60-$70.

The Westin Bonaventure (404 South Figueroa Street, 90071; 624-1000, Fax 612-4800, 800-228-3000) 1,475 rooms and suites, restaurant, outdoor swimming pool, spa, exercise facilities, shopping center, in-room refrigerators, 24-hour room service, fax service, business center, meeting facilities for 1,500, transportation to area attractions, wheelchair access, exercise center, tennis, pets allowed, car rental. SGL/DBL$150-$190, STS$325-$2,000+.

Wilshire Koreana Hotel (3513 Wilshire Boulevard, 90010; 381-7411, Fax 386-7379, 800-233-1234) 388 rooms and suites, two restaurants, lounge, outdoor swimming pool, valet laundry, child care, fax service, wheelchair access, no-smoking rooms, beauty and barber shop, car rental. SGL/DBL$130-$170, STS$250-$550.

Wilshire Royale Hotel (2619 Wilshire Boulevard, 90057; 387-5311, Fax 380-8174, 800-421-8072) 200 rooms and suites, restaurant, outdoor swimming pool, spa, kitchenettes, valet laundry, child care, fax service, complimentary newspaper, beauty and barber shop, gift shop, tennis. SGL/DBL$65-$80, STS$95-$150.

Hollywood Area

Best Western Sunset Plaza Hotel (8400 Sunset Boulevard, 90069; 654-0750, 800-528-1234) 86 rooms, restaurant, lounge, complimentary breakfast, heated swimming pool, no pets, VCRs, children under 12 free. SGL$69-$79, DBL$75-$165.

Dunes Sunset Motel (5625 Sunset Boulevard, 90028; 467-5171, Fax 469-1962, 800-452-3863, 800-443-8637 in California) 57 rooms, restaurant, lounge, room service, airport courtesy car, free parking. SGL$54-$59, DBL$59+.

Park Sunset Hotel (8462 Sunset Boulevard, 90069; 654-6470, Fax 654-6470, 800-821-3660) 84 rooms and suites, restaurant, swimming pool, in-room refrigerators and safes, kitchenettes, valet laundry, babysitting services, fax and business services, airport transportation, no-smoking rooms, beauty and barber shop, free parking. SGL/DBL$79-$89, STS$139-$169+.

Sunset Palms Motel (7160 Sunset Boulevard, 90046; 874-6660) 40 rooms. SGL$33-$38, DBL$36-$40.

Sunset Plaza Hotel (8400 Sunset Boulevard, 90069; 654-0750, 800-421-3653, 800-252-0645 in California) 86 rooms and suites, swimming pool, airport transportation, free parking. SGL$67-$78, DBL$77-$82, STS$119-$140.

Westside Area

Best Western Royal Palace Hotel (2528 Sepulveda Boulevard, 90064; 310-477-9066, Fax 478-4133, 800-528-1234) 55 rooms and suites, complimentary breakfast, outdoor swimming pool, spa, whirlpool, in-room refrigerators, kitchenettes, fax service, laundry room, child care, exercise facilities, free parking, car rental, no pets. SGL$55-$75, STS$70-$81.

Beverly Grand Hotel (7257 Beverly Boulevard, 90036; 939-1653, Fax 930-0176, 800-899-2383 in California) 41 rooms and suites, restaurant, complimentary breakfast, no-smoking rooms, free parking. SGL/DBL$48-$90, STS$120-$135.

Beverly Hillcrest Hotel (1224 South Beverly Drive, 90035; 277-2800, 800-421-3212, 800-252-0174 in California) 150 rooms and suites, restaurant, in-room refrigerators, outdoor swimming pool, fax service, child care, valet laundry. SGL$110-$125, DBL$125-$140, STS$250-$420.

Beverly Plaza Hotel (8384 West Third Street, 90048; 658-6600, Fax 653-3464, 800-624-6835, 800-334-6835 in California) 116 suites, restaurant, lounge, outdoor swimming pool, sauna, exercise facilities, valet laundry, 24-hour room service, fax service, complimentary newspaper, transportation to airport and local attractions, beauty and barber shop, wheelchair access, no-smoking rooms. SGL/DBL$98-$168.

Beverly Hills Comstock Hotel (10300 Wilshire Boulevard, 90024; 275-5575, 800-343-2184) 106 rooms and suites, restaurant, outdoor swimming pool, spa, in-room safes, complimentary newspaper, kitchenettes, exercise facilities, airport transportation, fax service, babysitting services, valet laundry, car rental, gift shop, complimentary newspaper, STS$95-$290.

Bevonshire Lodge Motel (7575 Beverly Boulevard, 90036; 936-6154) 25 rooms and suites, kitchenettes, babysitting services, swimming pool, airport transportation, free parking. SGL/DBL$30-$45, STS$86-$96.

Carlyle Inn (1119 South Robertson Boulevard, 90035; 275-4445, Fax 850-0496, 800-3-CARLYL) 32 rooms and suites, restaurant, complimentary breakfast, spa, computer hookups, valet services, fax services, transportation to local attractions, complimentary afternoon tea and newspaper, no-smoking rooms. SGL/DBL$95-$130, STS$140+.

Century Plaza Hotel and Tower (2025 Avenue of the Stars, 90067; 277-2000, Fax 551-3355, 800-228-3000) 996 rooms and suites, four restaurants, lounges, two outdoor swimming pools, whirlpools, spa, exercise facilities, fax and business services, wheelchair access, in-room refrigerators, meeting facilities for 3,000, room service, pets allowed, no-smoking rooms, tennis, car rental, gift shop, travel agency. SGL/DBL$180-$295, STS$300-$5,000.

Century Wilshire Hotel (10776 Wilshire Boulevard, 90024; 474-4506, Fax 474-2535, 800-421-7223) 130 rooms and suites, swimming pool, free parking. SGL$65-$75, DBL$75-$85, STS$85-$150.

Crest Motel (7701 Beverly Boulevard, 90036; 931-8100) 28 rooms, outdoor swimming pool, located within walking distance of the Farmers Market, free parking. SGL/DBL$34-$38.

Days Inn Wilshire (3900 Wilshire Boulevard, 90010; 736-5222, Fax 736-5038, 800-325-2525) 86 rooms and suites, restaurant, lounge, swimming pool, whirlpools, car rental, fax service, gift shop, children under 12 free, wheelchair access, no-smoking rooms, gift shop, free parking. SGL$59-$79, STS$85-$140.

Dunes Wilshire Motor Hotel (4300 Wilshire Boulevard, 90010; 938-1962, Fax 469-1962, 800-452-3863, 800-443-8637 in California) 58 rooms, restaurant, kitchenettes, valet laundry, outdoor swimming pool, airport transportation, free parking. SGL/DBL$53-$67.

Four Seasons Hotel (300 South Doheny Drive, 90048; 273-2222, Fax 859-3824, 800-332-3442) 285 rooms and suites, restaurant, outdoor swimming pool, spa, exercise facilities, in-room safes and mini-bars, valet laundry, fax service, complimentary newspaper, transportation to Rodeo Drive, free parking, wheelchair access, no-smoking rooms, car rental, gift shop. SGL/DBL$250-$315, STS$355-$2000.

Holiday Inn Brentwood (170 North Church Lane, 90049; 310-476-6411, Fax 310-472-1157, 800-HOLIDAY) 211 rooms and suites, restaurant, lounge, outdoor heated swimming pool, valet laundry, fax service, laundry room, airport transportation, exercise facilities, pets allowed, free parking. SGL$98-$150, STS$210+.

Holiday Inn Westwood (10740 Wilshire Boulevard, 90024; 475-8711, Fax 475-5220, 800-472-8556, 800-HOLIDAY) 296 rooms and suites, restaurant, lounge, outdoor swimming pool, spa, in-room refrigerators and mini-bars, valet laundry, fax and business services, transportation to area attractions, gift shop, wheelchair access, no-smoking rooms, exercise center, tours, meeting facilities for 300, free parking, car rental. SGL$120-$140, STS$225.

Hotel Bel Air (701 Stone Canyon Road, 90077; 472-1211, Fax 854-0926, 800-648-4097) 75 rooms and suites, restaurant, swimming pool, airport transportation, wheelchair access. SGL$225-$395, STS$500-$2,000.

Capri Motel (9620 Airport Boulevard, 90045; 645-7700) 51 rooms, swimming pool, airport courtesy car. SGL$36-$40, DBL$40-$60.

Hotel Del Capri (10587 Wilshire Boulevard, 90024; 474-3511, Fax 824-0594, 800-444-6835) 82 rooms and suites, complimentary breakfast, outdoor heated swimming pool, in-room refrigerators, kitchenettes, valet laundry, fax service, transportation available to local area, airport transportation, pets allowed, free parking, car rental. SGL$85-$105, STS$110-$140.

Hotel Nikko (465 South La Cienega Boulevard, 90048; 247-0400, Fax 247-0315, 800-645-5687) 344 rooms and suites, restaurant, lounge, complimentary breakfast, outdoor swimming pool, spa, valet laundry, 24-hour room service, child care, wheelchair access, no-smoking rooms, gift shop, car rental. SGL/DBL$220-$320, STS$325-$1,200.

Nutel Motel (1906 West Third Street, 90057; 483-6681, Fax 483-9793) 137 rooms and suites, restaurant, airport transportation, room service, tours, free parking. SGL$30-$34, DBL$36-$44, STS$60-$85.

Park Plaza Lodge (6001 West Third Street, 90036; 931-1501) 49 rooms, restaurant, lounge, complimentary breakfast, outdoor swimming pool, exercise facilities, free parking, airport transportation. SGL$45-$55.

St. Regis Motor Hotel (11955 Wilshire Boulevard, 90025; 477-6021, Fax 273-2162) 80 rooms and suites, restaurant, kitchenettes, outdoor swimming pool. SGL/DBL$45-$60, STS$60-$80.

Skyways Airport Hotel (9250 Airport Boulevard, 90045; 670-2900, Fax 410-1787, 800-336-0024) 95 rooms, restaurant, exercise facilities, airport transportation, no-smoking rooms, pets allowed. SGL$45-$50, DBL$50-$58+.

Hotel Sofitel Ma Maison (8555 Beverly Boulevard, 90048; 278-5444, Fax 657-2816, 800-221-4542) 311 rooms and suites, restaurant, outdoor swimming pool, spa, exercise facilities, in-room refrigerators and mini-bars, valet laundry, 24-hour room service, fax service, complimentary newspaper, gift shop, wheelchair access, no-smoking rooms, car rental. SGL/DBL$185-$205, STS$250-$450.

J.W. Marriott Hotel at Century City (2151 Avenue of the Starts, 90067; 277-2777, Fax 785-9240, 800-228-9290, 800-447-9966 in California) 475 rooms and suites, restaurant, lounge, 24-hour room service, gift shop, indoor and outdoor swimming pools, concierge, transportation to local attractions, exercise facilities, no-smoking rooms, wheelchair access. SGL$239-$259, DBL$269-$289, STS$326-$2,500.

Ramada Hotel Beverly Hills (1150 South Beverly Drive, 90035; 553-6561, Fax 277-4463, 800-272-6232) 260 rooms and suites, restaurant, in-room refrigerators and microwaves, fax service, transportation to local attractions, complimentary newspaper, children under 18 free, outdoor swimming pool, exercise facilities, no-smoking rooms, gift shop, free parking. SGL/DBL$115-$165, STS$180-$250.

TraveLodge West (10740 Santa Monica Boulevard, 90025; 310-474-4576, Fax 310-470-3117, 800-255-3050) 55 rooms, complimentary breakfast, outdoor heated swimming pool, in-room refrigerators, complimentary newspaper, fax service, complimentary newspaper, free parking, no-smoking rooms, no pets. SGL$62-$90.

Wilshire Comfort Inn (3400 West Third Street, 90020; 385-0061, Fax 385-8517, 800-228-5150 in California) 130 rooms, restaurant, lounge, babysitting services, outdoor swimming pool, tour bus service, laundry room, free parking. SGL/DBL$49-$54.

Bel Age Hotel (1020 North San Vincente, 90069; 854-1111, Fax 476-5890) 191 suites, restaurant, swimming pool, airport transportation, wheelchair access. SGL/DBL$245-$500+.

Best Western Eagle Rock Inn (2911 Colorado Boulevard, 90041; 256-7711, Fax 255-6750, 800-528-1234) 50 rooms, complimentary breakfast, swimming pool, in-room refrigerators, complimentary newspaper, whirlpool, fax service, wheelchair access, no-smoking rooms. SGL/DBL$65-$75.

Best Western Hollywood (6141 Franklin Avenue, 90028; 464-5181, Fax 962-0536, 800-528-1234) 82 rooms, restaurant, swimming pool, free parking, children under 12 free, pets allowed. SGL$55-$75, DBL$60-$85.

Best Western Hotel Tokyo (328 East First Street, 90012; 617-2000, Fax 895-0623, 800-228-6596, 800-228-6596 in California) 164 rooms and suites, restaurant. SGL$78-$95, DBL$88-$105, STS$170.

Best Western Pacific Hotel (11250 Santa Monica Boulevard, 90025; 310-478-1400, 800-528-1234) 78 rooms, complimentary breakfast, exercise facilities, children under 18 free, fax service, wheelchair access, no-smoking rooms, no pets. SGL/DBL$54-$89.

Best Western Willow Tree Inn (1919 West Artesia Boulevard, 90220; 310-537-6700, 800-528-1234) 96 rooms, restaurant, complimentary breakfast, swimming pool, children under 12 free, airport transportation, no-smoking rooms, no pets. SGL/DBL$48-$65.

Brandon Hotel (733-35 South Hartford Avenue, 90017; 483-0632) 80 rooms and efficiencies, exercise facilities, airport courtesy car, free parking. SGL$23-$32, DBL$25-$36.

Brentwood Suites Hotel (199 North Church Lane, 90049; 476-6255) 60 suites, swimming pool, exercise facilities, laundry room, kitchenettes, pets allowed, free parking. STS$85-$175.

Chesterfield Hotel Century City-Beverly Hills (10320 Olympic Boulevard, 90064; 556-2777, Fax 203-0563) 134 rooms and suites, restaurant, exercise facilities, wheelchair access, no-smoking rooms. SGL$125-$164, DBL$135-$185, STS$185-$225.

Clark Hotel (426 South Hill Street, 90013; 624-4121, 800-223-9868) 518 rooms and suites, restaurant, lounge, airport courtesy car, kitchenettes, babysitting service, tours, SGL$35-$45, DBL$35-$50, STS$60.

Clark Plaza Motel (141 South Clark Drive, 90048; 278-9310, Fax 274-5786, 800-421-0745, 800-252-0268 in California) 105 1- and 2-bedroom suites, complimentary breakfast, swimming pool. 1BR$125-$145, 2BR$150-$180.

Clarion Carriage House Inn (927 Hilgard Avenue, 90024; 208-3945, 800-221-2222) 47 rooms, restaurant, complimentary breakfast, swimming pool, whirlpools wheelchair access, free parking, no pets. SGL$90-$95, DBL$95-$100.

Other Areas

Comfort Inn (17111 Clark Avenue, 90706; 920-8853, 800-221-2222) 70 rooms, restaurant, complimentary breakfast, swimming pool, wheelchair access, no pets. SGL/DBL$39-$47.

Czoschke Bed and Breakfast (Bed and Breakfast International) 2 rooms, complimentary breakfast, no smoking. SGL/DBL$68.

Days Inn (21725 East Gateway Drive, 91765; 714-860-5440, Fax 714-860-8224. 800-325-2525) 184 rooms, restaurant, swimming pool, airport transportation, wheelchair access, no-smoking rooms. SGL$59-$85, DBL$69-$95.

Eastlake Victorian Inn (1442 Kellam Avenue, 90026; 250-1620) 9 rooms and suites, bed and breakfast, complimentary breakfast, no-smoking, free parking. SGL/DBL$49-$99, STS$125-$150.

Econo Lodge (457 South Mariposa Avenue, 90020; 380-6910, 800-424-4777) 47 rooms, outdoor swimming pool, sauna, whirlpool, exercise facilities, wheelchair access, children under 18 free. SGL/DBL$45-$55.

Executive Motor Inn Mariposa (458 South Mariposa Avenue, 90020; 380-6910, 800-453-4511) 50 rooms and suites, restaurant, swimming pool, room service, laundry room, exercise facilities, free parking. SGL$40, DBL$45, STS$59.

Highland Gardens Hotel (7047 Franklin Avenue, 90028; 850-0536) 70 rooms and suites, in-room refrigerators, kitchenettes, fax service, laundry room, outdoor swimming pool, free parking. SGL/DBL$60-$70, STS$70-$100.

The Huntington Hotel (752 South Main Street, 90014; 627-3186) 100 rooms and suites, restaurant, lounge, laundry room, tours, SGL$27-$32, DBL$34-$45, STS$70-$125.

Jerry's Motel (285 South Lucas Avenue, 90026; 481-0921) 10 rooms, restaurant, laundry room, tours, room service, free parking. SGL$32-$45, DBL$37-$40.

Le Dugy Hotel (1000 Westmount Drive, 90069; 657-7400, Fax 854-6744, 800-424-4443) 103 suites, restaurant, swimming pool, no-smoking rooms. SGL/DBL$150-$225

Le Parc (733 North West Knoll Drive, 90069; 855-8888, Fax 659-7812) 154 suites, restaurant, swimming pool, lighted tennis courts, exercise facilities, no-smoking rooms. SGL/DBL$165-$255.

Loyola Marymount University (Loyola Boulevard and 80th Street, 90045; 642-2975, Fax 338-1808) 1,500 rooms, restaurant, laundry room, babysitting services, swimming pool, spa, exercise facilities, tennis, free parking.

Mitchell Hotel (1072 West Sixth Street, 90017; 481-2477) 61 rooms and efficiencies. SGL/DBL$23-$28.

Mid-Wilshire Guest House (716 South Bronson Avenue, 90005; 738-1817) 4 rooms, bed and breakfast, complimentary breakfast, no-smoking rooms, free parking. SGL/DBL$35-$60.

Park Plaza Hotel (607 South Park View, 90057; 384-5281) 40 rooms and suites, restaurant, indoor swimming pool, exercise facilities, valet laundry, babystting services, beauty and barber shop, laundry room, free parking. SGL/DBL$35-$65, STS$55-$75+.

Hotel Los Angeles (1255 West Temple Street, 90266; 250-8925) 30 rooms, restaurant, jacuzzis, tours, laundry room, free parking. SGL$54-$60, DBL$62-$68, STS$70-$92.

Quality Inn (7330 Eastern Avenue, 90201; 928-3452, Fax 928-9851, 800-221-2222) 128 rooms and suites, restaurant, complimentary breakfast, outdoor swimming pool, spa, whirlpool, exercise center, meeting facilities, car rental, in-room refrigerators, laundry room, no-smoking rooms, free parking, no pets. SGL/DBL$60-$90, STS$70-$90+.

Salisbury House (2273 West 20th Street, 90018) 5 rooms and suites, bed and breakfast, complimentary breakfast, no-smoking rooms, free parking. SGL/DBL$65-$85, STS$80-$90.

Sunset Marquis Hotel and Villas (1200 North Alta Loma Road, 90069; 657-1333, Fax 652-5300, 800-858-9758) 120 suites and villas, restaurant, two swimming pools, spa, exercise facilities, in-room refrigerators, mini-bars and safes, valet laundry, fax services, complimentary newspaper, complimentary limo service within seven miles, gift shop, laundry room, no-smoking rooms, free parking, car rental. SGL/DBL$215-$1,000.

Terrace Manor (1353 Alvarado Terrace, 90006; 381-1478) 4 rooms and suites, bed and breakfast, complimentary breakfast, free parking. SGL/DBL$70-$100.

UCLA Conference Services (310 DeNeve Drive, 90024; 825-5305, Fax 206-7122) 2,375 rooms and suites, restaurant, swimming pool, exercise facilities, airport transportation. SGL$40-$60, STS$48-$124.

University of Southern California Summer Conferences (642 West 34th Street, 90089; 743-2022, Fax 749-0578) 1,250 rooms and suites, kitchen units, wheelchair access, indoor and outdoor swimming pools, laundry room, travel agency. SGL$21-$27, DBL$14-$17, STS$17-$27.

Westwood Marquis Hotel and Gardens (930 Hilgard Avenue, 90024; 208-8765, Fax 824-0355, 800-421-2317) 258 suites, restaurant, two outdoor swimming pools, spa, airport transportation, no-smoking rooms, in-room fax and computer hookups, valet laundry, 24-hour room service, transportation to local areas, beauty and barber shop, exercise facilities, pets allowed, car rental. STS$220-$650.

Los Banos

Area Code 209
Los Banos Chamber of Commerce
402 West Pacheco Boulevard
Los Banos CA 93635
826-2495

Bonanza Motel (349 West Pacheco Boulevard, 93635; 826-3872) 38 rooms, swimming pool, no-smoking rooms. SGL$30, DBL$35-$45.

Los Olivos

Area Code 805

Los Olivos Grand Hotel (2860 Grand Avenue, 93441; 688-7788, Fax 688-1942, 800-446-2455) 21 rooms, restaurant, complimentary breakfast, swimming pool, airport transportation, no-smoking rooms. SGL/DBL$150-$235.

Zaca Lake Resort (Box 187, 93441; 688-4891) 15 rooms, complimentary breakfast, wheelchair-access rooms. SGL/DBL$75-$125+.

Los Osos

Area Code 805

Best Western Sea Pines Golf Resort (1945 Solano Avenue, 93402; 528-5252, Fax 528-8231, 800-528-1234) 20 rooms, restaurant, golf, no-smoking rooms, no pets. SGL/DBL$79-$99.

Lost Hills

Area Code 805

Economy Inns of America (14684 Aloma Street, 93249; 797-2371, 800-826-0778) 76 rooms, swimming pool. SGL/DBL$24-$38.

Motel 6 (14685 Warren Street, 93249; 797-2371, 505-891-6161) 46 rooms. SGL/DBL20-$26.

Lynwood

Area Code 310
Lynwood Chamber of Commerce
Box 763
Lynwood CA 90262
537-8143

TraveLodge (11401 Long Beach Boulevard, 90262; 763-4029, 800-255-3050) 49 rooms, restaurant, swimming pool, tours, meeting facilities for 72. SGL/DBL$35-$60.

Madera

Area Code 209
Madera Chamber of Commerce
131 West Yosemite Avenue
Madera CA 93637
673-3563

Best Western Madera Valley Inn (317 North G Street, 93637; 673-5164, Fax 661-8426, 800-528-1234) 95 rooms, restaurant, lounge, swimming pool, no-smoking rooms, complimentary newspaper, meeting facilities, fax service, pets allowed. SGL/DBL$50-$61.

Economy Inns of America (1855 West Cleveland Avenue, 93637; 661-1131, 800-826-0778) 80 rooms, swimming pool, wheelchair access, pets allowed. SGL/DBL$35-$40.

Gateway Inn (Avenue 16 and Highway 99, 93637; 674-8817) 49 rooms and kitchenettes, swimming pool, pets allowed. SGL/DBL$36-$45.

Malibu

Area Code 213

Casa Malibu Motel (22752 Pacific Coast Highway, 90265; 456-2219) 21 rooms, swimming pool. SGL/DBL$75-$110.

Malibu Beach Inn (22878 Pacific Coast Highway, 90265; 456-6444, Fax 456-1499, 800-255-1007) 47 rooms and suites, bed and breakfast, complimentary breakfast, swimming pool, in-room refrigerators, private balconies, valet laundry, fax service, wheelchair access, free parking. SGL/DBL$125-$200, STS$200-$300.

Malibu Country Inn (6506 Westward Beach Road, 90265; 457-9622, Fax 457-1349) 16 rooms and suites, restaurant, complimentary breakfast, swimming pool, free parking, wheelchair-access rooms, no-smoking rooms, pets allowed. SGL/DBL$125, STS$175+.

Manhattan Beach

Area Code 213

Barnabey's Hotel (3501 Sepulveda Boulevard, 90266; 545-8466, Fax 545-5849, 800-552-5285, 800-421-0341) 128 rooms and suites, restaurant, complimentary breakfast, indoor swimming pool, spa, kitchenettes, in-room mini-bars, valet laundry, fax service, complimentary newspaper, no-smoking rooms, airport courtesy car, gift shop, laundry room, free parking. SGL/DBL$104-$134, SGL$225-$295.

Comfort Inn Manhattan Beach (850 North Sepulveda Boulevard, 90266; 318-1020, Fax 376-3545, 800-221-2222) 45 rooms, restaurant, complimentary breakfast, outdoor swimming pool, spa, walking distance to the beach, in-room refrigerators, fax services, complimentary newspaper, laundry room, wheelchair-access rooms, free parking, no pets. SGL/DBL$60-$85.

Marriott Residence Inn (1700 North Sepulveda Boulevard; 546-7627, Fax 545-1327, 800-331-3131) one- and two-bedroom suites, complimentary breakfast, outdoor swimming pool, spa, in-room microwaves, kitchenettes, valet laundry, fax service, transportation to local attractions, complimentary newspaper, laundry room, airport courtesy car, meeting facilities for 35, wheelchair-access rooms, pets allowed, free parking, car rental. SGL/DBL$85-$180.

Radisson Plaza Hotel and Golf Course (1400 Parkview Avenue, 90266; 546-7511, Fax 546-7520) 400 rooms, restaurant, exercise facilities, airport transportation, golf. SGL$115-$135, DBL$120-$155.

Sea Horse Motel (233 North Sepulveda Boulevard, 90266; 376-7951, 800-233-8057) 37 rooms and suites, restaurant, outdoor swimming pool, within walking distance of the beach, in-room refrigerators, no-smoking rooms, free parking, car rental. SGL$40-$48, DBL$48-$58, STS$58-$70.

Sea View Inn At The Beach (3400 Highlands Avenue, 90266; 545-1504) 9 rooms, swimming pool. SGL/DBL$65-$75.

Maricopa

Area Code 805

Best Western Inn (600 Poso Street, 93252; 769-8291, 800-528-1234) 41 rooms, restaurant, complimentary breakfast, swimming pool, jacuzzi, children under 12 free, no-smoking rooms, no pets. SGL/DBL$45-$75.

Oak Meadows Too (Box 619, 95338; 742-6161) 6 rooms, bed and breakfast, complimentary breakfast. SGL$45, DBL$55.

Marina

Area Code 408

The Best Inn (3280 Dunes Drive, 93933; 384-1800) 142 rooms. SGL/DBL$25-$65.

Comfort Inn (3290 Dunes Drive, 93933; 883-0300, 800-221-2222) 84 rooms, restaurant, complimentary breakfast, wheelchair-access rooms, no pets. SGL/DBL$39-$89.

El Matador Motel (420 Reservation Road, 93933; 384-5121) 27 rooms, swimming pool. SGL/DBL$35-$55.

Motel 6 (100 Reservation Road, 93933; 384-1000) 126 rooms. SGL/DBL$30-$45.

Marina del Rey

Area Code 213
Marina del Rey Chamber of Commerce
4629 Admiralty Way
Marina del Rey CA 90292
821-0555

Best Western Jamaica Bay Inn (4175 Admiralty Way, 90292; 310-823-5333, Fax 310-823-1325, 800-528-1234) 42 rooms, restaurant, lounge, swimming pool, spa, whirlpools, in-room refrigerators and microwaves, fax service, laundry room, beach, no pets. LS SGL/DBL$90-$100; HS SGL/DBL$135-$145.

Doubletree Hotel Marina Del Ray (4100 Admiralty Way, 90292; 301-3000, Fax 301-6890, 800-528-0444) 338 rooms and suites, three restaurants, lounge, outdoor heated swimming pool, exercise facilities, fax and business service, in-room refrigerators and mini-bars, room service, transportation to local attractions, gift shop, airport courtesy car, beach, meeting and conference facilities for 650, free parking, wheelchair-access rooms, no-smoking rooms. SGL/DBL$170-$210, STS$245-$1,225.

Foghorn Harbor Inn (4140 Via Marina, 90290; 823-4626, Fax 578-1964, 800-624-7351) 24 rooms, complimentary breakfast, in-room refrigerators, complimentary newspaper, airport transportation, free parking. SGL/DBL$70-$130.

Jamaica Bay Inn (4175 Admiralty Way, 90292, 823-5333) 42 rooms. SGL$90, DBL$90-$140.

The Jolly Roger Motel (2904 Washington Boulevard, 90291; 822-2904, Fax 301-9461, 800-822-2904) 87 rooms, restaurant, lounge, complimentary breakfast, outdoor swimming pool, spas, fax service, meeting facilities for 40. SGL/DBL$59-$79.

The Mansion Inn Marina Del Ray (327 Washington Boulevard, 90291; 821-255, Fax 827-0289, 800-828-0688) 33 rooms and suites, complimentary breakfast, in-room refrigerators, wheelchair-access rooms, valet laundry, fax service, complimentary newspaper, travel agency, car rental, free parking. SGL/DBL$79-$89, STS$119+.

Marina Beach Hotel (4100 Admiralty Way, 90292; 301-3000) 300 rooms and suites, restaurant, water-view, airport courtesy car. SGL/DBL$160-$300, STS$250-$1,400.

Marina Del Ray Hotel (13534 Bali Way, 90292; 301-1000, Fax 301-8167, 800-882-4000, 800-777-1700, 800-8-MARINA in California) 159 rooms and suites, two restaurants, lounge, outdoor swimming pool, balconies, meeting facilities, airport courtesy car, ocean view, valet laundry, 24-hour room service, child care, fax service, gift shop, car rental, free parking, wheelchair-access rooms, no-smoking rooms. SGL$120-$185, DBL$140-$205.

Marina Del Ray Marriott (13480 Maxella Avenue, 90292; 822-8555, Fax 823-2996, 800-228-9290) 283 rooms, restaurant, outdoor swimming pool, spa, in-room refrigerators, valet laundry, fax service, complimentary newspaper, airport transportation, pets allowed, gift shop, free parking. SGL$139, DBL$159.

Marina International Hotel and Bungalows (4200 Admiralty Way, 90292; 301-2000, Fax 301-6687, 800-882-4000, 800-8-MARINA in California) 135 rooms, suites and bungalows, restaurant, outdoor swimming pool, spa, in-room refrigerators, valet laundry, complimentary newspaper, free parking, airport courtesy car, no-smoking rooms, gift shop, car rental. SGL$100-$160, DBL$120-$180.

Marriott Hotel (13480 Maxella Avenue, 90292; 822-8555, Fax 823-2996) 283 rooms, restaurant, airport courtesy car, tennis, wheelchair-access rooms, no-smoking rooms. SGL/DBL$140-$170.

Oakwood Apartments (4111 South Via Marina, 90292; 578-6100) one- and two-bedroom apartments, tennis, swimming pool, exercise facilities. 1BR$65-$85, 2BR$90-$100.

The Ritz-Carlton Marina Del Ray (4375 Admiralty Way, 90292; 823-1700, Fax 823-2403, 800-241-3333) 306 rooms and suites, two restaurants, lounge, outdoor swimming pool, spa, in-room mini-bars and safes, valet laundry, 24-hour room service, child care, fax service, exercise facilities, no-smoking rooms, wheelchair-access rooms, lighted tennis courts, airport courtesy car, car rental, gift shop, SGL/DBL$165-$255, STS$410-$1,200.

Sea Lodge of Marina Del Ray (327 Washington Street, 90291; 821-2557) 48 rooms and suites, restaurant, complimentary breakfast, wheelchair access. free parking. SGL/DBL$75-$87, STS$98+.

Maywood

Area Code 213

Budget Host Inn (5445 Atlantic Avenue, 90270; 560-8848) 37 rooms. SGL/DBL$45-$50.

Merced

Area Code 209
Merced City Chamber of Commerce
732 West 18th Street
Merced CA 95344
722-3864

Merced Convention and Visitors Bureau
1880 N Street
Merced CA 95344
384-3333

All-Star Inn (1215 R Street, 95340; 722-2737) 36 rooms. SGL/DBL$25-$30.

Best Western Inn (1033 Motel Drive, 94340; 723-2163, Fax 384-7272, 800-528-1234) 42 rooms, restaurant, lounge, complimentary breakfast, swimming pool, in-room refrigerators, fax service, no pets. SGL/DBL$36-$55.

Best Western Pine Cone Inn (1213 V Street, 95340; 723-3711, Fax 722-8551, 800-528-1234) 98 rooms, restaurant, lounge, swimming pool, meeting facilities, fax service, pets allowed, wheelchair-access rooms, no-smoking rooms. SGL/DBL$53-$68.

Motel 6 (1410 V Street, 95340; 384-2181) 77 rooms. SGL/DBL$25-$30.

Motel 6 (1983 East Childs Avenue, 95340; 384-3802) 80 rooms. SGL/DBL$25-$30.

TraveLodge (200 East Childs Avenue, 95340; 723-3121, Fax 723-0127, 800-255-3050) 110 rooms and suites, restaurant, lounge, swimming pool, in-room refrigerators, meeting facilities for 75, no pets. SGL/DBL$51-$66.

Mission Viejo

Area Code 714

Hampton Inn (26328 Oso Parkway, 92691; 582-7100, Fax 582-3287, 800-950-1099, 800-HAMPTON) 147 rooms, complimentary breakfast, exercise center, swimming pool, meeting facilities, airport transportation, pets allowed. SGL/DBL$73-$90.

Mojave

Area Code 619
Mojave Chamber of Commerce

15835 Sierra Highway
Mojave CA 93501
824-2481

Econo Lodge (2145 Highway 58, 93501; 824-2463, Fax 824-9508, 800-446-6900) 33 rooms, swimming pool, no-smoking rooms, children under 18 free, complimentary newspaper, pets allowed. SGL/DBL$28-$45.

Friendship Inn (15620 Sierra Highway, 93501; 824-4523, 800-424-4777) 30 rooms, swimming pool, kitchenettes, children under 18 free. SGL/DBL$25-$35.

Motel 6 (16958 Sierra Highway, 93501; 824-4571) 121 rooms. SGL/DBL$25-$30.

Scottish Inn (16352 Sierra Highway, 93501; 805-824-9317, 800-251-1962) 41 rooms, swimming pool, wheelchair-access rooms, hot tubs, no-smoking rooms. SGL$29-$31, DBL$31-$40.

Monrovia

Area Code 818
Monrovia Chamber of Commerce
620 South Myrtle Avenue
Monrovia CA 91016
358-1159

Holiday Inn (924 West Huntington Drive, 91016; 357-1900, 800-HOLIDAY) 174 rooms, restaurant, lounge, swimming pool, pets allowed, meeting facilities for 400, SGL/DBL$70-$112.

Howard Johnson (700 West Huntington Drive, 91016; 818-357-5211, Fax 818-357-2786, 800-654-2000) 150 rooms, restaurant, outdoor heated swimming pool, jacuzzi, valet laundry, meeting facilities for 350, fax service, exercise center, no-smoking rooms, airport transportation, no pets. SGL$65-$85, DBL$80-$100.

Oak Tree Inn (788 West Huntington Drive, 91016; 358-8981, Fax 301-0657) 56 rooms, complimentary breakfast, swimming pool, jacuzzi, meeting facilities for 65. airport transportation, wheelchair access, no-smoking rooms. SGL/DBL$40-$60.

Montecito

Area Code 805

San Ysidro Ranch (900 San Ysidro Lane, 93108; 969-5046) 43 cottages, restaurant, complimentary breakfast, swimming pool, tennis, pets allowed. SGL/DBL$160-$425.

Monterey and Monterey Park

Area Code 408
Monterey Peninsula Chamber of Commerce
& Visitors and Convention Bureau
380 Alvarado Street
Monterey CA 93942
649-1770

RENTAL SOURCES: Bay Lodging Reservations (177 Webster Street, 93940; 655-1426) rental condos in the Monterey area; **Bed and Breakfast International** (Box 282910, 94128; 696-1690, Fax 696-1699, 800-872-4500) represents bed and breakfast accommodations throughout California. Accommodations available in private homes, houseboats on the Bay and inns. All rates include complimentary breakfast. SGL/DBL$50-$125; **Inns By The Sea** (624-0101, 800-433-4732, 800-422-4732 in California) represents seven inns on the Monterey peninsula; **The Inns of Monterey** (800-232-4141, 800-225-2902 in California) represents the Spindrift, Monterey Bay and Victorian Inns.

The Arbor Inn (1058 Munras Avenue, 93940; 372-3381, 800-351-8811) 56 rooms, complimentary breakfast, sauna, hot tubs, free parking, wheelchair access, no-smoking rooms, no pets. SGL$59-$79, DBL$69-$89.

The Artist's Loft Bed and Breakfast (Bed and Breakfast International) 1 room, complimentary breakfast, no smoking. SGL$88.

Bay Park Hotel (1425 Munras Avenue, 93940; 649-1020, Fax 373-4258, 800-338-3565) 80 rooms, restaurant, swimming pool, pets allowed, no-smoking rooms. SGL$59-$102, DBL$69-$109.

Bayside Inn (2055 Fremont Street, 93940; 372-8071) 21 rooms, swimming pool. SGL/DBL$45-$75.

Best Western Beach Hotel (2600 Sand Dunes Drive, 93940; 394-3321, Fax 393-1912, 800-528-1234) 196 rooms, restaurant, swimming pool, free parking, beach, no-smoking rooms. LS SGL/DBL$79-$89; HS SGL/DBL$169-$179.

Best Western Monterey Park Inn (420 North Atlantic Boulevard, 91754; 818-289-5090, Fax 818-281-6499, 800-528-1234) 56 rooms, restaurant, lounge, complimentary breakfast, swimming pool, spa, wheelchair-access rooms, no-smoking rooms, laundry room, fax service, SGL/DBL$44-$64.

Best Western Park Crest Inn (1100 Munras Avenue, 93940; 372-4576, Fax 372-2317, 800-528-1234) 53 rooms and suites, restaurant, complimentary breakfast, swimming pool, whirlpool, fax service, hot tub, water view, no-smoking rooms, no pets. LS SGL/DBL$42-$58; HS SGL/DBL$72-$95.

Best Western Monterey Inn (825 Abrego Street, 93940; 373-5345, Fax 373-3246, 800-528-1234) 80 rooms, restaurant, swimming pool, free parking, wheelchair-access rooms, no-smoking rooms, no pets. LS SGL/DBL$63-$78; HS SGl/DBL$93-$118.

Best Western Monterey Beach (2600 Sand Dunes Drive, 93950; 394-3321) 196 rooms and suites, restaurant, airport courtesy car, tennis, golf, wheelchair-access rooms, no-smoking rooms. SGL/DBL$90-$170, STS$250+.

Best Western Park Hotel (434 Potrero Grande Drive, 91754; 213-728-8444, Fax 213-722-0710, 800-528-1234) 78 rooms, restaurant, lounge, complimentary breakfast, spa, sauna, meeting facilities, children under 12 free, fax service, no-smoking rooms. SGL/DBL$46-$85.

Best Western Ramona Inn (2332 Fremont Street, 93940; 373-2445, 800-528-1234) 34 rooms, restaurant, complimentary breakfast, swimming pool, whirlpool, no pets. LS SGL/DBL$50-$65; HS SGL/DBL$75-$90.

Best Western Steinbeck Lodge (1300 Munras Avenue, 93940; 373-3203, 800-528-1234) 32 rooms, restaurant, complimentary breakfast, swimming pool, free local telephone calls, children under 12 free, no-smoking rooms, no pets. LS SGL/DBL$42-$58; HS SGL/DBL$70-$90.

Best Western Victorian Inn (487 Foam Street, 93940; 373-8000, Fax 373-4815, 800-528-1234) 68 rooms, complimentary breakfast, free parking, wheelchair-access rooms, fireplaces, children under 18 free, fax service, no-smoking rooms, pets allowed. LS SGL/DBL$89-$99; HS SGL/DBL$139-$149.

California Motel (2042 North Fremont Street, 93940; 372-5851) 47 rooms, swimming pool, wheelchair access. SGL/DBL$30-$109.

Cannery Row Inn (200 Foam Street, 93940; 649-8580, Fax 649-2566) 32 rooms, complimentary breakfast, free parking, wheelchair-access rooms, no-smoking rooms. SGL/DBL$65-$140.

Carmel Hill Motor Lodge (1374 Munras Avenue, 93942; 373-3252) 38 rooms, swimming pool. SGL/DBL$48-$85.

Casa Munras Garden Hotel (700 Munras Avenue, 93942; 375-2411, Fax 375-1365, 800-222-2558, 800-222-2446 in California) 151 rooms, restaurant, swimming pool, wheelchair-access rooms. SGL$71-$124, DBL$139-$350.

Clarion Carriage House Inn (406 Alvarado Street, 93940; 375-3184, 800-221-2222) 45 rooms, complimentary breakfast, meeting facilities, wheelchair-access rooms, no pets, no-smoking rooms. SGL/DBL$105-$145.

Colton Inn (707 Pacific Street, 93940; 649-6500, Fax 373-6987, 800-848-7007, 800-221-2222) 50 rooms, free local telephone calls, airport courtesy car, no-smoking rooms, wheelchair-access rooms, no pets, SGL$78-$106, DBL$84-$225.

Come-On Inn (1560 Monterey Pass Road, 91754; 263-9888, Fax 268-0353) 54 rooms and suites, outdoor swimming pool, spa, in-room refrigerators, airport courtesy car, free parking. SGL/DBL$33-$41.

Comfort Inn (1262 Munras Avenue, 93940; 372-8088, 800-221-2222) 36 rooms, restaurant, complimentary breakfast, swimming pool, no pets. LS SGL/DBL$45-$65; HS SGL/DBL$60-$110.

Comfort Inn Carmel Hill (1262 Munras Avenue, 93940; 372-2908, 800-221-2222) 29 rooms, restaurant, complimentary breakfast, swimming pool, wheelchair-access rooms, no pets. LS SGL/DBL$45-$65; HS SGL/DBL$65-$110.

Comfort Inn Del Monte Beach (2401 Del Monte Avenue, 93940; 373-7100) 47 rooms, restaurant, complimentary breakfast, swimming pool, no-smoking rooms, wheelchair-access rooms, no pets. LS SGL/DBL$45-$89; HS SGL/DBL$50-$129.

Cypress Gardens Inn (1150 Munras Avenue, 93940; 373-2761, Fax 624-2967, 800-422-4731 in California) 46 rooms, complimentary breakfast, swimming pool, no-smoking rooms, pets allowed. SGL/DBL$49-$99.

Cypress Tree Inn of Monterey (2227 North Fremont Street, 93940; 372-7586, Fax 372-2940) 55 rooms, restaurant. SGL/DBL$52-$195.

Days Inn (1400 Del Monte Boulevard, 93940; 394-5335, Fax 394-7125) 143 rooms, restaurant, swimming pool, wheelchair-access rooms, no-smoking rooms. SGL$65-$85, DBL$75-$100.

Del Monte Beach Inn (1110 Del Monte, 93940; 649-4410) 19 rooms, bed and breakfast, complimentary breakfast. SGL/DBL$40-$75.

Del Monte Pines Motel (1298 Munras Avenue, 93940; 375-2323) 19 rooms, complimentary breakfast, swimming pool, SGL/DBL$49-$124.

Doubletree Hotel (2 Portola Plaza, 93940; 649-4511, Fax 372-0620, 800-528-0444) 375 rooms and suites, two restaurants, lounge, outdoor heated swimming pool, spa, meeting facilities for 1,000, tennis, wheelchair-access rooms, no-smoking rooms. SGL$120-$175, DBL$150-$190.

Driftwood Motel (2362 North Fremont Street, 93940; 372-5059) 14 rooms. SGL/DBL$35-$115.

El Adobe Inn (936 Munras Avenue, 93940; 372-5409, Fax 624-2967, 800-422-4732) 26 rooms, complimentary breakfast, no-smoking rooms, pets allowed. SGL/DBL$49-$79.

El Castell Motel (2102 North Fremont Street, 93940; 372-8176, Fax 649-6187, 800-629-1094 in California) 50 rooms, swimming pool, no-smoking rooms. SGL/DBL$33-$83.

Fairway Motel (2075 Fremont Street, 93940; 373-5551) 42 rooms. SGL/DBL$30-$100.

Franciscan Inn (2058 North Fremont Street, 93940; 375-9511) 47 rooms. SGL/DBL$40-$95.

Hillside House Bed and Breakfast (Bed and Breakfast International) 1 rooms, complimentary breakfast, no smoking. SGL$95.

Holiday Inn (1000 Aquajito Road, 93940; 373-6141, Fax 655-8608, 800-HOLIDAY, 800-234-5697) 204 rooms, restaurant, swimming pool, meeting facilities for 300, wheelchair-access rooms, pets allowed. SGL/DBL$89-$200.

Holiday Inn (443 Wave Street, 93940; 372-1800, Fax 372-1969, 800-HOLIDAY) 43 rooms, restaurant, complimentary breakfast, swimming pool, meeting facilities for 300, wheelchair-access rooms, no pets. SGL/DBL$102-$172.

Hyatt Regency Resort and Conference Center (One Old Golf Course Road, 93940; 372-1234, Fax 375-3960, 800-824-2196 in California) 579 rooms, restaurant, swimming pool, airport transportation, wheelchair-access rooms, exercise facilities, tennis, golf, free parking. SGL$135-$175, DBL$150-$200.

The Jabberwock Inn (598 Laine Street, 93940; 372-4777) 7 rooms, bed and breakfast, complimentary breakfast, no-smoking rooms. SGL/DBL$95+.

Lone Oak Motel (2221 North Fremont Street, 93940; 372-4924) 46 rooms and efficiencies. SGL/DBL$38-$82.

Los Altos Bed and Breakfast (Bed and Breakfast International) 1 room, complimentary breakfast, no smoking. SGL$95.

Mariposa Inn (1386 Munras Avenue, 93940; 649-1414, Fax 646-5937) 51 rooms, complimentary breakfast, swimming pool, golf, wheelchair-access rooms, no-smoking rooms. SGL$68-$160, DBL$110-$165.

Marriott Hotel (350 Calle Principal, 93940; 649-4234) 341 rooms, restaurant, swimming pool, wheelchair access, exercise facilities. SGL/DBL$119-$170.

Merritt House Inn (386 Pacific Street, 93940; 646-9686, Fax 624-5345) 25 rooms, complimentary breakfast. SGL/DBL$120+.

Monterey Bay Inn (242 Cannery Row, 93940; 373-6242, Fax 373-7603) 47 rooms, restaurant, complimentary breakfast, exercise facilities, no-smoking rooms, wheelchair-access rooms. SGL/DBL$95-$260.

Monterey Beach Hotel (2600 Sand Dunes Drive, 93940; 394-3321) 196 rooms, restaurant, swimming pool, wheelchair access. SGL/DBL$99-$179.

Monterey Hotel (406 Alvarado Street, 93940; 375-3184) 44 rooms, complimentary breakfast. SGL/DBL$110-$185.

Monterey Downtown TraveLodge (675 Munras Avenue, 93940; 373-1876, Fax 373-8693) 49 rooms, no-smoking rooms, wheelchair-access rooms. SGL/DBL$49-$99.

Monterey Motor Lodge (55 Camino Aquajito, 93940; 372-8057) 45 rooms, complimentary breakfast, swimming pool, pets allowed. SGL/DBL$55-$110.

Monterey Pines (1288 Munras Avenue, 93940; 375-2165) 47 rooms. SGL/DBL$150-$250.

Monterey Plaza Hotel (400 Cannery Row, 93940; 646-1700, Fax 646-0285, 800-334-3999) 290 rooms and suites, restaurant, lounge, gift shop, valet laundry, no pets. wheelchair-access rooms, no-smoking rooms. SGL/DBL$150-$280.

Monterey Sheraton Hotel (350 Calle Principal, 93940; 649-4243, Fax 372-2968, 800-325-3535) 344 rooms, two restaurants, lounge, outdoor heated swimming pool, jacuzzi, sauna, meeting facilities for 1,255, beauty shop, gift shop, airport transportation, wheelchair-access rooms, no-smoking rooms. SGL$85-$195, DBL$100-$210.

Montero Lodge (1240 Munras Avenue, 93940; 375-6002) 20 rooms, complimentary breakfast. SGL/DBL$39+.

Munras Lodge (1010 Munras Avenue, 93940; 646-9696) 29 rooms, complimentary breakfast. SGL/DBL$45-$199.

The Old Monterey Inn (500 Martin Street, 93940; 375-8284) 10 rooms, bed and breakfast, complimentary breakfast, no-smoking rooms. SGL/DBL$140-$200+.

The Otter Inn (571 Wave Street, 93940; 375-2299) 33 rooms, complimentary breakfast, wheelchair access. SGL/DBL$75-$190.

Pacific Hotel (300 Pacific Street, 93940; 373-5700, Fax: 373-6921) 103 rooms, restaurant, complimentary breakfast, wheelchair-access rooms, no-smoking rooms, pets allowed. SGL/DBL$144-$264.

Padre Oaks Motel (1278 Munras Avenue, 93940; 373-3741) 20 rooms, complimentary breakfast, swimming pool, no-smoking rooms. SGL/DBL$45-$55.

Pelican Inn (1182 Cass Street, 93940; 375-2679) 19 rooms, complimentary breakfast, swimming pool, no-smoking rooms, pets allowed. SGL/DBL$54-$116.

Rosedale Inn (775 Asilomar Avenue, Pacific Grove, 93950; 655-1000, Fax 655-0691, 800-822-5606) 19 rooms, complimentary breakfast, swimming pool, no-smoking rooms, wheelchair-access rooms. SGL$95-$125, DBL$95-$175.

San Carlos Inn (850 Abrego Street, 93940; 649-6332) 55 rooms, complimentary breakfast. SGL/DBL$65-$120.

Sand Dollar Inn (755 Abrego Street, 93940; 372-7551, Fax 372-0916, 800-982-1986) 63 rooms, restaurant, lounge, complimentary breakfast, outdoor heated swimming pool, spa, children under 12 free, in-room refrigerators, laundry room, no-smoking rooms, wheelchair-access rooms, pets allowed, free parking. SGL/DBL$74-$114.

Scottish Fairway Motel (2075 Fremont Street, 93940; 373-5551) 42 rooms, complimentary breakfast, swimming pool, wheelchair-access rooms, no-smoking rooms. SGL$33-$60, DBL$40-$84.

Sheraton Hotel (350 Calle Principal, 93940; 649-4234, Fax 372-2968) 344 rooms and suites, restaurant, swimming pool, exercise equipment, wheelchair-access rooms, no-smoking rooms. SGL$150-$175, DBL$150-$200.

Spindrift Inn (652 Cannery Row, 93940; 646-8900, Fax 646-5342, 800-841-1879) 41 rooms, restaurant, complimentary breakfast, airport transportation, wheelchair-access rooms, no-smoking rooms. SGL/DBL$139-$329.

Stagecoach Motel (1111 Tenth Street, 93940; 373-3632) 25 rooms, swimming pool, complimentary breakfast. SGL/DBL$32-$120.

Steinbeck Gardens Inn (443 Wave Street, 93940; 372-1800) 43 rooms, complimentary breakfast, wheelchair-access rooms, no-smoking rooms. SGL/DBL$75-$120.

Super 8 Motel (2050 North Fremont Street, 93940; 373-3081, 800-800-8000) 48 rooms, restaurant, spa, sauna, no pets, no-smoking rooms. SGL/DBL$42-$46.

TraveLodge At Monterey Fairgrounds (2030 North Fremont Street, 93940; 373-3381, Fax 649-8741, 800-255-3050) 103 rooms and suites, restaurant, lounge, swimming pool, beauty and barber shop, car rental, meeting facilities for 100, no pets, VCRs. LS SGL/DBL$49-$79; HS SGL/DBL$59-$85.

TraveLodge (675 Munras Street, 93940; 373-1876, Fax 373-8693, 800-255-3050) 49 rooms and suites, restaurant, lounge, swimming pool, in-room refrigerators and microwaves, meeting facilities for 20, airport transportation, golf, tennis, no pets. SGL/DBL$54-$79.

Vagabond Motel (2120 Fremont Street, 93940; 372-6066) 19 rooms. SGL/DBL$32-$110.

Victorian Inn (487 Foam Street, 93940; 373-8000, Fax 373-8000, 800-232-4141) 68 rooms, restaurant, complimentary breakfast, wheelchair-access rooms, pets allowed, no-smoking rooms. SGL/DBL$119-$299.

Way Station Inn (1200 Olmstead Road, 93940; 372-2945) 46 rooms. SGL/DBL$59-$119.

West Wind Lodge (1046 Munras Avenue, 93940; 373-1337, Fax 372-2451, 800-821-0805) 52 rooms and suites, complimentary breakfast, indoor heated swimming pool, spa, free local telephone calls, meeting facilities for 20, free parking, no pets. SGL$50-$95, DBL$65-$130, STS$95-$145.

Westerner Motel (2041 Fremont Street, 93940; 373-2911) 22 rooms. SGL/DBL$39+.

Willow House Bed and Breakfast (Bed and Breakfast International) 1 room, complimentary breakfast, no smoking. SGL$88.

Moreno Valley

Area Code 714
Moreno Valley Chamber of Commerce
12685 Perris Boulevard
Moreno Valley CA 92388
924-1928

Best Western Image Suites (24840 Elder Avenue, 92388; 924-4546, Fax 247-9337, 800-528-1234) 126 rooms, restaurant, complimentary breakfast, lounge, heated swimming pool, spa, meeting facilities for 150, wheelchair-access rooms, no-smoking rooms, no pets. SGL$45-$50, DBL$50-$80.

Comfort Inn (24412 Sunnymead Boulevard, 92388; 247-6699, 800-221-2222) 51 rooms, restaurant, swimming pool, whirlpool, wheelchair-access rooms, no pets. SGL/DBL$40-$60.

Econo Lodge (24810 Sunnymead Boulevard, 92388; 247-8582, 800-424-4777) 35 rooms, swimming pool, whirlpools, in-room refrigerators and microwaves, children under 18 free, wheelchair-access rooms, no pets. SGL/DBL$33-$47.

Ramada Inn (24630 Sunnymead Boulevard, 92553; 243-0088, Fax 243-0424, 800-2-RAMADA) 149 rooms, restaurant, lounge, swimming pool, jacuzzi, exercise facilities, meeting facilities for 200, wheelchair-access rooms, no-smoking rooms, pets allowed, free parking. SGL$45-$65, DBL$51-$71.

Rodeway Inn (23330 Sunnymead Boulevard, 92388; 242-0699, 800-424-4777) 86 rooms, complimentary breakfast, outdoor heated swimming pool, whirlpools, kitchenettes, VCRs, children under 18 free, meeting facilities, laundry room, complimentary newspaper, wheelchair-access rooms, no pets. SGL/DBL$40-$50.

TraveLodge (23120 Sunnymead Boulevard, 92553; 247-3434, Fax 247-1115, 800-255-3050) 69 rooms and suites, restaurant, complimentary breakfast, swimming pool, spa, in-room refrigerators, laundry room, meeting facilities for 25, no pets. SGL/DBL$36-$43.

Morro Bay

Area Code 805
Morro Bay Chamber of Commerce
895 Napa
Morro Bay CA 93442
772-4467 or 800-231-0592

Bay Breeze Motel (1148 Front Street, 93442; 772-5607) SGL/DBL$35-$65.

Bay View Lodge (225 Harbor Street, 93442; 772-2771, 800-742-8439 in California) 22 rooms, no-smoking rooms. SGL/DBL$60-$75.

Baywood Bed and Breakfast (1370 Second Street, 93442; 528-8888) complimentary breakfast, restaurant, no-smoking rooms. SGL/DBL$74-$125+.

Best Value Motel (220 Beach Street, 93442; 772-3333) wheelchair-access rooms, no-smoking rooms. SGL/DBL$35-$65.

Best Western El Rancho (2460 Main Street, 93442; 805-772-2212, 800-528-1234) 27 rooms, restaurant, heated swimming pool, children under 12 free, laundry room, no-smoking rooms, pets allowed. SGL$44-$64, DBL$49-$69.

Best Western San Marcos Motor Inn (250 Pacific Street, 93442; 805-772-2248, 800-528-1234) 32 rooms, restaurant, lounge, complimentary breakfast, in-room refrigerators, spa, no-smoking rooms, no pets. SGL/DBL$46-$99.

Best Western Tradewinds Motel (225 Beach Street, 93442; 805-772-7376, 800-528-1234) 24 rooms, whirlpool, pets allowed. SGL/DBL$39-$54.

Blue Sail Inn (851 Market Avenue, 93442; 772-7132, 800-336-0707 in California) 36 rooms, wheelchair-access rooms, no-smoking rooms, no pets. SGL/DBL$75-$100+.

Breakers Motel (Morro Bay Boulevard and Market Street, 93442; 772-7317, 800-932-8899 in California) 35 rooms, swimming pool, no-smoking rooms, pets allowed. SGL/DBL$75-$100+.

Coffey Break Bed and Breakfast (213 Dunes Street, 93442; 772-4378) bed and breakfast, complimentary breakfast, no smoking. SGL/DBL$75-$125.

El Morro Lodge (1206 Main Street, 93442; 772-5633, 800-527-6782 in California. 26 rooms, complimentary breakfast. SGL/DBL$75-$100+.

Embarcadero Inn (456 Embarcadero Street, 93442; 772-2700, 800-292-ROCK) 32 rooms, complimentary breakfast, spas, under 12 stay free, free local telephone calls, free parking, wheelchair-access rooms, no-smoking rooms. SGL/DBL$70-$160.

Fireside Inn (730 Morro Avenue, 93442; 772-2244, 800-444-0562) 24 rooms and efficiencies, complimentary breakfast, children under 12 free, fax service, laundry room, free parking, wheelchair-access rooms, no-smoking rooms, no pets. SGL/DBL$55-$85.

Gold Coast Motel (670 Main Street, 93442; 772-7740, 800-924-7740 in California) 17 rooms, pets allowed. SGL/DBL$35+.

Golden Pelican Inn (3270 Main Street, 93442; 772-7135) complimentary breakfast, pets allowed. SGL/DBL$40-$100.

Gray's Inn and Gallery (561 Embarcadero, 93442; 772-3911) rooms and efficiencies. SGL/DBL$75-$125.

Harbour House Inn (1095 Main Street, 93442; 772-2711) 46 rooms, restaurant, wheelchair-access rooms, no-smoking rooms. SGL/DBL$50-$75.

Harbor View Motor Lodge (215 Harbor Street; 772-2447) rooms and efficiencies, swimming pool. SGL/DBL$50-$100+.

Holland Inn Motel (2630 North Main Street, 93442; 772-2650) SGL/DBL$50-$100+.

The Inn At Morro Bay (19 Country Club Road, 93442; 772-5651, Fax 772-4779, 800-321-9655 in California) 96 rooms, restaurant, swimming pool, airport transportation, golf, wheelchair-access rooms, no-smoking rooms. SGL/DBL$85-$250.

La Serena Inn (990 Morro Avenue, 93442; 772-5665, 800-248-1511 in California) 37 rooms, complimentary breakfast, wheelchair-access rooms, no-smoking rooms. SGL/DBL$58-$90.

Marina Street (305 Marina, 93442; 772-4016) bed and breakfast, complimentary breakfast. SGL/DBL$75-$125.

Morro Bay Motel (1100 Main Street, 93442; 722-5609) wheelchair-access rooms, no-smoking rooms. SGL/DBL$50-$75.

Morro Gardens (440 Atascadero Road, 93442; 772-2817. rooms and efficiencies. SGL/DBL$40-$75.

Motel 6 (298 Atascadero Road, 93442; 772-5641) swimming pool, pets allowed. SGL/DBL$45-$55.

Rambler Rose (1029 Monterey, 93442; 772-5000) rooms and efficiencies. SGL/DBL$40-$75.

Sandpiper Motel (1050 Morro Avenue, 93442; 772-2381) rooms and efficiencies, pets allowed. SGL/DBL$50-$125.

Sea Air Inn (845 Morro Avenue, 93442; 772-4437) 25 rooms and suites, restaurant, airport courtesy car, no-smoking rooms. SGL/DBL$35-$75, STS$75-$85.

Sea Harbor Inn (645 Morro Avenue, 93442; 772-7335) rooms and efficiencies. SGL/DBL$75-$125+.

Sundown Motel (640 Main Street, 93442; 772-7335) SGL/DBL$35-$65.

TraveLodge (1080 Market Avenue, 93442; 805-772-1259, Fax 805-772-2157, 800-255-3050) 31 rooms and suites, restaurant, lounge, swimming pool, meeting facilities for 15, SGL/DBL$35-$55.

The Twin Dolphin (590 Morro Avenue, 93442; 772-4483) 31 rooms and suites, complimentary breakfast, wheelchair-access rooms, no-smoking rooms. SGL/DBL$60-$65, STS$90+.

Villager Motel (1098 Main Street, 93442; 772-1235, 800-444-0782) 22 rooms, restaurant, no-smoking rooms. SGL/DBL$35-$100.

Mountain View

Area Code 415
Mountain View Chamber of Commerce
580 Castro Street
Mountain View CA 94042
968-8378

Ambassador Business Inns (860 El Camino Real, 94040; 940-1000, Fax 968-7870, 800-538-1600) 91 rooms and suites, lounge, complimentary breakfast, outdoor heated swimming pool, spa, children under 12 free, exercise facilities, laundry room, handicapped rooms, no-smoking rooms, no pets. SGL/DBL$58-$66.

Best Western Inn (93 West El Camino Real, 94040; 967-6957, Fax 967-4834, 800-445-7776, 800-528-1234) 58 rooms, complimentary breakfast, swimming pool, exercise facilities, no-smoking rooms, no pets. SGL$60-$70, DBL$65-$75.

Best Western Mountain View Inn (2300 El Camino Real, 94040; 962-9912, Fax 962-9011, 800-528-1234) 70 rooms, restaurant, complimentary breakfast, no-smoking rooms. SGL/DBL$64-$85.

Best Western Tropicana Lodge (1720 El Camino Real, 94040; 961-0220, Fax 961-1471, 800-528-1234) 59 rooms, restaurant, complimentary breakfast, swimming pool, pets allowed. SGL$55-$68, DBL$60-$74.

County Inn (850 Leong Drive, 94043; 961-1131, Fax 965-9099) 52 rooms, restaurant, swimming pool, whirlpool, sauna, exercise facilities, wheelchair-access rooms, no pets, no-smoking rooms. SGL/DBL$65-$98.

Marriott Residence Inn (18545 El Camino Real, 94040; 940-1300, Fax 969-4997, 800-331-3131) in-room microwaves, wheelchair-access rooms, no-smoking rooms, pets allowed.

Mountain View Comfort Inn (1561 West El Camino Real, 94040; 967-7888, Fax 967-3579, 800-228-5150) 37 rooms, complimentary breakfast, swimming pool, wheelchair-access rooms, no-smoking rooms. SGL$55-$75, DBL$65-$75.

Residence Inn (1854 El Camino Real West, 94040; 940-1300, Fax 969-4997, 800-331-3131) 112 rooms and efficiencies, restaurant, complimentary breakfast, exercise facilities, wheelchair-access rooms, no-smoking rooms, pets allowed. SGL/DBL$120-$160.

Rodeway Inn (55 Fairchild Drive, 94043; 967-6856, Fax 964-4542, 800-228-2000, 800-424-4777) 50 rooms, complimentary breakfast, swimming pool, whirlpool, meeting facilities, children under 18 free, wheelchair-access rooms, no-smoking rooms. SGL$54-$65, DBL$59-$70.

National City

Area Code 619
National City Chamber of Commerce
711 A Avenue
National City CA 92050
477-9339

Best Pacific Inn (1640 East Plaza Boulevard, 92050; 474-9202, 800-872-2434 in California) 70 rooms, swimming pool. SGL$30-$35, DBL$39-$45.

Comfort Inn Naval Station (1645 Plaza Boulevard, 92050; 474-8696, 800-228-5150) 92 rooms. SGL/DBL$39-$54.

Econo Lodge (1640 East Plaza, 91950; 474-9202, 800-446-6900, 800-424-4777) 70 rooms, swimming pool, wheelchair-access rooms, no pets, children under 18 free. SGL/DBL$36-$43.

Radisson Inn (700 National City Boulevard, 92050; 336-1100, 800-333-3333) 180 rooms, restaurant, swimming pool, airport transportation, wheelchair-access rooms, no-smoking rooms. SGL/DBL$59-$69.

Newhall

Area Code 805
Santa Clarita Valley Chamber of Commerce
24275 Walnut Street
Newhall CA 91321
259-4787

Hampton Inn Valencia (25259 The Old Road, 91321; 253-2400, Fax 253-1683, 800-HAMPTON, 800-426-7866) 130 rooms, swimming pool, pets allowed, free parking. SGL$65-$71, DBL$72-$78.

Needles

Area Code 619
Needles Chamber of Commerce
Box 705
Needles CA 92363
326-2050

Best Motel (1900 West Broadway, 92536; 326-3824) 29 rooms, restaurant, swimming pool, pets allowed. SGL/DBL$30-$37.

Best Western Overland (712 Broadway, 92363; 619-326-3821, Fax 619-326-3274, 800-528-1234) 41 rooms and suites, restaurant, lounge, swimming pool, children under 12 free, no-smoking rooms, wheelchair-access rooms, pets allowed. SGL$33-$52, DBL$39-$95.

Days Inn (1111 Pashard Street, 92363; 619-326-5660, Fax 619-326-4002, 800-325-2525) 60 rooms, swimming pool, jacuzzi, fax service, children under 12 free, pets allowed, no-smoking rooms. SGL$40-$50, DBL$50-$60.

Friendship Inn (1707 West Broadway, 92363; 326-3839) 27 rooms, restaurant, swimming pool, airport courtesy car, wheelchair-access rooms, no-smoking rooms. SGL/DBL$26-$37.

New Cuyama

Area Code 805

Cuyama Buckhorn (4923 Primero, 93254; 766-2591) 22 rooms, restaurant, swimming pool. SGL/DBL$45-$75.

Newport Beach

Area Code 714
Newport Beach Convention and Visitors Bureau
4340 Campus Drive #211
Newport Beach CA 92663
756-2072

Newport Harbor Area Chamber of Commerce
1470 Jamboree Road
Newport Beach CA 92660
644-8211

Best Western Bay Shores Inn (1800 West Balboa Boulevard, 92663; 675-3463, Fax 675-4977, 800-222-6675, 800-528-1234) 20 rooms, restaurant, complimentary breakfast, ocean view, complimentary newspaper, VCRs, children under 12 free, no-smoking rooms, no pets. SGL$75-$82, DBL$82-$109, STS$129-$169.

Country Side Inn (325 Bristol, 92658; 549-0300, 800-332-9992 in California) 350 rooms and one-bedroom suites, complimentary breakfast, restaurant, swimming pool, airport transportation, exercise facilities. SGL$68-$88, DBL$78-$98.

Doryman's Inn (2102 West Ocean Front, 92663; 675-7300) 10 rooms, bed and breakfast, complimentary breakfast, restaurant, no-smoking rooms. SGL$/DBL$135-$200.

Four Seasons Hotel (690 Newport Center Drive, 92660; 759-0808, Fax 759-0568, 800-332-3442) 319 rooms and suites, restaurant, swimming pool, airport courtesy car, balconies, 24-hour room service, exercise facilities, pets allowed, wheelchair-access rooms, no-smoking rooms, lighted tennis courts. SGL$185-$250, DBL$210-$270, STS$300-$1,500.

Hyatt Newport (1107 Jamboree Road, 92660; 729-1234, Fax 644-1552, 800-233-1234) 410 rooms and suites, two restaurants, lounges, three heated swimming pools, jacuzzis, meeting facilities for 600, exercise facilities, airport courtesy car, wheelchair-access rooms, no-smoking rooms, lighted tennis courts, golf. SGL$115-$165, DBL$135-$185+.

Le Meridian Newport Beach (4500 MacArthur Boulevard, 92660; 476-2001, 800-543-4300) 435 rooms and one-bedroom suites, restaurant, swimming pool, lighted tennis courts, exercise facilities, airport transportation, wheelchair-access rooms, no-smoking rooms, SGL/DBL$130-$190, 1BR$800+.

Marriott Suites (500 Bayview Circle, 92660; 854-4500, Fax 854-3937) 251 suites, restaurant, complimentary breakfast, swimming pool, exercise facilities, airport transportation, pets allowed, no-smoking rooms, wheelchair-access rooms. SGL$149, DBL$169.

Newport Beach Marriott Hotel and Tennis Club (900 Newport Center Drive, 92660; 640-4000, Fax 640-5055, 800-228-9290) 602 rooms, restaurant, swimming pool, exercise facilities, airport transportation, pets allowed, wheelchair-access rooms.

Newport Channel Inn (6030 West Coast Highway, 92663; 642-3030, 800-457-8614, 800-255-8614) 30 rooms, children under 12 free, meeting facilities for 10, laundry room, wheelchair access, no-smoking rooms, no pets. SGL/DBL$57-$90.

Newport Classic Inn (2300 West Coast Highway, 92663; 722-2999, Fax 631-5659, 800-633-3199) 50 rooms and suites, restaurant, complimentary breakfast, lounge, outdoor heated swimming pool, valet laundry, exercise facilities, airport courtesy car, meeting facilities for 30, free parking, wheelchair-access rooms, no-smoking, no pets. SGL/DBL$55-$76.

Portofino Beach Hotel (2306 West Oceanfront, 92663; 673-7030, Fax 723-4370) 20 rooms and suites, complimentary breakfast. SGL/DBL$100-$150, STS$210-$235.

Rodeway Inn (6208 West Pacific Coast Highway, 92663; 642-8552, 800-424-4777) 71 rooms, swimming pool, VCRs, children under 18 free, no pets. SGL/DBL$52-$63.

Sheraton Newport Beach Hotel (4545 MacArthur Boulevard, 92660; 833-0570, 800-325-3535) 348 rooms and suites, three restaurants, lounge, complimentary breakfast, outdoor swimming pool, spa, meeting facilities for 1,000, gift shop, wheelchair-access rooms, no-smoking rooms, airport courtesy car, lighted tennis courts. SGL/DBL$98-$145.

The Westin South Coast Plaza (666 Anton Boulevard, Costa Mesa, 92626; 540-2500, Fax 540-4432, 800-228-3000) 394 rooms, restaurant, swimming pool, airport transportation, pets allowed, wheelchair-access rooms, no-smoking rooms, tennis. SGL$129-$149.

Norco

Area Code 714
Norco Chamber of Commerce
3900 Acacia Norco CA 91760
737-2531

Howard Johnson Lodge (1695 Hammer Avenue, 91760; 278-8886, 800-654-2000) 55 rooms and suites, complimentary breakfast, swimming pool, laundry, fax service, meeting facilities, wheelchair-access rooms, no pets. SGL$42-$72, DBL$48-$68.

North Fork

Area Code 209
North Fork Chamber of Commerce
Box 782
North Fork CA 93643
877-2410

Ye Olde South Fork Inn (Box 731, 93643; 877-7025) 8 rooms, bed and breakfast, complimentary breakfast. SGL/DBL$45-$68.

Norwalk

Area Code 310

All-Star Inn (10646 East Rosecrans Avenue, 90650; 864-2567) 55 rooms. SGL/DBL$30-$38.

Best Western Inn (10902 Firestone Boulevard, 90650; 929-8831, Fax 929-4027, 800-528-1234) 88 rooms, complimentary breakfast, swimming pool, whirlpool, in-room refrigerators, laundry room, no-smoking rooms, no pets, free parking. SGL$/DBL$40-$54.

Comfort Inn (12512 Pioneer Boulevard, 90650; 868-3453, Fax 868-5385, 800-221-2222) 79 rooms, restaurant, whirlpool, sauna, wheelchair-access rooms, no-smoking rooms, no pets. SGL/DBL$40-$50.

Econo Lodge (12225 East Firestone Boulevard, 90650; 868-0791, 800-424-4777) 43 rooms, swimming pool, whirlpool, wheelchair-access rooms, children under 18 free, no pets. SGL/DBL$39-$49.

Park Inn International (12500 East Firestone Boulevard, 90650; 868-0401, Fax 929-3569) 256 rooms. SGL/DBL$50-$70.

Saddleback Inn (12500 East Firestone Boulevard, 90650; 868-0401, 800-272-6232, 800-367-0401) 256 rooms and suites, restaurant, swimming pool, airport transportation, pets allowed, free parking. SGL$110-$125, DBL$125-$135, STS$150+.

Sheraton Norwalk Hotel (13111 Sycamore Drive, 90650; 213-863-6666, Fax 213-868-4486, 800-325-3535, 800-652-3535) 185 rooms and suites, restaurant, lounge, outdoor heated swimming pool, whirlpools, exercise facilities, meeting facilities for 750, business services, wheelchair-access rooms, no-smoking rooms, free parking. SGL$75-$105, DBL$85-$115.

Oakhurst

Area Code 209
Southern Yosemite Area Tourism Council
Box 1410
Oakhurst CA 93644
683-7766

Best Western Yosemite Gateway Inn (40530 California Highway 41, 93644; 683-2378, Fax 683-5654) 110 rooms and efficiencies, swimming pool, wheelchair access, no-smoking rooms, pets allowed. LS SGL/DBL$46-$58; HS SGL/DBL$66-$78.

Chateau Du Sureau (Box 577, 93644; 683-6860) 9 rooms, bed and breakfast, complimentary breakfast, swimming pool, wheelchair-access rooms. DBL$250-$340.

Days Inn (40662 Highway 41, 93644; 642-2525, 800-325-2525) 41 rooms, swimming pool, no-smoking rooms. LS SGL/DBL$55-$85; HS SGL/DBL$65-$92.

Oakhurst Lodge (Box 24, 93644; 683-4417, 800-521-4447 in California) 60 rooms, no-smoking rooms, pets allowed. LS SGL/DBL$50; HS SGL/DBL$55.

Ople's Guest House (41118 Highway 41, 93644; 683-2800) 3 rooms, bed and breakfast, complimentary breakfast. SGL$40.

Pine Rose Inn (Box 2341, 93644; 642-2800) 8 rooms, bed and breakfast, complimentary breakfast, no-smoking rooms, pets allowed. LS SGL/DBL$47-$85; HS SGL/DBL$55-$99.

Shilo Inn (406-44 Highway 41, 93644; 683-3555, 800-222-2244) 80 rooms and suites, complimentary breakfast, outdoor swimming pool, spa, sauna, in-room refrigerators, complimentary newspaper, exercise facilities, pets allowed. LS SGL/DBL$69-$96; HS SGL/DBL$85-$109.

Snowline Lodge (42150 Highway 41, 93644; 683-5854) 6 rooms, no-smoking rooms, pets allowed. LS DBL$38; HS DBL$47.

Oceano

Area Code 805

RENTAL SOURCES: Beachfront Vacation Homes (1298 Strand Avenue, 93448; 773-4771) represents private home rentals.

Oceanside

Area Code 619
Oceanside Chamber of Commerce
512 Fourth Street
Oceanside CA 92054
722-1534

RENTAL SOURCES: Wessex Beach Houses (400 South Strand; 722-3677) home rentals. $365W+.

The Beach House (412 South Strand, 92054; 714-497-2982) one- and two-bedroom condos. LS 1BR$350W, 2BR$650W; HS 1BR$600W, 2BR$1,200W.

Best Western Marty's Valley Inn (3240 East Mission Avenue, 92054; 757-7700, Fax 439-3311, 800-528-1234) 111 rooms, restaurant, complimentary breakfast, heated swimming pool, children under 12 free, fax service, wheelchair-access rooms, no-smoking rooms, no pets. SGL$53-$59, DBL$59-$66.

Best Western Oceanside Inn (1680 Oceanside Boulevard, 92054 722-1821, Fax 967-8969, 800-528-1234, 800-443-9995 in California) 80 rooms, complimentary breakfast, swimming pool, free local telephone calls, complimentary newspaper, meeting facilities, in-room refrigerators and microwaves, VCRs, no-smoking rooms, wheelchair-access rooms, no pets. SGL/DBL$59-$80.

Comfort Inn (1440 Mission Avenue, 92054; 967-4100, 800-228-5150, 800-350-SURF, 800-221-2222) 67 rooms, restaurant, complimentary breakfast, meeting facilities, wheelchair access, no-smoking rooms, no pets. SGL/DBL$48-$58.

El Camino Inn (3170 Vista Way, 92056; 757-2200, 800-458-6064, 800-350-SURF) 42 rooms, complimentary breakfast, outdoor swimming pool, exercise facilities, free parking, no-smoking rooms, pets allowed. SGL/DBL$54-$70.

Motel 6 (3708 Plaza Drive, 92056; 941-1011, 505-891-6161) 136 rooms. SGL/DBL$27-$33.

Motel 6 (1403 Mission Avenue, 92054; 721-6662, 505-891-6161) 79 rooms. SGL/DBL$30-$36.

Sandman Motel (1501 Carmelo Drive, 92054; 722-7661, 850-SURF) 82 rooms, restaurant, swimming pool, wheelchair access, pets allowed, marina. SGL$40-$50, DBL$45-$55.

TraveLodge (1401 North Hill Street, 92054; 722-1244, Fax 722-3228, 800-255-3050) 45 rooms and suites, restaurant, laundry room, fax service, no-smoking rooms, no pets. SGL/DBL$38-$49.

Villa Marina Resort (2008 Harbor Drive, North, 92054; 722-1561, Fax 439-9758, 800-252-2033) 57 rooms and suites, complimentary breakfast, outdoor heated swimming pool, sauna, jacuzzi, fax service, no-smoking rooms. SGL/DBL$70, STS$90-$140.

Ojai

Area Code 805
Ojai Valley Chamber of Commerce
338 East Ojai Avenue
Ojai CA 93023
646-3000

Best Western Casa Ojai (1302 Ojai Avenue, 93023; 646-8175, Fax 640-8247, 800-528-1234) 45 rooms and suites, restaurant, complimentary breakfast, swimming pool, whirlpool, tennis, children under 12 free, golf, wheelchair-access rooms, no-smoking rooms, pets allowed. SGL/DBL$55-$110.

The Oaks At Ojai (122 East Ojai Avenue, 93023; 646-5573, Fax 640-1504) 46 rooms, restaurant, complimentary breakfast, swimming pool, exercise facilities, airport transportation, no-smoking rooms. SGL/DBL$175+.

Ojai Manor Hotel (210 East Matilja Street, 93020; 646-0961) 6 rooms, complimentary breakfast. SGL/DBL$80-$90.

Ojai Rancho (615 West Ojai Avenue, 93020; 646-1434) 17 rooms, swimming pool. SGL/DBL$35-$85.

Ojai Valley Inn and Country Club (Country Club Road, 93023 646-5511, Fax 646-7969, 800-422-OJAI) 218 rooms and suites, restaurant, swimming pool, lighted tennis courts, golf, wheelchair-access rooms, no-smoking rooms, pets allowed. SGL/DBL$180-$240, STS$310-$350.

Ontario

Area Code 714
Greater Ontario Visitors and Convention Bureau
123 West D Street
Ontario CA 91671
984-2458

Best Western Ontario Airport Motel (209 North Vineyard Avenue, 91764; 983-9600, Fax 395-9219, 800-528-1234) 150 rooms, restaurant, lounge, complimentary breakfast, heated swimming pool, spa, laundry room, children under 12 free, meeting facilities, fax service, airport courtesy car, wheelchair-access rooms. SGL/DBL$44-$70.

Clarion Hotel Ontario Airport (2200 East Holt Boulevard, 91764; 896-8811, 800-284-8811) 300 rooms and suites, restaurant, swimming pool, lighted tennis, courts, exercise facilities, airport courtesy car, wheelchair-access rooms, no-smoking rooms. SGL/DBL$80-$101, STS$325-$450+.

Comfort Inn Airport (2301 East Euclid Avenue, 91762; 986-3556, 800-221-2222) 45 rooms, restaurant, outdoor swimming pool, spa, whirlpools, meeting facilities, wheelchair-access rooms, no pets. SGL/DBL$35-$49.

Days Inn (1405 Fourth Street, 91006; 983-7411, Fax 391-1216, 800-325-2525) 50 rooms, restaurant, complimentary breakfast, jacuzzi, meeting facilities, children under 12 free, fax service, wheelchair-access rooms, no-smoking rooms, no pets. SGL$39-$50, DBL$45-$55.

Doubletree Club Hotel (429 North Vineyard Avenue, 91769; 391-6411, Fax 391-2369, 800-528-0444) 171 rooms, restaurant, lounge, complimentary breakfast, heated outdoor swimming pool, spa, meeting facilities for 50, exercise facilities, airport courtesy car, wheelchair access, no-smoking rooms, free parking. SGL$67-$79, DBL$77-$89.

Econo Lodge South (724 South San Antonio Avenue, 91764; 988-7969, 800-424-4777) 45 rooms, complimentary breakfast, swimming pool, free local telephone calls, wheelchair-access rooms, children under 18 free. SGL/DBL$40-$50.

Fairfield Inn -Marriott (3201 East Center Lake Drive, 91764; 395-9300) 117 rooms. SGL/DBL$45+.

Hilton Ontario Airport (700 North Haven, 91764; 980-0400, Fax 948-9309) 309 rooms and suites, restaurant, outdoor swimming pool, jacuzzi, meeting facilities for 700, business services, airport courtesy car, exercise facilities, wheelchair-access rooms, no-smoking rooms. SGL$100-$135, DBL$115-$145, STS$150+.

Holiday Inn International Airport (1801 East G Street, 91762; 983-3604, Fax 986-4724, 800-HOLIDAY) 292 rooms, restaurant, swimming pool, meeting facilities for 200, wheelchair-access rooms, airport transportation, no-smoking rooms, pets allowed. SGL$61-$63, DBL$70-$72.

Howard Johnson Lodge (2425 South Archibald Avenue, 91761; 923-2728) 61 rooms and suites, restaurant, complimentary breakfast, swimming pool, jacuzzis, no-smoking room, fax service, valet laundry, meeting facilities. SGL/DBL$42-$72.

Innsuites Apartments (3400 Shelby Street, 91764; 466-9600, Fax 941-1445) 150 suites. SGL/DBL$68-$99.

Lexington Hotel Inn Suites (231 North Vineyard, 91764; 983-8484, Fax 983-0858, 800-53-SUITE) 150 rooms and suites, restaurant, complimentary breakfast, outdoor heated swimming pool, spa, valet laundry, child care, fax service, gift shop, laundry room, airport courtesy car, wheelchair-access rooms, no-smoking rooms, free parking. SGL/DBL$68-$105.

Marriott Residence Inn (2025 East D Street, 91764; 983-6788, Fax 983-3843, 800-331-3131) restaurant, complimentary breakfast, airport transportation, swimming pool, jacuzzi, meeting facilities for 60, in-room microwaves and VCRs, wheelchair-access rooms, no-smoking rooms, pets allowed. SGL/DBL$109-$119.

Motel 6 (1560 East Fourth Street, 91761; 984-2424, 505-891-6161) 71 rooms. SGL/DBL$31-$37.

Motel 6 (1515 North Mountain Avenue, 91762; 986-6632, 505-891-6161) 60 rooms. SGL/DBL$29-$45.

Ontario Airport Hilton (700 North Haven, 91764; 980-0400, Fax 980-1675, 800-654-1379) 319 rooms and suites, restaurant, swimming pool, airport transportation, exercise facilities, wheelchair access, no-smoking rooms.

Ontario Motor Inn (1522 West Mission Boulevard, 91762; 984-6789) 33 rooms. SGL/DBL$32-$50.

Quality Inn (1818 East Holt Boulevard, 91767; 988-8466, 800-221-2222) 107 rooms, restaurant, lounge, complimentary breakfast, swimming pool, sauna, whirlpool, airport transportation, wheelchair-access rooms, no pets. SGL/DBL$49-$76.

Red Lion Inn (222 North Vineyard, 91762; 983-0909, Fax 983-8851, 800-547-8010) 343 rooms and suites, restaurant, swimming pool, airport courtesy car, exercise facilities, wheelchair-access rooms, pets allowed, no-smoking rooms. SGL$110-$130, DBL$120-$150, STS$300-$500.

The Residence Inn (2025 East O Street, 91764; 983-6788, Fax 983-3843, 800-331-3131) 200 rooms, complimentary breakfast, swimming pool, meeting facilities for 60, wheelchair access, airport transportation, pets allowed. SGL$109, DBL$129.

Roadway Inn (2359 South Grove Avenue, 92671; 983-7721) 65 rooms. SGL/DBL$45-$80.

Super 8 Motel (514 North Vineyard Avenue, 983-2886, Fax 988-2115, 800-800-8000) 135 rooms, restaurant, complimentary breakfast, outdoor swimming pool, spa, airport courtesy car, free local telephone calls, complimentary newspaper, meeting facilities, fax service, transportation to local attractions, laundry room, wheelchair-access rooms, no-smoking rooms, no pets. SGL/DBL$47-$54.

TraveLodge (1655 East Fourth Street, 91764; 986-8898, 800-255-3050) 80 rooms, restaurant, swimming pool, spa, tours, car rental, meeting facilities for 80, airport transportation, no pets. SGl/DBL$45-$48+.

TraveLodge (2441 South Euclid Avenue, 91762; 983-7721, Fax 983-0755, 800-255-3050) 53 rooms, restaurant, swimming pool, whirlpool, fax service, kitchenettes, no pets. SGL/DBL$34-$45.

TraveLodge (755 North Euclid Avenue, 91762; 984-1775, 800-255-3050) 33 rooms, restaurant, swimming pool, whirlpool, pets allowed. SGL/DBL$42-$52.

Orange

Area Code 714
Orange Chamber of Commerce
80 Plaza Square
Orange CA 92666
538-3581

Best Western El Camino Inn (3191 Tustin Avenue, 92665; 998-0360, 800-528-1234) 56 rooms, restaurant, complimentary breakfast, swimming pool, children under 12 free, meeting and conference facilities, no pets, no-smoking rooms. SGL$42-$49, DBL$45-$54.

Doubletree Hotel (100 The City Drive, 92668; 634-4500, Fax 978-3839, 800-528-0444) 460 rooms and suites, two restaurants, lounge, outdoor swimming pool, whirlpool, meeting facilities for 850, concierge, exercise facilities, tennis, airport courtesy car, wheelchair access, no-smoking rooms, pets allowed, free parking. SGL/DBL$110-$130, STS$250+.

Hilton Suites (400 North State College Boulevard, 92668; 938-1111, Fax 938-0930, 800-HILTONS) 230 suites, restaurant, complimentary breakfast, swimming pool, meeting facilities for 140, exercise facilities, wheelchair-access rooms, no-smoking rooms. STS$140-$180.

Howard Johnson (1930 East Katella, 92667; 639-1121, 800-654-2000) 30 rooms, restaurant, swimming pool, jacuzzi, no-smoking rooms. SGL$35-$40, DBL$40-$45.

Marriott Residence Inn (201 North State College Boulevard, 92668; 978-7700, 800-331-3131) 105 rooms and efficiencies, restaurant, complimentary breakfast, exercise facilities, wheelchair access/room, meeting facilities for 65, in-room microwave and VCRs, convenience store, car rental, transportation to local attractions, no-smoking rooms, pets allowed. SGL$100-$120, DBL$100-$155.

Motel 6 (2920 West Chapman Avenue, 92668; 634-2441) 171 rooms. SGL/DBL$29-$35.

Ramada Inn (101 North State College Boulevard, 92668; 634-9500, Fax 634-4751) 143 rooms. SGL/DBL$40-$56.

TraveLodge of Orange (1302 West Chapman Avenue, 92668; 633-7720, Fax 633-9469, 800-255-3050) 32 rooms and suites, restaurant, lounge, swimming pool, in-room refrigerators, fax service, wheelchair access, tennis, no pets. SGL/DBL$40-$55.

Woodfin Suites (720 City Drive South, 92668; 740-2700, Fax 971-1692, 800-237-8811) 123 suites, restaurant, lounge, outdoor heated swimming pool, sauna, in-room refrigerators, meeting facilities for 90, no pets, free parking. wheelchair-access rooms, no-smoking rooms. SGL/DBL$79-$109.

Oxnard

Area Code 805
Oxnard Chamber of Commerce
325 Esplanade Drive
Oxnard CA 93030
485-8833

Casa Sirena Marina Resort (3605 Peninsula Road, 93035; 985-6311, Fax 985-4329, 800-228-6026, 800-44-RELAX) 272 rooms and suites, restaurant, swimming pool, in-room refrigerators and mini-bars, valet laundry, fax service, transportation to local attractions, airport courtesy car, exercise facilities, meeting facilities for 500, gift shop, bike rentals, lighted tennis courts, wheelchair-access rooms, no-smoking rooms, free parking. SGL/DBL$79-$99, STS$139-$250.

Crown Sterling Suites (2101 Mandalay Beach Road, 93035; 984-2500, Fax 984-8339, 800-433-4600) 250 suites, restaurant, complimentary breakfast, swimming pool, tennis, airport transportation. SGL/DBL$135-$270.

Financial Plaza Hilton (600 Esplanade Drive, 93030; 485-9666, Fax 485-2061, 800-44-RELAX, 800-HILTONS) 160 rooms and suites, restaurant, outdoor heated swimming pool, spa, jacuzzi, in-room refrigerators, free parking, meeting facilities for 600, wheelchair-access rooms, pets allowed. SGL$75-$90, DBL$85-$100, STS$100-$175.

Friendship Inn Regal Lodge (1012 South Oxnard Boulevard, 93030; 486-8381, 800-424-4777) 33 rooms, two restaurants, swimming pool, kitchenettes, meeting facilities, children under 18 free, no pets. SGL/DBL$36-$68.

Mandalay Beach Resort-Embassy Suites (2101 Mandalay Beach Road, 93030; 984-2500, Fax 984-8339, 800-582-3000 in California) 250 suites, restaurant, swimming pool, tennis, free parking. SGL$100-$170, DBL$120-$180, STS$160-$500.

Radisson Suite Hotel (2101 West Vineyard Avenue, 93030; 988-0130, Fax 983-4470) 250 suites, restaurant, complimentary breakfast, swimming pool, airport courtesy car, lighted tennis courts, wheelchair-access rooms, no-smoking rooms. STS$85-$130.

Vagabond Inn (1245 North Oxnard Boulevard, 93030; 983-0251, Fax 988-9638, 800-522-1555) 70 rooms, restaurant, complimentary breakfast, swimming pool, no-smoking rooms, pets allowed, airport transportation, free local telephone calls, no-smoking rooms, children under 18 free, fax service, complimentary newspaper. SGL$45-$58, DBL$50-$58.

Wagon Wheel Motor Inn (2751 Wagon Wheel Road, 93030; 485-3131) 83 rooms, swimming pool. SGL/DBL$29-$39.

Pacific Beach

Area Code 619

Catamaran Resort Hotel (3999 Mission Boulevard, 92109; 488-1081, Fax 488-0901, 800-228-0770) 314 rooms and suites, restaurant, swimming pool, airport transportation, exercise facilities, beach, wheelchair-access rooms, no-smoking rooms. SGL/DBL$120-$180, STS$175-$250.

Pacific Shores Inn (4802 Mission Boulevard, 92109; 483-6300, Fax 483-9276) 55 rooms, swimming pool, pets allowed. SGL$75-$85, DBL$80-$95.

Pacific Terrace Inn (610 Diamond Street, 92109l 581-3500, Fax 274-3341, 800-334-3370 in California) 73 rooms and suites, restaurant, complimentary breakfast, swimming pool, wheelchair-access rooms. SGL$150-$170, DBL$150-$180, STS$225+.

Pacific Grove

Area Code 408
Pacific Grove Chamber of Commerce
Forest and Central Avenues
Pacific Grove CA 93950
373-3304

Asilomar Conference Center (800 Asilomar Boulevard; 372-8016, Fax 372-7227) 320 rooms, restaurant, complimentary breakfast, swimming pool, free parking, wheelchair-access rooms. SGL$55-$65, DBL$65-$65, STS$110+.

Best Western Butterfly Trees Lodge (1150 Lighthouse Avenue, 93950; 372-0503, Fax 372-4385, 800-528-1234) 68 rooms, restaurant, complimentary breakfast, swimming pool, spa, sauna, fireplaces, fax service, meeting facilities, no-smoking rooms, wheelchair-access rooms, pets allowed. SGL$59-$99, DBL$79-$109.

Bide-A-Wee Motel (221 Asilomar Boulevard, 93950; 372-2330) 17 rooms. SGL/DBL$50-$80.

Butterfly Grove Inn (1073 Lighthouse Avenue, 93950; 373-4921) 28 rooms, swimming pool, no-smoking rooms. SGL/DBL$55-$95.

Centrella Hotel (612 Central Avenue, 93950; 372-3372, 800-233-3372) 26 rooms and cottages, bed and breakfast, complimentary breakfast, airport transportation, free parking, no smoking, wheelchair-access rooms. SGL/DBL$95-$185.

The Executive Lodge (660 Dennett Avenue, 93950; 373-8777, 800-221-9323 in California) 30 rooms, complimentary breakfast, wheelchair-access rooms, free parking. SGL/DBL$95-$150.

Gatehouse Inn (225 Central Avenue, 93950; 649-8436, 800-753-1881) 8 rooms, bed and breakfast, complimentary breakfast, wheelchair-access rooms, free parking. SGL/DBL$95-$170.

Gosby House Inn (643 Lighthouse Avenue, 93950; 375-1287) 22 rooms, bed and breakfast, complimentary breakfast, no-smoking rooms. SGL/DBL$85-$130.

Green Gables (104 Fifth Street, 93950; 375-2095) 11 rooms, complimentary breakfast, no-smoking rooms. SGL/DBL$100-$160.

Lakewood Inn (740 Crocker Avenue, 93950; 373-1114) 25 rooms. SGL/DBL$52-$72.

Lighthouse Lodge (1249 Lighthouse Avenue, 93950; 655-2111) 30 rooms, restaurant, complimentary breakfast, wheelchair access. SGL/DBL$99-$199.

Martine Inn (255 Ocean View Boulevard, 93950; 373-3388) 19 rooms, bed and breakfast, complimentary breakfast, wheelchair-access rooms, no-smoking rooms, free parking. SGL/DBL$115-$225.

Old Saint Angela Inn (321 Central Avenue, 93950; 372-3246) 9 rooms, bed and breakfast, complimentary breakfast, no-smoking. SGL/DBL$75-$135.

Pacific Gardens Inn (701 Asilomar Boulevard, 93950; 646-9414) 28 rooms, complimentary breakfast. SGL/DBL$70-$150.

Pacific Grove Inn (581 Pine Avenue, 93950; 375-2825) 10 rooms, bed and breakfast, complimentary breakfast, wheelchair-access rooms, no-smoking. SGL/DBL$75-$90.

Pacific Grove Motel (Lighthouse at Grove Acres, 93950; 373-3741) 20 rooms, swimming pool. SGL/DBL$40-$90.

Pacific Grove Plaza (620 Lighthouse Avenue, 93950; 373-0562) 33 rooms. SGL/DBL$120+.

Pine Acres Lodge (1150 Jewell Avenue, 93950; 372-6651, Fax 372-0392) 13 rooms. SGL/DBL$65-$175.

Quality Inn (1111 Lighthouse Avenue, 93950; 646-8885, 800-221-2222) 49 rooms, complimentary breakfast, swimming pool, sauna, whirlpools, meeting facilities, wheelchair-access rooms, no pets, free parking. SGL$70-$150, DBL$90-$190.

Rosedale Inn (775 Asilomar Avenue, 93950; 655-1000, Fax 655-0691) 28 rooms. SGL/DBL$95-$165.

Roserox Country Inn By The Sea (557 Ocean View Boulevard, 93950; 373-7673) 8 rooms, bed and breakfast, complimentary breakfast, free parking. SGL/DBL$125-$205.

Seven Gables Inn (555 Ocean View Boulevard, 93950; 372-4341) 14 rooms, bed and breakfast, complimentary breakfast, no-smoking. SGL/DBL$100-$185.

Sunset Motel (133 Asilomar Boulevard, 93950; 375-3936) 20 rooms and suites. SGL/DBL$55-$90, STS$75-$90.

Terrace Oaks Inn (1095 Lighthouse Avenue, 93950; 373-4382) 11 rooms, complimentary breakfast. SGL/DBL$48-$73.

Wilkie's Motel (1038 Lighthouse Avenue, 92950; 372-5960) 24 rooms, complimentary breakfast, no-smoking rooms. SGL/DBL$65-$85.

Palmdale

Area Code 805
Palmdale Chamber of Commerce
712 East Palmdale Boulevard
Palmdale CA 93550
273-3232

Best Western (38630 Fifth Street, 93550; 947-8055, Fax 947-9957, 800-325-2525) 150 rooms and suites, restaurant, swimming pool, wheelchair-access rooms, no-smoking rooms. SGL$45-$60, DBL$50-$65, STS$75-$120.

Days Inn (38630 Fifth Street West, 93550; 947-8055, Fax 947-9957, 800-325-2525) 150 rooms, restaurant, lounge, swimming pool, spa, valet laundry, gift shop, meeting facilities, children under 12 free, fax service. SGL$44-$60, DBL$50-$85.

Holiday Inn (38630 Fifth Street, 93550; 947-8055, Fax 947-9957, 800-HOLIDAY) 153 rooms, restaurant, lounge, swimming pool, spa, car rental, exercise facilities, airport transportation.

Ramada Inn (300 West Palmdale Boulevard, 93550; 273-1200, Fax 947-9593, 800-228-2828) 135 rooms and suites, restaurant, lounge, outdoor swimming pool, jacuzzi, airport transportation, free parking, valet laundry, fax service, meeting facilities for 300, children under 18 free, room service, wheelchair-access rooms, no-smoking rooms. SGL$57-$70, DBL$62-$75.

Super 8 Motel (200 West Palmdale Boulevard, 93550; 273-8000, Fax 266-4521, 800-800-8000) 94 rooms, restaurant, outdoor heated swimming pool, spa, meeting facilities, fax service, in-room refrigerators, wheelchair-access rooms, no-smoking rooms, no pets. SGL/DBL$32-$40.

Vagabond Inn (130 East Palmdale Boulevard, 93550; 273-1400, Fax 272-9473, 800-522-1555) 100 rooms, restaurant, complimentary breakfast, heated swimming pool, wheelchair-access rooms, in-room refrigerators, car rental, pets allowed, airport transportation, free local telephone calls, no-smoking rooms, children under 18 free, fax service, complimentary newspaper. SGL$35, DBL$35-$38.

Palomar

Area Code 619

Palomar Mountain Lodge (2228 Crestline Road, 92060; 742-1543) 10 rooms, restaurant, wheelchair-access rooms. SGL/DBL$45-$65.

Palm Desert

Area Code 619
Desert Resorts Convention and Visitors Bureau
44-100 Monterey Avenue #203
Palm Desert CA 92260
568-1886

Palm Desert Chamber cf Commerce
74-004 Highway 111
Palm Desert CA 92260
346-6111

RENTAL SOURCES: Century 21 Emery Rentals (73130 El Paseo, 92260; 568-1891, 800-635-8617) rental condos. LS $75-$120; HS $130-$240; **Continental Vacation Rentals** (73-091 Country Club Drive, 92260; 773-9951, 800-869-1129) rental condos. LS $125-$250/$650W-$1,150W; HS $150-$325/$800W-$1,300W; **Cove Condo Rentals** (77622 Country Club Drive, 92260; 360-6565, 800-777-2615) rental condos. LS$75-$120; HS$135-$210; **Desert Sunshine Rentals** (72-655 Highway 111, 92260; 568-9629, 800-654-8754) rentals condos and private homes. LS $67-$135; HS$135-$350; **Desert Vacation Rentals** (44-250 Monterey Avenue, 92260; 776-5430, 800-776-1245) rental condos. LS $90-$225; HS $190-$425; **Lobland-Waring Property Management** (73-350 El Paseo, 92260; 568-0777, 800-753-3325) rental condos and private homes. $1,000W; **Sunrise Company Vacation Rentals** (76-300 Country Club Drive, 92260; 345-5695, 800-869-1130) rental condos. LS $140-$245; HS $195-$330.

Casa Larrea Motel (73-771 Larrea Street, 92260; 568-0311) 20 rooms and efficiencies, complimentary breakfast, swimming pool, sauna, no pets. SGL/DBL$35-$64.

Palm Desert

Embassy Suites Hotel (74-700 Highway 111, 92260; 340-6600, Fax 340-9519, 800-633-2834, 800-223-1679 in California) 195 suites, restaurant, complimentary breakfast, swimming pool, spa, putting green, lighted tennis courts, exercise equipment, meeting facilities for 800, wheelchair-access rooms, no-smoking rooms. STS$59-$139.

Erawan Garden (Highway 111, 92260; one- and two-bedroom suites, restaurant, swimming pool, tennis, golf, wheelchair-access rooms, no-smoking rooms. 1BR$180+; 2BR$250+.

Gala Villa (73-721 Shadow Mountain Drive; 346-6121) 21 rooms, swimming pool. LS SGL/DBL$40-$48; HS SGL/DBL$64-$72.

Holiday Inn (74675 Highway 111, 92260; 619-340-4303, Fax 619-340-4303, 800-HOLIDAY) 129 rooms, restaurant, complimentary breakfast, swimming pool, sauna, balconies, whirlpools, jacuzzi, exercise facilities, tennis, airport transportation, no pets. SGL/DBL$89-$190.

Howard Johnson Hotel (74675 Highway 11, 92260; 619-340-4303, Fax 619-340-4303, 800-654-2000) 132 rooms and one- and two-bedroom suites, restaurant, complimentary breakfast, outdoor swimming pool, saunas, lighted tennis courts, fax service, valet laundry, balconies, wheelchair-access rooms, no pets. SGL/DBL$35-$175.

The Inn At Deep Canyon (74-470 Abronia Trail, 92260; 346-8061) 30 rooms, swimming pool, wheelchair access, no-smoking rooms. SGL/DBL$85-$150.

International Lodge (74-380 El Camino, 92260; 346-6161) 51 rooms and efficiencies, swimming pool. SGL/DBL$45-$85.

Marriott's Desert Springs Resort and Spa (74-855 County Club Drive, 92260; 619-341-2211, Fax 341-1872, 800-228-9290) 891 rooms, restaurant, swimming pool, golf, lighted tennis courts, exercise facilities, wheelchair-access rooms, no-smoking rooms, pets allowed. LS SGL/DBL$150-$230;HS SGL/DBL$350-$495.

Palm Desert Biltmore Hotel (73-850 Highway 111, 92260; 346-6088) 16 rooms, swimming pool. SGL$85, DBL$96-$105.

Palm Desert Resort and Country Club (77-333 Country Club Drive, 92260; 345-2781) 300 rooms and suites, restaurant, swimming pool, lighted tennis courts.

Shadow Mountain Resort (45750 San Luis Rey, 92260; 472-3713, Fax 346-6518, 800-472-3713) 125 condos and suites, restaurant, swimming pool, lighted tennis courts, golf, no-smoking rooms. LS SGL/DBL$80-$235; HS SGL/DBL$130-$395.

The Traveler's Inn (Highway 111, 92260; 341-9100, Fax 773-3515, 800-633-8300) 115 rooms, complimentary breakfast, swimming pool, airport courtesy car, wheelchair-access rooms, no-smoking rooms. SGL/DBL$62-$87.

Vacation Inn Hotel (74-715 Highway 111, 92260; 619-340-4441, 800-231-8675) 133 rooms, restaurant, outdoor heated swimming pool, spa, children under 16 free, tennis, exercise facilities, meeting facilities for 80, airport transportation, free parking, wheelchair access, no-smoking rooms, no pets. SGL/DBL$39-$85.

Palm Springs

Area Code 619
Palm Springs Convention and Visitors Bureau
Airport Park Plaza
Palm Springs CA 92262
327-8411

RENTAL SOURCES: National Reservation Bureau, Inc. (19510 Ventura Boulevard, Tarzana CA 91357; 818-344-6776, 800-537-7666) represents hotels and inns in the Anaheim area. SGL/DBL$30-$200.

Arrowhead Arms Motel (715 San Lorenzo Road, 92264; 325-9723) 15 rooms and suites, swimming pool, airport transportation. SGL/DBL$40-$90, STS$90+.

Autry Resort Hotel (4200 East Palm Canyon Drive, 92264; 328-1171, Fax 324-7280, 800-443-6328) 173 rooms and cottage suites, restaurant, complimentary breakfast, swimming pool, exercise facilities, airport transportation, wheelchair-access rooms, no-smoking rooms, pets allowed. SGL/DBL$125-$195, STS$185+.

The Bahama Hotel (2323 North Palm Canyon Drive, 92262; 325-8190) 28 rooms, swimming pool. SGL/DBL$35-$65.

Best Western Aloha Tropics Hotel (411 East Palm Canyon Drive, 92262; 327-1391, Fax 323-3493, 800-367-6858, 800-528-1234) 92 rooms, restaurant, lounge, swimming pool, spa, laundry room, gift shop, children under 12 free, pets allowed. SGL$64-$89, DBL$64-$200.

Best Western Host Hotel (1633 South Palm Canyon Drive, 92264; 325-9177, Fax 325-9177, 800-528-1234, 800-222-4678) 72 rooms, restaurant, lounge, complimentary breakfast, swimming pool, spa, children under 12 free, tours, no-smoking rooms, no pets. LS SGL$69-$78, DBL$89-$98; HS SGL$125-$150, DBL$225-$250.

Best Western Royal Sun Hotel (1700 South Palm Canyon Drive, 92264; 327-1564, Fax 322-1796, 800-338-1188, 800-528-1234) 66 rooms, restaurant, lounge, complimentary breakfast, swimming pool, hot tubs, spa, laundry room, children under 12 free, no-smoking rooms, no pets. SGL/DBL$49-$64.

Casa Cody Bed and Breakfast Country Inn (175 South Cahailla Road, 92262; 320-9346, Fax 325-8610, 800-231-CODY) 17 rooms and suites, bed and breakfast, complimentary breakfast, kitchenettes, fireplaces, courtesy car, wheelchair-access rooms, two swimming pools, spa, free parking. LS SGL/DBL$35-$105, STS$70-$160; HS $65-$160, STS$80+.

Cambridge Inn (1277 South Palm Canyon Drive, 92264; 325-5026, 800-843-2128 in California) 65 rooms, swimming pool. SGL/DBL$59-$79.

Canyon Hotel Racquet and Golf Resort (2850 South Palm Canyon Drive, 92262; 323-5656) 465 rooms and suites, restaurant, swimming pool, tennis courts, golf course.

Cathedral Canyon Resort (34567 Cathedral Canyon Drive, 92264; 321-9000, 800-824-8224 in California) 162 suites, restaurant, swimming pool, tennis courts. LS SGL/DBL$65-$85; MS SGL/DBL$95-$135; HS SGL/DBL$150-$190.

Club Trinidad Resort (1900 East Palm Canyon Drive, 92264; 327-1161) 44 rooms. SGL/DBL$85-$200.

Comfort Inn (950 North Indian Avenue, 92262; 325-2707; 800-638-2657, 800-228-5150) 52 rooms and efficiencies, complimentary breakfast, restaurant, swimming pool, airport transportation.

Courtyard by Marriott (1200 Tahquitz Canyon Way, 92262; 322-6100, Fax 322-6091) 149 rooms and suites, restaurant, swimming pool, airport courtesy car, exercise facilities, wheelchair-access rooms, no-smoking rooms. SGL/DBL$130-$140, STS$140+.

Days Inn (69-151 East Palm Canyon Drive, 92234; 324-5934, Fax 324-3034, 800-325-2525) 97 one- and two-bedroom suites, swimming pool, wheelchair-access rooms, no-smoking rooms, no pets. LS 1BR$69-$89, 2BR$115-$125; HS 1BR$93-$113, 2BR$144-$147.

Doubletree Resort (Landau Boulevard, 92263; 322-7000, Fax 322-6853, 800-528-0444) 280 rooms and suites, two restaurants, lounge, swimming pool, sauna, meeting facilities for 1,200, putting green, exercise facilities, golf, tennis, airport courtesy car, free parking. SGL/DBL$80-$205, STS$160-$750.

El Rancho Lodge (1330 East Palm Canyon Drive, 92264 327-1339, 800-869-1138) 19 rooms and suites, restaurant, complimentary breakfast, swimming pool, airport courtesy car. SGL/DBL$55-$75, STS$120+.

Four Seasons Apartments (290 San Jacinto Drive, 92262; 325-6427) 20 rooms and suites, swimming pool, no-smoking rooms. SGL/DBL$95, STS$125+.

Friendship Inn (950 North Indian Avenue, 92262; 325-2707, 800-453-4511) 86 rooms, restaurant, swimming pool. SGL/DBL$39-$65.

Golden Palm Villa (601 Grenfall Road, 92264; 327-1408) 21 rooms and efficiencies, swimming pool, airport courtesy car, no children. SGL/DBL$60-$90.

Hampton Inn (2000 North Palm Canyon Drive, 92262; 320-0555, Fax 320-2261, 800-HAMPTON) 95 rooms, complimentary breakfast, swimming pool, meeting facilities, wheelchair-access rooms, no-smoking rooms. SGL/DBL$64-$71.

Hilton Hotel (400 East Tahquitz Canyon Way, 92262; 320-6868, Fax 320-2126) 260 rooms and suites, restaurant, swimming pool, airport courtesy car, lighted tennis courts, meeting facilities for 1,500, business services, airport transportation, wheelchair-access rooms, no-smoking rooms, pets allowed. SGL/DBL$175-$275, STS$275+.

Holiday Inn (155 South Belardo Road, 92262; 325-1301, Fax 691-323-8937, 800-622-9451, 800-HOLIDAY) 121 rooms, restaurant, lounge, swimming pool, spa, putting green, in-room refrigerators and microwaves, meeting facilities for 250, exercise center, wheelchair-access rooms, airport transportation, no pets. SGL/DBL89-$119.

Hyatt Regency Suites (285 North Palm Canyon Drive, 92262; 322-9000, Fax 325-4027, 800-233-1234) 194 one- and two-bedroom suites, restaurant, lounge, swimming pool, whirlpools, sauna, golf, balconies, in-room refrigerators, airport courtesy car, exercise facilities, wheelchair-access rooms, no-smoking rooms. STS$195-$400+.

Ingleside Inn (200 West Ramon Road, 92264; 325-0046, Fax 325-0710, 800-772-6655, 800-826-4162 in California) 29 rooms and suites, restaurant, complimentary breakfast, swimming pool, airport courtesy car. SGL/DBL$85-$275, STS$300-$500+.

La Mancha Private Villas and Court Club (444 Avenida Caballeros, 92263; 323-1773, Fax 323-5928, 800-854-1298, 800-255-1773) 54 suites and villas, restaurant, outdoor heated swimming pool, jacuzzi, in-room refrigerators and microwaves, fax service, meeting facilities for 30, lighted tennis courts, exercise facilities, airport courtesy car, wheelchair-access rooms, no pets. SGL/DBL/STS$135-$695.

La Siesta Villa (247 West Stevens Road, 92262; 325-2269) one- and two-bedroom villas, complimentary breakfast, swimming pool, no-smoking rooms. SGL/DBL$100-$175.

Las Brisas (222 South Indian Canyon Drive, 92262; 325-4372, Fax 320-1371, 800-346-5714) 90 rooms and suites, complimentary breakfast, swimming pool, airport courtesy car, wheelchair access, no-smoking rooms. SGL/DBL$100-$115, STS$170-$190.

Lawrence Welk's Desert Oasis (34567 Cathedral Canyon Drive, 92234; 321-9000, Fax;: 321-6200, 800-542-4253, 800-824-8224 in California) 165 suites and efficiencies, restaurant, swimming pool, airport transportation, lighted tennis courts, golf, wheelchair access, no-smoking rooms. STS$170-$250.

Lexington Hotel Suites (69-151 East Palm Canyon Drive, 92234; 324-5939, Fax 324-3034, 800-53-SUITES) 97 suites, complimentary breakfast, swimming pool, airport transportation, wheelchair access, no-smoking rooms. 1BR$110-$120, 2BR$125-$165.

Mira Loma Hotel (1420 North Indian Avenue, 92262; 320-1178) 14 rooms and suites, swimming pool, airport courtesy car. SGL/DBL$50-$65, STS$85-$95.

Motel 6 (595 East Palm Canyon Drive, 92262; 325-6129, 505-891-6161) 125 rooms. SGL/DBL$27-$38.

Motel 6 (660 South Palm Canyon Drive, 92262; 327-4200, 505-891-6161) 149 rooms. SGL/DBL$30-$42.

Oasis Water Resort Villa Hotel (4190 East Palm Canyon Drive, 92264; 328-1499, Fax 324-8659, 800-247-4664) 110 rooms, complimentary breakfast, swimming pool, tennis, airport transportation, no-smoking rooms. SGL/DBL$160-$329.

Orchard Tree Inn (261 South Belardo Road, 92262; 325-2791, 800-733-3435) 35 rooms, bed and breakfast, complimentary breakfast. SGL/DBL$65-$225.

Palm Springs Marquis Hotel and Villas (150 South Indian Avenue, 92262; 322-2121, 800-458-6679, 800-223-1050 in California) 264 rooms and suites, restaurant, lounge, two outdoor swimming pools, jacuzzi, children under 12 stay free, gift shop, valet laundry, meeting facilities for 1,000, exercise facilities, lighted tennis courts, wheelchair-access rooms, no-smoking rooms, no pets. SGL/DBL$60-$90, STS$130-$155.

Palm Tree Motel (1590 East Palm Canyon Drive, 92264; 327-1293) 15 rooms, complimentary breakfast, swimming pool, airport transportation. SGL/DBL$55-$120.

The Palms at Palm Springs (572 North Indian Avenue, 92262; 325-1111, Fax 327-0867) 37 rooms, restaurant, complimentary breakfast, swimming pool, exercise facilities. SGL$180-$210, DBL$119-$150.

Park Inn Club and Breakfast Palm Springs (415 South Belardo Road, 92262; 320-4117, Fax 323-3303) 50 rooms and cottage suites, complimentary breakfast, three swimming pools, spa, meeting facilities for 60, kitchenettes, airport courtesy car, no-smoking rooms. SGL/DBL$55-$100.

Quality Inn (1269 East Palm Canyon Drive, 92264; 323-2775, Fax 323-4234, 800-221-2222, 800-472-4339) 124 rooms, restaurant, lounge, swimming pool, whirlpool, airport courtesy car, wheelchair access, no-smoking rooms, no pets. SGL/DBL$39-$175.

Racquet Club of Palm Springs (400 East Tahquitz-McCallum, 92262; 320-6868, Fax 320-2126, 800-HILTONS) 265 rooms, restaurant, swimming pool, tennis, airport transportation, wheelchair access, no-smoking rooms, pets allowed. SGL$180-$210, DBL$120-$150.

Radisson Palm Springs Resort and Conference Center (1600 North Indian Avenue, 92262; 327-8311, Fax 327-4323) 480 rooms and suites, restaurant, swimming pool, lighted tennis courts, airport courtesy car, exercise facilities, wheelchair-access rooms, no-smoking rooms. SGL/DBL$130-$180, STS$190-$500.

Ramada Resort (2800 South Palm Canyon Drive, 92264; 323-1711, Fax 322-1075, 800-245-6904) 255 rooms and suites, restaurant, two swimming pools, spa, children under 18 free, airport transportation, exercise facilities, wheelchair-access rooms, free parking, no-smoking rooms. SGL/DBL$80-$140, STS$125-$200.

Ramada Hotel Resort (1800 East Palm Canyon Drive, 92264; 323-1711, Fax 322-1075, 800-2-RAMADA) 255 rooms, restaurant, lounge, swimming pool, whirlpools, exercise facilities, children under 18 free, balconies, gift shop, airport transportation, wheelchair-access rooms, no-smoking rooms. SGL/DBL$49-$139.

Racquet Club of Palm Springs (2743 North Indian Avenue, 92263; 325-1281, Fax 325-4529, 800-367-0946, 800-423-6588 in California) 150 rooms and suites, restaurant, swimming pool, airport courtesy car, lighted tennis courts, exercise facilities, wheelchair-access rooms, no-smoking rooms, pets allowed. SGL/DBL$130-$170, STS$200+.

Riviera Resort and Racquet Club (1600 North Indian Canyon Drive, 92262; 327-8311, Fax 327-4323) 516 rooms. SGL/DBL$70-$195.

Shilo Inn Palms Springs Desert Resort (1875 North Palm Canyon Drive, 92262; 320-7676, 800-222-2244) 124 rooms, restaurant, complimentary breakfast, two swimming pools, spa, sauna, complimentary newspaper, laundry room, airport courtesy car, in-room refrigerators, wheelchair-access rooms, no-smoking rooms, exercise facilities. LS SGL/DBL$55-$85; HS SGL/DBL$90-$129.

Smoke Tree Inn (1800 Smoke Tree Lane, 92264; 327-8355, 800-331-1306 in California) 51 rooms, complimentary breakfast, swimming pool, wheelchair access. SGL/DBL$100+.

Spa Hotel and Mineral Springs (100 North Indian Avenue, 92263; 854-1279, Fax 325-3344, 800-854-1279, 800-472-4371 in California) 230 rooms and suites, restaurant, airport courtesy car, swimming pool, free parking, lighted tennis courts, exercise facilities, wheelchair-access rooms, no-smoking rooms. SGL/DBL$98-$185, STS$253-$400+.

Sundance Villas (303 West Cabrillo Road, 92262; 325-3888) 19 villas, swimming pool, airport courtesy car, lighted tennis courts, exercise facilities. SGL/DBL$350-$500+.

Super 8 Motel (1900 North Palm Canyon Drive, 92262; 322-3757, Fax 323-5290, 800-800-8000) 63 rooms and suites, restaurant, complimentary breakfast, outdoor heated swimming pool, spa, free local telephone calls, fax service, in-room refrigerators, wheelchair-access rooms, no-smoking rooms, pets allowed. SGL/DBL$55-$66.

TraveLodge Palm Springs (333 East Palm Canyon Drive, 92264; 327-1211, Fax 320-4672, 800-255-3050) 158 rooms, restaurant, lounge, complimentary breakfast, swimming pool, whirlpool, balconies, laundry room, no pets. LS SGL/DBL$29; HS SGL/DBL$49.

Vagabond Inn (1699 South Palm Canyon Drive, 92264; 325-7211, Fax 322-9269, 800-522-1555) 120 rooms, heated restaurant, sauna, swimming pool, in-room refrigerators, no-smoking rooms, airport transportation, free local telephone calls, no-smoking rooms, children under 18 free, fax service, complimentary newspaper. SGL$35-$75, DBL$39-$79.

Villa Royale (1620 Indian Trail, 92264; 327-2314, 800-245-2314) 34 rooms and efficiencies, restaurant, complimentary breakfast, swimming pool, airport transportation. SGL/DBL$65-$150, EFF$135.

Westward Ho Hotel (701 East Palm Canyon Drive, 92264; 320-2700, 800-854-4345) 208 rooms, restaurant, lounge, outdoor swimming pool, jacuzzi, no-smoking rooms, airport transportation. SGL/DBL$40-$80.

Wyndham Palm Springs (888 East Tahquitz Canyon Way, 92262; 322-6000, Fax 322-5351) 410 rooms and suites, restaurant, lounge, swimming pool, sauna, whirlpool, meeting facilities for 1,800, free parking, airport courtesy car, exercise facilities, tennis, golf, wheelchair-access rooms, no-smoking rooms. SGL/DBL$180-$230, STS$200-$230.

Pasadena and South Pasadena

Area Code 818
Pasadena Chamber of Commerce
199 South Los Robles Avenue #210
Pasadena CA 91101
795-335

Pasadena Convention and Visitors Bureau
171 South Los Robles Avenue
Pasadena CA 91101
795-9311

South Pasadena Chamber of Commerce
1005 Fair Oaks Avenue
South Pasadena CA 91030
799-7161

RENTAL SOURCES: Apartments For Travelers (The Valley; 952-1336) rental source for one- and two-bedroom apartments in the Burbank area. SGL/DBL$65-$100.

Best Western Colorado Inn (2156 East Colorado Boulevard, 91107; 793-9339, Fax 568-2731, 800-528-1234) 77 rooms and suites, restaurant, lounge, complimentary breakfast, swimming pool, jacuzzi, meeting facilities for 35, in-room refrigerators, complimentary newspaper, whirlpool, laundry room, fax service, wheelchair-access rooms. SGL/DBL$54-$86.

Best Western Pasadena Inn (3570 East Colorado Boulevard, 91107; 796-9100, Fax 9948, 800-528-1234) 63 rooms, restaurant, complimentary breakfast, swimming pool, spa, sauna, in-room refrigerators, airport transportation, valet laundry, children under 12 free, laundry room. SGL/DBL$36-$61.

Best Western Pasadena Royale Inn (3600 East Colorado Boulevard, 91107; 793-0950, Fax 568-2827, 800-528-1234) 63 rooms and suites, restaurant, valet laundry, meeting facilities, fax service, complimentary breakfast, swimming pool. SGL$44-$78, DBL$50-$83.

Comfort Inn East (2462 East Colorado Boulevard, 91107; 405-0811, 800-221-2222) 50 rooms, complimentary breakfast, swimming pool, spa, jacuzzi, sauna, in-room refrigerators and microwaves, exercise facilities, no-smoking rooms, wheelchair-access rooms, no pets. LS SGL$49-$57, DBL$54-$57; HS SGL/DBL$110.

Days Inn Pasadena (3500 Colorado Boulevard, 91107; 792-1363, Fax 792-9213, 800-325-2525) 101 rooms and suites, restaurant, swimming pool, whirlpool, beauty salon, valet laundry, fax service, children under 12 free, wheelchair-access rooms, no-smoking rooms. SGL$49-$65, DBL$60-$75, STS$65-$95.

Donnymac Irish Inn (119 North Meredith Avenue, 91106; 440-0066) 4 rooms, bed and breakfast, complimentary breakfast, no-smoking rooms. SGL/DBL$85+.

Doubletree Hotel at Plaza Las Fuentes (191 North Los Robles, 91101; 792-2727, Fax 795-7669, 800-528-0444) 362 rooms and suites, restaurant, outdoor swimming pool, sauna, business services, meeting facilities for 500, airport transportation, exercise facilities, no-smoking rooms, pets allowed. SGL$79-$135, DBL$89-$149, STS$250-$750.

Econo Lodge (1203 East Colorado Boulevard, 91106; 449-3170, 800-424-4777) 53 rooms and efficiencies, swimming pool, kitchenettes, children under 18 free. SGL/DBL$36-$175.

Hilton Inn (150 South Los Robles Avenue, 91101; 855-1000, Fax 584-3148, 800-HILTONS) 300 rooms and suites, restaurant, swimming pool, meeting facilities for 1,000, tennis, wheelchair-access rooms, no-smoking rooms. SGL/DBL$125-$170.

Holiday Inn (303 East Cordova Street, 91101; 449-4000, Fax 584-1390, 800-457-7940, 800-HOLIDAY) 318 rooms and suites, restaurant, swimming pool, meeting facilities for 300, gift shop, car rental, tennis, airport transportation, pets allowed. SGL$89-$108, DBL$101-$120, STS$125-$150.

Livingston Hotel and Apartments (139 South Los Robles Avenue, 91101; 795-3311) 27 rooms and suites, restaurant. SGL/DBL$45-$50.

Pasadena Inn (400 South Arroyo Parkway, 91105; 795-8401, Fax 577-2629) 62 rooms, restaurant, outdoor swimming pool, in-room refrigerators, meeting facilities for 100, pets allowed, fax service, car rental, free parking. SGL/DBL$40-$60.

Regal Inn Motel (3800 East Colorado Boulevard, 91107; 448-4743) 35 rooms and efficiencies, swimming pool, in-room refrigerators. SGL/DBL$33-$38.

Ritz Carlton Huntington Hotel (1401 South Oak Knoll Avenue, 91106; 568-3900, Fax 568-3159) 401 rooms and suites, restaurant, swimming pool, spa, exercise facilities, lighted tennis courts, airport transportation, wheelchair-access rooms, meeting facilities for 1,000, no-smoking rooms, pets allowed. SGL/DBL$135-$210, STS$230-$2,500.

Rodeway Inn (3321 East Colorado Boulevard, 91107; 796-9291, 800-424-4777) 73 rooms and suites, indoor and outdoor swimming pools, whirlpool, in-room refrigerators, meeting facilities for 20, jacuzzi, in-room refrigerators, no-smoking rooms, meeting facilities, wheelchair-access rooms, children under 18 free. SGL$45-$49, DBL$53-$105.

Saga Motor Hotel (1633 East Colorado Boulevard, 91106; 795-0431) 69 rooms, complimentary breakfast, swimming pool. SGL$49-$55, DBL$53-$59.

TraveLodge (2131 East Colorado Boulevard, 91107; 796-3121, Fax 793-4713, 800-255-3050) 84 rooms and suites, restaurant, lounge, swimming pool, whirlpool, airport transportation, in-room refrigerators, no pets. SGL/DBL$40-$70.

Vagabond Inn Pasadena (2863 East Colorado Boulevard, 91107; 449-3020, Fax 578-9791, 800-522-1555) 88 rooms, restaurant, complimentary breakfast, heated swimming pool, in-room refrigerators, free parking, car rental, pets allowed, airport transportation, free local telephone calls, no-smoking rooms, children under 18 free, fax service, complimentary newspaper. SGL$40-$46, DBL$45-$66.

Paso Robles

Area Code 805
Paso Robles Chamber of Commerce
1113 Spring Street
Paso Robles CA 93446
238-0506

Adelaide Motor Inn (1215 Ysabel Avenue, 93446; 238-2770, Fax 238-3497, 800-549-PASO in California) 67 rooms, restaurant, swimming pool, airport courtesy car, wheelchair access, no-smoking rooms. SGL$35-$48, DBL$46-$50.

Best Western Black Oak Motor Lodge (1135 24th Street, 93446; 238-4740, Fax 238-0726, 800-528-1234) 110 rooms, restaurant, lounge, swimming pool, spa, in-room refrigerators and microwaves, whirlpool, laundry room, airport transportation, wheelchair access, no-smoking rooms. no pets. SGL/DBL$54-$64.

Lake Nacimiento Resort (Lake Nacimiento Road, 93446; 238-3256, 800-323-3839) 19 rooms and efficiencies, restaurant, swimming pool, wheelchair-access rooms, no-smoking rooms. SGL/DBL$60-$125+.

Melody Ranch (939 Spring Street, 93446; 238-3911) 19 rooms, restaurant, swimming pool. SGL/DBL$30-$42.

Paso Robles Inn (1103 Spring Street, 93446; 238-2660, Fax 238-4707) 70 rooms, restaurant, swimming pool, exercise facilities, airport transportation, wheelchair access, no-smoking rooms, free parking. SGL/DBL$45-$60.

TraveLodge (2701 Spring Street, 93446; 238-0078, 800-255-3050) 31 rooms, restaurant, lounge, swimming pool, in-room microwaves, airport transportation. LS SGL/DBL$39-$65; HS SGL/DBL$42-$66.

Pismo Beach

Area Code 805
Pismo Beach Chamber of Commerce
581 Dolliver Street
Pismo Beach CA 93449
773-4382

Adams Motel (1000 Dolliver, 93449; 773-2065) 20 rooms and efficiencies, kitchenettes. SGL/DBL$50-$125.

Amber Motel (490 Dolliver Street, 93449; 773-3275) 20 rooms and two-bedroom suites, complimentary breakfast, heated outdoor swimming pool, airport transportation, beach nearby, pets allowed. SGL$35-$65, DBL$50-$95.

Beachcomber Motel (100 Ocean View, 93449; 800-773-4994, 800-662-5545 in California) 20 rooms, swimming pool, beach nearby, wheelchair-access rooms. SGL/DBL$45-$100.

Best Western Shelter Cove Lodge (2651 Price Street, 93449; 773-3511, 800-528-1234) 52 rooms, complimentary breakfast, restaurant, lounge, swimming pool, in-room refrigerators, meeting facilities, beach, children under 18 free, ocean view, wheelchair-access rooms, no-smoking rooms, no pets. LS SGL/DBL$83-$93; HS SGL$145-$155, DBL$155-$165.

Best Western Shore Cliff Lodge (2555 Price Street, 93449; 773-4671, Fax 773-2341, 800-528-1234, 800-441-8885) 99 rooms, restaurant, lounge, swimming pool, kitchenettes, ocean view, lighted tennis courts, meeting facilities, fax service, no pets. LS SGL/DBL$83-$93, HS SGL$95-$100, DBL$185-$210.

Blue Seal Inn (230 Dolliver Street, 93449; 773-2403) 26 rooms and efficiencies, complimentary breakfast. SGL/DBL$35-$45.

The Cliffs At Shell Beach (2757 Shell Beach Road, 93449; 773-5000, Fax 773-0764, 800-826-5838, 800-826-7827 in California) 176 rooms and suites, restaurant, swimming pool, ocean view, gift shop, conference facilities, airport courtesy car, exercise facilities, wheelchair-access rooms, no-smoking rooms. SGL/DBL$98-$185, STS$150-$255.

Dolphin Cove Lodge (170 Main Street, 93449; 773-4706) 22 rooms and efficiencies. SGL/DBL$50-$150.

Edgewater Motel (280 Wadsworth, 93449; 773-4811, 800-634-5858 in California) 93 rooms and efficiencies, heated swimming pool, jacuzzis. SGL/DBL$50-$150.

El Pismo Inn (230-240 Pomeroy, 93449; 773-4529) 22 rooms, free parking, no pets. SGL/DBL$45-$65.

Knight's Rest (2351 Price Street, 93449; 773-4617) 35 units and efficiencies, swimming pool, sauna, ocean view, wheelchair access. SGL/DBL$50-$100.

Kon Tiki Inn (1621 Price Street, 93449; 773-4833, Fax 773-6541) 86 rooms, restaurant, swimming pool, ocean view, exercise facilities, beach, lighted tennis courts, wheelchair-access rooms, no-smoking rooms. SGL/DBL$68-$88.

Ocean Palms Motel (390 Ocean View, 93449; 773-4669) 22 rooms, swimming pool, pets allowed. SGL/DBL$35-$50.

Palomar Motel (1601 Shell Beach Road, 93449; 773-1104) 12 rooms and efficiencies. SGL/DBL$30-$50.

Pismo Bay Motor Lodge (371 Pismo, 93449; 773-2554) 12 rooms and efficiencies, no-smoking rooms. SGL/DBL$35-$50.

Pismo Coast Inn (1111 Price Street, 93449; 773-4928) 11 rooms and efficiencies, pets allowed. SGL/DBL$50-$100.

Pismo Landmark (701 Price Street, 93449; 773-5566, 800-262-7557 in California) 19 rooms, bed and breakfast, kitchenettes, complimentary breakfast, wheelchair access.

Quality Suites (651 Five Cities Drive, 93440; 773-3773, 800-221-2222) 133 rooms, restaurant, heated swimming pool, whirlpool, in-room refrigerators and microwaves, putting green, wheelchair-access rooms, gift shop, no-smoking rooms, no pets. LS SGL$79-$109, DBL$89-$119; HS SGL$82-$112, DBL$92-$142.

Sandlecastle Inn (100 Stimson Avenue, 93449; 773-2422, 800-822-6606) 59 rooms and suites, complimentary breakfast, wheelchair-access rooms, heated spa, balconies, no-smoking rooms, beach. SGL/DBL$95-$155, STS$175-$200.

Sea Crest Resort Motel (2241 Price Street, 93449; 773-4608, 800-728-8400 in California) 160 rooms and suites, restaurant, swimming pool, beach, conference facilities, airport transportation, wheelchair-access rooms. SGL/DBL$65-$90.

Sea Garden Motel (340 Stimson, 93449; 773-2216) 19 rooms and efficiencies. SGL/DBL$50-$100.

Sea Gypsy (1020 Cypress Street, 93449; 773-1801, 800-422-1091, 800-592-5923 in California) 77 rooms and efficiencies, swimming pool, beach. SGL/DBL$35-$100.

Sea Venture Motel (100 Ocean View, 93449; 773-4994, Fax 773-4693, 800-237-4693, 800-662-5545 in California) 52 rooms, restaurant, complimentary breakfast, swimming pool, in-room refrigerators, airport transportation, beach, wheelchair-access rooms, no-smoking rooms. SGL/DBL$80-$160.

Sea View Motel (230 Five Cities Drive, 93449; 773-1841) 100 rooms, complimentary breakfast, heated outdoor swimming pool, jacuzzis, pets allowed. SGL/DBL$35-$50.

Spyglass Inn (2705 Spyglass Drive, 93449; 773-4855, 800-824-2612 in California) 82 rooms, restaurant, swimming pool, jacuzzis, ocean view, miniature golf course, airport courtesy car, no-smoking rooms. SGL/DBL$70-$120.

Surf Motel (250 Main Street, 93449; 773-2070) 33 rooms, complimentary breakfast, indoor heated swimming pool, whirlpools, airport transportation, wheelchair access, pets allowed. SGL$35-$65, DBL$50-$95.

Tides Motel (2121 Price Street, 93449; 773-2493) 26 rooms, swimming pool. SGL/DBL$50-$150.

Whalers Inn (2411 Price Street, 93449; 773-2411, 800-245-2411 in California) 140 rooms, heated swimming pool, spa, beach, ocean view, meeting facilities. SGL/DBL$50-$150.

Placentia

Area Code 714

Fairfield Inn (710 West Kimberly Avenue, 92670; 996-4410) 135 rooms. SGL/DBL$45+.

Marriott Residence Inn (700 West Kimberly, 92670; 996-0555, Fax 993-1043, 800-331-3131) 112 suites, restaurant, complimentary breakfast, meeting facilities for 25, in-room microwave, convenience store, wheelchair-access rooms, no-smoking rooms, pets allowed. SGL/DBL$69-$139.

Quality Hotel (118 East Orangethorpe Avenue, 92670; 528-7778, 800-221-2222) 102 rooms, restaurant, complimentary breakfast, swimming pool, exercise facilities, wheelchair-access rooms, no pets. SGL/DBL$45-$59.

Pomona

Area Code 714

All Star Inn (2470 South Garey Avenue, 91766; 591-1871) 153 rooms. SGL/DBL$31-$37.

Ha'Penny Inn (310 East Foothill Boulevard, 91767; 593-7617, Fax 596-1786) 80 rooms, swimming pool, no-smoking rooms. SGL/DBL$35-$55.

Pomona Hilltop Suites Hotel (3101 Temple Avenue, 91768; 598-7666, 800-222-2244) 130 suites, restaurant, complimentary breakfast, swimming pool, exercise facilities, airport courtesy car. SGL/DBL$109-$119.

Sheraton Suites Fairplex (1101 West McKinley Avenue, 91768; 622-2220, 800-325-3535) 255 suites, restaurant, lounge, heated swimming pool, spa, sauna, meeting facilities for 800, business services, exercise facilities, wheelchair-access rooms, no-smoking rooms, airport courtesy car.

Shilo Inn (3200 Temple, 91768; 598-0073, 800-222-2244) 130 suites, restaurant, complimentary breakfast, swimming pool, exercise facilities, airport courtesy car, wheelchair-access rooms, no-smoking rooms. SGL/DBL$79-$95.

Shilo Inn Hilltop (3101 Temple Avenue, 91768; 598-7666. Fax 598-5654) 215 rooms, restaurant, swimming pool, exercise facilities, airport transportation. SGL/DBL$91-$141.

Porterville

Area Code 209
Porterville Chamber of Commerce
36 West Cleveland
Porterville CA 93257
784-7502

The Sundance Inn (676 North Main Street, 93257; 784-7920) 44 rooms, swimming pool, airport transportation, no-smoking rooms. SGL$26, DBL$30+.

Port Hueneme

Area Code 805
Port Hueneme Chamber of Commerce
220 North Market Street
Port Hueneme CA 93041
488-2023

The Country Inn At Port Hueneme (350 East Hueneme Road, 93041; 986-5353, Fax 986-4399, 800-44-RELAX) 135 rooms and suites, complimentary breakfast, heated swimming pool, spa, in-room refrigerators and microwaves, meeting facilities, wheelchair access, no-smoking rooms. SGL/DBL$75-$85, STS$150.

Poway

Area Code 619

Poway Country Inn (13845 Poway Road, 92064; 748-6320) 44 rooms. SGL/DBL$41-$54.

TraveLodge (12448 Poway Road, 92064; 784-7311, 800-255-3050) 47 rooms, restaurant, lounge, swimming pool, whirlpool, meeting facilities, no pets. SGL/DBL$39-$44.

Ramona

Area Code 619

Ramona Valley Inn (416 Main Street, 92065; 789-6433) 39 rooms, complimentary breakfast, swimming pool, wheelchair access, no-smoking rooms. SGL$40-$50, DBL$45-$55.

San Vincente Inn and Golf Club (24157 San Vincente, 92065; 789-3788, 800-776-1289 in California) 28 rooms, restaurant, swimming pool, wheelchair-access rooms. SGL/DBL$65-$105.

Rancho Mirage

Area Code 619

All Star Inn (69-570 Highway 11, 92270; 324-8475) 66 rooms. SGL/DBL$31-$37.

Marriott's Rancho Las Palmas Resort (41000 Bob Hope Drive, 92270; 568-2727, Fax 568-5845, 800-228-9290) 456 rooms and suites, restaurant, swimming pool, airport transportation, golf, exercise facilities, wheelchair-access rooms, no-smoking rooms, pets allowed. SGL/DBL$70-$250.

The Ritz Carlton (68-900 Frank Sinatra Drive, 92270; 321-8282, Fax 328-3167, 800-241-3333) 240 rooms and suites, restaurant, swimming pool, airport courtesy car, golf, exercise facilities, lighted tennis courts, wheelchair-access rooms, no-smoking rooms. SGL/DBL$275-$375, STS$725-$1,700.

The Westin Mission Hills Resort (71333 Dinah Shore Drive, 92270; 328-5955, Fax 321-2955, 800-228-3000) 512 rooms and suites, restaurant, swimming pool, golf, lighted tennis courts, exercise facilities, airport transportation, wheelchair-access rooms, no-smoking rooms, pets allowed, free parking. LS SGL/DBL$135-$250; HS SGL/DBL$250-$385.

Rancho Santa Fe

Area Code 619

The Inn At Rancho Santa Fe (5951 Linea del Cielo, 92067; 756-1131, Fax 759-1604, 800-654-2928) 80 rooms, suites and cottages, restaurant, lounge, outdoor heated swimming pool, exercise equipment, children under 16 free, in-room refrigerators, fax service, meeting facilities for 120, laundry room, free parking, wheelchair access, tennis, pets allowed. SGL$80-$180, 1BR$140, 2BR$255-$425.

Rancho Valencia Resort (5921 Valencia Circle, 92067; 756-1123, Fax 756-0165, 800-548-3664) 43 villas and suites, restaurant, complimentary breakfast, swimming pool, airport transportation, tennis, wheelchair access, no-smoking rooms. SGL/DBL$295-$600.

Redlands

Area Code 714
Redlands Chamber of Commerce
One East Redlands Boulevard
Redlands CA 92373
793-2546

Best Western Sandman Motel (1120 West Colton Avenue, 92373; 793-2001, Fax 792-7612, 800-528-1234) 66 rooms, restaurant, complimentary breakfast, swimming pool, kitchenettes, fax service, whirlpools, no-smoking rooms, no pets. SGL/DBL$39-$54.

Budget Host Terrace Motel (102 The Terrace Avenue, 91770; 793-2408, 800-283-4678) 35 rooms. SGL/DBL$30-$40.

Morey Mansion (190 Terracina Boulevard, 92373; 793-7970) 5 rooms, bed and breakfast, complimentary breakfast.

Motel 6 (1160 Arizona Street, 92374; 792-3175. 505-891-6161) 80 rooms. SGL/DBL$25-$32.

Redondo Beach

Area Code 310
Redondo Beach Chamber of Commerce
1215 North Catalina Avenue
Redondo Beach CA 90277
376-6913

RENTAL SOURCES: ABC Travel Agency (18039 Crenshaw Boulevard, Torrance 90504; 376-3704, Fax 379-6615) rents ocean-front rental homes and apartments in the Redondo Beach area.

Best Western Galleria Inn (2740 Artesia Boulevard, 90278; 370-4353, Fax 793-7135, 800-528-1234) 39 rooms and suites, spa, complimentary breakfast, in-room refrigerators, valet laundry, airport courtesy car, fax service, wheelchair-access rooms, no-smoking rooms, free parking, car rental. SGL/DBL$52-$68, STS$90-$100.

Best Western Beach Inn (1850 South Pacific Coast Highway, 90277; 540-3700, Fax 540-3675, 800-528-1234) 108 rooms, restaurant, lounge, fax service, meeting facilities, heated swimming pool, jacuzzi, sauna, lighted tennis courts, exercise facilities. SGL/DBL$74-$89.

Best Western Sunrise Hotel-King Harbor Marina (400 North Harbor Drive, 90277; 376-0746, Fax 376-7384, 800-528-1234) 111 rooms and suites, restaurant, outdoor swimming pool, spa, exercise facilities, ocean view, in-room refrigerators, valet laundry, transportation to local attractions, fax service, complimentary newspaper, laundry room, wheelchair-access rooms, no-smoking rooms, free parking. SGL/DL$75-$100+.

Holiday Inn Crowne Plaza (300 North Harbor Drive, 90277; 318-8888, Fax 376-1930, 800-HOLIDAY) 343 rooms and suites, restaurant, lounge, outdoor swimming pool, spa, exercise facilities, in-room refrigerators and mini-bars, valet laundry, 24-hour room service, child care, fax and business services, transportation to local attractions, lighted tennis courts, meeting facilities for 700, complimentary newspaper, wheelchair-access rooms, no-smoking rooms, beauty and barber shop, gift shop, car rental. SGL/DBL$130-$183, STS$235-$625.

Palos Verdes Inn (1700 South Pacific Highway, 90277; 316-4211, 800-421-9241, 800-352-0385) 114 rooms and suites, restaurant, swimming pool, free parking. SGL$77-$85, DBL$85-$93, STS$110-$162.

Portofino Inn Redondo Beach (260 Portofino Way, 90277; 379-8481, Fax 372-7329, 800-468-4292) 168 rooms and suites, restaurant, lounge, swimming pool, ocean view, in-room refrigerators and mini-bars, 24-hour rooms service, fax service, complimentary evening snacks, gift shop, wheelchair-access rooms, no-smoking rooms, beach, exercise facilities. SGL/DBL$140-$200, STS$275+.

Sheraton At Redondo Beach (300 North Harbor Drive, 90277; 318-8888, Fax 376-1930, 800-325-3535) 339 rooms and suites, restaurant, lounge, outdoor heated swimming pool, spa, sauna, exercise facilities, tennis, meeting facilities for 600, business service, wheelchair-access rooms, no-smoking rooms, beach. SGL$115-$160, DBL$135-$180, STS$275-$600.

TraveLodge (2740 Artesia Boulevard, 90278; 370-4353, 800-255-3050, 800-233-8059) 50 rooms and suites, restaurant, swimming pool, whirlpool, fax service, balconies, ocean view, car rental, free parking. SGL$49-$55, DBL$52-$66, STS$75-$95.

TraveLodge (206 South Pacific Coast Highway, 90277; 318-1811, Fax 379-0190, 800-255-3050) 37 rooms and suites, restaurant, complimentary breakfast, outdoor swimming pool, spa, exercise facilities, valet laundry, fax service, no-smoking rooms, wheelchair-access rooms, free parking, tennis, no pets. SGL$49-$60, DBL$52-$64, STS$85-$95.

Vagabond Inn Redondo Beach (6226 Pacific Coast Highway, 90277; 378-8555, Fax 791-7034, 800-522-1555) 40 rooms and suites, restaurant, complimentary breakfast, outdoor heated swimming pool, free parking, pets allowed, airport transportation, free local telephone calls, no-smoking rooms, children under 18 free, fax service, complimentary newspaper. SGL$50-$57, DBL$55-$67.

Reedley

Area Code 209
Reedley District Chamber of Commerce
1613 12th Street
Reedley CA 93654
638-3548

Hotel Burgess (1726 11th Street, 93654; 638-6315) 19 rooms, no-smoking rooms. SGL$28-$50, DBL$26-$60.

Rialto

Area Code 714
Rialto Chamber of Commerce
120 North Riverside Avenue
Rialto CA 92376
875-5364

Best Western Empire Inn (475 West Valley Road, 92376; 877-0690, 800-528-1234) 100 rooms, restaurant, complimentary breakfast, swimming pool, sauna, exercise facilities, meeting facilities, no-smoking rooms, no pets. SGL$45-$55, DBL$55-$85.

TraveLodge (425 Foothills Boulevard, 92367; 820-0705, 800-255-3050) 50 rooms, restaurant, lounge, swimming pool, whirlpool, in-room refrigerators and microwaves, no pets. SGL/DBL$36-$45.

Ridgecrest

Area Code 619
Ridgecrest Chamber of Commerce
301 South China Lake Boulevard
Ridgecrest CA 93555
375-8331

Carriage Inn of Ridgecrest (901 China Lake Boulevard, 93555; 446-7910, Fax 446-6408, 800-854-2608, 800-542-6082 in California) 163 rooms, restaurant, swimming pool, exercise equipment, airport transportation, meeting facilities, wheelchair access, no-smoking rooms. SGL/DBL$70-$86.

Econo Lodge (210 Inyo-Kern road, 93555; 446-2551, 800-424-4777) 54 rooms, in-room refrigerators, children under 18 free, no pets. SGL/DBL$44-$50.

El Rancho Motel (507 South China Lake Boulevard, 93555; 375-9731) 88 rooms and efficiencies, swimming pool, pets allowed. SGL/DBL$35-$40.

Heritage Inn (1050 North Norma, 93555; 446-6543) 172 rooms, restaurant, swimming pool, pets allowed. SGL/DBL$55+.

Motel 6 (535 China Lake Boulevard, 93555; 375-6866, 505-891-6161) 76 rooms. SGL/DBL$21-$27.

Ridgecrest Motor Inn (329 Ridgecrest Boulevard, 93555; 375-1542) 62 rooms, swimming pool. SGL/DBL$30-$40.

Riverside

Area Code 714
Greater Riverside Chamber of Commerce
4261 Main Street
Riverside CA 92501
683-7100

Riverside Convention and Visitors Bureau
3443 Orange Street
Riverside CA 92501
787-7950

All Star Inn (1260 University Avenue, 92507; 784-2131) 54 rooms, swimming pool. SGL/DBL$27-$33.

Best Western Inn (10518 Magnolia Avenue, 92505; 359-0770, Fax 359-6749, 800-528-1234) 62 rooms, restaurant, lounge, swimming pool, in-room refrigerators, whirlpool, children under 12 free, wheelchair-access rooms, no-smoking rooms. SGL/DBL$47-$62.

Riverside

Days Inn (10545 Magnolia, 92507; 523-4914, 800-325-2525) 66 rooms and suites, complimentary breakfast, swimming pool, jacuzzis, children under 12 free, fax service, wheelchair-access rooms, no-smoking rooms, no pets. SGL/DBL$39-$60, STS$45-$70.

Days Inn (1510 University Avenue, 92507; 788-8989, Fax 787-6783, 800-325-2525) 163 rooms, restaurant, lounge, swimming pool, spa, valet laundry, gift shop, meeting facilities, wheelchair-access rooms, no-smoking rooms, children under 12 free, fax service, no pets. SGL/DBL$49-$85.

Econo Lodge (1971 University Avenue, 92507; 684-6363, Fax 684-9228, 800-424-4777) 45 rooms and efficiencies, restaurant, swimming pool, in-room refrigerators, wheelchair-access rooms, children under 18 free, no pets, no-smoking rooms. SGL/DBL$35-$55.

Econo Lodge (9878 Magnolia Avenue, 92503; 687-3090, 800-424-4777) 32 rooms, restaurant, complimentary breakfast, swimming pool, in-room refrigerators, children under 18 free, wheelchair-access rooms, no pets. SGL/DBL$39-$55.

Hampton Inn (1590 University Avenue, 92507; 683-6000, Fax 782-8052, 800-HAMPTON) 120 rooms, complimentary breakfast, swimming pool, meeting facilities, wheelchair access, no-smoking rooms. SGL/DBL$45-$49.

Holiday Inn Hotel and Conference Center (1200 University Avenue, 92507; 682-8000, Fax 682-7095, 800-HOLIDAY) 182 rooms, restaurant, lounge, swimming pool, meeting facilities for 700, children under 18 free, wheelchair-access rooms, exercise facilities, airport transportation, no-smoking rooms, pets allowed.

Howard Johnson Lodge (1199 University Avenue, 92507; 682-9011, Fax 369-6645, 800-654-2000) 102 rooms, restaurant, lounge, swimming pool, room service, laundry room, meeting facilities for 100, wheelchair-access rooms, no-smoking rooms. LS SGL$32-$50, DBL$37-$55; HS SGL$42-$60, DBL$47-$65.

Motel 6 (3663 La Sierra Avenue, 92505; 351-0764, 505-891-6161) 149 rooms. SGL/DBL$24-$30.

Motel 6 (4045 University Avenue, 92501; 686-6666, 505-891-6161) 53 rooms. SGL/DBL$24-$30.

Motel 6 (6830 Valley Way, 92509; 681-6666, 505-891-6161) 140 rooms. SGL/DBL$22-$28.

Mission Inn (3649 Seventh Street; 784-0300) 240 rooms and suites, restaurant, swimming pool, exercise facilities, airport courtesy car. SGL$95, DBL$110.

Sheraton Riverside Hotel (3400 Market Street, 92501; 784-8000, Fax 369-7127, 800-325-3535) 296 rooms and suites, two restaurants, lounge, swimming pool, spa, meeting facilities for 750, gift shop, airport courtesy car, wheelchair-access rooms, no-smoking rooms.

Super 8 Motel (1199 University Avenue, 92507; 682-9011, Fax 369-6645) 103 rooms. SGL/DBL$30-$36.

TraveLodge (11043 Magnolia Avenue, 92505; 688-5000, Fax 785-5655, 800-255-3050) 42 rooms and suites, restaurant, lounge, complimentary breakfast, swimming pool, whirlpool, meeting facilities for 12, kitchenettes, tennis, no pets. SGL/DBL$49-$79.

Rosemead

Area Code 213

Motel 6 (1001 San Gabriel Boulevard, 91770; 572-6076) 130 rooms. SGL/DBL$30-$40.

Rodeway Inn (8832 Glendon Way, 91770; 288-9801, 800-424-4777) 53 rooms, complimentary breakfast, swimming pool, whirlpool, wheelchair-access rooms, children under 18 free. SGL/DBL$35-$45.

Sheraton Rosemead Hotel (888 Montebello Boulevard, 91770; 722-8800, Fax 721-8028, 800-325-3535) 147 rooms and suites, restaurant, lounge, outdoor heated swimming pool, spa, sauna, meeting facilities for 300, gift shop, exercise facilities, airport transportation, wheelchair-access rooms, no-smoking rooms.

TraveLodge (8463 East Garvey Avenue, 91770; 818-571-5555, Fax 818-572-7416, 800-255-3050) 56 rooms and suites, restaurant, lounge, swimming pool, whirlpool, complimentary newspaper, meeting facilities, tours, in-room refrigerators, car rental, airport transportation, free parking, no pets. SGL$40-$42, DBL$46-$48, STS$75-$85.

TraveLodge (2146 San Gabriel Boulevard, 91770; 818-280-0501, 800-255-3050) 50 rooms and suites, restaurant, lounge, whirlpool, laundry room, meeting facilities for 16, in-room refrigerators, airport transportation, no pets. SGL/DBL$35-$49.

Vagabond Inn Rosemead (3633 North Rosemead Boulevard, 91770; 288-6661, Fax 288-6661, 800-468-2251, 800-522-1555) 100 rooms, restaurant, lounge, complimentary breakfast, outdoor swimming pool, spa, valet laundry, fax service, complimentary newspaper, wheelchair-access rooms, no-smoking rooms, pets allowed, car rental, free parking. SGL$42-$47, DBL$42-$57.

Rowland Heights

Area Code 818

Best Western Executive Inn (18880 East Gale Avenue, 91748; 810-1818, Fax 810-3222, 800-528-1234) 135 rooms, restaurant, lounge, complimentary breakfast, swimming pool, laundry room, whirlpools, children under 12 free, tours, fax service, meeting facilities, no-smoking rooms. SGL$59-$83, DBL$62-$86.

Motel 6 (18970 East Labin Court, 91748; 964-5333, 505-891-6161) 125 rooms. SGL/DBL$27-$35.

Salinas

Area Code 408
Salinas Area Chamber of Commerce
Box 1170
Salinas CA 93902
424-7611

All Star Inn (140 Kern Street, 93901; 753-1711) 121 rooms. SGL/DBL$30-$36.

Best Western Airport Motor Inn (555 Airport Road, 93905; 424-1741, Fax 424-1741, 800-528-1234) 96 rooms, restaurant, lounge, complimentary breakfast, swimming pool, VCRs, children under 12 free, jacuzzi, no-smoking rooms, pets allowed. SGL/DBL$32-$95.

Comfort Inn (144 Kern Street, 93905; 758-8850, 800-221-2222) 32 rooms, restaurant, complimentary breakfast, wheelchair-access rooms. SGL$49-$98, DBL$54-$110.

El Dorado Motel (1351 North Main Street, 93906; 449-2442, 800-523-6506) 44 rooms and suites, no-smoking rooms, pets allowed. SGL/DBL$28-$56, STS$58-$78.

Laurel Inn Motel (801 West Laurel Drive, 93906; 449-2474, Fax 449-2476, 800-354-9831) 145 rooms, restaurant, lounge, outdoor heated swimming pool, in-room refrigerators, meeting facilities for 25, free parking, wheelchair-access rooms, no-smoking rooms, no pets. SGL$48-$68, DBL$58-$80.

Motel 6 (1257 De La Toree Boulevard, 93950; 757-3077, 505-891-6161) 128 rooms. SGL/DBL$27-$33.

Motel 6 (1010 Fairview Avenue, 93905; 758-3077, 505-891-6161) 58 rooms. SGL/DBL$25-$31.

Ramada Inn (808 North Main Street, 93906; 424-8661, Fax 424-5628, 800-228-2828) 70 rooms, restaurant, lounge, swimming pool, free parking, wheelchair-access rooms, no-smoking rooms. SGL$39-$69, DBL$69-$89.

Vagabond Inn (131 Kern Street, 93905; 758-4693, Fax 758-9835, 800-522-1555) 70 rooms, restaurant, heated swimming pool, wheelchair-access rooms, pets allowed, airport transportation, free local telephone calls, no-smoking rooms, children under 18 free, fax service, complimentary newspaper. SGL$39-$44, DBL$44-$54.

San Bernadino

Area Code 714
San Bernardino Area Chamber of Commerce
546 West Sixth Street
San Bernadino CA 92402
885-7515

Astro Motel (111 South E Street, 92401; 889-0417) 31 rooms. SGL$25-$28, DBL$32-$37.

Best Western Sands (606 North H Street, 92410; 889-8391, Fax 889-8394, 800-528-1234, 800-331-4409 in California) 54 rooms, restaurant, swimming pool, children under 12 free, whirlpools, no-smoking rooms, pets allowed. SGL/DBL$40-$52.

Comfort Inn (1909 South Business Center, 92408; 889-0090, 800-221-2222) 50 rooms, restaurant, complimentary breakfast, swimming pool, wheelchair-access rooms, no pets. SGL$47-$66, DBL$52-$71.

Econo Lodge (688 Fairway Drive, 92408; 825-7750, 800-446-6900, 800-424-4777) 134 rooms, restaurant, lounge, swimming pool, meeting facilities, children under 18 free, no pets. SGL$35-$85, DBL$41-$85.

E-Z 8 Motel (1750 Waterman Avenue, 92408; 888-4827) 118 rooms. SGL/DBL$27-$39.

Highland Inn Motel (1386 East Highland Avenue, 92404; 881-1702) 51 rooms, restaurant, swimming pool.

Hilton Hotel (285 East Hospitality Lane, 92408; 889-0133, Fax 381-4299, 800-445-8667) 247 rooms and suites, restaurant, outdoor swimming pool, jacuzzi, meeting facilities for 700, business service, airport courtesy car, wheelchair access, no-smoking rooms. SGL/DBL$70-$160+, STS$125-$300.

Inland Empire Hilton (285 East Hospitality Lane, 92504 889-0133) 244 rooms and suites, restaurant, swimming pool, exercise facilities, golf. SGL/DBL$70+.

La Quinta Inn (205 East Hospitality Lane, 92408; 888-7571, 800-531-5900) 153 rooms, restaurant, lounge, swimming pool, wheelchair access, meeting facilities, pets allowed. SGL$45-$50, DBL$50-$55+.

Maruko Hotel and Convention Center (295 North E Street, 92401; 381-6181, Fax: 381-5288, 800-472-3353) 238 rooms and suites, restaurant, swimming pool, airport courtesy car, free parking. SGL/DBL$100+.

Motel 6 (1960 Ostrems Way, 92407; 887-8191, 505-891-6161) 104 rooms. SGL/DBL$24-$30.

Motel 6 (111 Redlands Boulevard, 92408; 825-6666) 120 rooms. SGL/DBL$24-$30.

Oak Creek Inn Villa Viejo (777 West Sixth Street, 93407; 889-3561, Fax 884-7127, 800-228-9669) 57 rooms, restaurant, complimentary breakfast, swimming pool, no-smoking rooms. SGL/DBL$35-$45.

Ramada Inn (2000 Ostrems Way, 93407; 887-3001, Fax 880-3792, 800-228-2828) 116 rooms and suites, restaurant, lounge, heated swimming pool, spa, meeting facilities, children under 18 free, free parking, airport transportation, wheelchair-access rooms, no-smoking rooms. SGL$49-$89, DBL$59-$99.

San Bernadino Hilton (294 East Hospitality Lane, 92408; 889-0133, Fax 381-4299) 261 rooms and suites, restaurant, swimming pool, exercise facilities. SGL/DBL$85-$145.

Super 8 Motel (294 East Hospitality Lane, 92408; 381-1681, Fax 888-5120, 800-800-8000) 81 rooms, restaurant, complimentary breakfast, outdoor heated swimming pool, spa, complimentary newspaper, free local telephone calls, kitchenettes, meeting facilities, wheelchair-access rooms, no-smoking rooms, no pets. SGL/DBL$52-$56

Super 8 Motel (215 Freeway, 92410; 889-3561, Fax 884-7127, 800-800-8000) 58 rooms, restaurant, complimentary breakfast, outdoor heated swimming pool, spa, free local telephone calls, kitchenettes, complimentary newspaper, fax service, wheelchair-access rooms, no-smoking rooms, no pets. SGL/DBL$35-$38.

TraveLodge (225 East Hospitality Lane, 92408; 888-6777, Fax 885-6925, 800-255-3050) 91 rooms, restaurant, lounge, complimentary breakfast, swimming pool, car rental, transportation to local attractions, VCRs, in-room refrigerators and microwaves, free local telephone calls, airport transportation, no pets. SGL/DBL$40-$55.

San Clemente

Area Code 714
San Clemente Chamber of Commerce
1100 North El Camino Real
San Clemente CA 92672
492-1131

Beachcomber Motel (522 Avenida Victoria, 92672; 492-5457) studio and one-bedroom apartments, room service. LS SGL/DBL$65-$85, 1BR$90-$110; HS SGL/DBL$125, 1BR$150.

Casa Tropicana (610 Avenida Victoria, 92672; 492-1234) 8 rooms, bed and breakfast, complimentary breakfast, restaurant, balconies, beach, wheelchair-access rooms. SGL/DBL$140-$240.

Casablanca Inn (1601 North El Camino Real, 92672; 361-1644, Fax 361-3825, 800-752-9726) 42 rooms and suites, spa, jacuzzis, in-room refrigerators and microwaves, meeting facilities for 125, free parking, children under 18 free, no-smoking rooms, wheelchair-access rooms, no pets. SGL/DBL$59-$109.

Comfort Suites (3700 El Camino Real, 92672; 361-6600, 800-221-2222) 60 rooms, restaurant, complimentary breakfast, swimming pool, whirlpools, meeting facilities, wheelchair-access rooms, no pets. SGL$49-$74, DBL$49-$79.

Econo Lodge (2002 El Camino Real, 92672; 361-2110, 800-446-6900, 800-424-4777) 31 rooms, swimming pool, spas, whirlpools, wheelchair-access rooms, children under 18 free, ocean view, no pets. SGL/DBL$45-$60.

Holiday Inn (111 South Avenue, 92672; 361-3000, Fax 361-2472, 800-HOLIDAY) 65 rooms and suites, restaurant, swimming pool, spa, in-room refrigerators, balconies, whirlpools, ocean view, wheelchair-access rooms, exercise facilities, pets allowed. SGL/DBL$65-$135.

Quality Suites (2481 El Camino Real, 92672; 366-1000, Fax 336-1030, 800-221-2222) 66 rooms and suites, restaurant, lounge, complimentary breakfast, swimming pool, whirlpools, ocean view, wheelchair-access rooms, no pets. SGL$69-$89, DBL$79-$99.

Ramada Inn (35 Calle de Industrias, 92672; 498-8800, 800-228-2828) 110 rooms and suites, restaurant, lounge, complimentary breakfast, outdoor heated swimming pool, children under

18 free, meeting facilities for 300, beach, free parking, car rental, wheelchair-access rooms, ocean view, no-smoking rooms. SGL/DBL$73-$79, DBL$83-$89, STS$150+.

San Clemente Beach AYH Hostel (233 Avenida Granada, 92672; 714-492-2848) 50 beds, kitchen, SGL$8.

San Clemente Motor Lodge (2222 South El Camino Real, 92672; 492-4992) 15 rooms, pets allowed. SGL$30-$45, DBL$35-$65.

Sea Horse Inn (602 Avenida Victoria, 92672; 492-1720, Fax 498-8857) LS SGL/DBL$80-$85, 1BR$95-$105, 2BR$115-$135; HS SGL/DBL$90-$95, 1BR$105-$125, 2BR$135-$155.

Trade Winds Motel (2001 South El Camino Real, 92672; 492-8888) 11 rooms, no-smoking rooms. SGL/DBL$35+.

TraveLodge (2441 South El Camino Real, 92672; 498-5954, Fax 498-5954, 800-255-3050, 800-346-6441) 23 rooms, restaurant, complimentary breakfast, whirlpool, VCRs, in-room refrigerators, balconies, no-smoking rooms, ocean view, no pets. SGL/DBL$35-$49.

TraveLodge (1301 North El Camino Real, 92672; 361-0636, Fax 492-1140, 800-255-3050) 43 rooms and suites, restaurant, lounge, complimentary breakfast, free parking, ocean view, in-room refrigerators, fax service, wheelchair-access rooms, no-smoking rooms, no pets. LS SGL/DBL$43-$58; HS SGL/DBL$48-$63.

San Diego

Area Code 619
San Diego Convention and Visitors Bureau
1200 Third Avenue #824
San Diego CA 92101
232-3101

San Diego Visitor Information Center
2688 East Mission Bay Drive
San Diego CA 92109
276-8200

Bed and Breakfast International (1181B Solana Avenue, Albany, 94706; 525-4569, 800-872-4500) represents bed and breakfasts in the San Diego area.

Bed and Breakfast International (Box 28290, 94128, San Francisco 94128; 415-696-1650, Fax 415-696-1699) -represents bed and breakfasts in the San Diego area.

National Reservation Bureau, Inc. (19510 Ventura Boulevard, Tarzana CA 91357, 818-344-6776, 800-537-7666) represents hotels and inns in the San Diego area. SGL/DBL$30-$200.

Bahia Resort Hotel (998 West Mission Bay Drive, 92109; 288-0770, Fax 488-1512, 800-288-0770) 325 rooms, restaurant, lounge, swimming pool, whirlpool, gift shop, meeting facilities, car rental, lighted tennis courts, beach, no-smoking rooms, free parking. SGL/DBL$95+.

Balboa Park Inn (3402 Park Boulevard, 92103; 298-0823, Fax 294-8080) 42 rooms and suites, complimentary breakfast. SGL/DBL$80-$100, STS$95-$135+.

The Bay Club Hotel and Marina (2131 Shelter Island Drive, 92106; 224-8888, Fax 225-1604, 800-672-0800, 800-833-6565 in California) 105 rooms, restaurant, complimentary breakfast, airport courtesy car, wheelchair-access rooms, no-smoking rooms. SGL$98, DBL$112.

Beachcomber Motel (907 Turquoise Street, 92109; 488-4442) 33 rooms and efficiencies. SGL/DBL$39.

Beach Haven Inn (4740 Mission Boulevard, 92109; 272-3812, Fax 231-8026) 22 rooms. SGL/DBL$72-$100.

Bed and Breakfast #1: complimentary breakfast, SGL$55 (Bed and Breakfast International/SF)

Bed and Breakfast #2: SGL$55-$80 (Bed and Breakfast International/SF)

Best Western Airport Inn (2901 Nimitz Boulevard, 92106; 224-3655, Fax 224-4025, 800-528-1234) 105 rooms, restaurant, lounge, swimming pool, meeting facilities, children under 12 free, fax service, no-smoking rooms, airport courtesy car. SGL/DBL$60-$72.

Best Western Bayside Inn (555 West Ash Street, 92101; 233-7500, Fax 239-8060, 800-528-1234) 122 rooms, restaurant, lounge, complimentary breakfast, swimming pool, children under 12 free, fax service, wheelchair-access rooms, airport courtesy car, no-smoking rooms. SGL$67-$73, DBL$73-$83.

Best Western Blue Sea Lodge (7070 Pacific Beach Drive, 92109; 488-4700, Fax 488-7276, 800-BLUESEA, 800-528-1234) 100 rooms, restaurant, lounge, complimentary breakfast, beach, swimming pool, kitchenettes, ocean view, wheelchair-access rooms, no pets. LS SGL$95-$105, DBL$110-$120; HS SGL$115-$125, DBL$185-$210.

Best Western Hacienda Suites of Old Town (4041 Harney Street, 92110; 298-4707, Fax 298-4707, 800-528-1234) 149 rooms and suites, restaurant, lounge, swimming pool, VCRs, meeting facilities, laundry room, fax service, in-room microwaves, ocean view, airport transportation. LS SGL$89-99, DBL$99-$109; HS SGL/DBL$99-$119.

Best Western Hotel Kearny Mesa (3805 Murphy Canyon Road, 92123; 277-1199, Fax 277-3442, 800-528-1234) 176 rooms, restaurant, lounge, complimentary breakfast, swimming pool, spa, in-room refrigerators, fax service, exercise facilities. SGL/DBL$69-$119.

Best Western Inn (9310 Kearny Mesa Road, 92126; 578-6600, Fax 536-1368, 800-528-1234) 101 rooms, restaurant, lounge, complimentary breakfast, heated, whirlpool, meeting facilities for 50, in-room refrigerators and microwaves, fax service, swimming pool, exercise facilities, no pets. SGL$55-$74, DBL$59-$80.

Best Western Posada Inn (5005 North Harbor Drive, 92106; 224-3254, Fax 224-2186, 800-528-1234) 112 rooms, restaurant, lounge, swimming pool, children under 12 free, fax service, airport courtesy car, exercise facilities, no-smoking rooms. SGL/DBL$63-$91.

Best Western Rancho Bernardo (17065 West Bernardo Drive, 92127; 485-6530, Fax 485-6530, 800-528-1234) 181 rooms, restaurant, lounge, complimentary breakfast, swimming pool, spa, laundry room, meeting facilities, fax service, exercise facilities, no pets. SGL$77-$88, DBL$98-$200.

Best Western Seven Seas (411 Hotel Circle South, 92108; 291-1300, Fax 291-6933, 800-528-1234) 309 rooms, restaurant, lounge, swimming pool, gift shop, tours, free local telephone call, laundry room, transportation to local attractions, meeting facilities, fax service, no-smoking rooms, pets allowed. SGL/DBL$55-$80.

Best Western Shelter Island Marina Inn (2051 Shelter Island Drive, 92106; 222-0561, Fax 222-9760, 800-528-1234) 97 rooms, restaurant, swimming pool, no pets. LS SGL$70-$80, DBL$75-$85; HS SGL$115-$140, DBL$135-$155.

Bristol Court Hotel (1055 First Avenue, 92101; 232-6141, Fax 232-0228, 800-662-4477, 800-932-4848 in California) 99 rooms and suites, restaurant, lounge, exercise facilities, children under 12 free, valet laundry, fax service, meeting facilities for 300, wheelchair-access rooms, no-smoking rooms, pets allowed. SGL$99-$125, STS$250.

The Britt House (406 Maple Street, 92103; 234-2926) 10 rooms, bed and breakfast, complimentary breakfast, no-smoking rooms. SGL/DBL$95-$120.

Budget Motels of America (641 Camino Del Rio South, 92108; 295-6886, 800-624-1257) 56 rooms, no-smoking rooms, in-room refrigerators and microwaves, laundry room, no-smoking rooms. SGL$31+.

Camel Highland Golf and Tennis Resort (14455 Penasquiotos Drive, 92129; 672-9100, Fax 672-9166, 800-622-9223) 177 rooms, restaurant, swimming pool, exercise facilities, airport transportation, tennis, golf, wheelchair access, pets allowed. SGL$120-$160, DBL$160+.

Catamaran Resort Hotel (3999 Mission Boulevard, 92109; 488-1081, 800-288-0770) 315 rooms and suites, restaurant, lounge, airport transportation, swimming pool, whirlpool, convention and meeting facilities, bicycle rentals, gift shop, car rental, exercise facilities, wheelchair-access rooms, no-smoking rooms. SGL/DBL$105+.

Clarion Hotel at Balboa Park (2223 El Cajon Boulevard, 92104; 296-2101, 800-843-9988, 800-423-1935 in California) 142 rooms and suites, restaurant, lounge, complimentary breakfast, outdoor heated swimming pool, whirlpools, wheelchair-access rooms. SGL$98-$138, DBL$118-$148.

Comfort Inn (8000 Parkway Drive, 91942; 698-7747, 800-221-2222) 128 rooms, restaurant, complimentary breakfast, swimming pool, whirlpool, wheelchair-access rooms, no pets. SGL$44-$55, DBL$50-$60.

Comfort Inn Airport (1955 San Diego Avenue, 92110; 543-1130, 800-221-2222) 121 rooms and suites, restaurant, complimentary breakfast, whirlpool, wheelchair-access rooms, no pets. SGL$40-$60, DBL$47-$67.

Comfort Inn Downtown (719 Ash Street, 92101; 232-2525, 800-221-2222) 67 rooms, restaurant, complimentary breakfast, swimming pool, meeting facilities, free parking, airport courtesy car, wheelchair-access rooms, no pets. SGL/DBL$45-$70.

Comfort Inn Mission Bay (3747 Midway Drive, 92110; 225-1295, 800-221-2222) 63 rooms, restaurant, complimentary breakfast, whirlpool, wheelchair-access rooms, no pets. SGL/DBL$40-$67.

Comfort Inn Naval Station (1645 Plaza Boulevard, 91950; 474-8696, 800-221-2222) 92 rooms, restaurant, complimentary breakfast, swimming pool, whirlpool, meeting facilities, wheelchair-access rooms, no pets. SGL$33-$53, DBL$38-$58.

Comfort Suites Mission Valley (631 Camino Del Rio South, 92108; 294-3444, Fax 260-0746) 122 rooms, restaurant, complimentary breakfast, swimming pool, whirlpool, airport transportation, meeting facilities, wheelchair-access rooms, no pets. SGL$59-$74, DBL$67-$82.

Comfort Suites North (12979 Rancho Penasquitos Boulevard, 92129; 484-3300, 800-221-2222) 104 rooms, restaurant, complimentary breakfast, swimming pool, whirlpools, meeting facilities, wheelchair-access rooms. SGL$54-$59, DBL$59-$74.

The Cottage (3829 Albatross Street, 92103; 299-1564) 2 rooms, bed and breakfast, complimentary breakfast. SGL$65, DBL$75.

Dana Inn and Marina (1710 West Mission Bay Drive, 92109; 222-6440, 800-345-9995, 800-445-3339) 196 rooms, restaurant, lounge, outdoor heated swimming pool, jacuzzis, children under 18 free, laundry room, free parking, tennis, no-smoking rooms. SGL/DBL$80-$130.

Days Inn (543 South Hotel Circle, 92108; 297-8800, Fax 298-6029, 800-325-2525) 283 rooms and efficiencies, restaurant, heated swimming pool, spa, free local telephone calls, laundry room, kitchenettes, children under 12 free, fax service, wheelchair-access rooms, no-smoking rooms, no pets. SGL/DBL$40-$60, EFF$57-$59.

Days Inn (3350 Rosecrans Street, 92110; 224-9800, Fax 224-0928, 800-325-2525) 159 rooms and suites, complimentary breakfast, heated swimming pool, jacuzzi, in-room refrigerators and microwaves, VCRs, children under 12 free, fax service, no pets, wheelchair-access rooms, no-smoking rooms. SGL/DBL$54-$74, STS$74-$89.

Del Mar Hilton San Diego (1355 Harbor Drive, 92101; 232-3861, Fax 232-4924, 800-HILTONS) 256 rooms and suites, restaurant, swimming pool, meeting facilities for 900, beach, business services, tennis, golf, airport transportation, wheelchair access, no-smoking rooms. SGL$105-$120, DBL$110-$140, STS$225-$650.

Diamond Head Inn (605 Diamond Street, 92109; 273-1900, Fax 231-8026) 21 rooms. SGL/DBL$75-$100.

Doubletree Hotel (901 Camino del Rio South, 92108; 543-9000, Fax 543-9358, 800-528-0444) 350 rooms and suites, restaurant, lounge, complimentary breakfast, heated outdoor swimming pool, whirlpool, sauna, meeting facilities for 750, business services, exercise equipment, airport transportation, wheelchair access, no-smoking rooms, free parking. SGL$77-$99, DBL$89-$110.

Doubletree Resort (14455 Penasquitos Drive, 92129; 672-9100, Fax 672-9166, 800-528-0444) 185 rooms and suites, two restaurants, lounge, outdoor heated swimming pools, spas, meeting facilities for 450, golf, lighted tennis courts, exercise facilities, wheelchair access, no-smoking rooms. SGL/DBL$100-$165, STS$200-$400.

Doubletree Club Hotel (11915 El Camino Real, 92130; 481-5900, Fax 481-0990, 800-528-0444) 230 rooms and suites, restaurant, lounge, outdoor swimming pool, whirlpool, meeting facilities for 150, exercise center, free parking. SGL/DBL$100-$155, STS$200-$400.

Doubletree Club Hotel (11611 Bernardo Plaza Court, 92128; 485-9250, Fax 451-7948, 800-528-0444) 211 rooms and suites, restaurant, lounge, complimentary breakfast, outdoor heated swimming pool, spa, meeting facilities for 100, airport transportation, exercise center, wheelchair-access rooms, no-smoking rooms, free parking. SGL$79-$99, DBL$89-$109, STS$150+.

Econo Lodge By The Bay (1655 Pacific Highway, 92101; 232-6391, Fax 235-4622, 800-446-6900) 35 rooms, swimming pool, no-smoking rooms, pets allowed. SGL$38-$43, DBL$48-$58.

Embassy Suites Downtown (601 Pacific Highway, 92101; 239-2400, Fax 239-1520, 800-362-2779) 337 suites, restaurant, complimentary breakfast, indoor swimming pool, whirlpool, sauna, airport courtesy car, meeting facilities for 250, bay-view, gift shop, valet laundry, exercise facilities, wheelchair access, no-smoking rooms. STS$120-$190.

Embassy Suites Hotel (4550 La Jolla Village Drive, 92122; 453-0400, 800-EMBASSY) 335 suites, restaurant, complimentary breakfast, indoor swimming pool, whirlpool, sauna, exercise equipment, wheelchair-access rooms, meeting facilities for 200, gift shop, room service, valet laundry, no-smoking rooms.

Executive Hotel and Suites (3888 Greenwood, 92110; 299-6633, Fax 291-8333, 800-638-6336) 220 rooms and suites, complimentary breakfast, swimming pool, exercise facilities, airport transportation, wheelchair access, no-smoking rooms. SGL/DBL$60-$68.

E-Z 8 Motel (3333 Channel Way, 92100; 223-9500, 800-326-6835) 119 rooms. SGL/DBL$29-$41.

E-Z 8 Motel (4747 Pacific Highway, 92110; 294-2512, 800-326-6835) 127 rooms. SGL/DBL$27-$39.

E-Z 8 Motel (1010 Outer Road, 92154; 575-8808, 800-326-6835) 89 rooms. SGL/DBL$27-$39.

E-Z 8 Motel (2484 Hotel Circle Place, 92108; 291-8252, 800-326-6835) 111 rooms. SGL/DBL$29-$41.

Fabulous Inn (2485 Hotel Circle Place, 92108; 291-7700, Fax 297-6179, 800-824-0950, 800-647-1982 in California) 175 rooms and suites, complimentary breakfast, outdoor heated swimming pool, jacuzzis, children under 16 free, meeting facilities for 350, laundry room, airport courtesy car, no-smoking, wheelchair-access rooms, no pets. SGL/DBL$46-$75, STS$69-$109.

Friendship Inn (4345 Mission Bay Drive, 92109; 273-1121, 800-424-4777) 40 rooms, restaurant, lounge, wheelchair-access rooms, children under 18 free, no pets. SGL$35-$48, DBL$39-$51.

Golden West Hotel (720 Fourth Avenue, 92101; 233-7595) 50 rooms. SGL/DBL$15-$31.

Grosvenor Inn (3145 Sports Arena Boulevard, 92110; 225-9999, Fax 225-0958, 800-232-1212, 800-222-2929 in California) 206 rooms and suites, restaurant, swimming pool, airport courtesy car, wheelchair access, no-smoking rooms. SGL/DBL$60-$75, STS$150-$250.

Hampton Inn Kearney Mesa (5434 Kearny Mesa Road, 92111; 292-1482, Fax 292-4410, 800-HAMPTON) 151 rooms, swimming pool, meeting facilities. SGL/DBL$68-$73.

Hanelei Hotel (2270 Hotel Circle North, 92108; 297-1101, Fax 297-6049, 800-882-0858, 800-542-6082 in California) 424 rooms and suites, three restaurants, two swimming pools, exercise center, meeting facilities for 350, wheelchair-access rooms, no-smoking rooms, tennis, golf, pets allowed. SGL/DBL$90-$120, STS$225-$350+.

The Handlery Hotel and Country Club (950 Hotel Circle North, 92108; 298-0511, Fax 298-9793, 800-223-0888) 216 rooms, 3 restaurants, 3 swimming pools, exercise room, golf, meeting facilities, car rental, gift shops. SGL$60-$80, DBL$70-$90.

Harbor Hill Guest House (2330 Albatross Street, 92101; 233-0638) 5 rooms, bed and breakfast, complimentary breakfast, free parking. SGL$50+.

Hawaiian Gardens Suite Hotel (1031 Imperial Beach Boulevard, 91932; 429-5303, 800-334-3071) 40 rooms, complimentary breakfast, outdoor heated swimming pool, spa, kitchenettes, in-room refrigerators, laundry room, free parking, no-smoking rooms. SGL/DBL$59-$93.

Heritage Park Inn (2470 Heritage Park Row, 92110; 295-7088) 9 rooms, bed and breakfast, complimentary breakfast, free parking. SGL/DBL$80-$120.

Hilton Beach and Tennis Resort (1775 East Mission Bay Drive, 92109; 276-4010, Fax 275-7992) 354 rooms and suites, restaurant, swimming pool, airport courtesy car, exercise facilities, wheelchair access, no-smoking rooms, pets allowed, boat rentals. SGL$125-$200, DBL$150-$225, STS$250-$550.

Holiday Inn (1355 North Harbor Drive, 92101; 232-3861, Fax 232-4924, 800-HOLIDAY) 600 rooms and suites, restaurant, lounge, outdoor heated swimming pool, jacuzzi, gift shop, balconies, meeting facilities for 600, airport transportation. SGL$105-$120, DBL$110-$140.

Holiday Inn Harbor View (1617 First Avenue, 92101; 239-6171, Fax 233-6228, 800-HOLIDAY) 205 rooms, restaurant, lounge, meeting facilities, wheelchair access, airport courtesy car, no pets. SGL$60, DBL$70+.

Holiday Inn Montgomery Field (8110 Aero Drive, 92123; 277-8888, 800-992-1441, 800-HOLIDAY) 225 rooms and suites, restaurant, swimming pool, meeting facilities for 400, gift shop, tours, exercise room, airport transportation. SGL$74-$94, DBL$82-$105.

Holiday Inn Mission Valley (595 Hotel Circle South, 92108; 291-5720, Fax 297-7362, 800-HOLIDAY) 322 rooms, restaurant, lounge, gift shop, routs, car rental, exercise facilities, no pets. SGL$56-$65, DBL$63-$72, STS$85-$92.

Holiday Inn Sea World (3950 Jupiter Street, 92110; 226-8000, 800-HOLIDAY) 70 rooms and efficiencies, restaurant, swimming pool, spa, meeting facilities for 20, wheelchair-access rooms, airport transportation, pets allowed. SGL/DBL$75-$100.

Horton Grand Hotel (311 Island Avenue, 92101; 544-1186, Fax 239-3823, 800-999-1886) 134 rooms and suites, restaurant, exercise facilities, wheelchair access, no-smoking rooms. SGL/DBL$100-$130, STS$150-$190.

Hotel San Diego (339 West Broadway, 92101; 234-0221, Fax 232-1305, 800-621-5380, 800-824-1244 in California) 220 rooms and suites, restaurant, airport courtesy car, no-smoking rooms. SGL/DBL$50-$70, STS$100-$110.

Howard Johnson Hotel (1430 Seventh Avenue, 92101; 696-0911, Fax 234-9416, 800-654-2000) 134 rooms, restaurant, outdoor heated swimming pool, meeting facilities, transportation to local attractions, valet laundry, car rental, fax service, exercise facilities, no-smoking rooms, no pets. SGL$52-$80, DBL$62-$90.

Howard Johnson Lodge (4545 Waring Road, 92120; 286-7000, 800-654-2000) 93 rooms, restaurant, complimentary breakfast, balconies, valet laundry, fax service, free parking, in-room refrigerators and microwaves, wheelchair access, no-smoking rooms. SGL$45-$85, DBL$55-$95.

Howard Johnson Lodge (1631 Hotel Circle South, 92108; 293-7792, Fax 298-5321, 800-876-8937, 800-654-2000) 81 rooms, swimming pool, spa, meeting facilities for 25, wheelchair-access rooms, no-smoking rooms, no pets. SGL/DBL$49-$69.

Humphrey's Half Moon Inn (2302 Shelter Island Drive, 92106; 224-3411, Fax 224-3478, 800-345-9995) 182 rooms and suites, restaurant, swimming pool, airport courtesy car, wheelchair access, no-smoking rooms, marina. SGL$79-$105, DBL$99-$125.

Hyatt Regency (820 West F Street, 92101; 232-1234, Fax: 239-5678, 800-233-1234) 875 rooms, restaurant, lounge, outdoor swimming pool, whirlpool, meeting facilities, exercise facilities, tennis. SGL/DBL$85-$145.

Innsuites Pacific Beach (4760 Mission Boulevard, 92109; 483-6782, Fax 270-9472) 90 rooms. SGL/DBL$55-$85.

Kings Inn (1333 Hotel Circle South, 92108; 297-2231, 800-542-6082 in California) 140 rooms, restaurant, swimming pool, exercise center, meeting facilities, tennis, golf. SGL$57-$67, DBL$61-$71.

La Quinta Inn (10185 Paseo Montril, 92129; 484-8800, Fax 538-0476, 800-531-5900) 140 rooms, restaurant, swimming pool, wheelchair-access rooms, meeting facilities, no-smoking rooms, pets allowed. SGL$46-$51, DBL$51-$65.

Loma Lodge (3202 Rosecrans Street, 92110; 222-0511, 800-266-0511) 43 rooms, complimentary breakfast, swimming pool. SGL$30-$53, DBL$45-$89.

Marriott Hotel and Marina (333 West Harbor Boulevard, 92101; 234-1500, 800-228-9290) 1,355 rooms and suites, 4 restaurants, lounge, swimming pool, spa, meeting facilities for 25, in-room microwaves, balconies, concierge, tennis, marina, airport courtesy car, pets allowed. SGL/DBL$155-$190, STS$300+.

Marriott Mission Valley (8757 Rio San Diego Drive, 92108; 692-3800, Fax 692-0769, 800-842-5329) 350 rooms and suites, restaurant, swimming pool, exercise facilities, tennis, airport transportation, wheelchair-access rooms, no-smoking rooms, pets allowed. SGL$130-$145, DBL$145-$160, STS$275-$2,800.

Marriott Residence Inn (11002 Rancho Carmel Drive, 92127; 800-331-3131) restaurant, complimentary breakfast, wheelchair-access rooms, pets allowed. SGL/DBL$69-$139.

Marriott Residence Inn (5400 Kearny Mesa Road, 92111; 278-2100, Fax 268-3926, 800-331-3131) airport transportation, wheelchair-access rooms, meeting facilities for 35, in-room microwaves, pets allowed. SGL/DBL$115-$149.

The Maryland Hotel (630 F Street, 92101; 239-9243, Fax 235-8968) 50 rooms, swimming pool, no-smoking rooms. SGL$20-$27, DBL$30-$40.

Mission Valley Inn (875 Hotel Circle South, 92108; 298-8281, Fax 295-5610, 800-854-2608) 210 rooms, restaurant, three swimming pools, exercise facilities, tennis, meeting facilities for 200. SGL$49-$69, DBL$49-$79.

Monet's Garden (7039 Casa Lane, 91945; 464-8296) 5 rooms, bed and breakfast, complimentary breakfast. SGL$35, DBL$40.

Motel 6 (5592 Clairemont Mesa Boulevard, 92117; 268-9758, 505-891-6161) 65 rooms. SGL/DBL$35-$41.

Motel 6 (2424 Hotel Circle North, 92108; 296-1612, 505-891-6161) 92 rooms. SGL/DBL$36-$42.

Old Town Inn (4444 Pacific Coast Highway, 92110; 260-8042, Fax 295-4532, 800-225-9610) 84 rooms and suites, kitchenettes, in-room refrigerators, laundry room, no-smoking rooms. SGL/DBL$30-$53, STS$52-$81.

Omni San Diego Hotel (910 Broadway Circle, 92101; 239-2200, Fax 250-0509, 800-THE-OMNI) 450 rooms, restaurant, lounge, swimming pool, jacuzzi, business services, exercise facilities, lighted tennis courts, airport transportation, wheelchair access, no-smoking rooms. SGL/DBL$160-$185, STS$300+.

Pacific Shores Inn (4802 Mission Boulevard, 92109; 483-9276, Fax 483-9276, 800-367-6467) 55 rooms, outdoor heated swimming pool, pets allowed. SGL$75-$85, DBL$80-$95.

Pacific Terrace Inn (610 Diamond Street, 92109; 581-3500) 73 rooms and suites, restaurant, complimentary breakfast, swimming pool, wheelchair-access rooms, no-smoking rooms. SGL/DBL$110-$250.

Pan Pacific Hotel (400 West Broadway, 92101; 239-4500, Fax 239-4527, 800-373-8585 in California) 450 rooms and suites, restaurant, swimming pool, airport courtesy car, wheelchair access, no-smoking rooms. SGL/DBL$125-$170, STS$250+.

Park Manor Residential Hotel (525 Spruce Street, 92103; 291-0999, Fax 291-8844) 35 rooms, restaurant, airport transportation, no-smoking rooms, pets allowed. SGL/DBL$65-$165.

Plaza International Hotel (1515 Hotel Circle South, 92108; 291-8790) 220 rooms, swimming pool, exercise facilities, airport transportation. SGL/DBL$125-$235.

Point Loma Inn (2933 Fenelon Street, 92106; 222-4704, Fax 295-4532, 800-225-9610) 14 rooms. SGL$38-$75, DBL$40-$85.

Princess Resort (1404 West Vacation Road, 92109; 274-4630, Fax 581-5929) 563 rooms, restaurant, lounge, swimming pool, meeting facilities, fax service, valet laundry, no-smoking rooms, no pets. SGL/DBL$115-$185.

Quality Inn Stadium (5343 Adobe Falls Road, 92120; 287-1911, 800-221-2222) 96 rooms, restaurant, swimming pool, whirlpools, no pets. SGL$49-$69, DBL$59-$89.

Quality Suites (9880 Mira Mesa Boulevard, 92131; 530-2000, 800-221-2222) 130 rooms, restaurant, lounge, complimentary breakfast, swimming pool, wheelchair-access rooms. SGL$79-$89, DBL$89-$99.

Radisson Suite Hotel (11520 West Bernardo Court, 92127; 451-6600, Fax 592-0253, 800-333-3333) 177 suites, restaurant, swimming pool, airport courtesy car, wheelchair access, no-smoking rooms, pets allowed. STS$75-$130.

Radisson Hotel Harbor View (1646 Front Street, 92101; 239-6800, Fax 238-9461, 800-333-3333) 333 rooms, restaurant, swimming pool, exercise facilities, airport transportation, wheelchair-access rooms, no-smoking rooms, pets allowed. SGL/DBL$89-$129, STS$149-$279.

Ramada Hotel Bayview (660 K Street, 92101; 696-0234, Fax 231-8199, 800-766-0234) 312 rooms, restaurant, exercise facilities, jacuzzi, children under 18 free, meeting facilities for 200, airport transportation, exercise facilities, wheelchair access, no-smoking rooms. SGL$73-$113, DBL$83-$123.

Ramada Inn (5550 Kearny Mesa Road, 92111; 278-0800, Fax 277-6585, 800-2-RAMADA) 150 rooms, restaurant, lounge, heated swimming pool, spa, airport courtesy car, free parking, free local telephone calls, children under 18 free, wheelchair-access rooms, no-smoking rooms. SGL$52-$89, DBL$57-$99.

Ramada Inn (2435 Jefferson Street, 92110; 260-8500, Fax 297-2078, 800-2-RAMADA) 151 rooms and suites, restaurant, lounge, complimentary breakfast, swimming pool, spa, children under 12 free, free parking, airport transportation, in-room refrigerators and microwaves, wheelchair-access rooms, no-smoking rooms. SGL$51-$99, DBL$61-$109.

Ramada Inn (2151 Hotel Circle South, 92108; 291-6500, Fax 294-7531, 800-345-9995) 183 rooms, restaurants, lounge, swimming pool, children under 18 free, car rental, free parking, wheelchair-access rooms, no-smoking rooms. SGL$52-$99, DBL$62-$99.

Rancho Bernardo Inn (17550 Bernardo Oaks Drive, 92128; 800-542-6096 in California) 287 rooms and suites, restaurant, swimming pool, pets allowed, golf, lighted tennis courts. SGL/DBL$105+.

Red Lion Hotel (7450 Hazard Center Drive, 92108; 297-5466, 800-547-8010) 300 rooms and suites, restaurant, lounge, indoor and outdoor swimming pools, spa, room service, gift shop, car rental, exercise facilities, tennis courts, airport courtesy car, pets allowed. SGL/DBL$125-$165.

Regency Plaza Hotel (1515 Hotel Circle, 92108; 291-8790, Fax 260-0147) 216 rooms. SGL/DBL$89-$99.

Rodeway Inn (833 Ash Street, 92101; 239-2285, 800-424-4777) 45 rooms, restaurant, meeting facilities, beauty shop, whirlpools, no pets. SGL$44-$69, DBL$49-$69.

San Diego Princess Resort (1404 West Vacation Road, 92109; 274-4630, 800-542-6275) 460 rooms and cottage suites, 3 restaurants, lounges, five swimming pools, exercise center, pets allowed, tennis, marina, boat rentals, meeting and conventional facilities. SGL$110-$145, DBL$125-$180, STS$185-$345.

Seapoint Hotel (4875 North Harbor Drive, 92106; 224-3621, Fax 224-3629, 800-345-9995) 243 rooms, restaurant, swimming pool, exercise facilities, airport transportation, marina, tennis, wheelchair-access rooms, no-smoking rooms. SGL$55-$110, DBL$65-$120.

Sheraton Grand On Harbor Island (1590 Harbor Island Drive, 92101; 291-6400, Fax 294-9627, 800-325-3535) 350 rooms and suites, restaurant, swimming pool, exercise facilities, tennis, airport courtesy car, wheelchair-access rooms, no-smoking rooms SGL$125-$170, DBL$145-$190, STS$250-$950.

Sheraton Harbor Island (1380 Harbor Island Drive, 92101; 291-2900, Fax 294-3279, 800-325-3535) 711 rooms and suites, restaurant, swimming pool, exercise facilities, airport courtesy car, wheelchair-access rooms, no-smoking rooms. SGL$125-$170, DBL$146-$190, STS$250-$950.

Hotel St. James (830 Sixth Avenue, 92101; 234-0155, Fax 235-9410, 800-338-1616) 107 rooms and suites, restaurant, exercise facilities, wheelchair access, no-smoking rooms. SGL/DBL$60-$120, STS$85-$400+.

Sommerset Hotel Suites (606 Washington Street, 92103; 692-5200, Fax 299-6065, 800-356-1787 in California) 81 suites, complimentary breakfast, swimming pool, airport transportation, wheelchair access. SGL/DBL$90-$150.

Super 8 Motel (1403 Rosecrans, 92106; 225-9461, Fax 225-9461, 800-800-8000) 86 rooms, restaurant, outdoor heated swimming pool, laundry room, car rental, meeting facilities, kitchenettes, in-room refrigerators, airport transportation, wheelchair-access rooms, no-smoking rooms, no pets. LS SGL/DBL$50-$60; HS SGL/DBL$56-$66.

Super 8 Motel (4540 Mission Bay Drive, 92109; 274-7888, Fax 274-7888, 800-800-8000) 117 rooms, outdoor heated swimming pool, spa, car rental, transportation to local attractions, fax service, airport transportation, wheelchair-access rooms, no-smoking rooms, no pets. SGL$44-$48, DBL$51-$60.

Surfer Motor Lodge (711 Pacific Beach Drive, 92109; 483-7070) 52 rooms, restaurant, swimming pool. SGL/DBL$65+.

Town and Country Hotel and Convention Center (500 Hotel Circle North, 92108; 291-7131, Fax 291-3584, 800-845-2608, 800-542-6082 in California) 1,000 rooms and suites, four restaurants, swimming pool, sauna, exercise facilities, airport transportation, meeting facilities for 3,000, lighted tennis courts, golf, wheelchair access, no-smoking rooms. SGL$80-$130, STS$250-$450.

TownHouse Lodge Friendship Inn (810 Ash Street, 92101; 233-8826, 800-982-2020) 57 rooms, swimming pool, pets allowed. SGL/DBL$45-$65.

TraveLodge (2353 Pacific Highway, 92101; 232-8931, Fax 237-07765, 800-255-3050) 74 rooms and suites, restaurant, lounge, complimentary breakfast, swimming pool, transportation to local attractions, tours, car rental, meeting facilities, airport transportation, no pets. LS SGL/DBL$39-$59; HS SGL/DBL$44-$59.

TraveLodge Airport (5103 North Harbor Drive, 92106; 223-8171, Fax 222-7330, 800-255-3050) 45 rooms and suites, restaurant, lounge, complimentary breakfast, swimming pool, tours, car rental, laundry room, airport transportation, no pets. SGL/DBL$39-$59.

TraveLodge (1267 Eleventh Avenue, 92101; 232-7601, 800-255-3050) 25 rooms, restaurant, lounge, tours, car rental, no pets. SGL/DBL$35-$52.

TraveLodge (840 Ash Street, 92101; 234-8477, 800-255-3050) 30 rooms and suites, restaurant, lounge, tours, no pets. SGL/DBL$39-$49.

TraveLodge (1505 Pacific Highway, 92101; 239-9185, 800-255-3050) 24 rooms, restaurant, no pets. SGL/DBL$39-$52.

TraveLodge (5550 Clairemont Mesa Boulevard, 92115; 560-4551, Fax 268-4354, 800-255-3050) 88 rooms, restaurant, lounge, complimentary breakfast, fax service, in-room refrigerators and microwaves, laundry room, no pets. SGL/DBL$39-$50.

TraveLodge (1305 Pacific Highway, 92101; 233-0398, 800-255-3050) 18 rooms, restaurant, lounge, no pets. SGL/DBL$39-$55.

TraveLodge (1960 Harbor Island Drive, 92101; 291-0694, Fax 293-0694, 800-255-3050) 208 rooms and suites, restaurant, lounge, swimming pool, sauna, airport transportation, meeting facilities for 300, tours, car rental, no pets, room service. SGL/DBL$109-$119.

TraveLodge (4610 DeSoto Street, 92109; 483-9800) 86 rooms, restaurant, lounge, swimming pool, whirlpool, tours, laundry room, fax service, no pets. SGL/DBL$39-$69.

TraveLodge (16929 West Bernardo Drive, 92127; 487-0445, Fax 673-2062, 800-255-3050) 49 rooms and suites, restaurant, lounge, complimentary breakfast, swimming pool, meeting facilities for 25. SGL/DBL$46-$70.

TraveLodge (3737 Sports Arena Boulevard, 92110; 226-3711, Fax 224-9248, 800-255-3050) 307 rooms and suites, restaurant, lounge, swimming pool, whirlpool, airport transportation, room service, kitchenettes, meeting facilities for 200, no pets. SGL/DBL$52-$79.

TraveLodge (4760 Mission Boulevard, 92109; 483-6780, Fax 270-9471, 800-255-3050) 48 rooms and suites, restaurant, lounge, kitchenettes, laundry room, fax service, tours, car rental. SGL/DBL$49-$69.

TraveLodge (1101 Hollister Street, 92154; 429-7600) 60 rooms and suites, restaurant, swimming pool, tours, car rental, kitchenettes, no pets. SGL/DBL$33-$38.

TraveLodge (2380 Moore Street, 92110; 291-9100, Fax 291-4717, 800-255-3050) 72 rooms and suites, restaurant, lounge, complimentary breakfast, swimming pool, whirlpool, sauna, in-room refrigerators and microwaves, laundry room, tours, fax service, kitchenettes, no pets. SGL/DBL$44-$59.

TraveLodge (1201 Hotel Circle South, 92108; 297-2271, Fax 542-1510, 800-255-3050) 100 rooms, restaurant, lounge, swimming pool, tours, VCRs, fax service. SGL/DBL$49-$64.

TraveLodge (1345 10th Avenue, 92101; 234-6344, 800-255-3050) 30 rooms, restaurant, lounge, car rental, tours, no pets. SGL/DBL$35-$47.

TraveLodge (840 A Street, 92101; 234-8277, 800-255-3050) 28 rooms and suites, restaurant, tours, no pets. SGL/DBL$39-$55.

TraveLodge (1943 Pacific Highway, 92101; 232-7551, Fax 239-1108, 800-255-3050) 29 rooms, restaurant, lounge, no pets. SGL/DBL$35-$51.

U.S. Grant Hotel (326 Broadway, 92101; 232-3121, Fax 232-6947, 800-334-6957) 283 rooms and suites, restaurant, complimentary breakfast, exercise facilities, airport transportation, wheelchair-access rooms, pets allowed. SGL$135-$155, DBL$155-$175, STS$245-$1,000.

Vacation Inn Old Town (3900 Old Town Avenue, 92110; 299-7400, Fax 299-9009, 800-451-9864 in California) 125 rooms and suites, complimentary breakfast, swimming pool. LS SGL/DBL$79-$119; HS SGL/DBL$99-$140.

Vagabond Inn (1325 Scott Street, 92106; 224-3371, Fax 223-0646, 800-522-1555) 39 rooms, restaurant, heated swimming pool, pets allowed, in-room refrigerators, kitchenettes, airport transportation, free local telephone calls, no-smoking rooms, children under 18 free, fax service, complimentary newspaper. SGL$47-$51, DBL$52-$61.

Vagabond Inn (6440 El Cajon Boulevard, 92115; 286-2040, Fax 286-2517, 800-522-1555) 50 rooms, restaurant, swimming pool, pets allowed, in-room refrigerators, pets allowed, airport transportation, free local telephone calls, no-smoking rooms, children under 18 free, fax service, complimentary newspaper. SGL$39, DBL$42-$49.

Vagabond Inn (625 Hotel Circle South, 92108; 297-1691, Fax 692-9009, 800-522-1555) 87 rooms, restaurant, two swimming pools, pets allowed, airport transportation, free local telephone calls, no-smoking rooms, children under 18 free, fax service, complimentary newspaper. SGL$41-$48, DBL$46-$48.

Wayfarer's Inn (3275 Rosecrans Street, 92110; 224-2411, Fax 222-2123, 800-266-2411) 44 rooms, outdoor swimming pool, children under 18 free. SGL$34-$40, DBL$45-$55.

Welcomin (1550 East Washington Street, 92103; 298-8215) 32 rooms. SGL/DBL$40-$49.

Westgate Hotel (1055 Second Avenue, 92101; 238-1818) 223 rooms, restaurant. SGL/DBL$124-$154+.

Wyndham Garden Hotel North San Diego (5975 Lusk Boulevard, 92121; 558-1818, Fax 558-0421, 800-822-4200) 180 rooms, restaurant, lounge, outdoor heated swimming pool, meeting facilities for 500, exercise facilities, wheelchair access, no-smoking rooms. SGL$49-$108, DBL$50-$118, STS$70-$128.

San Dimas

Area Code 714
San Dimas Chamber of Commerce
111 South Monte Vista
San Dimas CA 91773
592-3818

Best Western Inn (204 North Village Court, 91773; 599-2362, Fax 592-7903, 800-528-1234) 134 rooms, restaurant, lounge, complimentary breakfast, swimming pool, in-room refrigerators, complimentary newspaper, meeting facilities, children under 18 free, no-smoking rooms. SGL$55-$85, DBL$60-$90.

Comfort Suites (501 West Bonita Avenue, 91773; 592-0500, 800-221-2222) 60 rooms, complimentary breakfast, swimming pool, whirlpools, meeting facilities, wheelchair-access rooms, no pets. SGL$69-$84, DBL$74-$94.

Motel 6 (502 West Arrow Highway, 91773; 592-5631, 505-891-6161) 42 rooms. SGL/DBL$28-$34.

San Gabriel

Area Code 818
San Gabriel Chamber of Commerce
534 West Mission Drive
San Gabriel CA 91776
576-2525

Quality Inn (1114 East Las Tunas Drive, 91776; 285-0921, 800-221-2222) 42 rooms, complimentary breakfast, swimming pool, whirlpools, wheelchair-access rooms. SGL/DBL$50-$60.

Sanger

Area Code 209
Sanger District Chamber of Commerce
1700 7th Street
Sanger CA 93657
875-4575

Townhouse Motel (1308 Church Street, 93657; 875-5531) 19 rooms, swimming pool, no-smoking rooms. SGL$35-$40, DBL$42-$57.

San Juan Capistrano

Area Code 714
San Juan Capistrano Chamber of Commerce
31682 El Camino Real
San Juan Capistrano 92675
493-4700

Best Western Capistrano Inn (27174 Ortega Highway, 92675; 493-5661, Fax 661-8293, 800-441-9438, 800-528-1234) 108 rooms, restaurant, lounge, complimentary breakfast, swimming pool, whirlpool, children under 12 free, kitchenettes, fax service, no-smoking rooms, pets allowed. SGL/DBL$59-$77.

Edgewater Inn (34744 Coast Highway, 92625; 240-0150, Fax 493-3692) 35 rooms and suites, restaurant, free parking, wheelchair access. SGL/DBL$85-$125, STS$100-$125.

TraveLodge (28742 Camino Capistrano, 92675; 364-0342, Fax 364-1684, 800-255-3050) 33 rooms and suites, restaurant, lounge, tours, whirlpool, kitchenettes, tennis, no pets. SGL/DBL$39-$59.

San Luis Obispo

Area Code 805
San Luis Obispo Chamber of Commerce
1039 Chorro Street
San Luis Obispo, CA 93401
543-1328

San Luis Obispo County Visitors and Conference Bureau
1041 Chorro Street
San Luis Obispo CA 93401
541-8000

The Adobe Inn (1473 Monterey Street, 93401; 549-0321) 15 rooms, bed and breakfast, complimentary breakfast, no-smoking rooms. SGL$35-$55, DBL$45-$85.

All Star Inn (1625 Calle Joaquin, 93401; 541-6992) 117 rooms. SGL/DBL$30-$36.

Apple Farm Court and Inn (2015 Monterey Street, 93401; 544-2040, Fax 541-5497, 800-255-2040) 67 rooms, restaurant, swimming pool, airport transportation, wheelchair access, no-smoking rooms. SGL/DBL$70-$150+.

Best Western Olive Tree Inn (1000 Olive Street, 93405; 544-2800, 800-528-1234) 46 rooms, restaurant, swimming pool, pets allowed. SGL$43-$53, DBL$45-$82.

Best Western Royal Oak Motor Hotel (214 Madonna Road, 93405; 544-4410, Fax 544-3026, 800-528-1234) 99 rooms, restaurant, swimming pool, meeting facilities, children under 12 free, fax service, no-smoking rooms, wheelchair-access rooms, pets allowed. SGL$57-$78, DBL$63-$78.

Best Western Somerset Manor (1895 Monterey Street, 93401; 544-0973, Fax 541-2805, 800-528-1234) 39 rooms, restaurant, lounge, swimming pool, spa, whirlpool, fax service, no pets. SGL/DBL$36-$49

Campus Motel (404 Santa Rosa Street, 93405; 544-0881, 800-447-8080 in California) 35 rooms, swimming pool, wheelchair-access rooms, pets allowed. SGL/DBL$48-$68.

Cuesta Canyon Lodge (1800 Monterey, 93401; 544-8600, Fax 541-4698, 800-544-8601 in California) 104 rooms, complimentary breakfast, swimming pool, airport transportation, wheelchair-access rooms. SGL/DBL$58+.

Embassy Suites Hotel (333 Madonna Road, 93405; 549-0800, Fax 543-5273, 800-422-9495) 196 suites, restaurant, complimentary breakfast, indoor swimming pool, whirlpools, gift shop, car rental, room service, meeting facilities for 700, valet laundry, laundry room, exercise facilities, airport transportation, wheelchair access, no-smoking rooms. SGL/DBL$119-$129.

Garden Street Inn (1212 Garden Street, 93401; 545-9802) 13 rooms, bed and breakfast, complimentary breakfast, private baths, wheelchair-access rooms. SGL/DBL$$50-$150.

Howard Johnson Lodge (1585 Calle Joaquin, 93450; 544-5300, Fax 541-2823, 800-654-2000) 64 rooms, restaurant, outdoor heated swimming pool, in-room refrigerators, VCRs, laundry room, wheelchair-access rooms, no-smoking rooms, airport courtesy car, pets allowed. SGL$49-$69, DBL$54-$74.

La Cuesta Motor Inn (2074 Monterey Street, 93401; 543-2777, 544-0696, 800-543-2777) 72 rooms, complimentary breakfast, outdoor swimming pool, jacuzzis, children under 12 free, fax service, free local telephone calls, airport transportation, free parking, wheelchair access, no-smoking rooms, no pets. SGL$70-$81.

LampLighter (1604 Monterey Street, 93401; 543-3709, 800-843-6882, 800-843-6882) 42 rooms and efficiencies, complimentary breakfast, airport transportation, swimming pool, no-smoking rooms. SGL$37-$64, DBL$39-$65.

San Luis Obispo

Madonna Inn (100 Madonna Road, 93401; 543-3000, 800-543-9666) 109 rooms, restaurant, airport transportation. SGL/DBL$72-$170.

Midtown Motel (475 Marsh Street, 93401; 543-4533) 16 rooms. SGL/DBL$42-$75.

Motel 6 (1433 Calle Joaquin, 93401; 549-9595) 87 rooms. SGL/DBL$28-$34.

Peach Tree Inn (2001 Monterey Street, 93401; 543-3170, 800-227-6396 in California) 39 rooms, complimentary breakfast. SGL/DBL$40-$60.

Quality Inn and Suites (1631 Monterey Street, 93401; 541-5001, 800-221-2222) 138 rooms, restaurant, complimentary breakfast, swimming pool, whirlpool, in-room refrigerators and microwaves, VCRs, meeting facilities, wheelchair-access rooms, no pets. LS SGL$89-$99, DBL$103-$123; HS SGL$99-$119, DBL$109-$129.

Sands Motel and Suites (1930 Monterey Street, 93401; 544-0500, Fax 544-3529, 800-441-4655) 70 rooms and suites, complimentary breakfast, outdoor heated swimming pool, free local telephone calls, children under 12 free, in-room refrigerators and microwaves, VCRs, meeting facilities for 120, airport courtesy car, wheelchair-access rooms, no-smoking rooms, pets allowed. SGL$45-$69, DBL$54-$79, STS$55-$89.

Super 8 Motel (1951 Monterey Street, 93401; 544-7895, 800-800-8000) 49 rooms, complimentary breakfast, outdoor heated swimming pool, wheelchair-access rooms, free local telephone calls, in-room refrigerators and microwaves, no-smoking rooms, no pets. SGL/DBL$39-$59.

TraveLodge (1825 Monterey Street, 93401; 543-5110, 800-255-3050) 38 rooms, restaurant, lounge, swimming pool. SGL/DBL$35-$47.

TraveLodge (950 Olive Street, 93401; 544-8886, 800-255-3050) 32 rooms and suites, restaurant, kitchenettes, whirlpool, no pets. SGL/DBL$36-$48.

Vagabond Inn (210 Madonna Road, 93401; 544-4710, Fax 541-1949, 800-522-1555) 60 rooms, restaurant, heated swimming pool, pets allowed, airport transportation, free local telephone calls, no-smoking rooms, children under 18 free, fax service, complimentary newspaper. SGL$47-$52, DBL$52-$64.

Villa San Luis Motel (1670 Monterey Street, 93401; 543-8071) 24 rooms, swimming pool. SGL/DBL$33-$43.

San Marcos and Lake San Marcos

Area Code 619
San Marcos Chamber of Commerce
904-4 West San Marcos Boulevard
San Marcos CA 92069
744-1270

Lake San Marcos Resort-Quail Inn (1025 La Bonita Drive, 92069; 744-0120, Fax 744-0748, 800-447-6556) 142 rooms and suites, three restaurants, lounge, outdoor heated swimming pool, spa, jacuzzi, children under 12 free, in-room refrigerators, meeting facilities for 350, tennis, golf, airport transportation, gift shop, valet laundry, wheelchair access, no-smoking rooms, pets allowed. SGL/DBL$85-$115, STS$125-$225.

TraveLodge (517 San Marcos Boulevard, 92069; 471-2800, 800-255-3050) 85 rooms and suites, restaurant, lounge, swimming pool, laundry room, kitchenettes, meeting facilities for 35, no pets. SGL/DBL$35-$37+.

San Miguel

Area Code 805

Ranch Bed and Breakfast (Box 3653, 93451; 463-2320) 4 rooms, complimentary breakfast and dinner, swimming pool, airport transportation. SGL$60-$90, DBL$90-$120.

San Pedro

Area Code 310
San Pedro Peninsula Chamber of Commerce
390 West Seventh Street
San Pedro CA 90733
832-7272

Best Western San Pedro Grand Hotel (111 South Gaffey Street, 90731; 514-1414, Fax 831-8262, 800-528-1234) 60 rooms and suites, restaurant, lounge, outdoor swimming pool, spa, complimentary breakfast, wheelchair-access rooms, children under 12 free, fax service, no-smoking rooms, no pets, free parking. SGL/DBL$69-$104, STS$159+.

Best Western Sunrise At Ports O'Call (525 South Harbor Boulevard, 90731; 548-1080, Fax 519-0380, 800-528-1234) 110 rooms, restaurant, lounge, complimentary breakfast, swimming pool, transportation to local attractions, fax service, children under 12 free, wheelchair-access rooms, airport courtesy car, no pets. SGL/DBL$68-$78.

Compri Hotel Los Angeles Harbor (2800 Via Cabrillo Marina, 90731; 514-3344, Fax 514-8945) 226 rooms and suites, restaurant, swimming pool, airport transportation, exercise facilities, pets allowed, free parking. SGL$80-$99, DBL$90-$109, STS$175-$325.

Doubletree Hotel and Conference Center (2800 Via Cabrillo Marina, 90731; 514-3344, Fax 514-8945, 800-528-0444, 800-426-6774) 226 rooms and suites, three restaurants, lounge, swimming pool, whirlpool, sauna, lighted tennis courts, exercise facilities, meeting facilities for 550, marina. SGL/DBL$110-$140.

Econo Lodge (411 South Pacific Avenue, 90731; 831-0195, 800-424-4777) 35 rooms, restaurant, complimentary newspaper, wheelchair-access rooms, children under 18 free, no pets. SGL/DBL$40-$50.

The Grand Cottages (809 South Grand Avenue, 90731; 548-1240) 4 suites, bed and breakfast, complimentary breakfast, no-smoking. SGL/DBL$90, STS$105.

Grand Hotel San Pedro (111 South Gaffey Street, 90731; 514-1414, 800-248-3188, 800-225-3135 in California) 64 rooms and suites, restaurant, complimentary breakfast, lounge, outdoor swimming pool, jacuzzi, children under 12, meeting facilities for 100, valet laundry, free parking, no pets, wheelchair-access rooms, no-smoking rooms. SGL/DBL$69-$95, STS$169-$199.

Los Angeles International AYH-Hostel (3601 South Gaffey, 90731; 831-8109) 70 beds, kitchen, no-smoking rooms, free parking. SGL$11-$15.

The Pacific Inn (516 West 38th Street, 90731; 514-1247) 24 rooms and efficiencies, wheelchair access. SGL$50-$68, DBL$63-$73.

Ramada Inn (850 East Dominguez Street, 90746; 538-5500, 800-228-2828) 167 rooms and suites, restaurant, swimming pool. SGL$65-$75, DBL$75-$80.

Sheraton San Pedro Hotel (601 South Palos Verdes Street, 90731; 519-8200, Fax 519-8421, 800-325-3535) 232 rooms and suites, restaurant, swimming pool, exercise facilities, airport transportation, wheelchair-access rooms, no-smoking rooms. SGL/DBL$60-$120, STS$135-$695.

The Vagabond Inn San Pedro (215 South Gaffey Street, 90731; 831-8911, 831-2649, 800-522-1555) 74 rooms, restaurant, complimentary breakfast, outdoor heated swimming pool, in-room refrigerators, pets allowed, free parking, airport transportation, free local telephone calls, no-smoking rooms, children under 18 free, fax service, complimentary newspaper. SGL$55, DBL$60-$65.

West Adams Bed and Breakfast Inn (1650 Westmoreland Boulevard, 90006; 737-5041) 4 rooms, bed and breakfast, complimentary breakfast, free parking. SGL$70, DBL$75, STS$100.

San Ramon

Area Code 415

Marriott Residence Inn (1071 Market Place, 94583; 277-9292, Fax 277-0687, 800-331-3131) restaurant, complimentary breakfast, meeting facilities for 30, exercise facilities, wheelchair-access rooms, no-smoking rooms, pets allowed. SGL/DBL$69-$145.

San Ramon Marriott-Bishop Ranch (2600 Bishop Drive, 9458;3; 867-9200, Fax 275-9443, 800-228-9290) 372 rooms and suites, restaurant, swimming pool, exercise facilities, wheelchair access, no-smoking rooms, pets allowed. SGL$109-$135, DBL$109-$145, STS$250-$500.

San Simeon

Area Code 805
San Simeon Chamber of Commerce
Box 1
San Simeon CA 93452, 927-3500

San Simeon

Best Western Cavalier Inn (9415 Hearst Drive, 93452; 927-4688, Fax 927-0497, 800-528-1234) 90 rooms, restaurant, swimming pool, exercise facilities, wheelchair access, no-smoking rooms, pets allowed. LS SGL/DBL$59-$69; HS SGL/DBL$105-$115.

Best Western Green Tree Inn (9450 Castillo Drive, 93452; 927-4691, Fax 927-1473, 800-528-1234) 117 rooms and suites, restaurant, heated indoor swimming pool, spa, kitchenettes, laundry room, children under 18 free, fax service, tennis, wheelchair-access rooms, no-smoking rooms, free parking. SGL/DBL$60-$90, STS$135-$210.

California Sea Coast Lodge (9215 Hearst Drive; 927-3878, 800-451-9900 in California) 57 rooms and suites, complimentary breakfast, swimming pool, wheelchair access, no-smoking rooms. SGL/DBL$70-$110, STS$125-$175.

El Rey Inn (9260 Castillo Drive, 93452; 927-3998, 800-322-8029, 800-821-7914) 56 rooms and suites, restaurant, complimentary breakfast, outdoor heated swimming pool, spas, free local telephone calls, laundry room, free parking, wheelchair-access rooms, no pets. SGL/DBL$65-$75, STS$99-$159.

Holiday Inn (9070 Castillo Drive, 93452; 927-8691, 800-HOLIDAY) 100 rooms, restaurant, lounge, outdoor heated swimming pool, laundry room, meeting facilities for 25, children under 18 free, wheelchair-access rooms, pets allowed. SGL/DBL$65-$130.

Pines Resort (7200 Moonstone Beach Drive, 93452; 927-4502) 38 rooms, restaurant, swimming pool. SGL/DBL$50+.

Ragged Point Inn (Box 110, 93452; 927-4502) 20 rooms, restaurant. SGL/DBL$84-$95.

San Simeon Pines Resort (7200 Moonstone Beach Drive, 93452; 927-4648) 60 rooms, swimming pool, wheelchair access, no-smoking rooms. SGL/DBL$65-$95.

Sands Motel (9355 Hearst Drive, 93452; 927-3243, 800-444-0779) 33 rooms, restaurant, complimentary breakfast, swimming pool, no-smoking rooms. SGL/DBL$45-$70.

Silver Surf Motel (9390 Castillo Drive, 93452; 927-4661, 800-736-1353) 73 rooms, swimming pool, pets allowed. SGL/DBL$59-$85.

Santa Ana

Area Code 714
Santa Ana Chamber of Commerce
600 West Santa Ana Boulevard
Santa Ana CA 92702
541-5353

RENTAL SOURCES: Bed and Breakfast International (Box 282910, 94128; 696-1690, Fax 696-1699, 800-872-4500) represents bed and breakfast accommodations throughout California. Accommodations available in private homes, houseboats and inns. All rates include complimentary breakfast. SGL/DBL$50-$125.

Best Western Santa Ana Inn (2600 North Main Street, 92701; 836-5141, Fax 543-0841, 800-528-1234) 125 rooms, restaurant, lounge, swimming pool, spa, children under 18 free, meeting facilities, in-room refrigerators, fax service, wheelchair access/room, no-smoking rooms. SGL$48-$56, DBL$54-$80.

Best Western Irvine Host Hotel (1717 East Dyer Road, 92705; 261-1515, Fax 261-1265, 800-433-4374, 800-528-1234) 148 rooms, restaurant, complimentary breakfast, swimming pool, no-smoking rooms, airport courtesy car. SGL/DBL$58-$70.

Comfort Suites Airport (2620 Hotel Terrace Drive, 92705; 966-5200, 800-221-2222) 130 rooms and suites, restaurant, complimentary breakfast, swimming pool, whirlpool, meeting facilities, in-room refrigerators, airport courtesy car, wheelchair-access rooms, no pets. SGL/DBL$59-$78.

Courtyard By Marriott (3002 South Harbor Boulevard, 92704; 545-1001, Fax 545-0841, 800-321-2211) 157 rooms, restaurant, meeting facilities, no pets. SGL/DBL$76+.

Crown Sterling Suites (1325 East Dyer Road, 92705; 241-3800, 800-433-4600) 308 suites, restaurant, complimentary breakfast, swimming pool, airport courtesy car, wheelchair access, no-smoking rooms. SGL/DBL$100-$150.

Days Inn (1600 E First Street, 92701; 835-3051, Fax 543-0856, 800-325-2525) 146 rooms and suites, restaurant, lounge, swimming pool, sauna, whirlpool, exercise facilities, gift shop, meeting facilities, fax service, valet laundry, children under 12 free, pets allowed, no-smoking rooms. SGL$50-$70, DBL$55-$75.

Doubletree Club Hutton Centre (7 Hutton Centre Drive, 92707; 751-2400, Fax 662-7935, 800-528-0444) 170 rooms and suites, restaurant, lounge, complimentary breakfast, outdoor heated swimming pool, spa, meeting facilities for 50, exercise center, airport courtesy car, free parking. SGL/DBL$90-$120, STS$150-$200.

Embassy Suites (1325 East Dyer Road, 92075; 241-3800, Fax 662-1651, 800-EMBASSY) 308 suites, restaurant, complimentary breakfast, airport transportation, wheelchair access, no-smoking rooms.

Howard Johnson (2700 Hotel Terrace, 92705; 432-8888, Fax 434-6228, 800-654-2000) 144 rooms, complimentary breakfast, outdoor heated swimming pool, spa, wheelchair-access rooms, airport courtesy car, no-smoking rooms. SGL/DBL$51-$70.

Howard Johnson (939 East 17th Street, 92701; 558-3700, 800-654-8778, 800-654-2000) 145 rooms, restaurant, outdoor swimming pool, whirlpool, sauna, meeting facilities, airport courtesy car, wheelchair access/room, no-smoking rooms. SGL/DBL$32-$56.

Motel 6 (1623 East First Street, 92701; 558-0500, 505-891-6161) 33 rooms. SGL/DBL$31-$37.

Quality Suites Airport (2701 Hotel Terrace Drive, 92705; 957-9200, 800-221-2222) 177 rooms, restaurant, complimentary breakfast, lounge, swimming pool, whirlpool, in-room refrigerators and microwaves, VCRs, airport courtesy car, wheelchair-access rooms, no pets. SGL/DBL$85-$94.

Radisson Suite Hotel (2720 Hotel Terrace Drive, 97205; 556-3838, Fax 241-1008) 122 suites. SGL/DBL$79-$89.

Ramada Hotel (2726 South Grand Avenue, 92705; 966-1955, Fax 966-1889, 800-228-2828) 194 rooms, restaurant, lounge, swimming pool, spa, exercise facilities, free parking, airport transportation, wheelchair-access rooms, no-smoking rooms. SGL/DBL$69-$99.

Ricker Bed and Breakfast (Bed and Breakfast International) 1 room, complimentary breakfast, no smoking. SGL/DBL$65.

Rodeway Inn (1104 North Harbor Boulevard, 92703; 554-1177, 800-424-4777) 90 rooms, restaurant, heated swimming pool, spa, whirlpools, wheelchair-access rooms, in-room refrigerators, tours, airport courtesy car, transportation to local attractions, meeting facilities. SGL/DBL$46-$58.

TraveLodge (1400 Southeast Bristol, 92707; 557-8700, Fax 557-9164, 800-255-3050) 102 rooms, restaurant, complimentary breakfast, swimming pool, exercise facilities, airport transportation, no pets. SGL/DBL$40-$49.

Vagabond Inn (1519 First Street, 92701; 547-9426, Fax 547-4327, 800-522-1555) 52 rooms, restaurant, swimming pool, no-smoking rooms, pets allowed. SGL/DBL$45-$62.

Woolley's Petite Suites Hotel (2721 Hotel Terrace Road, 92705; 540-1111, Fax 662-1643, 800-762-2597) 184 suites, lounge, outdoor heated swimming pool, valet laundry, room service, kitchenettes, fax service, gift shop, laundry room, wheelchair-access rooms, no-smoking rooms, exercise facilities, free parking. SGL/DBL$49-$62.

Santa Barbara

Area Code 805
Santa Barbara Conference and Visitors Bureau
1330 State Street
Santa Barbara CA 93102
965-3023

RENTAL SERVICES: Accommodations Santa Barbara (3344 State Street, 93101; 800-292-2222) represents hotels in the Santa Barbara area.

Ala Mar Motel (102 West Cabrillo Boulevard, 93101; 962-9208) 19 rooms and efficiencies, wheelchair-access rooms. SGL/DBL$75-$125.

Adobe Motel (26 East Haley Street, 963-9194) 17 rooms and efficiencies, no-smoking rooms, pets allowed. SGL/DBL$55-$75+.

Alpine Motel (2824 State Street, 93105; 687-2821) 10 rooms, restaurant, exercise facilities, no-smoking rooms. SGL/DBL$50-$60.

Ambassador By The Sea Motel (202 West Cabrillo Boulevard, 93101; 965-4577) 32 rooms and efficiencies, complimentary breakfast, swimming pool. SGL/DBL$90-$160.

Arlington Inn (1136 De La Vina, 93101; 965-6532, 800-428-3912 in California) 43 rooms, bed and breakfast, complimentary breakfast, free parking. SGL/DBL$50-$85.

Bath Street Inn (1720 Bath Street, 93101; 682-9680) 7 rooms, bed and breakfast, complimentary breakfast, free parking. SGL/DBL$75-$125.

Bayberry Inn (111 West Valerio Street, 93101; 682-3199) 8 rooms, bed and breakfast, complimentary breakfast, no-smoking rooms, pets allowed. SGL/DBL$75-$125.

Beach House Motel (320 West Yanonali Street, 93101; 966-1126) 12 rooms and efficiencies, complimentary breakfast, SGL/DBL$55-$125.

Best Western El Patio Beachside Inn (336 West Cabrillo Boulevard, 93101; 805 965-6556, Fax 805 966-6626, 800-528-1234) 60 rooms, restaurant, lounge, swimming pool, room service, fax service, beach, tennis, no pets. LS SGL$78-$88, DBL$84-$94; HS SGL$114-$124, DBL$120-$130.

Best Western Encina Lodge and Suites (2220 Bath Street, 93105; 805 682-7277, Fax 805 563-9319, 800-528-1234) 121 rooms and suites, restaurant, lounge, swimming pool, spa, beauty and barber shop, gift shop, in-room refrigerators, fax service, airport transportation, wheelchair-access rooms, no-smoking rooms. LS SGL/DBL$92-$106; HS SGL/DBL$102-$116, STS$112-$126.

Best Western Pepper Tree Inn (3850 State Street, 93150; 805 687-5511, Fax 805 682-2410, 800-528-1234) 150 rooms, restaurant, lounge, two outdoor heated swimming pools, spas, in-room refrigerators and safes, complimentary newspaper, fax service, transportation to local attractions, beauty and barber shop, gift shop, laundry room, airport transportation, no-smoking rooms, exercise facilities, free parking. SGL/DBL$96-$134.

Blue Quail Inn and Cottages (1908 Bath Street, 93101; 687-2300, 800-676-1622, 800-549-1622 in California) 9 rooms, bed and breakfast, complimentary breakfast, in-room refrigerators, children under 12 free, no smoking, free parking, no pets. SGL/DBL$82-$165.

Blue Sands Motel (421 South Milpas Street, 93103; 965-1624) 11 rooms and efficiencies, swimming pool, pets allowed. SGL/DBL$50-$100.

Cabrillo Inn At The Beach (931 East Cabrillo Boulevard, 93101; 966-1641, 800-648-6708) 40 rooms and suites, restaurant, swimming pool, free parking. SGL/DBL$75-$150, STS$135-$185.

California Hotel (35 State Street, 93101; 966-7153) 96 rooms. SGL/DBL$55.

Cathedral Oaks Lodge (4770 Calle Real, 93110; 964-3511, Fax 964-0075, 800-654-1965, 800-228-4581 in California) 126 rooms and suites, complimentary breakfast, outdoor heated swimming pool, jacuzzi, children under 12 free, free local telephone calls, meeting facilities for 85, in-room refrigerators, laundry room, free parking, airport transportation, wheelchair access/room, no pets, no-smoking rooms. SGL/DBL$74-$98, STS$110-$150.

Cheshire Cat Inn (36 West Valerio Street, 93101; 569-1610, Fax 682-1876) 14 rooms, bed and breakfast, complimentary breakfast, free parking, no smoking. SGL/DBL$109-$179.

Coast Village Inn (1188 Coast Village Road, 93108; 969-3266) 25 rooms, swimming pool, no-smoking rooms. SGL/DBL$60-$85.

Colonial Motel (206 Castillo Street, 93101; 963-4317) 22 rooms and efficiencies, complimentary breakfast, swimming pool, no-smoking rooms. SGL/DBL$50-$75.

Eagle Inn (232 Natoma Avenue, 93101; 965-3586) 17 rooms and efficiencies, complimentary breakfast. SGL$75-$125.

East Beach Lodge (1029 Orilla Del Mar Street, 93103; 965-0546) 32 rooms and efficiencies, restaurant, swimming pool, pets allowed. SGL/DBL$55-$125.

El Encanto Hotel and Garden Villas (1900 Lasuen Road, 93103; 687-5000, Fax 687-3903, 800-346-7039 in California) 100 cottages, restaurant, swimming pool, airport courtesy car, tennis. SGL/DBL$120-$300.

El Prado Motor Inn (1601 State Street, 93101; 966-0807) 70 rooms and efficiencies, swimming pool, wheelchair access, no-smoking rooms. SGL/DBL$50-$80.

Fess Parker's Red Lion Resort (633 East Cabillo Boulevard, 93103; 564-4333, Fax 962-8198, 800-879-2929) 360 rooms and suites, restaurant, lounge, swimming pool, sauna, spa, concierge, meeting and convention facilities, tennis, exercise equipment, golf, free parking, airport courtesy car, wheelchair access, laundry room, no-smoking rooms. SGL/DBL$180-$280, STS$225-$700.

Four Season Biltmore Hotel (1260 Channel Drive, 93108; 969-2261, Fax 969-4682, 800-332-3442) 236 rooms and cottages, restaurant, swimming pool, exercise facilities, wheelchair-access rooms, no-smoking rooms, pets allowed. SGL/DBL$240-$290.

Franciscan Inn (109 Bath Street, 93101; 963-8845) 53 rooms, restaurant, complimentary breakfast, swimming pool, wheelchair access, no-smoking rooms. SGL/DBL$75-$145.

Glenborough Inn And Cottage (1327 Bath Street, 93101; 966-0589) 9 rooms, bed and breakfast, complimentary breakfast, no-smoking rooms. SGL/DBL$60-$100+.

Hacienda Motel (3643 State Street, 93105; 687-6461) 31 rooms and efficiencies. SGL/DBL$35-$50.

Harbor House (104 Bath Street, 93101; 962-9745) 10 rooms, airport transportation, pets allowed. SGL/DBL$30-$60.

Harbor View Inn (28 West Cabrillo Boulevard, 93101; 963-0780, Fax 963-7967) 64 rooms, restaurant, complimentary breakfast, swimming pool, wheelchair access. SGL/DBL$89-$119.

Harbour Carriage House (420 West Montecito Street, 93101; 962-8447, 800-594-4633) 9 rooms, bed and breakfast, complimentary breakfast, private baths, fireplaces, jacuzzis, fax service, no children, no smoking, no pets, free parking, wheelchair-access rooms. SGL/DBL$85-$185.

Holiday Lodge (2325 State Street, 93105; 687-6800) 11 rooms and efficiencies. SGL/DBL$35-$45.

Hope Ranch Motel (4111 State Street, 93110; 967-2901) 16 rooms and efficiencies. SGL/DBL$30-$45.

Hotel State Street (121 State Street, 93101; 966-6586) 53 rooms. SGL/DBL$30-$55.

Ivanhoe (1406 Castillo Street, 93101; 963-8832) 5 rooms, bed and breakfast, complimentary breakfast, pets allowed. SGL/DBL$125+.

Kings Inn of Santa Barbara (128 Castillo Street, 93101; 934-4471) 45 rooms, swimming pool, no-smoking rooms. SGL/DBL$50-$100.

La Rancho Motel (316 West Montecito Street, 93101; 962-0181) 22 rooms and efficiencies. SGL/DBL$30-$55.

Marina Beach Motel (21 Bath Street, 93101; 963-9311) 31 rooms and efficiencies. SGL/DBL$55-$140, EFF$65-$175.

Mason Beach Inn (324 West Mason Street, 93101; 962-3203, 800-446-0444 in California) 34 rooms. SGL/DBL$58-$105.

Miramar Resort Hotel (1555 South Hameson Lane, 93102; 969-2203) 202 rooms and efficiencies, restaurant, swimming pool, exercise facilities. SGL/DBL$70-$125, EFF$150+.

Modoc Motel (4455 Hollister Avenue, 93110; 967-6504) 8 rooms. SGL/DBL$30-$45.

Montecito Inn (1295 Coast Village Road, 93108; 969-0780, Fax 969-0623, 800-843-2017) 52 rooms and suites, restaurant, complimentary breakfast, exercise facilities, swimming pool. SGL/DBL$135-$168.

Motel 6 (3505 State Street, 93105; 687-5400, 505-891-6161) 60 rooms, swimming pool, no-smoking rooms, pets allowed. SGL/DBL$35-$55.

Motel 6 (443 Corona Del Mar Drive, 93103; 564-1392, 505-891-6161) 32 rooms, swimming pool, wheelchair access, pets allowed. SGL/DBL$35-$50.

Mountain View Motel (3055 De La Vina Street, 93105; 687-6636) 34 rooms, complimentary breakfast, swimming pool. SGL/DBL$60-$70.

New Faulding Hotel (15 East Haley Street, 93101; 963-9191) 80 rooms, no-smoking rooms. SGL/DBL$55-$65.

Oak Lodge Motel (302 West Mission Street, 93101; 687-9389) 6 rooms and efficiencies. SGL/DBL$35-$60.

Ocean Palms Hotel (232 West Cabillo Boulevard, 93101; 966-9133, Fax 965-7882, 800-350-2326) 36 rooms and suites, outdoor heated swimming pool, kitchenettes, in-room refrigerators, valet laundry, child care, fax service, free parking. SGL/DBL$50-$120, STS$90-$160.

Old Yacht Club Inn (431 Corona Del Mar Drive, 93103; 962-1277, Fax 962-3989, 800-676-1676, 800-549-1676) 9 rooms, bed and breakfast, complimentary breakfast, private baths, free parking, fax service, no pets, no smoking, SGL/DBL$80-$140.

Olive House (1604 Olive Street, 93101; 962-4902) 6 rooms, bed and breakfast, complimentary breakfast, no-smoking rooms. SGL/DBL$75-$125+.

Pacific Crest Motel (433 Corona Del Mar Drive, 93103; 966-3103) 26 rooms and efficiencies, no-smoking rooms, pets allowed. SGL/DBL$35-$100.

Pacific Park Motel (122 West Cabrillo Boulevard, 93101; 963-0405) 19 rooms. SGL/DBL$50-$100.

The Parsonage (1600 Olive Street, 93101; 962-9336) 6 rooms, bed and breakfast, complimentary breakfast. SGL/DBL$75-$125+.

Plaza Inn (3885 State Street, 93105; 687-3217) 12 rooms. SGL/DBL#35-$65.

Polynesian Motel (433 West Montecito Street, 93101; 963-7851, 962-9428, 800-626-1986) 41 rooms, outdoor heated swimming pool, jacuzzis, kitchenettes, fax service, free parking, laundry room, no-smoking rooms, pets allowed. SGL/DBL$48-75.

Presidio Motel (1620 State Street, 93101; 963-1355) 16 rooms, complimentary breakfast, no-smoking rooms. SGL/DBL$35-$85.

Quality Suites (5490 Hollister Avenue, 93111; 805 683-6722, 800-221-2222) 75 rooms, restaurant, complimentary breakfast, swimming pool, whirlpool, meeting facilities, wheelchair-access rooms, no pets. LS SGL$95-$125, DBL$105-$145; HS SGL$115-$155, DBL$125-$165.

Radisson Suite Hotel (232 West Cabrillo Boulevard, 93101; 966-9133, 800-333-3333) 47 rooms. SGL/DBL$90-$150.

Ramada Suites (2050 North Preisker Lane, 93545; 928-6000, 800-272-6232) 210 suites, restaurant, lounge, swimming pool.

San Ysidro Ranch (900 San Ysidro Lane, 93108; 969-5046, Fax 565-1995) 43 cottages, restaurant, swimming pool, tennis, pets allowed. SGL/DBL$175-$255.

Sandman At The Beach (18 Bath Street, 93101; 963-4418) 20 rooms, complimentary breakfast, wheelchair access. SGL/DBL$65+.

Sandman Inn (3714 State Street, 93105; 687-2468, Fax 687-6581, 800-457-2880) 111 rooms, restaurant, complimentary breakfast, swimming pool, exercise facilities, airport courtesy car, wheelchair-access rooms, pets allowed. SGL/DBL$74-$84.

Sandpiper Lodge (3525 State Street, 93105; 687-5326) 75 rooms and efficiencies, no-smoking rooms. SGL/DBL$35-$65.

Santa Barbara Inn (901 East Cabrillo Boulevard, 93103; 966-2285) 71 rooms, restaurant, lounge, swimming pool, ocean view, in-room refrigerators, valet laundry, airport transportation, wheelchair-access rooms, no-smoking rooms, free parking. SGL/DBL$65-$125.

Santa Barbara Miramar Resort (1555 South Jameson Lane, 93108; 969-2203, Fax 969-3163, 800-322-6983) 126 rooms, restaurant, swimming pool, exercise facilities, tennis. SGL/DBL$70-$125, STS$100-$400+.

Schooner Inn (533 State Street, 93101; 965-4572) 96 rooms, complimentary breakfast. SGL/DBL$55-$65.

Sheraton Santa Barbara (1111 East Cabrillo Boulevard, 93103; 963-0744) 174 rooms and suites, restaurant, lounge, outdoor heated swimming pool, jacuzzi, sauna, meeting facilities for 300, gift shop, beach, wheelchair-access rooms, exercise facilities, no-smoking rooms. SGL/DBL$125+.

Simpson House Inn (121 East Arrellage, 93101; 963-7067, 800-676-1280) 10 rooms and suites, bed and breakfast, complimentary breakfast, private baths, fax service, free parking, airport transportation, wheelchair-access rooms, no smoking, no pets. SGL/DBL$80-$185.

Sunset Motel (3504 State Street, 93105; 687-3813) 12 rooms, pets allowed. SGL/DBL$35-$40.

Tides Motel (116 Castillo Street, 93101; 963-9772) 25 rooms and efficiencies. SGL/DBL$35-$50.

Tiffany Inn (1323 De La Vina Street, 93101; 963-2283) 6 rooms, bed and breakfast, complimentary breakfast, no-smoking. SGL/DBL$70-$195.

Traveler's Motel (3222 State Street, 93105; 687-6009) 13 rooms and efficiencies, no-smoking rooms, pets allowed. SGL/DBL$35-$45.

TraveLodge (22 Castillo Street, 93101; 805 965-8527, Fax 805 965-6125, 800-255-3050) 19 rooms, restaurant, lounge, no pets. SGL/DBL$55-$80.

TraveLodge City Center (1816 State Street, 93101; 805 569-2205, 800-255-3050) 23 rooms, restaurant, lounge, no pets. SGL/DBL$45-$65.

Tropicana Inn (223 Castillo Street, 93101; 966-2219) 31 rooms, restaurant, swimming pool, wheelchair-access rooms, no-smoking rooms. SGL/DBL$125+.

The Upham Hotel and Garden Cottages (1404 De La Vina Street, 93101; 962-0058, 800-727-0876) 42 rooms and suites, bed and breakfast, restaurant, complimentary breakfast, free parking. SGL/DBL$95-$165, STS$150-$300.

Vagabond Inn Midtown (1920 State Street, 93101; 569-1521, Fax 682-6854, 800-522-1555) 46 rooms, complimentary breakfast, swimming pool, pets allowed, airport transportation, free local telephone calls, no-smoking rooms, children under 18 free, fax service, complimentary newspaper. SGL$50-$55, DBL$55-$65.

Vagabond Inn (2819 State Street, 93105; 687-6444, Fax 687-4432, 800-522-1555) 55 rooms, complimentary breakfast, swimming pool, in-room refrigerators, pets allowed, airport transportation, free local telephone calls, no-smoking rooms, children under 18 free, fax service, complimentary newspaper. SGL$49-$61, DBL$54-$71.

Villa Rosa (15 Chapal Street, 93101; 966-0851) 18 rooms and efficiencies, complimentary breakfast, swimming pool. SGL/DBL$70-$195.

West Beach Inn (306 W. Cabrillo Boulevard, 93101; 963-4277, Fax 564-4210, 800-423-5991, 800-233-5743 in California) 44 rooms and efficiencies, complimentary breakfast, swimming pool, wheelchair-access rooms, no-smoking rooms, pets allowed. SGL/DBL$120-$145.

Santa Clara

Area Code 408
Santa Clara Convention and Visitors Bureau
1515 El Camino Real
Santa Clara CA 95052
296-7111

Best Western Santa Clara Holiday Lodge (4341 El Camino Real, 95051; 244-3366, Fax 244-3366, 800-528-1234) 50 rooms, restaurant, lounge, complimentary breakfast, swimming pool, wheelchair-access rooms, no-smoking rooms, no pets. SGL/DBL$50-$65.

Biltmore Hotel and Suites (2151 Laurel Wood Road, 95054; 988-8411, 800-255-9925) 250 rooms and suites, restaurant, lounge, swimming pool, transportation to local attractions, free parking, airport courtesy car. SGL/DBL$49-$79+.

Capri Motel (2465 El Camino Real, 95051; 243-8173) 39 rooms, swimming pool. SGL/DBL$35-$42.

Casa Clara Motel (455 El Camino Real, 95041; 296-6979) 28 rooms, swimming pool. SGL/DBL$30-$35.

Days Inn (4200 Great American Way Parkway, 95054; 980-1525, Fax 988-0976, 800-325-2525) 168 rooms, restaurant, swimming pool, jacuzzi, valet laundry, gift shop, children under

12 free, fax service, airport courtesy car, wheelchair-access rooms, no-smoking rooms. SGL$49-$79, DBL$59-$89.

Doubletree Hotel (5101 Great America Parkway, 95054; 986-0700, Fax 986-1838, 800-528-0444) 520 rooms and suites, two restaurants, lounge, swimming pool, spa, sauna, meeting facilities for 880, exercise facilities, airport transportation, golf, tennis, pets allowed, free parking. SGL$143-$163, DBL$158-$178.

Econo Lodge (2930 El Camino Real, 95051; 241-3010, 800-446-6900, 800-424-4777) 70 rooms and efficiencies, restaurant, complimentary breakfast, swimming pool, free parking, airport courtesy car, pets allowed. SGL/DBL$46-$78.

Embassy Suites Hotel (2885 Lakeside Drive, 95054; 496-6400, Fax 988-7529, 800-EMBASSY) 257 suites, complimentary breakfast, free parking, indoor swimming pool, spa, sauna, airport transportation, meeting facilities for 100, room service, valet laundry, wheelchair-access rooms, no-smoking rooms. STS$160-$180.

E-Z 8 Motel (3550 El Camino Real, 95051; 246-3119, 800-326-6835) 66 rooms. SGL/DBL$30-$42.

Granada Inn (2515 El Camino Real, 95051; 241-2841, Fax 241-8559, 800-448-6444) 60 rooms and efficiencies, complimentary breakfast, airport transportation, no-smoking rooms. SGL$47, DBL$47-$51.

Howard Johnson Motor Lodge (5405 Stevens Creek Boulevard, 95051; 257-8600, Fax 257-8600, 800-654-2000) 96 rooms and suites, restaurant, heated swimming pool, meeting facilities, laundry room, wheelchair-access rooms, no-smoking rooms, airport transportation. SGL$64-$89, DBL$74-$99.

Kings Highway Motel (1031 El Camino Real, 95050; 296-3544) 19 rooms and efficiencies. SGL/DBL$45-$48.

Santa Clara

Madison Street Inn (1390 Madison Street, 95050; 249-5541) 3 rooms, bed and breakfast, complimentary breakfast, swimming pool, no-smoking. SGL/DBL$60-$80.

Mariani's Inn (2500 El Camino Real, 95051; 243-1431, 800-553-8666) 126 rooms and suites, restaurant, lounge, complimentary breakfast, outdoor heated swimming pool, jacuzzis, children under 18 free, free local telephone calls, laundry room, exercise equipment, meeting facilities for 150, free parking, airport courtesy car, wheelchair access, no-smoking rooms, pets allowed. SGL$66, DBL$68, STS$71-$79.

Marriott Hotel (2700 Mission College Boulevard, 95054; 988-1500, Fax 727-4353) 754 rooms and suites, restaurant, swimming pool, exercise facilities, airport courtesy car, tennis, pets allowed. SGL$125, DBL$140, STS$160.

Mission Inn Motel (1150 El Camino Real, 95050; 247-6077) 25 rooms and efficiencies. SGL/DBL$32-$36.

Motel 6 (3208 El Camino Real, 95051; 241-022, 505-891-6161) 99 rooms, swimming pool. SGL$45-$48, DBL$50-$56.

Quality Suites Hotel (3100 Lakewood Drive, 95054; 748-9800, 800-221-2222) 221 rooms, restaurant, complimentary breakfast, swimming pool, whirlpools, wheelchair-access rooms, free parking, exercise facilities, no pets. SGL$89-$139, DBL$99-$149.

St. Francis Motel (2222 The Alameda, 95050; 296-4330) 27 rooms and efficiencies. SGL/DBL$45.

Sterling Motel (2234 The Alameda, 95050; 249-7651) 86 one- and two-bedroom suites, restaurant, complimentary breakfast, swimming pool, exercise facilities, no-smoking rooms. SGL/DBL$65+.

TraveLodge (3477 El Camino Real, 95051; 984-3364, 800-255-3050) 43 rooms, restaurant, lounge, meeting facilities for 30, VCRs. SGL/DBL$42-$58.

The Vagabond Inn (3580 El Camino Real, 95051; 241-0771, Fax 247-3386, 800-522-1555) 70 rooms, restaurant, complimentary breakfast, heated swimming pool, no-smoking rooms, in-room refrigerators and microwaves, pets allowed, airport transportation, free local telephone calls, children under 18 free, fax service, complimentary newspaper. SGL$53-$59, DBL$53-$65.

Western Motel (2250 El Camino Real, 95050; 296-6551) 31 rooms, swimming pool. SGL$36-$38, DBL$42-$44.

Woodmark Hotel (5415 Stevens Creek Boulevard, 95051; 446-3030, 800-223-0888) 60 rooms and suites, restaurant, complimentary breakfast, free parking, wheelchair-access rooms, no-smoking rooms. SGL/DBL$120-$220+.

Santa Cruz

Area Code 408
Santa Cruz Chamber of Commerce, Conference and Visitors Center
105 Cooper Street
Santa Cruz CA 95061
423-1111

Santa Cruz County Convention and Visitors Bureau
740 Front Street
Santa Cruz CA 95061
423-6927

Aladdin's Inn (50 Front Street, 95060; 426-3575) 22 rooms and efficiencies, free parking, in-room refrigerators and microwaves, free parking. LS SGL/DBL$32-$55; HS SGL/DBL$40-$95.

Babbling Brook Inn (1025 Laurel Street, 95060; 427-2437, Fax 427-2457, 800-866-1131) 12 rooms, bed and breakfast, complimentary breakfast, balconies, fireplaces, jet tubs, meeting facilities, airport transportation, wheelchair access, no-smoking rooms, free parking. SGL/DBL$85-$125.

Santa Cruz

Best Inn (370 Ocean Street, 95060; 458-9220) 53 rooms, free parking, wheelchair access, free parking. LS SGL/DBL$22-$64; HS SGL/DBL$44+.

Best Western All Suite Inn (500 Ocean Street, 95060; 408 458-9898, Fax 408 429-1902, 800-528-1234) 40 suites, restaurant, lounge, complimentary breakfast, swimming pool, sauna, laundry room, jacuzzis, in-room refrigerators and microwaves, free parking, wheelchair access, no-smoking rooms. LS SGL/DBL$75-$150; HS SGL/DBL$115-$175.

Best Western Inn (126 Plymouth Street, 95060; 405-425-4717, 800-528-1234) 26 rooms and suites, restaurant, lounge, complimentary breakfast, heated swimming pool, sauna, tennis, putting green, kitchenettes, jacuzzis, wheelchair-access rooms, no pets. LS SGL/DBL$45-$135; HS SGL/DBL$60-$175.

Best Western Torch-Lite Inn (500 Riverside Avenue, 95060; 405-426-7575, 800-528-1234) 38 rooms, swimming pool, free parking, tennis, putting green, wheelchair access, balconies, free parking, kitchenettes, no-smoking rooms, pets allowed. LS SGL/DBL$55-$125; HS SGL/DBL$70-$125.

Candlelite Inn (1101 Ocean Street, 95060; 427-1616) 42 rooms, restaurant, swimming pool, in-room refrigerators, wheelchair access, no-smoking rooms, free parking. LS SGL/DBL$40-$75; HS SGL/DBL$65-$110.

Capri Motel (337 Riverside Avenue, 95060; 426-4611) 17 rooms and suites, swimming pool, free parking. LS SGL/DBL$24-$45; HS SGL/DBL$32-$120.

Carousel Motel (110 Riverside Avenue, 95060; 425-7090) 34 rooms, complimentary breakfast, free parking, balconies, hot tubs, wheelchair access. LS SGL/DBL$49-$90; HS SGL/DBL$80-$120.

Casa Blanca Motel (101 Main, 95060; 423-1570, Fax 423-0235) 27 rooms, restaurant, airport transportation, meeting and banquet facilities, in-room refrigerators and microwaves, meeting facilities, balconies, beach, free parking, wheelchair access. LS SGL/DBL$58-$185; HS SGL/DBL$78-$185.

Chaminade at Santa Cruz (One Chaminade Lane, 95065; 475-5600, Fax 476-4798, 800-283-6569) 152 rooms, restaurant, swimming pool, sauna, jacuzzis, wheelchair access, hot tubs, meeting facilities, airport transportation, free parking, exercise facilities. LS SGL/DBL$99+; HS SGL/DBL$145+.

Chateau Victorian (118 First Street, 95060; 458-9458) 7 rooms, bed and breakfast, complimentary breakfast, fireplaces, meeting facilities, private baths, free parking. SGL/DBL$99-$131.

Cliff Crest Bed and Breakfast (407 Cliff Street, 95060; 427-2609) 5 rooms, bed and breakfast, complimentary breakfast, fireplaces, private baths, solarium. SGL/DBL$80-$135.

Comfort Inn (110 Plymouth Street, 95060; 408 426-2664, Fax 426-0923, 800-221-2222) 63 rooms, complimentary breakfast, swimming pool, sauna, spa, free parking, wheelchair-access rooms, no pets. LS SGL/DBL$65-$140; HS SGL/DBL$75-$150.

The Darling House (314 West Cliff Drive, 90560; 458-1958) 8 rooms, bed and breakfast, complimentary breakfast and dinners, fireplaces, jacuzzis, meeting facilities, private baths, no-smoking rooms. LS SGL/DBL$50-$195; HS SGL/DBL$85-$195.

The Dream Inn On The Beach (175 West Cliff Drive, 9506; 426-4330, Fax 427-2025, 800-662-3838 in California) 164 room, restaurant, swimming pool, sauna, spa, beach, hot tubs, rooms service, no-smoking rooms. LS SGL/DBL$99-$145; HS SGL/DBL$109-$245.

Edgewater Beach Motel (525 Second Street, 95060; 423-0440) 20 rooms and efficiencies, swimming pool, free parking, ocean view, wheelchair access. LS SGL/DBL$48+; HS SGL/DBL$75+.

Edric Motel (124 First Street, 95060; 423-8087) 11 rooms and efficiencies, beach. LS SGL/DBL$65-$110; HS SGL/DBL$75-$120.

Harbor Inn (645 Seventh Avenue, 95062; 479-9731) 12 rooms, efficiencies and suites, free parking, wheelchair access. LS SGL/DBL$45-$75; HS SGL/DBL$65-$130.

Hitching Post Motel (1717 Soquel Avenue, 95062; 423-4608) 31 rooms and efficiencies, swimming pool, free parking. LS SGL/DBL$40-$70; HS SGL/DBL$50-$100.

Holiday Inn (611 Ocean Street, 95060; 426-7100, Fax 429-1044; 800-241-1555 in California, 800-HOLIDAY) 169 rooms, restaurant, outdoor heated swimming pool, hot tub, meeting facilities for 400, room service, children under 18 free, free parking, wheelchair access. LS SGL/DBL$77-$96; HS SGL/DBL$99-$125.

Inn At Pasatiempo (555 Highway 17, 95060; 423-5000, Fax 426-1737, 800-834-2546) 57 rooms and suites, restaurant, lounge, complimentary breakfast, swimming pool, meeting facilities, jacuzzis, airport transportation, golf, wheelchair access, no-smoking rooms. LS SGL/DBL$70-$175; HS SGL/DBL$80-$175.

Lanai Motor Lodge (550 Second Street, 95060; 426-3626) 20 rooms, efficiencies and suites, heated swimming pool, ocean view, balconies. LS SGL/DBL$30-$140; HS SGL/DBL$35-$165.

Magic Carpet Motel (130 West Cliff Drive, 95060; 429-7737, Fax: 429-6200) 28 rooms and efficiencies, restaurant, balconies, hot tubs, laundry room. LS SGL/DBL$28-$95; HS SGL/DBL$34-$165.

Mardi Gras Motel (338 Riverside Avenue, 95060; 426-3707) 24 rooms and efficiencies, heated swimming pool, balconies, balconies, free parking. LS SGL/DBL$25-$48; HS SGL/DBL$32-$115.

Mission Inn (2250 Mission Street, 95060; 425-5455) 42 rooms, wheelchair access, no-smoking rooms. SGL/DBL$65-$110.

Monterey Manor Hotel (325 Pacific Avenue, 95060; 423-8564, Fax 423-0149) 36 rooms and apartments, complimentary breakfast, heated swimming pool. LS SGL/DBL$45-$95; HS SGL/DBL$65-$145.

Ocean Echo Motel and Cottages (401 Johans Beach Drive, 95062; 462-4192) 15 rooms and cottages, swimming pool, balconies, beach, wheelchair access, free parking, pets allowed. LS SGL/DBL$45-$85; HS SGL/DBL$60-$125.

Pleasure Point Bed and Breakfast (2-3665 East Cliff Drive, 95062; 475-4657) 3 rooms, bed and breakfast, complimentary breakfast, balconies, fireplaces, private baths, free parking. SGL/DBL$95-$125.

Riverside Garden Inn (600 Riverside Avenue, 95060; 458-9660, 800-527-3833) 79 rooms, complimentary breakfast, swimming pool, balconies, hot tubs, meeting facilities, wheelchair-access rooms, no-smoking rooms. LS SGL/DBL$48-$101; HS SGL/DBL$52-$149.

Santa Cruz Inn (2950 Soquel Avenue, 95062; 475-6322) 20 rooms, jacuzzis, fireplaces. LS SGL/DBL$39-$95; HS SGL/DBL$49-$99.

Sea and Sand Inn (201 West Cliff Drive, 95060; 427-2400) 20 rooms, efficiencies and suites, hot tubs, complimentary breakfast, free parking. LS SGL/DBL$75-$190; HS SGL/DBL$105-$190.

St. Charles Court (902 Third Street, 95060; 423-2091) 8 rooms and efficiencies, swimming pool, balconies, free parking, no-smoking rooms, no pets. LS SGL/DBL$30-$85; HS SGL/DBL$55-$140.

Sunny Cove Motel (2-1610 East Cliff Drive, 95062; 475-1741) 13 rooms and efficiencies, swimming pool, pets allowed, free parking. LS SGL/DBL$30-$70; HS SGL/DBL$40-$100.

Sunset Inn (2424 Mission Street, 95060; 423-3471) 28 rooms and efficiencies. LS SGL/DBL$40-$65; HS SGL/DBL$55-$95.

Terrace Court Motel (125 Beach Street, 95060; 423-3031) 40 rooms and efficiencies, swimming pool, balconies, LS SGL/DBL$62-$98; HS SGL/DBL$66-$105.

TraveLodge (525 Ocean Street, 95060; 408 426-2300, Fax 408 426-1126, 800-255-3050) 55 rooms and suites, restaurant, swimming pool, balconies, free parking, no-smoking rooms, tennis, no pets. LS SGL/DBL$50-$95; HS SGL/DBL$65-$130.

TraveLodge (619 Riverside Avenue, 95060; 408 423-9525, 800-255-3050) 63 rooms and suites, restaurant, complimentary breakfast, swimming pool, tennis, no pets. SGL/DBL$40-$80.

Villa Vista (2-2800 East Cliff Drive, 95062; 866-2626) two- and three-bedroom condos. LS $1,200W; HS $1,800W.

Santa Fe Springs

Area Code 310
Santa Fe Springs Chamber of Commerce
11736 East Telegraph Road
Santa Fe Springs CA 90670
868-6736

Best Western Sandman Motel (13530 East Firestone Boulevard, 90670; 921-8571, Fax 921-2451, 800-528-1234) 56 rooms, restaurant, complimentary breakfast, swimming pool, laundry room, complimentary newspaper, in-room refrigerators, wheelchair-access rooms, no-smoking rooms, no pets. SGL/DBL$42-$47.

Days Inn (13420 East Firestone Boulevard, 90670; 213-404-4114, 800-325-2525) 105 rooms, restaurant, swimming pool, jacuzzi, children under 12 free, fax service, pets allowed, wheelchair-access rooms, no-smoking rooms. SGL$45, DBL$50+.

Santa Maria

Area Code 805

Hilton Santa Maria Airport (3455 Skyway Drive, 93455; 928-8000, Fax 928-5252, 800-HILTONS) 190 rooms, restaurant, lounge, outdoor swimming pool, meeting facilities for 425, business services. SGL/DBL$68-$108.

Best Western Big America Hotel (1725 North Broadway, 93454; 922-5200, Fax 922-9865, 800-528-1234) 123 rooms, restaurant, lounge, swimming pool, whirlpool, meeting facilities, fax service, airport courtesy car, in-room refrigerators, pets allowed, wheelchair-access rooms. SGL/DBL$55-$90.

Howard Johnson Lodge (210 South Nicholson Avenue, 93454; 922-5891, Fax 928-9222, 800-654-2000) 64 rooms, restaurant, swimming pool, valet laundry, meeting facilities, fax service, pets allowed. SGL/DBL$47-$79.

Hunter's Inn (1514 Broadway, 93454; 922-2123, Fax 925-1523) 76 rooms. SGL/DBL$52-$95.

Motel 6 (2040 North Preisker Lane, 93454; 928-0811) 126 rooms. SGL/DBL$25-$31.

Motel 6 (839 Main Street, 93454; 925-2551) 60 rooms. SGL/DBL$23-$29.

Ramada Suites (2050 North Preisker Lane, 93454; 928-6000, Fax 928-0356, 800-228-2828) 210 suites, kitchenettes, restaurant, lounge, heated swimming pool, airport transportation, free parking, children under 12 free, wheelchair-access rooms, no-smoking rooms. SGL$68-$128, DBL$76-$128.

Santa Maria Inn (801 South Broadway, 93454; 928-7777, Fax 928-5690, 800-44-RELAX) 180 rooms and suites, restaurant, lounge, swimming pool, spa, meeting facilities for 400, SGL/DBL$69-$135.

Western Host Motel (1007 East Main Street, 93454; 922-4505) 81 rooms, swimming pool, tennis, no-smoking rooms. SGL/DBL$40-$60.

Santa Monica

Area Code 415
Santa Monica Convention and Visitors Bureau
Box 5278
Santa Monica CA 90405
393-7593

Santa Monica Visitors Center
1400 Ocean Avenue
Santa Monica CA 90401

RENTAL SOURCES: Bed and Breakfast International (Box 282910, 94128; 696-1690, Fax 696-1699, 800-872-4500) represents bed and breakfast accommodations in the Santa Monica area. Accommodations available in private homes, houseboats and inns. All rates include complimentary breakfast. SGL/DBL$50-$125.

American Motel (1243 Lincoln Boulevard, 90401; 458-1411) rooms and efficiencies, SGL/DBL$40-$50.

Bayside Hotel (2001 Ocean Avenue, 90405; 396-6000) 45 rooms and efficiencies, ocean view. SGL/DBL$54-$61.

Bay View Plaza Holiday Inn (530 Pico Boulevard, 90405; 399-9344, 800-465-4329) 339 rooms and suites, restaurant, exercise facilities, laundry room, car rental, tours, meeting facilities for 500, free parking. SGL$65-$116, DBL$65-$125, STS$225-$250.

Belle Blue Inn (1670 Ocean Avenue, 90401; 393-6295) rooms and efficiencies, SGL/DBL$55-$65.

Best Western Gateway Hotel (1920 Santa Monica Boulevard, 90404; 310-829-9100, Fax 310-829-9211, 800-528-1234) 122 rooms, restaurant, lounge, swimming pool, meeting facilities, wheelchair-access rooms, exercise center, fax service, airport courtesy car, in-room refrigerators, no-smoking rooms. LS SGL/DBL$69-$79; HS SGL/DBL$84-$94.

Cal Mar Hotel Suites (220 California Avenue, 90403; 395-5555, 800-776-0667 in California) 35 suites, swimming pool. SGL$60-$68, DBL$70-$78.

Carmel Hotel (201 Broadway, 90401; 451-2469, 800-445-8695) 110 rooms and suites, restaurant, lounge, children under 12 free, airport courtesy car, free parking, no pets. SGL$50, DBL$60-$65, STS$100.

The Channel Road Inn (219 West Channel Road, 90402; 459-1920, Fax 454-9920) 16 rooms and suites, complimentary breakfast, fax service, ocean view, child care, complimentary newspaper, laundry room, wheelchair-access rooms, no-smoking rooms, free parking. SGL/DBL$95-180, STS$165, $185+.

Comfort Inn (2815 Santa Monica Boulevard, 90404; 310-828-5516, 800-221-2222, 800-228-5150) 101 rooms and efficiencies, restaurant, swimming pool, no pets. SGL$55-$85, DBL$65-$95.

Days Inn (3007 Santa Monica Boulevard, 90404; 829-1983, 800-325-2525) 72 rooms, spa, children under 12 free, fax service, pets allowed. SGL$59-$69, DBL$69-$79.

Hotel Georgian Julia Maria (1414 Ocean Avenue, 90401; 395-3332, Fax 451-3374, 800-727-HOTEL) 35 rooms, restaurant, complimentary breakfast. SGL$83-$93, DBL$93-$103.

Guest Quarters Suite Hotel (1707 Fourth Street, 90401; 395-3332, Fax 452-7399, 800-424-2900) 253 suites, restaurant, outdoor swimming pool, spa, exercise facilities, ocean view, valet laundry, child care, complimentary newspaper, fax service, no-smoking rooms, airport courtesy car, car rental. SGL/DBL$135-$185.

Holiday Inn (120 Colorado Avenue, 90401; 213-451-0676, Fax 213-393-7145, 800-HOLIDAY) 138 rooms, restaurant, ocean view, swimming pool, no-smoking rooms. SGL/DBL$100-$140.

Holiday Inn Bayview Plaza (530 West Pico Boulevard, 90405; 399-9344, Fax 399-2504, 800-HOLIDAY) 309 rooms and suites, restaurant, outdoor swimming pool, spa, exercise facilities, ocean view, fax service, complimentary breakfast, beauty and barber shop, gift shop, laundry room, no-smoking rooms, airport transportation, free parking. SGL/DBL$99-$139, STS$225-$250.

International Guest House (1032 Seventh Street, 90303; 458-6233) 30 rooms, bed and breakfast, complimentary breakfast. SGL$20, DBL$35.

Loews Santa Monica Beach Hotel (1700 Ocean Avenue, 90401; 458-6700, Fax 458-2813, 800-223-0888) 360 rooms and suites, two restaurants, lounge, indoor and outdoor swimming pool, spa, exercise facilities, ocean view, in-room computer hookups, valet laundry, child care, fax and business services, complimentary newspaper, wheelchair-access rooms, beauty and barber shop, gift shop, no-smoking rooms, car rental. SGL/DBL$175-$300, STS$300-$1,500.

Miramar-Sheraton (101 Wilshire Boulevard, 90401; 394-3731, Fax 458-7912, 800-325-3535) 365 rooms and suites, two restaurants, lounge, outdoor swimming pool, spa, room service, beauty and barber shop, car rental, meeting facilities for 900, in-room safes, wheelchair-access rooms, ocean view, no-smoking rooms, 24-hour room service, fax service, complimentary newspaper, car rental, airport transportation. SGL$110-$155, DBL$130-$175, STS$200-$500.

Ocean Lodge (1667 Ocean Avenue, 90401; 395-6295) 43 rooms. SGL/DBL$40-$80.

Oceana Hotel (849 Ocean Avenue, 90423; 393-0486, Fax 458-1162, 800-777-0758) 60 suites, swimming pool, exercise facilities, free parking. STS$89-$160.

Pacific Sands Motel (1515 Ocean Avenue, 90401; 395-6133) 169 rooms. SGL/DBL$45-$65.

Pacific Shore Hotel (1819 Ocean Avenue, 90401; 451-8711, Fax 394-6657, 800-241-3848) 169 rooms and suites, restaurant, lounge, outdoor swimming pool, spa, in-room safes, valet laundry, transportation within five miles, ocean view, laundry room, gift shop, car rental, free parking. SGL/DBL$100-$135, STS$155-$175.

Palm Motel (2020 14th Street, 90405; 452-3861) rooms and efficiencies. SGL/DBL$38-$70.

Park Hyatt Santa Monica (One Pico Boulevard, 90405; 392-1234, 800-228-9000, 800-233-1234) 196 rooms and efficiencies, restaurant, swimming, exercise facilities. SGL/DBL$125-$155.

Radisson Huntley Hotel (1111 Second Street, 90403; 394-5454, Fax 458-9776, 800-556-4012, 800-556-4011 in California) 213 rooms and suites, restaurant, lounge, valet laundry, ocean view, fax service, child care, wheelchair-access rooms, no-smoking rooms, free parking, beauty and barber shop, gift shop, car rental. SGL/DBL$125-$140, STS$150-$250+.

Santa Monica Hotel (3102 Pico Boulevard, 90405; 450-5766, 800-231-7679, 800-826-7141 in California) 100 rooms, in-room refrigerators, kitchenettes, fax service, meeting facilities, laundry room, airport transportation, free parking, no-smoking, no pets. SGL$59, DBL$69.

Santa Monica International AYH Hostel (1436 Second Street, 90401; 393-9913) 230 beds, 10 rooms, kitchen, no-smoking rooms, wheelchair-access rooms, free parking. SGL$12-$15.

Shangri-la Hotel (1301 Ocean Avenue, 90401; 394-2791, Fax 451-3351) 55 rooms and suites, complimentary breakfast, ocean view, kitchenettes, valet laundry, child care, fax service, transportation to local attractions, complimentary newspaper, laundry room, airport transportation, free parking. SGL/DBL$110-$135, STS$140-$450.

Sheraton Miramar Hotel (101 Wilshire Boulevard, 90401; 213-394-3731, Fax 213-458-7912, 800-325-3535) 305 rooms and suites, restaurant, swimming pool, wheelchair-access rooms, no-smoking rooms, beach. SGL/DBL$65-$125.

The Sovereign Hotel and Suites At Santa Monica Bay (205 Washington Avenue, 90403; 395-9921, Fax 458-3085, 800-331-0163) 86 rooms and suites, complimentary breakfast, kitchenettes, laundry room, meeting facilities for 50, fax service, airport transportation, free parking. SGL/DBL$79-$129, STS$99-$199.

Stardust Motel (3202 Wilshire Boulevard, 90403; 828-4584) 14 rooms. SGL/DBL$45-$75.

TraveLodge (1525 Ocean Avenue, 90401; 213-451-0761, 800-255-3050) 29 rooms and restaurant, lounge, outdoor swimming pool, free parking. SGL/DBL$65-$90.

Village Motel (2624 Santa Monica Boulevard, 90404; 828-9230) rooms and efficiencies. SGL/DBL$40-$45.

Woerner Bed and Breakfast (Bed and Breakfast International) 1 room, complimentary breakfast, no smoking. SGL/DBL$75.

Santa Paula

Area Code 805

TraveLodge (650 South Peck Road, 93060; 525-1561, Fax 525-4230, 800-255-3050) 52 rooms and suites, restaurant, complimentary breakfast, swimming pool, whirlpool, car rental, in-room refrigerators, fax service, no pets. SGL/DBL$45-$67.

Santee

Area Code 619
Santee Chamber of Commerce
10315 Mission Gorge Road
 Santee CA 92071
449-6572

Santee Inn (10155 Mission Gorge Road, 92071; 258-2020) rooms, swimming pool, in-room refrigerators and microwaves. SGL/DBL$60-$83.

Best Western Santee (10726 Woodside Avenue, 92071; 449-2626, 800-528-1234) 47 rooms and suites, restaurant, heated swimming pool, meeting facilities, children under 12 free, no-smoking rooms. SGL$40-$50, DBL$49-$90.

Santa Maria

Area Code 805
Santa Maria Visitor and Convention Bureau
614 South Broadway
Santa Maria CA 93454
925-2403

Best Western Big America (1725 North Broadway, 93545; 922-5200, Fax 922-9865, 800-528-1234) 106 rooms and suites, restaurant, swimming pool, no-smoking rooms. LS SGL/DBL$54-$68; HS SGL/DBL$68-$78, STS$78-$88.

Colonial Motel (1866 Broadway, 93545; 925-8601) 30 rooms and efficiencies, no-smoking rooms. SGL$28-$32, DBL$36-$39, EFF$35-$45.

Howard Johnson Lodge (210 South Nicholson Avenue, 93454; 922-5891, Fax 925-9222, 800-654-2000) 62 rooms, complimentary breakfast, swimming pool, wheelchair-access rooms. SGL/DBL$49-$79.

Hunter's Inn (1514 South Broadway, 93454; 922-2123, Fax 925-1523, 800-950-2123 in California) 70 rooms, restaurant, swimming pool, no-smoking rooms. SGL/DBL$45-$60.

Ramada Suites (2050 North Preisker Lane, 93454; 928-6000, Fax 928-0356, 800-272-6232) 210 suites, restaurant, swimming pool, exercise facilities, wheelchair access, pets allowed. SGL/DBL$68-$128.

Santa Maria Airport Hilton (3455 Skyway Drive, 93455; 928-8000, Fax 928-5251, 800-445-8667) restaurant, swimming pool, airport transportation, exercise facilities, golf, wheelchair access, no-smoking rooms. SGL$55-$92, DBL$62-$102, STS$165-$225.

Santa Maria Inn (801 South Broadway, 93454; 928-7777, Fax 925-5690, 800-462-2476) 168 rooms and suites, restaurant, swimming pool, airport courtesy car, exercise facilities, wheelchair-access rooms, no-smoking rooms. SGL/DBL$65-$130, STS$135+.

Western Host Motor Hotel (1007 East Main Street, 93454; 922-4505) 81 rooms, restaurant, swimming pool, wheelchair access, no-smoking rooms, tennis. SGL/DBL$40-$50+.

Santa Ynez

Area Code 805

Santa Cota Motel (3099 Mission Drive, 93460; 688-5525) 23 rooms. SGL/DBL$35-$55.

San Ysidro

Area Code 619

Best Western Valli Hi Hotel (655 West San Ysidro Boulevard, 92074; 449-2626, 800-528-1234) SGL/DBL$32-$48.

Economy Inns of America (230 Via de San Ysidro, 92073; 428-6191, 800-423-3018) 22 rooms, restaurant, swimming pool, wheelchair access, no-smoking rooms, pets allowed. SGL/DBL$25-$30.

Mexico Gateway Inn (701 East San Ysidro Boulevard, 92073; 428-2251) 35 rooms, complimentary breakfast, airport transportation, wheelchair access, no-smoking rooms, pets allowed. SGL$40-$45, DBL$45-$55.

Motel 6 (160 East Calle Primaro, 92173; 690-6663, 505-891-6161) 103 rooms. SGL/DBL$23-$29.

Rodeway Inn (815 West San Ysidro Boulevard, 92073; 428-5521, Fax 428-0693. 800-221-2222, 800-424-4777) 125 rooms and suites, restaurant, swimming pool, whirlpools, laundry room, transportation to local attractions, in-room refrigerators, children under 18 free, wheelchair access, no-smoking rooms, no pets. SGL$34-$40, DBL$36-$48, STS$35-$55.

TraveLodge (643 San Ysidro Boulevard, 92173; 428-2800, 800-255-3050) 68 rooms, no pets. SGL/DBL$44-$72.

Seal Beach

Area Code 310

Radisson Inn (600 Marina Drive; 493-7501, 800-333-3333) 71 rooms, restaurant, complimentary breakfast, swimming pool, wheelchair-access rooms, no-smoking rooms. SGL$85-$105, DBL$100-$120.

The Seal Beach Inn and Gardens (212 Fifth Street, 90704; 493-2416) 23 rooms and one-bedroom suites, bed and breakfast, complimentary breakfast, swimming pool, no-smoking rooms, free parking. SGL/DBL$100-$155, STS$145+.

Seaside

Area Code 408
Seaside Chamber of Commerce
505 Broadway Avenue
Seaside CA 93955
394-6501

Best Western Magic Carpet Lodge (1875 Fremont Boulevard, 93955; 899-4221, 800-528-1234) 40 rooms, restaurant, complimentary breakfast, heated swimming pool, no-smoking rooms, fax service, no pets. SGL/DBL$45-$70.

Days Inn (1400 Del Monte Boulevard, 93955; 394-5335, Fax 394-7125, 800-325-2525) 143 rooms, restaurant, swimming pool, hot tubs, valet laundry, gift shop, children under 12 free, fax service, pets allowed, wheelchair access, no-smoking rooms. SGL$49-$69, DBL$59-$79.

Selma

Area Code 209

Best Western John Jay Inn (2799 Floral Avenue, 93622; 891-0300, 800-528-1234) 58 rooms and suites, restaurant, lounge, complimentary breakfast, swimming pool, laundry room, fax service, wheelchair-access rooms, exercise facilities, no-smoking rooms. SGL/DBL$40-$65.

Super 8 Motel (3142 South Highland Avenue, 93662; 896-2800, 800-800-8000) 40 rooms and suites, restaurant, complimentary breakfast, outdoor swimming pool, free local telephone calls, wheelchair-access rooms, no-smoking rooms, pets allowed. SGL/DBL$37-$45.

Sepulveda

Area Code 818

All-Star Inn (15711 Roscoe Boulevard, 91343; 894-9341) 23 rooms, swimming pool. SGL/DBL$35-$40.

Comfort Inn (8647 Sepulveda Boulevard, 91343; 893-3776, 800-221-2222) 59 rooms, complimentary breakfast, swimming pool, wheelchair-access rooms, no pets. SGL/DBL$43-$65.

Howard Johnson (9401 Sepulveda Boulevard, 91343; 892-0751, Fax 893-3150, 800-654-2000) 52 rooms, swimming pool, meeting facilities, kitchenettes, no-smoking rooms, no pets. SGL/DBL$36-$45, DBL$39-$48.

Rodeway Inn (8525 Sepulveda Boulevard, 91343; 894-5721, 800-424-4777) 75 rooms, restaurant, swimming pool, meeting facilities, children under 18 free, wheelchair-access rooms, no-smoking rooms, no pets. SGL/DBL$40-$50.

Sequoia National Park

Area Code 209

Giant Forest Lodge (Generals Highway, 93262; 561-3314, Fax 561-3135) 180 rooms, restaurant, wheelchair access. SGL/DBL$65+.

Montecito-Sequoia Lodge (Generals Highway, 93262; 565-3388, 800-227-9900) 45 rooms, restaurant, swimming pool, children under 12 free, no-smoking rooms, no pets. SGL/DBL$84.

Stony Creek Lodge (Highway 180, 93262; 561-3314, Fax 561-3135).

Sherman Oaks

Area Code 818
Sherman Oaks Chamber of Commerce
14241 Ventura Boulevard
Sherman Oaks CA 91423
906-1951

Valley Hilton Hotel (15433 Ventura Boulevard, 91403; 981-5400, Fax 981-3175, 800-248-0446, 800-HILTONS, 800-356-6196 in California) 215 rooms and suites, restaurant, complimentary breakfast, outdoor swimming pool, spa, meeting facilities for 450, exercise facilities, no-smoking rooms, airport transportation. SGL/DBL$75-$115, STS$150-$495.

Shoshone

Area Code 619

Shoshone Inn (852-4335) 25 rooms, swimming pool. SGL/DBL$30-$44.

Simi Valley

Area Code 805
Simi Valley Chamber of Commerce
250 Easy Street
Simi Valley CA 93065
526-3900

Clarion Hotel (1775 Madera Road, 93065; 584-6300, Fax 527-9969, 800-221-2222) 120 rooms and suites, restaurant, complimentary breakfast, outdoor heated swimming pool, spa, in-room refrigerators, fax service, room service, complimentary newspaper, laundry room, exercise facilities, wheelchair-access rooms, no pets, car rental. SGL$59-$98, STS$88-$250.

Motel 6 (2566 North Erringer Road, 93065; 526-3533, 505-891-6161) 60 rooms. SGL/DBL$35-$41.

Radisson Hotel (999 Enchantment Way, 93065; 583-2000, Fax 583-2779, 800-583-2000) 195 rooms and suites, restaurant, complimentary breakfast, swimming pool, airport transportation, exercise facilities, wheelchair access, no-smoking rooms, pets allowed. SGL$75-$85, DBL$85-$95, STS$129+.

TraveLodge (2550 Erringer Road, 93065; 584-6006, Fax 527-5629, 800-255-3050) 97 rooms and suites, restaurant, lounge, swimming pool, sauna, exercise facilities, laundry room, fax service, meeting facilities for 200, no pets. SGL/DBL$60-$90.

Solano Beach

Area Code 619
Solano Beach Chamber of Commerce
210 West Plaza
Solano Beach CA 92075
755-4775

Ramada Inn (717 South Highway 101, 92075; 792-8200, Fax 792-2370, 800-228-2828) 115 rooms, complimentary breakfast, swimming pool, spa, free parking, exercise facilities, meeting facilities for 75, wheelchair-access rooms, no-smoking rooms, beach. SGL$85-$115, DBL$93-$120.

Winners Circle Beach and Tennis Resort (550 Via de la Valle, 92075; 755-6666) 94 rooms. SGL/DBL$75+.

Soledad

Area Code 408
Soledad Chamber of Commerce

515 Front Street
Soledad CA 93960
678-2278

Best Western Valley Harvest Inn (1155 Front Street, 93960; 678-3833, Fax 678-3011, 800-528-1234) 60 rooms, restaurant, lounge, heated swimming pool, jacuzzi, laundry room, meeting facilities, laundry room, fax service, children under 12 free, wheelchair-access rooms, no-smoking rooms, no pets. SGL$44-$56, DBL$52-$80.

Solvang

Area Code 805
Solvang-Santa Ynez Valley Visitors Bureau
490 First Street
Solvang CA 93463
688-1981

The Alisal Ranch (1054 Alisal Road, 93463; 688-6411, Fax 688-2510) 66 rooms and suites, restaurant, complimentary breakfast, heated swimming pool, spa, riding stables, lake, conference facilities for 150, tennis, golf, wheelchair access. SGL$195-$250, DBL$250-$280, STS$250-$500.

Best Western King Frederik Motel (1617 Copenhagen Drive, 93463; 688-5515, 800-528-1234) 45 rooms, restaurant, lounge, complimentary breakfast, heated swimming pool, children under 12 free, spa, no pets. SGL/DBL$49-$68.

Chimney Sweep Inn (1554 Copenhagen Drive, 93463; 688-2111, 800-824-6444 in California) 2 rooms and cottage suites, spa, complimentary breakfast, wheelchair access, no-smoking rooms. DBL$65-$100, STS$185-$215.

The Danish Country Inn (1455 Mission Drive, 93463; 688-2018, Fax 688-1156, 800-44-RELAX) 82 rooms, restaurant, complimentary breakfast, heated swimming pool, jacuzzi, spa, meeting facilities, in-room refrigerators, VCRs, wheelchair-access rooms, no-smoking rooms. SGL/DBL$89-$106, STS$119-$190.

Dannebrog Inn (1450 Mission Drive, 93463; 688-3210) 75 rooms and suites, complimentary breakfast, indoor heated swimming pool, spas. SGL/DBL$$50-$74, STS$95-$145.

Denmark Motel (279 Alisal Road, 93463) 12 rooms and efficiencies. SGL/DBL$35+.

Hamlet Motel (1532 Mission Drive, 93463; 688-4413) 14 rooms, complimentary breakfast. SGL/DBL$38-$80.

Kronborg Inn (1440 Mission Drive, 93463) 39 rooms, complimentary breakfast, heated pool, spa, balconies. SGL/DBL$50-$85.

Meadowlark Motel (2644 Mission Drive, 93463; 688-4631) 20 rooms and efficiencies, swimming pool, no-smoking rooms, pets allowed. SGL/DBL$35-$55.

Petersen Village Inn (1576 Mission Drive, 93463; 688-3121, 800-321-8985 in California) 40 rooms and suites, restaurant, complimentary breakfast, swimming pool, no-smoking rooms, conference facilities. SGL/DBL$95-$145, STS$210.

Royal Copenhagen Motel (1579 Mission Drive, 93463; 688-5561, 800-624-6604 in California) 48 rooms, complimentary breakfast, heated swimming pool, no-smoking rooms. SGL/DBL$60-$85.

Sheraton Royal Scandinavian Inn (400 Alisal Road, 93464; 688-8000, Fax 688-0761, 800-325-3535) 133 rooms and suites, restaurant, lounge, heated swimming pool, spa, jacuzzi, meeting facilities for 300, wheelchair-access rooms, no-smoking rooms, free parking. SGL/DBL$75-$125, STS$205-$245.

Solvang Gaard Lodge (239 Alisal Road, 93436; 688-4404) 18 rooms. SGL/DBL$33-$48.

Svendsgaards Danish Lodge (1711 Mission Drive, 93463; 688-3277, 800-341-8000, 800-821-8757 in California) 49 rooms and efficiencies, complimentary breakfast, heated swimming pool, jacuzzi. SGL/DBL$45-$85.

Three Crowns Inn (1518 Mission Drive, 93436; 688-4702, 800-848-8484 in California) 27 rooms, complimentary breakfast. SGL/DBL$40-$90.

Tivoli Inn (1564 Copenhagen Drive, 93463; 688-0558, Fax 686-0032, 800-266-1484) 29 rooms and suites, restaurant, lounge, complimentary breakfast, children under 16 free, in-room refrigerators, meeting facilities for 20, free parking, no pets. SGL/DBL$85-$140, STS$135-$195.

Viking Motel (1506 Mission Drive, 93463; 688-4827) 12 rooms, complimentary breakfast. SGL/DBL$32-$80.

Spring Valley

Area Code 619
Spring Valley Chamber of Commerce
Box 1219
Spring Valley CA 92077
466-5736

TraveLodge (9603 Campo Road, 91977; 619-589-1111, Fax 619-460-7561, 800-255-3050) 45 rooms and suites, restaurant, lounge, kitchenettes, meeting facilities for 25, tennis, no pets. SGL/DBL$35-$49.

Squaw Valley

Area Code 209

BRAT Realty Management (Box 7101, Incline Village NV, 89450; 831-3318, Fax 831-8668, 800-869-8308, 800-468-2463) rents condos, chalets and private, lakefront homes in the Lake Tahoe and Squaw Valley areas. SGL/DBL$90-$750.

Resort At Squaw Creek (800-327-3353) 405 rooms and suites, restaurant, swimming pool.

Studio City

Area Code 818

Sportsmen's Lodge Hotel (12825 Ventura Boulevard, 91604; 769-4700, Fax 877-3898, 800-821-8511, 800-821-1625 in California) 193 rooms and suites, restaurant, outdoor swimming pool, spa, exercise facilities, valet laundry, child care, fax service, airport courtesy car, beauty and barber shop, car rental, gift shop, no-smoking rooms, free parking. SGL/DBL$94-$114, STS$153-$278.

Summerland

Area Code 805

Inn On Summer Hill (Box 376, 93067; 969-9998, 800-845-5566, 800-999-8999) 16 rooms, bed and breakfast, complimentary breakfast, wheelchair-access rooms. SGL/DBL$150-$175+.

Summerland Inn (Box 1209, 93067; 969-5225) 10 rooms, bed and breakfast, complimentary breakfast, wheelchair-access rooms. SGL/DBL$86-$120.

Sun City

Area Code 714

Sun Leisure Motel (27350 Highway 74, 92381; 928-3717) 18 rooms, swimming pool. SGL$25-$27, DBL$30.

Tecopa

Area Code 619

Tecopa Hot Springs Resort (Box 2, 92389; 852-4343) 14 rooms. SGL/DBL$38-$50.

Tehachapi

Area Code 805
Tehachapi Chamber of Commerce
209 East Tehachapi Boulevard
Tehachapi CA 93561
822-4180

Best Western Mountain Inn (416 West Tehachapi Boulevard, TraveLodge (500 Steuber Road, 93561; 823-8000, Fax 822-1337, 800-255-3050) 80 rooms and suites, restaurant, lounge, swimming pool, fax service, airport transportation, tennis, no pets. SGL/DBL$49-$59.

Spy Mountain Resort (18100 Lucaya Way, 93561; 822-5581, Fax 822-4055, 800-244-0864) 84 rooms and suites, restaurant, swimming pool, airport transportation, tennis, golf, wheelchair-access rooms, pets allowed. SGL/DBL$65-$150, STS$100-$250.

TraveLodge (500 Steuber Road, 93561; 823-8000, Fax 822-1337, 800-255-3050) 80 rooms and suites, restaurant, lounge, swimming pool, sauna, meeting facilities for 50, no pets. SGL/DBL$49-$59.

Temecula

Area Code 714

Temecula Valley Chamber of Commerce
27521 Ynez Road
Temecula CA 92390
676-5090

Best Western Guest House Motel (41873 Moreno Road, 92390; 676-5700, Fax 694-8520, 800-528-1234) 24 rooms, restaurant, lounge, swimming pool, fax service, wheelchair-access rooms, no-smoking rooms, no pets. SGL/DBL$43-$64.

Best Western Country Inn (27706 Jefferson Avenue, 92590; 676-7378, Fax 699-7995, 800-528-1234) 74 rooms, restaurant, lounge, swimming pool, fax service. SGL/DBL$45-$66.

Comfort Inn (27338 Jefferson Avenue, 92390; 699-5888, 800-221-2222) 72 rooms, restaurant, complimentary breakfast, swimming pool, whirlpool, exercise facilities, wheelchair-access rooms. SGL$46-$59, DBL$51-$59.

Doubletree Suites Hotel (29345 Rancho California Road, 92390; 676-5656, Fax 699-3928, 800-528-0444) 136 suites, restaurant, lounge, heated swimming pool, spa, meeting facilities for 70, exercise equipment, free parking. SGL/DBL$79-$99+.

Loma Vista Bed and Breakfast (33350 La Serena Way, 92591; 676-7047) 6 rooms, bed and breakfast, complimentary breakfast. SGL$55, DBL$65.

Motel 6 (41900 Moreno Road, 92590; 676-7199, 505-891-6161) 135 rooms. SGL/DBL$24-$30.

Ramada Inn (28980 Front Street, 92590; 676-8770, 800-228-2828) 70 rooms, restaurant, complimentary breakfast, swimming pool, in-room refrigerators and microwaves, meeting facilities, children under 18 free, wheelchair-access rooms, pets allowed, free parking, no-smoking rooms. SGL$39-$49, DBL$44-$54.

Rancho Motor Inn (28980 Front Street, 92390; 676-8770) 70 rooms, complimentary breakfast, swimming pool, wheelchair access, no-smoking rooms, pets allowed. SGL$34-$35, DBL$37-$42.

Temecula Creek Inn Resort (44501 Rainbow Canyon Road, 92592; 6767-5631, 800-962-7335) 84 rooms, restaurant, swimming pool, tennis, golf, airport transportation, wheelchair access, no-smoking rooms. SGL/DBL$105-$115+.

Templeton

Area Code 805

Country House Inn (91 Main Street, 93465; 434-1598) 6 rooms, bed and breakfast, complimentary breakfast, wheelchair-access rooms. SGL/DBL$50+.

Thousand Oaks

Area Code 805
Conejo Valley Chamber of Commerce
191 West Wilbur Road
Thousand Oaks CA 91360
497-1621

Best Western Oaks Lodge (12 Conejo Boulevard, 91360; 495-7011, Fax 495-0647, 800-528-1234) 76 rooms, restaurant, lounge, complimentary breakfast, swimming pool, children under 12 free, whirlpool, airport transportation, laundry room, fax service, no-smoking rooms, no pets. SGL$47-$57, DBL$52-$79.

Days Inn (1320 Newberry Road, 91320; 499-5910, Fax 498-5783, 800-325-2525) 124 rooms, restaurant, lounge, swimming pool, spa, fax service, no-smoking rooms. SGL/DBL$65-$70+.

Econo Lodge (1425 Thousand Oaks Boulevard, 91362; 496-0102, Fax 494-1295, 800-424-4777) 58 rooms, restaurant, complimentary breakfast, in-room refrigerators and microwaves, fax service, children under 18 free, beauty and barber shop, wheelchair-access rooms, no-smoking rooms, no pets, free parking. SGL/DBL$35-$50.

Holiday Inn Thousand Oaks (495 North Ventura Park Road, 91320; 498-6733, Fax 498-9789, 800-HOLIDAY) 159 rooms and suites, restaurant, outdoor swimming pool, spa, kitchenettes, in-room refrigerators and microwaves, room service, fax service, meeting facilities for 400, complimentary newspaper, wheelchair-access rooms, no-smoking rooms, car rental, free parking. SGL/DBL$60-$110, STS$75-$85.

Howard Johnson Hotel (75 West Thousand Oaks Boulevard, 91360; 497-3701, Fax 497-1875, 800-654-2000) 104 rooms and suites, restaurant, lounge, swimming pool, spa, in-room refrigerators and microwaves, valet laundry, fax service, room service, complimentary newspaper, wheelchair-access rooms, no-smoking rooms, free parking. SGL/DBL$49-$75, STS$135.

Three Rivers

Area Code 209

Best Western Holiday Lodge (40105 Sierra Drive, 93271; 561-4119, 800-528-1234) 45 rooms, complimentary breakfast, swimming pool, whirlpools, wheelchair-access rooms, no-smoking rooms, pets allowed. LS SGL/DBL$65-$70; HS SGL/DBL$68-$73.

Lazy J Ranch (39625 Sierra Drive, 93271; 561-4449) 19 rooms and cottage suites, swimming pool, pets allowed. SGL$40-$50, DBL$40-$56, STS$80-$140.

Sierra Lodge (43175 Sierra Drive, 93271; 561-3681, Fax 561-3264, 800-367-8879) 22 rooms and suites, restaurant, wheelchair access, free parking. SGL$42-$48, DBL$45-$42, STS$125+.

Torrance

Area Code 310

City Inn (3673 Torrance Boulevard, 90503; 316-5570, Fax 316-9349, 800-444-5111) 51 rooms and suites, complimentary breakfast, spa, kitchenettes, in-room refrigerators, computer hookups, fax service, wheelchair-access rooms, no-smoking rooms, free parking. SGL/DBL$49-$65, STS$68-$125.

Courtyard By Marriott (2633 Sepulveda Boulevard, 90505; 533-8000, 800-321-2211) 149 rooms and suites, restaurant, swimming pool, exercise facilities, wheelchair-access rooms, no-smoking rooms. SGL$85+, DBL$95+, STS$100+.

Holiday Inn (21333 Hawthorne Boulevard, 90503; 540-0500, Fax 540-2065, 800-HOLIDAY) 386 rooms and suites, restaurant, outdoor swimming pool, wheelchair-access rooms, meeting facilities for 450, exercise center.

Holiday Inn Torrance Gateway (19800 South Vermont, 90502; 781-9100, Fax 327-8296, 800-HOLIDAY, 800-465-4329) 338 rooms and suites, restaurant, wheelchair-access rooms, exercise facilities, no pets, free parking. SGL/DBL$89-$114, STS$150-$250.

Howard Johnson Lodge (2880 Pacific Coast Highway, 90505; 325-0660, Fax 775-6661, 800-654-2000) 88 rooms, restaurant, lounge, swimming pool, meeting facilities, laundry room, complimentary newspaper, no-smoking rooms, no pets. SGL$46-$84, DBL$52-$94.

Marriott Hotel (3635 Fashion Way, 90503; 316-3636, Fax 543-6076, 800-228-9290) 487 rooms and suites, restaurant, swimming pool, exercise facilities, meeting facilities for 80, in-room microwaves, airport transportation, pets allowed, wheelchair access, no-smoking rooms. SGL$145+, DBL$165+, STS$250+.

Marriott Residence Inn (3701 Torrance Boulevard, 90503; 543-4566, Fax 543-3026, 800-331-3131) 247 suites, complimentary breakfast, swimming pool. SGL/DBL$165-$235.

Quality Inn Torrance-Redondo Beach (4111 Pacific Coast Highway, 90505; 378-8511, Fax 378-8511, 800-221-2222) 90 rooms, restaurant, complimentary breakfast, outdoor swimming pool, spa, in-room refrigerators, kitchenettes, hot tubs, valet laundry, child care, fax service, transportation to local attractions, complimentary newspaper, laundry room, wheelchair-access rooms, no-smoking rooms, no pets, free parking, car rental. SGL/DBL$49-$65.

Summerfield Suites Hotel (19901 Prairie Avenue, 90503; 371-8525, Fax 542-9628, 800-833-4353) 144 one- and two-bedroom suites, complimentary breakfast, outdoor swimming pool, spa, exercise facilities, complimentary newspaper, laundry room, convenience store, airport transportation, pets allowed, no-smoking rooms, free parking. STS$95-$129.

TraveLodge (2448 Sepulveda Boulevard, 90501; 310-539-9888, Fax 310-539-6420, 800-255-3050) 53 rooms, restaurant, lounge, swimming pool, fax service, no pets. SGL/DBL$53-$68.

Tulare

Area Code 209
Tulare Chamber of Commerce
260 North L Street
Tulare CA 93274
686-1547

Best Western Town and Country Lodge (1051 North Blackstone Avenue, 93274; 688-7537, Fax 688-2163, 800-528-1234) 93 rooms and suites, restaurant, complimentary breakfast, swimming pool, wheelchair-access rooms, no-smoking rooms, pets allowed. SGL/DBL$42-$58.

360 Twentynine Palms

Economy Inns of America (1183 North Blackstone Street, 93274; 686-0985, 800-826-0778) 90 rooms, swimming pool. SGL$35-$38, DBL$40-$44.

Friendship Inn (26442 State Road 99, 93274; 688-0501, 800-424-4777) 55 rooms, restaurant, complimentary breakfast, swimming pool, wheelchair-access rooms, no-smoking rooms, pets allowed. SGL$30-$35, DBL$35-$40.

Mustang Inn Motel (1135 East Alpine Avenue, 93274; 686-7214) 31 rooms. SGL/DBL$25+.

Twentynine Palms

Area Code 619
Twentynine Palms Chamber of Commerce
6163 Adobe Road
Twentynine Palms CA 92277
367-3445

Bed and Breakfast (367-7936) 2 rooms, complimentary breakfast, fireplace, kitchenettes. SGL$45, DBL$55.

Best Western Gardens Motel (71487 Twentynine Palms Highway, 92277; 367-9141, Fax 367-2584, 800-528-1234) 72 rooms and suites, swimming pool, kitchenettes, whirlpools, fax service, no-smoking rooms, pets allowed. LS SGL/DBL$46-$66; HS SGL/DBL$76-$96.

Circle C (6340 El Rey Avenue, 92277; 367-7615, 800-545-9696) 11 rooms, bed and breakfast, complimentary breakfast, outdoor heated swimming pool, kitchenettes, no children, free local telephone calls, fax service, meeting facilities for 20, free parking, no-smoking rooms, no pets. SGL$70, DBL$85.

Civic Center Motel (6038 Bagley Avenue, 92277; 367-5074) 8 efficiencies. SGL/DBL$25/$130W.

Econo Lodge (72562 Twentynine Palms Highway, 92277; 367-2883, Fax 367-4965, 800-424-4777) 125 rooms, restaurant, swimming pool, whirlpools, meeting facilities, wheelchair-access rooms, children under 18 free, no-smoking rooms, no pets. SGL$33-$43, DBL$38-$50.

El Ranch Dolores (73352 Twentynine Palms Highway, 92277; 367-3528) 16 rooms and efficiencies, swimming pool. SGL/DBL$35+.

Motel 6 (367-2833) 63 rooms, restaurant, heated swimming pool, wheelchair-access rooms, laundry room, SGL$35, DBL$40.

Sunset Motel (73842 Twentynine Palms Highway, 92277; 367-3484) 9 rooms and efficiencies, swimming pool, in-room refrigerators, SGL/DBL$34-$45.

Tower Homestead (Amboy Road and Mojave; 367-7936) 6 rooms, bed and breakfast, complimentary breakfast. SGL/DBL$50.

Twentynine Palms Inn (73950 Inn Avenue, 92277; 367-3505, Fax 367-4425) 15 rooms, restaurant, lounge, complimentary breakfast, swimming pool, in-room refrigerators, airport transportation, pets allowed. SGL/DBL $35-$55.

Universal City

Area Code 818

Hilton Towers (555 University Terrace Parkway, 91608; 506-2500, Fax 509-2058, 800-HILTONS) 456 rooms, restaurant, swimming pool, exercise equipment, business services, meeting facilities for 1,500. SGL/DBL$115-$265.

Sheraton Universal Hotel (333 Universal Terrace Parkway, 91608; 980-1212, Fax 985-4980, 800-325-3535) 446 rooms and suites, restaurant, lounge, outdoor heated swimming pool, whirlpool, meeting facilities for 1,300, gift shop, wheelchair-access rooms, no-smoking rooms. SGL$145-$205, DBL$165-$225, STS$200-$575.

Upland

Area Code 714
Upland Chamber of Commerce
886 West Foothill Boulevard
Upland CA 91786
982-8816

Comfort Inn (1282 West 7th Street, 91783; 985-8115, 800-221-2222) 62 rooms, swimming pool, wheelchair-access rooms, no pets. SGL/DBL$36-$54.

Valencia

Area Code 805
Valencia Chamber of Commerce
23920 Valencia Boulevard
Valencia CA 91355
259-4787

Best Western Ranch House Inn (27413 North Tourney Road, 91355; 255-0555, Fax 255-2216, 800-528-1234) 185 rooms, restaurant, lounge, swimming pool, laundry room, transportation to local attractions, fax service, pets allowed, free parking, no-smoking rooms. SGL$59-$75, DBL$65-$95.

Valencia Hilton Garden Inn (27710 The Old Road, 91355; 254-8800, Fax 254-9399, 800-HILTONS, 800-445-8667) 152 rooms and suites, restaurant, lounge, outdoor heated swimming pool, spa, whirlpool, valet laundry, meeting facilities for 90, business services, room service, fax service, no-smoking rooms, wheelchair-access rooms, exercise equipment, free parking. SGL/DBL$79-$119, STS$158-$238.

Van Nuys

Area Code 818
Greater Van Nuys Area Chamber of Commerce
14545 Victory Boulevard
Van Nuys CA 91411
989-0300.

Best Western Airtel Plaza Hotel and Conference Center (7277 Valjean Avenue, 91406; 997-7676, Fax 785-8864, 800-350-1111) 268 rooms and suites, restaurant, complimentary breakfast, outdoor swimming pool, three spas, in-room refrigerators and mini-bars, valet laundry, fax service, transportation to local attractions, complimentary newspaper, gift shop, exercise facilities, no-smoking rooms, car rental, free parking. LS SGL/DBL$78-$89; HS SGL/DBL$135-$145.

Carriage Inn Motor Hotel (5525 Sepulveda Boulevard, 91411; 787-2300, Fax 782-9373, 800-854-2608, 800-542-6082 in California) 183 rooms and suites, restaurant, lounge, swimming pool, meeting facilities, no-smoking rooms. SGL$61-$71, DBL$60-$76.

Holiday Inn Mid-San Fernando Valley (8244 Orion Avenue, 91406; 989-5010, Fax 781-6453, 800-HOLIDAY, 800-465-4329) 128 rooms and suites, restaurant, outdoor heated swimming pool, tours, meeting facilities for 150, exercise equipment, valet laundry, fax service, laundry room, wheelchair-access rooms, no-smoking rooms, airport transportation, no pets, free parking. SGL/DBL$64-$96, STS$80-$118.

TraveLodge (6909 Sepulveda Boulevard, 91405; 787-5400, Fax 782-0239, 800-255-3050) 75 rooms and suites, restaurant, complimentary breakfast, swimming pool, meeting facilities for 40, wheelchair access, no-smoking rooms, no pets. SGL/DBL$45-$59.

Venice

Area Code 213
Venice Chamber of Commerce
13470 Washington Boulevard
Venica CA 90291
827-2366

Airport Hostel/Interclub (2221 Lincoln Boulevard, 90291; 305-0250, Fax 399-1930) 75 beds, kitchen, free parking. SGL$12.

Cadillac Hotel (401 Ocean Front Walk, 90291; 399-8876, Fax 822-1360) 41 rooms and suites, beach, valet laundry, fax service, tours, laundry rooms, sauna, exercise facilities, free parking. SGL/DBL$44-$59, STS$99+.

Folk's-Tel (15 Paloma Avenue, 90291; 392-7039) 30-apartments, airport transportation. $85W-$100W.

Jim's At The Beach (17 Brooks Avenue, 90291; 399-4018, Fax 399-4216) 8 rooms. SGL$13.

Jolly Roger Motor Hotel (2904 Washington Boulevard, 90291; 822-2904, Fax 301-9461, 800-822-2904) 82 rooms, restaurant, complimentary breakfast, swimming pool, free parking. SGL/DBL$47-$61.

Mansion Inn Marina Del Rey (327 Washington Boulevard, 90291; 821-2557) 43 rooms, complimentary breakfast, restaurant, free parking. SGL/DBL$89.

Marina Motel (3130 Washington Boulevard, 90291; 821-5086) 32 rooms, complimentary breakfast, no-smoking rooms. SGL$50-$70, DBL$60-$80.

Marina Pacific Hotel and Suites (1697 Pacific Avenue, 90291; 452-1111, Fax 452-5479, 800-421-8151) 92 rooms and one- and two-bedroom suites, restaurant, children under 13 free, in-room refrigerators, fax service, meeting facilities for 75, free parking, laundry room, airport transportation, wheelchair access, no-smoking rooms, no pets. SGL$80-$120, DBL$90-$130, STS$110-$185.

Share-Tel International Hostel (20 Brooks Avenue, 90291; 392-0325) 16 rooms, complimentary breakfast, no-smoking rooms, airport transportation. SGL$17/$105W.

Venice Beach Hotel-Motel (25 Windward Avenue, 90291; 399-7649) 30 rooms, restaurant, lounge, ocean view, airport courtesy car. SGL/DBL$15-$49.

Venice Beach House (15 30th Avenue, 90291; 823-1966) 9 rooms and suites, bed and breakfast, complimentary breakfast. SGL/DBL$75-$125.

Ventura

Area Code 805
Ventura Visitors and Convention Bureau
785 South Seward Avenue
Ventura CA 93001
648-2075

Bella Maggiore Inn (67 South California Street, 93001; 652-0277) 24 rooms, bed and breakfast, complimentary breakfast, wheelchair-access rooms. SGL$65, DBL$80.

Best Western Inn (708 East Thompson Boulevard, 93001; 648-3101, 800-528-1234) 75 rooms, restaurant, swimming pool, whirlpool, no-smoking rooms, no pets. LS SGL/DBL$48-$64; HS SGL/DBL$60-$68.

Clarion Carriage House Inn (181 East Santa Clara Street, 93001; 652-0141, 800-221-2222) 50 rooms, complimentary breakfast, swimming pool, wheelchair-access rooms, no pets. SGL$70-$95, DBL$80-$105.

The Cliff House (6602 West Pacific Coast Highway, 93001; 684-0025, Fax 651-1201) 27 rooms. SGL/DBL$75-$149.

The Clocktower Inn (181 East Santa Clara Street, 93001; 652-0141, 800-727-1027) 50 rooms, bed and breakfast, restaurant, complimentary breakfast, wheelchair-access rooms, free parking. SGL$70-$85, DBL$80-$95.

The Country Inn At Ventura (298 Chestnut Street, 93001; 653-1434, Fax 648-7126, 800-44-RELAX) 120 rooms and suites, restaurant, complimentary breakfast, heated swimming pool, spa, wheelchair access, no-smoking rooms. SGL$80-$90, DBL$90-$100.

Doubletree Hotel (2055 Harbor Boulevard, 93001; 643-6000, Fax 643-7137, 800-528-0444) 295 rooms and suites, restaurant, lounge, outdoor heated swimming pool, spa, sauna, meeting facilities for 875, beach, exercise facilities, free parking. SGL$89-$119, DBL$99-$129, STS$175-$350.

Harbortown Marina Resort (1050 Schooner Drive, 93001; 658-1212, 800-622-1212 in California) 155 rooms and suites, restaurant, swimming pool, tennis, free parking. SGL$55-$90, DBL$65-$100, STS$175+.

Holiday Inn (450 East Harbor Boulevard, 93001; 648-7731, Fax 653-0602, 800-842-0800, 800-HOLIDAY) 260 rooms and suites, two restaurants, lounge, swimming pool, spa, jacuzzi, meeting facilities for 500, ocean view, children under 18 free, wheelchair-access rooms. SGL$80-$90, DBL$90-$100.

Inn On The Beach (1175 South Seaward Avenue, 93001; 652-2000) 24 rooms, restaurant, complimentary breakfast, wheelchair access. SGL/DBL$60+.

La Mer (411 Poli Street, 93001; 643-3600) 5 rooms, bed and breakfast, complimentary breakfast, no-smoking. SGL$100-$160, DBL$105-$165.

La Quinta Inn (5818 Valentine Road, 93003; 658-6200, Fax 642-2840, 800-531-5900) 142 rooms, restaurant, lounge, complimentary breakfast, heated swimming pool, jacuzzi, meeting facilities, airport transportation, wheelchair access, pets allowed.

Motel 6 (2145 East Harbor Boulevard, 93001; 643-5100) 200 rooms. SGL/DBL$30-$36.

Pierpont Inn (550 San Jon Road, 93001; 643-6144, Fax 641-1501, 800-777-1700) 70 rooms and suites, restaurant, lounge, swimming pool, exercise facilities, wheelchair access, SGL$55-$60, DBL$60-$65.

TraveLodge (929 East Thompson Boulevard, 93001; 648-2557, Fax 653-1230, 800-255-3050) 37 rooms and suites, restaurant, lounge, swimming pool, fax service, no-smoking rooms, no pets. LS SGL/DBL$38-$58; HS SGL/DBL$44-$64.

Vagabond Inn (756 East Thompson Boulevard, 93001; 648-5371, Fax 648-5613, 800-522-1555) 82 rooms, restaurant, swimming pool, airport transportation, free local telephone calls, no-smoking rooms, children under 18 free, fax service, complimentary newspaper. SGL$46, DBL$48-$75.

Victorville

Area Code 619
Victorville Chamber of Commerce'
Box 996
Victorville CA 92392
245-6506

Best Western Green Tree Inn (14173 Green Tree Boulevard, 92392; 245-3461, Fax 245-7745, 800-528-1234) 168 rooms and suites, restaurant, lounge, swimming pool, children under 12 free, meeting facilities, jacuzzi, golf, no-smoking rooms, no pets. LS SGL/DBL$50-$61; HS SGL/DBL$68-$79, STS$68-$86.

E-Z Motel (15401 Park Avenue, 92392; 241-7516, 800-326-6835) 68 rooms. SGL/DBL$23-$33.

E-Z Motel (15366 La Paz Avenue, 92932; 243-2220, 800-326-6835) 81 rooms. SGL/DBL$20-$30.

Holiday Inn (15494 Palmdale Road, 92392; 245-6565, Fax 245-6649, 800-HOLIDAY) 160 rooms and suites, restaurant, lounge, swimming pool, meeting facilities for 750, wheelchair access, no-smoking rooms, pets allowed. SGL/DBL$45-$60.

Scottish Inn (15499 Village Drive, 92392; 243-5858, 800-251-1962) 21 rooms, swimming pool, whirlpool, kitchenettes, wheelchair-access rooms. SGL$28, DBL$32-$36.

TraveLodge (16868 Stoddard Wells Road, 92392; 243-7700, Fax 243-4432, 800-255-3050) 90 rooms and suites, restaurant, lounge, complimentary breakfast, swimming pool, whirlpool, meeting facilities, wheelchair-access rooms, no-smoking rooms, no pets. SGL/DBL$40-$51.

TraveLodge (13409 Mariposa Road, 92329; 241-1577, Fax 241-3627, 800-255-3050) 90 rooms and suites, restaurant, lounge, swimming pool, whirlpool, in-room refrigerators, meeting facilities for 40, fax service, airport transportation, tennis. SGL/DBL$33-$37.

Visalia

Area Code 209
Visalia Convention and Visitors Bureau
720 West Mineral King Avenue
Visalia CA 93291
734-5876.

Best Western Inn (623 West Main Street, 93277; 732-4561, Fax 738-0562, 800-528-1234) 40 rooms and suites, restaurant, complimentary breakfast, swimming pool, fax service, airport transportation, wheelchair-access rooms, pets allowed. SGL$44-$47, DBL$51-$53, STS$55-$64.

Capri Motel (1720 East Mineral King Avenue, 93291; 627-0494) 17 rooms, restaurant, kitchenettes, no pets. SGL/DBL$29-$32.

Econo Lodge (1400 South Mooney Boulevard, 93277; 732-6641, 800-424-4777) 48 rooms, restaurant, swimming pool, fax service, children under 18 free, no-smoking rooms, no pets. SGL$36-$46, DBL$40-$52.

El Rancho Motel (4506 West Mineral King Avenue, 93291; 734-9271) 16 rooms. SGL$27-$28, DBL$30-$32.

Holiday Inn Park Plaza (9000 West Airport Drive, 92377; 651-5000, 800-821-1127, 800-HOLIDAY) 259 rooms and suites, restaurant, lounge, swimming pool, meeting facilities for 1,800, children under 18 free, wheelchair-access rooms, exercise equipment, laundry room, airport transportation. SGL$75-$85, DBL$80-$90+.

Lamplighter Inn (3300 West Mineral King Highway, 93291; 732-4511, Fax 733-7946, 800-662-6692 in California) 100 rooms, restaurant, lounge, swimming pool, exercise center, airport courtesy car, children under 12 free, meeting facilities, wheelchair access, no-smoking rooms. SGL$65, DBL$75, STS$75+.

Marco Polo (4545 West Mineral King Avenue, 93277; 732-4591) 41 rooms, restaurant, lounge, outdoor swimming pool, meeting facilities, no pets. SGL$34-$45, DBL$36-$50.

Mooney Motel (2120 South Mooney Boulevard, 93277; 733-2666) 28 rooms, outdoor swimming pool, no pets. SGL$24-$26, DBL$26-$30.

Murphy's Motel (1102 East Mineral King Avenue, 93291; 734-5642) 20 rooms and efficiencies, outdoor swimming pool. SGL/DBL$43.

Oak Tree Inn (401 Woodland Drive, 93277; 732-8861) 43 rooms, swimming pool, airport transportation, no-smoking rooms, laundry room, pets allowed. SGL$28-$30, DBL$32-$44.

Parkway Inn (4801 West Mineral King Avenue, 93277; 627-2885) 38 rooms, outdoor, swimming pool, wheelchair-access rooms, no pets. SGL$33-$36, DBL$36-$40.

Radisson Hotel (300 South Court, 93291; 636-1111, Fax 636-8224, 800-333-3333) 201 rooms and suites, restaurant, outdoor swimming pool, exercise facilities airport transportation, wheelchair access, no-smoking rooms. SGL/DBL$75-$100, STS$200-$350.

Spalding House Inn (631 North Encina, 93291; 739-7866) 3 rooms, complimentary breakfast, no smoking. SGL/DBL$75-$85.

Sundance Inn (1400 South Mooney Boulevard, 93277; 732-6641, 800-242-4261) 50 rooms, restaurant, outdoor swimming pool. SGL$30-$34, DBL$34-$38.

TraveLodge (4645 West Mineral King Avenue, 93277; 732-5611, 800-255-3050) 78 rooms, outdoor swimming pool, kitchenettes, children under 18 free. SGL$38-$52, DBL$45-$57.

Vista

Area Code 619
Vista Chamber of Commerce
210 Washington Street
Vista CA 92083
726-1122

Best Western Hilltop Motor Lodge (330 Mar Vista Drive, 92083; 589-1111, 800-528-1234) 45 rooms. SGL/DBL$35-$55.

Econo Lodge (141 Nettleton Road, 92083; 941-9696, 800-424-4777, 800-446-6900) 35 rooms, swimming pool, wheelchair-access rooms, no-smoking rooms, children under 18 free, pets allowed. SGL/DBL$38-$48.

La Quinta Inn Motor Inn (630 Sycamore Avenue, 92083; 727-8180, Fax 598-1732, 800-531-5900) 106 rooms, restaurant, heated swimming pool, meeting facilities, wheelchair access, no-smoking rooms, pets allowed. SGL$42-$47, DBL$47-$52+.

Warner Springs

Area Code 619

Warner Springs Ranch (31652 Highway 79, 92086; 800-659-2763 in California) 250 one- and two-bedroom cottages, restaurant, swimming pool, golf, tennis, exercise facilities, wheelchair-access rooms, no-smoking rooms. SGL/DBL$75-$80, DBL$80+.

Wasco

Area Code 805
Wasco Chamber of Commerce
628 E Street
Wasco CA 93280
758-2748

Wasco Inn Motel (1126 Highway 46, 93280; 758-5317) 34 rooms, swimming pool, pets allowed. SGL$34-$38, DBL$38-$42.

West Covina

Area Code 818
West Covina Chamber of Commerce
811 South Sunset Avenue
West Covina CA 91790
338-8496

Best Western Inn (3275 East Garvey Avenue, 91791; 915-1611, Fax 332-6977, 800-528-1234) 126 rooms, restaurant, complimentary breakfast, swimming pool, jacuzzi, children under 12 free, meeting facilities, laundry room, fax service, no-smoking rooms. LS SGL/DBL$44-$58; HS SGL/DBL$135-$145.

Comfort Inn (2804 East Garvey Avenue, 91791; 915-6077, Fax 916077, 800-221-2222) 58 rooms, complimentary breakfast, swimming pool, whirlpools, meeting facilities, no-smoking rooms, no pets. SGL$36-$74, DBL$44-$79.

Embassy Suites (1211 East Garvey Street, 91724; 915-3411, Fax 331-0773, 800-362-2779) 264 suites, complimentary breakfast, swimming pool, airport courtesy car, exercise facilities, lighted tennis courts, wheelchair access, no-smoking rooms. STS$100-$140+.

Hampton Inn Airport (10300 La Cienega Boulevard, 90304; 310-337-1000, Fax 310-645-6925, 800-HAMPTON) 127 rooms, exercise facilities, airport transportation, pets allowed. SGL$65-$75, DBL$75-$88.

Holiday Inn (3223 East Garvey North, 91791; 966-8311, Fax 339-2850, 800-638-9938, 800-HOLIDAY) 134 rooms, restaurant, swimming pool, exercise facilities, wheelchair access, no-smoking rooms. no pets. SGL$50-$85, DBL$50-$87.

Westlake Village

Area Code 805
Westlake Village Chamber of Commerce
31838 Village Center Road
Westlake Village CA 91361
991-3101

RENTAL SOURCES: Bed and Breakfast Los Angeles (32074 Waterside Lane, 91361; 889-8870) reservation service for bed and breakfast inns and homestays in Los Angles, Orange counties and the coastal areas.

Hyatt Westlake Plaza (880 South Westlake Boulevard, 91361; 497-9991, Fax 379-9392, 800-233-1234) 256 rooms and suites, restaurant, complimentary breakfast, swimming pool, spa, 24-hour room service, concierge, fax service, complimentary newspaper, gift shop, exercise center, airport transportation, wheelchair access, no-smoking rooms, free parking. SGL/DBL$108-$155, STS$165-$350.

Westlake Village Hotel (31943 Agoura Road, 91361; 889-0230, Fax 879-0812, 800-535-9987 in California) 75 rooms and suites, restaurant, complimentary breakfast, swimming pool, lighted tennis courts, golf, no-smoking rooms. SGL$70-$75, DBL$75-$82, STS$175+.

Westminster

Area Code 714
Westminster Chamber of Commerce
14491 Beach Boulevard
Westminster CA 92683
898-9648

Best Western Inn (5744 Westminster Road, 92683; 898-4043, 800-528-1234) 45 rooms and efficiencies, swimming pool, children under 12 free, whirlpool, wheelchair-access rooms, pets allowed. SGL/DBL$38-$63, EFF$58-$72.

Motel 6 (6266 Westminster Avenue, 92683; 891-5366, 505-891-6161) 98 rooms. SGL/DBL$29-$35.

Motel 6 (13100 Goldenwest, 92683; 895-0042, 505-891-6161) 127 rooms. SGL/DBL$31-$37.

Sherwood Motor Inn (5921 Westminster Boulevard, 92683; 895-7099) 34 rooms, restaurant, swimming pool, wheelchair access, no pets. SGL/DBL$45-$75.

TraveLodge of Westminster (13659 Beach Boulevard, 92683; 373-3200, Fax 895-5801, 800-255-3050) 50 rooms and suites, swimming pool, whirlpool, meeting facilities for 45, no pets. SGL/DBL$39-$55.

Westminster Gateway TraveLodge (6601 Westminster Boulevard, 92683; 898-5598, Fax 818-895-2140, 800-255-3050) 60 rooms and suites, restaurant, lounge, swimming pool, whirlpool, meeting facilities for 25, no pets. SGL/DBL$39-$55.

Westwood Village

Area Code 310

Clarion Hotel (927 Hilgard Avenue, 90024; 208-3945, 800-252-7466) 47 rooms, complimentary breakfast, no-smoking rooms. SGL/DBL$85-$100.

Del Capri Hotel (10587 Wilshire Boulevard, 90024; 474-3511, 800-44-HOTEL) 81 rooms and suites, complimentary breakfast, swimming pool. SGL$85, DBL$$95, STS$100+.

Holiday Inn (10704 Wilshire Boulevard, 90024; 475-8711, 800-465-4329) 294 rooms and suites, restaurant, swimming pool, exercise facilities, wheelchair access, no-smoking rooms, pets allowed. SGL$120-$140, DBL$130-$145, STS$175-$250.

Westwood Marquis Hotel and Garden (930 Hilgard Avenue, 90024; 421-2317, Fax 824-0355) 258 suites, swimming pool, exercise facilities. SGL/DBL$220-$650.

Whittier

Area Code 310
Whittier Area Chamber of Commerce
8158 Painter Avenue
Whittier CA 90607
698-9554

RENTAL SOURCES: Cohost America Bed and Breakfasts (Box 9302, 90608; 699-8427) represents homestays in residential areas in the Whittier area.

Best Western Whittier Inn (14226 East Whittier Boulevard, 90606; 698-0323, Fax 945-7875, 800-528-1234, 800-344-5556) 46 rooms and suites, restaurant, lounge, complimentary breakfast, swimming pool, meeting facilities, fax service, free parking, no-smoking rooms. SGL/DBL$48-$56, STS$90-$96.

Coleen's California Casa (Box 9302, 90608; 699-8427) 3 rooms, bed and breakfast, complimentary breakfast, airport courtesy car, wheelchair-access rooms. SGL$100, DBL$125.

Days Inn Motel (14330 Telegraph Road, 90607; 213-944-4760, Fax 213-944-4376, 800-325-2525) 54 rooms, swimming pool, jacuzzis, wheelchair-access rooms, children under 12 free, fax service, no-smoking rooms. SGL$39-$55, DBL$49-$65.

Hilton Hotel (7320 Greeleaf Avenue, 90608; Fax 945-6018, 800-445-8667, 800-HILTONS) 202 rooms, lounge, restaurant, swimming pool, meeting facilities for 450, business services, exercise equipment, wheelchair access, no-smoking rooms. SGL/DBL$95-$130+.

TraveLodge (11530 Whittier Boulevard, 90601; 692-5555, 800-255-3050) 56 rooms and suites, restaurant, lounge, whirlpool, no pets. SGL/DBL$43-$48.

Vagabond Inn Whittier (14125 East Whittier Boulevard, 90605; 698-9701, Fax 698-8716, 800-522-1555) 49 rooms, complimentary breakfast, heated swimming pool, in-room refrigerators, pets allowed, free parking, airport transportation, free local telephone calls, no-smoking rooms, children under 18 free, fax service, complimentary newspaper. SGL$39-$44, DBL$44-$54.

Whittier Hilton Hotel (7320 Greenleaf Avenue, 90602; 945-8511, 800-443-1268) 206 rooms and suites, restaurant, swimming pool, airport transportation, fee parking. SGL$90-$100, DBL$100-$110, STS$375-$475.

Woodland and Woodland Hills

Area Code 916
Woodland Chamber of Commerce
520 Main Street
Woodland CA 95695
662-7327

Best Western Inn (21830 Ventura Boulevard, 91364; 340-1000, Fax 340-1020, 800-528-1234) 69 rooms. SGL/DBL$55-$75

Cinderella Motel (99 West Main Street, 95695; 662-1091) 30 rooms, swimming pool, no-smoking rooms. SGL$34, DBL$42-$44.

Comfort Inn (1562 Main Street, 95695; 443-6631, 800-221-2222) 51 rooms and suites, restaurant, swimming pool, sauna, whirlpool, laundry room, wheelchair-access rooms. SGL$36, DBL$40.

Farmhouse Motel (1021 Main Street, 95695; 662-8215) 18 rooms and efficiencies, swimming pool. SGL$26, DBL$28-$40.

Knights Inn Motel (53 West Main Street, 95695; 662-9335) 40 rooms, restaurant, swimming pool, pets allowed. SGL$30, DBL$35.

Hilton and Towers (6360 Canoga Avenue, 91367; 595-1000, Fax 595-1090, 800-445-8667) 327 rooms, restaurant, lounge, swimming pool, tennis, meeting facilities for 700, business services, exercise facilities. SGL/DBL$120-$170.

Holiday Inn (21101 Ventura Boulevard, 91364; 818-883-6110, Fax 818-340-6550, 800-HOLIDAY) 127 rooms, restaurant, lounge, swimming pool, laundry room, exercise facilities, no pets, free parking. SGL$70-$99, DBL$80-$108.

Oakland Apartments Woodland Hills (22122 Victory Boulevard, 91367; 595-3100) rental studio and one- and two-bedroom apartments, complimentary brunch, swimming pool, tennis. SGL/DBL$85+.

Phoenix Inn (1524 East Main Street, 95695; 666-3800) 53 rooms, restaurant. SGL$28, DBL$32.

Valley Oaks Inn (600 North East Street, 95695; 666-5511) 64 rooms, complimentary breakfast, swimming pool. SGL$37, DBL$41.

Vagabond Inn Woodland Hills (21057 Ventura Boulevard, 91364; 347-8080, Fax 716-5333, 800-522-1555) 100 rooms, restaurant, complimentary breakfast, outdoor swimming pool, spa, in-room refrigerators, fax service, complimentary newspaper, wheelchair access, no-smoking rooms, pets allowed, free parking. SGL$48-$54, DBL$53-$64.

Warner Center Hilton and Towers (6360 Canoga Avenue, 91367; 595-1000, Fax 595-1040, 800-922-2400, 800-445-8667) 318 rooms and suites, restaurant, outdoor swimming pool, exercise facilities, in-room refrigerators and mini-bars, laundry room, fax and business service, beauty and barber shop, gift shop, free parking, airport transportation, wheelchair access, no-smoking rooms, car rental. SGL/DBL$99-$139, STS$265-$850.

Warner Center Marriott Hotel (21850 Oxnard Street, 91367; 887-4800, Fax 347-0907, 800-228-9290) 472 rooms and suites, three restaurants, lounge, outdoor and indoor swimming pool, spa, exercise facilities, valet laundry, fax service, child care, pets allowed, no-smoking rooms, free parking, complimentary airport car service, gift shop, car rentals. SGL/DBL$89-$139, STS$350-$1,500.

Warner Gardens Motel (21706 Ventura Boulevard, 91364; 992-4426, Fax 704-1062, 800-824-9292) 42 rooms and suites, complimentary breakfast, swimming pool, wheelchair-access rooms, no-smoking rooms, valet laundry, in-room refrigerators and microwaves, fax services, free parking. SGL/DBL$46-$54, STS$58-$65.

Woodland Shadow Motel (584 North East Street, 95695; 666-1251) 129 rooms, restaurant, swimming pool. SGL/DBL$42-$44.

Woodland Hills Motor Lodge (22621 Ventura Boulevard, 91364; 884-7777) 41 rooms, swimming pool, airport transportation, pets allowed. SGL$37, DBL$46.

Yorba Linda

Area Code 714
Yorba Linda Chamber of Commerce
4854 Main Street
Yorba Linda CA 92686
777-3507

Country Side Suites (22677 Oakcrest Circle, 92687; 921-8688, Fax 283-3927, 800-336-0632) 112 rooms and suites, complimentary breakfast, outdoor heated swimming pool, jacuzzi, hot tubs, children under 12 free, fax service, gift shop, laundry room, free parking, wheelchair-access rooms, no-smoking, pets allowed. SGL$59-$75, DBL$69-$85, STS$89-$105.

Yucca Valley

Area Code 619
Yucca Valley Chamber of Commerce
56020 Sante Fe Trail
Yucca Valley CA 92284
365-6323

Desert View Motel (57471 Primrose Drive, 92285; 365-9706) 14 rooms. SGL/DBL$35-$50.

Super 8 Motel (57096 Twentynine Palms Highway, 92284 -619-228-1773, 800-800-8000) 48 rooms and suites, restaurant, complimentary breakfast, outdoor heated swimming pool, wheelchair-access rooms, free local telephone calls, no-smoking rooms, pets allowed. SGL/DBL$35-$43.

ADDITIONAL RESOURCES

Other travel books from Hunter Publishing

WHERE TO STAY IN NORTHERN CALIFORNIA
The most complete source available anywhere for every type of accommodation: B&Bs, country inns, condos and cottages for rent, hotels and motels. Over 3,500 places described, with prices, phones, special offers. 5 3/8 x 8 paperback/384 pp/$12.95/1-55650-573-6.

THE FLORIDA WHERE TO STAY BOOK
More than 4,000 places to stay in the #1 vacation destination in the country – condos for rent, inns, motels, hotels, even beach houses for rent by the week or month. Prices, descriptions, all details. 5 3/8 x 8 paperback/448 pp/$12.95/1-55650-539-6

THE GREAT AMERICAN WILDERNESS: TOURING AMERICA'S NATIONAL PARKS
The 41 most scenic parks, from Acadia to Yosemite, and how to see them: main access routes, where to stay, where to eat, which roads are most crowded or most beautiful, how much time to allow, what you can safely skip and what you must not miss. Special sections tell how to tour each park if you have only limited time – or if time is not a factor – and 11 detailed itineraries suggest ways to combine visits to several scenic areas in a single trip. Maps of each park included, showing all surrounding access roads. 5 3/8 x 8 paperback/288 pp/$11.95/1-55650-567-1

USA BY RAIL
Details what you will encounter on the 28 long-distance trains that criss-cross North America, describing points of interest along the way and spots where the trips can be broken. Station information, sightseeing, where to stay, route maps, excursions. Over 500 destinations, including 37 major cities, are covered. 5 3/8 x 8 paperback/320 pp/$15.95/1-55650-521-3

ADVENTURE GUIDE TO THE ALASKA HIGHWAY
A complete guide to what you will find along the highway, plus all worthwhile side-trips and approaches, such as the Alaska-Marine Highway, Klondike Highway, Top-of-the-World Highway. Maps & color photos. 5 3/8 x 8 paperback/288 pp/$14.95/1-55650-457-8

ADVENTURE GUIDE TO BAJA CALIFORNIA 2nd Edition
Thorough update of this classic tourguide to the peninsula, from Tijuana and Mexicali to Cabo San Lucas at the tip. The best driving routes, fascinating history, hotels, restaurants, all practical details. 5 3/8 x 8 paperback/288 pp/$13.95/1-55650-590-6

CANADIAN ROCKIES ACCESS GUIDE
The ultimate guide to outdoor adventure, from Banff to Lake Louise to Jasper National Park. Walking and canoeing routes, climbs, cycling itineraries. Maps, photos. 6 x 9 paperback/360 pp/$15.95/0-919433-92-8

HAWAII: A WALKER'S GUIDE
Walking the awesome Na Pali cliffs and climbing the Kilauea Volcano are just a few of the unforgettable adventures detailed here. Each hike is graded for difficulty, from multi-day excursions to scenic strolls. Detailed maps, color photos. 5 3/8 x 8 paperback/224 pp/$14.95/1-55650-215-X

THE GOLF RESORT GUIDES
Two updated volumes (EAST and WEST editions) describe the most rewarding golf resorts in every state, plus Canada, Mexico (in Western Edition), and the Caribbean (in Eastern Edition). All facilities are described and rated: golf courses, pro shop, tennis, ski, lodging, special packages offered, fees, restaurants, directions for arrival. Maps. 5 3/8 x 8 paperbacks/448 pp each/$13.95 each/EASTERN 1-55650-568-X; WESTERN 1-55650-569-8.

CALIFORNIA INSIDER'S GUIDE
Packed with stunning photographs and extensive historical & cultural background, combined with rich practical detail, the famous Insider's Guides cover the world. The California guide tells you where to stay, where to eat, what to see, how to get around, region-by-region. Large fold-out map included. Hun-

dreds of color photos. 5 5/8 x 8 3/4 paperback/256 pp/$14.95/1-55650-163-3

MEXICO INSIDER'S GUIDE
5 5/8 x 8 3/4 paperback/320 pp/$17.95/1-55650-454-3

CANADA WEST INSIDER'S GUIDE
5 5/8 x 8 3/4 paperback/256 pp/$17.95/1-55650-580-9

ADVENTURE GUIDE TO COSTA RICA
Biggest, most detailed guide on the market. Exhaustive coverage of history, people, customs, unique wildlife, restaurants, transport, where to stay. The best hiking trails, the national parks, a complete guide to San José and all other towns, with maps and photos. Offbeat, unusual adventure possibilities as well. 5 3/8 x 8 paperback/360 pp/$16.95/1-55650-456-X

ADVENTURE GUIDE TO BELIZE
Second edition. With some of the best diving in the world, 1000-foot waterfalls, virgin rainforest, 500 bird species, this is a naturalist's paradise. The latest and best guide available. Hotels, food, maps, color photos. 5 3/8 x 8 paperback/288 pp/$14.95/1-55650-493-4

ADVENTURE GUIDE TO THE DOMINICAN REPUBLIC
Miles of pristine beaches, jungles, soaring mountains and Old Santo Domingo, first Spanish capital of the Americas. A complete practical guide to every aspect of the island, from food to hiking, luxury hotels to budget travel bargains, shopping and transport. Maps. 5 3/8 x 8 paperback/256 pp/$13.95/1-55650-537-X

❧

Write Hunter Publishing, Inc., 300 Raritan Center Parkway, Edison NJ 08818 or call (908) 225 1900 for our complete free color catalog describing these and over 1,000 other unusual travel guides and maps to all parts of the world – from Africa to South America, from Europe to Asia. Find them in the best bookstores or you can order direct by sending your check to the address above (add $2.50 to cover shipping/handling).